Self in the World

SELF IN THE WORLD

Connecting Life's Extremes

Keith Hart

berghahn
NEW YORK · OXFORD
www.berghahnbooks.com

First published in 2022 by
Berghahn Books
www.berghahnbooks.com

Library of Congress Cataloging-in-Publication Data

Names: Hart, Keith, author.
Title: Self in the world : connecting life's extremes / Keith Hart.
Description: New York : Berghahn Books, 2022. | Includes bibliographical references and
   index. |
Identifiers: LCCN 2021042497 (print) | LCCN 2021042498 (ebook) |
   ISBN 9781800734203 (hardback) | ISBN 9781800734227 (paperback) |
   ISBN 9781800734210 (ebook)
Subjects: LCSH: Hart, Keith. | Anthropology. | Social history. | Humanities. | Progress. |
   Self (Philosophy) | Anthropologists--Great Britain--Biography.
Classification: LCC GN25 .H375 2022 (print) | LCC GN25 (ebook) |
   DDC 301--dc23/eng/20220107
LC record available at https://lccn.loc.gov/2021042497
LC ebook record available at https://lccn.loc.gov/2021042498

British Library Cataloguing in Publication Data

A catalogue record for this book is available from the British Library

ISBN 978-1-80073-420-3 hardback
ISBN 978-1-80073-422-7 paperback
ISBN 978-1-80073-421-0 ebook

For the magical twins, Louise and Constance,

Muriel Coldwell (1920–2018), my aunt, hero and friend

and

Friedrich Engels (1820–95), a great anthropologist and hero

Two things fill the mind with ever new and increasing admiration and awe, the more often and steadily we reflect upon them: the starry heavens above me and the moral law within me.

—Immanuel Kant's tombstone

Good writers have two things in common; they prefer to be understood rather than admired and they do not write for knowing and over-acute readers.

—Friedrich Nietzsche

Keep Ithaka always in your mind.
Arriving there is what you're destined for.
But don't hurry the journey at all.
Better if it lasts for years,
so you're old by the time you reach the island,
wealthy with all you've gained on the way,
not expecting Ithaka to make you rich.

—C.P. Cavafy

It was in 1989. The Berlin Wall came down. Me and a fellow student, we rented a car we drove to Berlin. Suddenly you could see all these people from East coming through. It was very touching, I mean it was difficult to understand, to be honest, the scope of what we were actually seeing. I said, If I'm somehow going to say something, I had better be myself.

Art is the world's ability to investigate and have an intimate relationship with itself. Gerd Richter, a German painter, said, 'Art is the highest form of hope'. At the bottom of my heart, I love making art. So why are you watching this episode? I am happy that you are here. But it is important that you think of yourself. What is in it for you? What are you actually doing here?

—Olafur Eliasson, *The Design of Art* (television series)

CONTENTS

Part III. World

Part IV. Lifelong Learning

PREFACE

I am sitting at the dining table. The view out of the living room window frames the laurel rose on the balcony. It is *la rentrée*, the first week of September when all Parisian children go back to school. Soon my wife and teenage daughter will leave this place to me during most weekdays. I have a refuge in our bedroom, but it is narrow, has no view and the Wi-Fi is weak there. I like to work where I can shut out their conversation, phone calls and YouTube clips while writing in the same room. I have reason to fear that absorption in my own thoughts will drive me away from everyone. Their babble beyond the wall of my concentration reassures me that I am connected. I have a family; I am not alone. I learned to do this from the beginning when my Mum, Dad, sister and I had one heated room in the winter. We used it for baking, eating, drying clothes, homework, sewing, sitting, talking, listening to the radio and keeping warm. If I wanted to read, I had to shut them out and I did. But they were there.

Our Paris flat is in an old winding street, rue du Faubourg Poissonnière, once the fish route to Les Halles. 'Faubourg' means outside the city walls. A market developed there for those who didn't want to pay entry fees.[1] A church was named for St Anne, the patron saint of Breton fishermen; she is *la Poissonnière*, the fishwife. The Gare du Nord is a few minutes' walk away, with the Eurostar to London and fast trains to Charles de Gaulle airport. The area was built up in the 1860s, during Louis Napoléon's *belle époque*. Humiliating defeat in the Franco-Prussian War closed off that decade. The buildings are more generous than Haussmann's post-war designs – the ironwork of the balconies is more ornate. Our neighbourhood has many specialist food shops, bars and small restaurants.

The original occupants of our flat would have been a middle-class bachelor or young couple. It has three big rooms, plus a nest of little spaces at the back and a good-sized cellar underground. Each room has mouldings indicating its function: books in the living room, flowers in the bedroom, fruit and vegeta-

---

1. H. Pirenne, *Medieval Cities* (1925).

bles in the dining room. The kitchen and beyond were the maid's workspace and personal quarters with water for washing and sewage. The master used a commode in his bedroom. An entry opening onto the staircase divides the two zones. Sophie and I have been here for twenty-three years.

A bottle of wine stands on my bedside table. I bought it in a Lancashire supermarket when visiting my Dad. The cheap *vin ordinaire* is well past its sell-by date. What is it doing there? The label says:

MANCHESTER UNITED
1995 CHARDONNAY
Premier League Champions
F.A. Cup Winners
OFFICIAL CLUB WINE

On the back it says:

This wine is exclusively bottled for Manchester United. Like everything else about the World's Greatest Football Club, it is unbeatable for quality and value. This 1995 Chardonnay is from the Languedoc region of Southern France and is fresh, crisp, with lots of fruit—another winner from United

VIN DE PAYS D'OC
Mise en bouteille par Domaine Lafayette, Beziers, France

United are emerging from a rough spell since their last great manager retired eight years ago. But they have the highest commercial turnover. This bottle is a symbol of my own journey. In 1950 no-one could imagine that United would one day flog cheap French plonk to their supporters. Nor that little Keithy from Old Trafford would end up as a writer in Paris.

Manchester formed me,[2] but there is little left to tie me there. My extended family of origin has died or moved on. I don't recognize the city now and I didn't like it much before. United and I have become 'world citizens'; but what and where is that? I cling to my roots by following their matches online. It is the only activity that links me to the place. The rest is just in my head.

Half the United team were killed in an air crash when I was 14 and they won nothing for a decade. Later, I too crashed and spent fifteen years recovering. I almost died five years ago and decided to write this book. I don't recall when I began wondering how I belong to humanity. But I explore that question here and I am not the only one asking it.

* * *

---

2. Hart, Appendix 2003c.

I woke up one day in October 2017 and found that Tom Petty had died in Los Angeles from a cardiac arrest aged 66. Tom Petty, leader of the Heartbreakers, died of a broken heart. For months I had immersed myself in his music, lyrics, live performances, biographies and documentaries while trying to launch this book. I thought I could approach writing my life story through his example. Before long the book moved on, but I mention my debt to him here. The *New York Times* said that his lyrics spoke for underdogs and *The Guardian* wrote:

> Petty was a music fan as much as he was a musician, aware that the style that had made him successful was based at least in part on borrowing and paying homage, smartly synthesizing the sound of artists he loved into something entirely his own.

Tom Petty's journey was about finding the freedom to be himself with and without his band. He never lost sight of where he came from, of where rock 'n' roll came from (the US South). He fought the corporate private property system twice and won both times. I too hate private property in the mind's products. I join the long human conversation about a better world that sustains us all. T.S. Eliot once wrote: 'The great poet immerses himself in his tradition and then writes the poem that is necessary to move it along'.[3] Bob Dylan and, not far behind, Tom Petty are the great poets of my lifetime. I am not a notable poet, but I am a fan of poetry, especially of songs produced in that great social crucible that is America.

The chorus of Tom Petty's 'Learning to Fly'[4] explains how he wants to learn to fly but doesn't have wings, and coming down is the hardest thing. I understand this. My story is not a variation of the Icarus myth, however. Like United, I have had rough times; and I am still there. This book is about learning and aspiration. I will explain what I mean in the Introduction. Nor is mine a huge success story. I have not sold eighty thousand albums. But I do know about wanting to fly.

My favourite anthropology teacher as an undergraduate was Audrey Richards. She came from an old colonial family and was very distinguished. She encouraged me to study cities in Africa and once granted me a personal tutorial. When I got married, she gave us a jam thermometer – 'every marriage needs a little sweetness'. She told my wife, 'If you see something you really like, buy four of them'. We had no money at the time. For the tutorial she asked me to write an essay which I then had to read out (this was Cambridge). She interrupted me a lot and kept asking for less abstraction, more detail. I had to write it again. I decided to write the most pedestrian

3. T.S. Eliot, *Notes Towards the Definition of Culture* (1948).

4. https://www.youtube.com/watch?v=4p_f7Df2-oM (accessed 8 September 2021).

piece I could. After reading it out, Audrey said, 'Now that we know you can walk, Mr Hart, we can discuss your aspiration to fly'. Tough love always goes straight to my heart.

* * *

I dedicate this book to Friedrich Engels, as well as to my daughters and aunt, because I finished it in his bicentenary year. He wrote a book on Manchester in 1844 in his mid-twenties, gave Karl Marx first-hand knowledge of the industrial working class, co-wrote the *German Ideology* and *Communist Manifesto* of 1848, tolerated Marx's defects, built him up as supreme leader and kept the movement going after his death. He enjoyed his wealth as the scion of a German transnational firm, drank champagne while hunting and considered marriage a bourgeois institution. For several decades he lived in Manchester faithfully with Mary Burns and, after her death, her sister Lizzie, both illiterate Irish working-class women with radical political views. He and Marx greeted with enthusiasm the publication of Lewis Henry Morgan's *Ancient Society* in 1877 for confirming their critique of the state and capitalism.[5] Engels's reworking of Morgan's argument later became a lynchpin of modern feminism.[6]

---

5. See Chapter 2.

6. F. Engels, *The Condition of the Working Class in England in 1844* (1845); *Socialism, Utopian and Scientific* (1880); *The Origin of the Family, Private Property and the State* (1884); G. McCrea, *Mrs. Engels* (novel, 2015).

ACKNOWLEDGEMENTS

This book has been through nine different versions, 2017–21. I shared each one with a large number of friends, too many to list here. Fortunately, many of them passed on making comments, either out of pressure of work or because they realized that the latest version, like its predecessors, was incomplete. Some hardy souls made the effort, however, a few of them at length and more than once. I divide these acknowledgements into those who helped me in various ways, not only as readers, and those who made a real difference to how this book turned out.

The first group includes Don Billingsley, Craig Calhoun, Jeanette Edwards, Bill Freund, Adam Kuper, Heonik Kwon, Alan Macfarlane, Bill Maurer, Ruben Oliven, Sherry Ortner, Vishnu Padayachee and Ted Powers. In the second were: Olu Abimbola, Kal Applbaum, Gabi Bockaj, John Bryden, Peter Clarke, John Comaroff, John Conroy, Sean Maliehe, Knut Nustad, Sandy Robertson and Gillian Tett. In summer 2019, a few close friends convened in Stockholm to discuss my work in general: Catherine Alexander, Sophie Chevalier, Gabriel Gbadamosi, Chris Hann, Ulf Hannerz, Vito Laterza, Horacio Ortiz, Ato Quayson, Theodoros Rakopoulos and Huon Wardle.[1] I thank all the above.

Tony Mason, my editor, has provided the enthusiasm and organization I needed to finish this book. I thank him and Marion Berghahn profusely for their confidence in it and me. Finally, I wrote most of this on the dining table in our living room, a crowded space that I share with Sophie and Constance. There are no words for what their tolerant support gave me throughout.

---

1. See https://culanth.org/fieldsights/swimming-into-the-current-the-movement-of-hu man-society-through-history (accessed 8 September 2021).

CHRONOLOGY

1943	Born
1943–60	Parents' home: Old Trafford, Manchester
1954–61	Manchester Grammar School
1960–72	Parents' home: Timperley, Cheshire
1961–69	St John's College, Cambridge
1965–68	Fieldwork, Ghana
1968–77	First marriage (one child)
1969–71	University of East Anglia, Norwich
1970	Cayman Islands mission
1971–75	Manchester University
1972–74	Economist Intelligence Unit
1972–2005	Parent's home: Kirkham, Lancashire
1972	Papua New Guinea mission
1975–79	Yale University
1976	Hong Kong mission
1979–81	University of Michigan
1979–82	West African agriculture
1981–82	McGill University
1983	University of Chicago
1984–98	Cambridge University
1986–88	University of the West Indies, Jamaica
1987–89	C.L.R. James in London
1992–98	African Studies Centre, Cambridge
1993–96	Prickly Pear Pamphlets
1994	Cambridge University teaching prize

1997–	Family home in Paris
1997–2018	In-laws home in Geneva
1998–2002	University of Pavia
1999–2001	*The Memory Bank* (*Money in an Unequal World*)
1999–2003	Arkleton Centre for Rural Development, Aberdeen
1999	University of Stellenbosch
2000	University of Chicago
2001–	Second marriage (one child)
2001	University of Chicago
2001–2	University of Oslo
2002–4	International Labour Office, Turin
2003	Northwestern University
2004–8	Goldsmiths, University of London
2008–	Second home, Durban
2008–13	University of Kwazulu Natal
2009	University of Chicago
2009–19	Open Anthropology Cooperative
2011–18	Human Economy Programme, Pretoria
2013–21	Berghahn Books Human Economy Series
2013–16	London School of Economics and Politics
2020–21	Coronavirus pandemic

INTRODUCTION

People have many sides, but I will focus here on two. Each of us is a biological organism with a historical personality that together make us a unique individual. But we cannot live outside society, which shapes us in unfathomable ways. Human beings must learn to be self-reliant (not self-interested) in small and large ways: no-one will brush your teeth for you or save you from being run over while crossing the street. We each must also learn to belong to others, merging personal identity in a plethora of social relations and categories. Modern ideology insists that being individual and mutual is problematic. The culture of capitalist societies anticipates a conflict between them. Yet they are inseparable aspects of human nature.

We embark on two life journeys – one out into the world, the other inward to the self. Society is mysterious to us because it dwells inside us, mostly inaccessible to thought. Writing brings the two into a mutual understanding that we can share. Lived society may become exposed to introspection in this way. Fragments of experience could then be combined into a whole, a world as singular as the self. There are as many worlds as individual journeys.[1] If there is only one world out there, each of us changes it whenever we move.

We like to imagine ourselves as competent actors with a singular identity. But it often feels that we are broken. We are out of touch in a world that is running away from us.[2] We feel disabled and lonely. We are parts, not wholes.

---

1. See 'Online Worlds and Virtual Reality' in Chapter 15, especially M. Heidegger.
2. E. Leach, *A Runaway World?* (1968).

What does it take to become fully human? Perhaps we will all eventually find our way to humanity. Now we are only part-human. We are deformed by class divisions and condemned to see the world through the cracked mirror of race.[3]

Self in the World

How did this come about? Why is human integrity so hard to achieve? Why do so many of us often feel lost in a vast and implacable universe? I wrote this book to find provisional answers, by examining my own experience and reflecting on what I have learned of the world. My guiding principle is that self and world, local and global, life and ideas, personal and impersonal, real and virtual are not as separate as they often seem. But it takes serious practical and intellectual effort to see how they are connected and to make them work for each of us.

I come from Manchester and took up socialism as a teenager. The two years I spent studying Ghana's street economy brought out another aspect of my upbringing. I found that I had considerable knowledge of markets and money. The 'informal economy' was a free market zone, operating outside the law.[4] I felt at home in it. This experience launched a dialogue within me, between the social and individual dimensions of human personality. My childhood offered support for both sides. Boys in the street and schoolyard combined gang behaviour with competitive individualism. A premium on conformity was matched by self-reliance and bravado. The neoliberal turn after 1980 convinced me that working-class solidarity had gone forever. But I discovered something similar in France – a republican tradition of taking to the streets in political protest (*manifestation*).[5]

The tension between belonging to a collective and individualism is a central theme of this book. After a long period as a Marxist, I immersed myself in classical liberalism.[6] Seventeenth- and eighteenth-century advocates of democratic revolution thought free movement would be the catalyst for a new society. Individual freedom could only be won though social engineering based on scientific knowledge. Their liberalism was at once individual and social. These have since become disconnected and need to be reunited. If I want to move freely in the world, I must find places whose public institutions support

---

3. See 'Resisting Alienation' in Chapter 3.
4. Hart, Appendix 1973, 2006c, 2015d.
5. Such as the *gilets jaunes* (yellow vests) protests of 2018–19.
6. Poets (Milton to Blake and Shelley) and philosophers (Locke, Rousseau, Smith, Jefferson, Kant).

free association. Learning how to combine liberalism and social democracy, freedom and equality, is a revolutionary project.

I trace my reinvention in midlife to spending two years in Jamaica during the late 1980s. Caribbean people, whose history has denied them the security of viewing the world from one place, developed a 'cubist' perspective on it, allowing participants to place themselves in the picture at multiple points.[7] The North Atlantic region is the crucible of modern world history; but it is not the world.

Self in the World is not an autobiography, but a reflection on the human condition in our times by one person. Individual freedom depends on being able to move; but nomadism also requires fixed points. Stability and movement are both essential to human life.[8] I am an anthropologist by profession, an amateur economist by inclination. I devour movies, novels, sport and all kinds of music. Most anthropologists discover the world by finding out what people do and think where they live.[9] I rely mainly on lifelong learning through reading, writing and varied world experience that includes eclectic immersion in high and low culture. I combine auto-ethnography[10] with world history and humanist philosophy. I teach what I have learned and learn from teaching.

Anthropology and the Humanities

Modern anthropology was born in the eighteenth century as one aspect of the drive to overthrow the Old Regime and instal democracy. Agrarian civilization was on its last legs and its class structure had no credible foundation. Rule by and for the people had to be based on what everyone had in common, their human nature. But what was that and how could nature and history, personal freedom and civic duty be reconciled? Democracy would require citizens to re-educate themselves in order to uphold it. The self, psychology, novels, newspapers and much else made their appearance then.

Anthropology has regressed since. In the nineteenth century, it became an explanation and support for Europeans taking over the world, ultimately a racist apologia for empire. But its method assumed that world history was unfinished. The senseless slaughter of 1914–18 required and found a new

---

7. J. Berger, *Success and Failure of Picasso* (1965).

8. See Chapter 13.

9. 'Ethnography' is literally writing about a people.

10. 'A form of qualitative research where an author uses self-reflection and writing to explore personal experience and connect this autobiography to wider cultural, political, and social understandings'. https://en.wikipedia.org/wiki/Autoethnography.

paradigm for the last century. We should join the people where they live in order to find out what they do, think and want. This is one half of what anthropology must become, but the other half – contemplating humanity's destiny on and beyond this planet – vanished from view. The anti-colonial revolution put paid to anthropology as the study of 'primitive' peoples, but most anthropologists have since clung to the narrow localism and ahistorical vision of 'fieldwork-based ethnography'. This focus had some fit with a world society composed of myopic nation states; but its aim was description, not prescription. Anthropologists struggled to catch up with global events that they did not understand nor could shape.

Universities focused on the task of bureaucratizing national capitalism have run out of steam. Having been tied to them hitherto, anthropologists will need to find other homes. The modernist project of compartmentalizing knowledge fights our pressing need to understand human beings who belong to humanity as a whole. Anthropology was never a 'discipline'. No-one could pull its range of interests together unless they were an unschooled human being in the first place. 'Anthropology' could be an umbrella term for several disciplines to pool their efforts while seeking to bridge the gap between formal education and wider public interests that are increasingly global.

In 2009, I met some younger anthropologists on Twitter who shared my dismay over how the leading professional organizations, especially the American Anthropological Association, had failed to keep up with the global and democratic potential of the internet. We formed the Open Anthropology Cooperative, which, in the next decade, acquired over twenty thousand members from around the world.[11] The membership generated many discussion groups, archives and other resources while promoting interaction across barriers of culture, social status and geography. The administrators found that calling ourselves 'open' did not mean that we could dispense with rules or avoid the threats posed by trolls, spammers and bots. We often descended into a half-hearted managerialism.

We never turned to anthropology for solutions to these problems. It was not intended to change the world; but it didn't help us to think about living in it either. When I started this book, I didn't set out to ignore contemporary academic anthropology apart from my own writings. It just happened that way. When I needed an example, I took it from my experience, reading outside my profession or popular culture. For intellectual inspiration I usually turned to books written before the modern discipline was invented. Yet in the course of writing this book, I began to focus on how anthropology might evolve beyond its present limitations by becoming a popular rather than aca-

---

11. Hart, Appendix 2015h. See Chapter 15.

demic pursuit. Above all, I hope that readers – with and without exposure to academic anthropology – will find here the means of reflecting on issues that matter to them.

If we wish to make a personal connection with the world, we must try to engage with the human condition as a whole. This was supposed to be anthropology's purpose, but is no longer. Being human is not something we inherit through our DNA. We have to work at becoming human, individually and collectively. *Becoming* is life, movement and process. Whatever stops developing has *become* – it is a state, a dead thing like this book. But it can live on in the minds of new readers. A focus on 'becoming human' – on emergence – favours a historical method. All the humanities are relevant: literature, the arts, history, ethnography, dialogical philosophy, rhetoric, religion and case law. But science must be their ally, not a threat. We need to know what is real and how things work.[12]

I have something to say here about how we might develop new social forms conducive to humanity's survival and progress. Improving education and the organization of knowledge is indispensable to that. The two sides of 'self' and 'world' inform each other here. We each need to place ourselves in history. Being human is not just about accounting for our own actions.

This book has some affinity with the romantic educational novel (*Bildungsroman*). It is about how I came to think the way I do, but also about the people, places and times I encountered along the way – a story of my formation. Life and ideas shape each other reflexively. Thought and action are intertwined and their social synthesis is communication. All the book's sections combine both, but the balance between them shifts. Writing about oneself is a humanist genre. Conventionally, the author describes their life as someone who rejects supernatural, natural and social conditioning. The scope for purposeful action is severely limited, however. We are exposed to natural disasters, social revolutions, wars and economic depressions. We depend on machines that few understand and on rules and ideas that we do not make ourselves. We offer token resistance to disabling pollution and environmental threats. The media reports disasters every day, inviting us to feel lucky that we missed that earthquake, air crash, massacre or flood.

The humanities once showed us our common history. They did this by delving deeply into particular persons, places, events and relationships. Religion has always connected thinking and feeling persons to the object world they share with everyone. Students now sign up for the social sciences, hoping to learn how to improve society. But they soon become confused and disillusioned. How does each of us relate to a world that seems to lack natural and social order? Personal connection to world society is currently unthinkable.

---

12. Hence the human sciences. See Chapter 20.

But unless we can each identify with it, how will humanity solve problems that we know are global in scope?

The Book's Organization

I spent my youth immersed in ancient languages and literature. Reading old books that made a difference is more rewarding than wading through untested ephemera. We learned that great human discoveries are made over many generations. This contrasts with the current mania for private property in ideas. Thought moves across time and space through stories and conversation. I know that a multitude have contributed to my working memory. This book is a rather egocentric exercise; but I am not its only begetter. I must introduce readers to the predecessors who have influenced me most.

My target audience is young students before they have been programmed by years of specialist higher education. I want them to understand, through my personal development, that learning is not just dead books or lectures imposed from above, but something we can acquire by teaching ourselves and learning from our friends at any stage of life. I discovered as a teacher that young people when starting out are more open-minded than students closed down by specialization. I hope too that curious members of the public will also find food for reflection here.

The Preface and this Introduction provide snapshots of the author and this book. Part I, 'Ancestors', surveys my main literary influences. It addresses three classes of authors in succession: writers about the self, anthropology and the anti-colonial intellectuals. I have worked in twenty-four countries on four continents. Part II, 'Self', is the story of this nomadic life, told as a chronological sequence in nine chapters. It is the longest section of the book. Part III, 'World', identifies themes that have shaped my understanding of humanity as a whole. These are: movement and its antithesis, inequality; the digital revolution; how economy can connect the local and global; and Africa's growing significance for the twenty-first-century world. Part IV, 'Lifelong Learning', brings self and world together as an extended education. Here I discuss my British origins; excursions into transnational history; money as a school for bridging life's extremes; and the relationship between learning, remembering and sharing. In the Afterword, I ask 'What question is this the answer to?' I reflect there on how and why I came to write this book.

Throughout it, I combine intellectual reflection with personal stories. The balance between ideas and life varies, as do the organization and style of each part. The front and back matter are written in a self-consciously non-academic way. Each of Parts I ('Ancestors') and III ('World') forms a set of related themes that draw heavily, but not exclusively, on my own and others' serious writing. They will appeal to more academically inclined readers and do not need to be read in a linear sequence. Part Two ('Self') is my life story and best read as a sequence. Part Four ('Lifelong Learning') consists of very different, experimental essays. The formal boundaries I observe in Parts I and III are mostly absent here.

I hope that the language of all parts is accessible and uncluttered, but a reader's engagement in any particular part is likely to fluctuate. Combining personal and impersonal aspects of a life in society usually requires different levels of formality, language and intellectual style. The book as a whole is an assemblage rather than a synthesis. Readers' attention to different parts and aspects of the book will vary depending on their background. I have included an unusual number of literary references. This is because I read a lot and, as a teacher, want to give those of you who are interested the chance to follow up. But some sections of the book can easily be read like a novel or documentary.

I summarize Part I more fully here since the book starts with my intellectual influences rather than with my life story. It comes first, but need not be read first or indeed at all. Some readers who care about the future of writing, anthropology or development may be more interested in this than in the story of my life. In Chapter 1, I list some of the authors who made writing about myself possible. They are: Michel de Montaigne (sixteenth-century); Jean-Jacques Rousseau, Benjamin Franklin and Edward Gibbon (all eighteenth-century); William Wordsworth and Henry Adams (from the long nineteenth century); Vladimir Nabokov and Chinua Achebe (twentieth-century). 'Writing the self' is different for each of these pioneers who were forced to reinvent the genre in order to express their own unique lives and historical circumstances. This book started out as a trade autobiography. But I needed to relate my explorations of the world to what I have experienced personally.

Chapter 2 draws attention to 'forgotten founders' of anthropology, only one of whom is recognized as a founder by today's academic anthropologists; but he is woefully misunderstood. Three are from the long eighteenth century. Giambattista Vico was a Neapolitan legal academic who taught Latin eloquence. His book, *Principi di Scienza Nuova* (*The New Science*) was wholly original, but Vico lacked position and resources and it was only taken up a century later. Immanuel Kant published the first introduction to anthropology in 1798.[13] It was intended to help his students monitor and organize their later life and was a bestseller. Rousseau founded what I call 'the anthropology of unequal society'.[14] The French maestro Claude Lévi-Strauss acknowledged

13. I. Kant, *Anthropology from a Pragmatic Point of View* (1798).
14. See Chapters 2 and 3.

Rousseau as his master;[15] but Rousseau and Kant have largely dropped out of academic histories of anthropology.

The other two span from the late nineteenth century to the mid-twentieth. W.H.R. Rivers was president of the British associations for both psychology and anthropology. His experience as a psychiatrist treating shell-shock victims in the First World War led him to synthesize his two sides as a public figure. He died prematurely in 1922. The 'functionalist revolution' of Malinowski and Radcliffe-Brown[16] downplayed Rivers's immense contribution. Living for two decades in Paris has led me to appreciate Emile Durkheim's nephew, Marcel Mauss, as the most important of anthropology's modern founders. He is well recognized by the Anglophone profession, but usually for the wrong reasons.

Chapter 3, on some intellectuals of the anti-colonial revolution, came later in my education. When the world turned in 1989–94 (the Soviet collapse, one-world capitalism, the rise of China and India and the internet going public), I asked what the other side in the overthrow of European empires might offer global anthropology. Its leaders had to imagine a post-racist world, then persuade the masses both to fight for it and to educate themselves to play an active part. Peoples coerced earlier into a world society made by and for Western imperialism now sought their own independent relationship to it. This was the most important political development of the last century. Anthropologists of that nationalist era did not draw on these social movements for their own vision. But we should. I was eventually drawn to study Pan-Africanism. Manchester played a significant part in its development. Three figures stand out: the American W.E.B. Du Bois, and two from the Caribbean, C.L.R. James, whom I think of as my mentor, and Frantz Fanon (1925–61), a psychiatrist who died tragically young. Turning to India and South Africa (now my second home), the greatest of these leaders, with most to teach us now, was Mohandas K. Gandhi (1869–1948); but he has lately fallen into some disrepute.

Part II starts with my early childhood in Manchester. I then jumped on the educational escalator to Manchester Grammar School and Cambridge University, where I abandoned classical languages and literature for social anthropology. Two years of fieldwork in a West African slum changed me more than any other single influence. I then combined teaching anthropology in Britain and the United States with part-time employment as a development consultant. My time in America was both liberating and harrowing

---

15. C. Lévi-Strauss, *Tristes Tropiques* (1955). See T. Luhrman, 'Our Master, Our Brother' (1990) on his debt to Rousseau.

16. B. Malinowski, *Argonauts of the Western Pacific* (1922); A. Radcliffe-Brown, *The Andaman Islanders* (1922).

for reasons explored in the final chapter on health. I returned to Cambridge and secondment in Jamaica allowed me to synthesize the different phases of my life when the world was turning in 1989–94. I moved to Paris in the late 1990s, took up writing and globetrotting and began an involvement with South Africa that lasts until now.

Part III considers some aspects of our world at this moment of history. The discussion embraces a scale far wider than my own life. But, where possible, I show how I have experienced what I describe. Where are we in history and what is wrong with it? The dominant social form of the last century was national capitalism, the attempt to regulate commerce in the interest of citizens. If capitalism is socially disorganized, its modern twin – the nation state – strengthens local social cohesion at the expense of a world society capable of addressing our common human needs and interests. Globalization has occurred several times in world history. The forces driving it now have undermined national capitalism. But inequality flourishes in our world today and is now entrenched everywhere.

In Chapter 13, I explain how legal, physical and cultural separation of unequal people has become universal. The antidote to this global 'apartheid' is freedom of movement. We should consider movement to be a human right, like other freedoms, subject to laws. Chapter 14 examines the digital revolution in communications from a personal point of view. It offers universal means to spread universal ideas. To be human is to depend on impersonal social conditions. By harnessing the most advanced technologies of our era, the digital revolution has enhanced the potential for economic democracy. The main threat to this is the growing power of transnational corporations. The chapter concludes with reflections on the sources of their power.

The idea of economy goes to the heart of my attempts to connect self and world. In Chapter 15, I review my own journey in economic investigation, taking in the informal economy and later the economic potential of virtual reality. The study of money shows how personal and impersonal dimensions of society are intertwined. I have recently focused on 'human economy'. It rests on two principles: human lives should be at the centre of economy and local affairs connected to humanity as a whole. In Chapter 16, I focus on the implications of Africa's current demographic explosion for the balance of world population and the world market. A similar explosion fuelled the age of European empires. This one could have more significant consequences for humanity and world society.

Part IV attempts a partial synthesis of self in the world and the idea of life-long learning. If I had to give one reason for doing anything that channels my energies over time, it would be that I hope to learn from doing it. This book is the strongest example of that principle. Chapter 17 asks how British post-war history has shaped me, especially its politics and higher education system.

Despite being an expatriate since before the millennium, I think and write a lot about how to fix the mess my country is in. Chapter 18 exhumes some undisciplined explorations into transnational history whose motivation was to blow up the nationalist history I had been fed from childhood. Chapter 19 addresses the topic of money that has occupied me most for three decades. I suggest that money is a means of communication that combines practically the two sides of us all, our own person and the widest reaches of our social universe. Money is – or should be – how we learn to be more fully human. Chapter 20, on learning, remembering and sharing, reverts to autobiographical mode and draws some provisional conclusions.

I have compiled this book from memory and from sources written by myself and others without any disciplinary focus. In middle age I learned how to inject some life into speech and prose shaped by formal education and to gain access to my unconscious mind. Everyone's memory becomes specialized with age, and mine accumulates images, facts and stories suitable for writing and teaching purposes.

Notes and References

Apart from Part II, my life story, the other three parts have many references to written sources. My system is a compromise between a book aimed at general readers and beginning students and one with an apparatus for professional academics. I have borrowed heavily from what I wrote before. My own papers that are accessible online are listed in an Appendix, with my name and only a year and a letter in the footnotes. All literary items mentioned in the text are listed with full details at the book's end. Each is included in a footnote on the same page, listing author, title and original year of publication, with shorter descriptions to follow. Books and articles listed only in footnotes are generally not included in the References.

The End of Something

I take a broader view of money than its current identification with finance.[17] The dominant form of society in the last century is now ending. Society is losing its national form and has not yet found a more inclusive one. After the financial crisis of 2008, leading governments sought to stave off economic collapse by using taxpayers' money to rescue the banks. Now the ability of central banks to use money as a tool of economic management is

17. See Chapter 19.

nearly exhausted; capital markets and national paper currencies have become unsustainable. The world is in the grip of a growing debt crisis fuelled by easy money. This is a turning point. Its denouement could be global depression, world war, fascism or democratic revolution.

The social form that dominated the last century, 'national capitalism', is a synthesis of industrial capitalism and nation states – the attempt to manage money, markets and accumulation through central bureaucracies representing the interests of citizens. G.W.F. Hegel articulated this programme in the 1820s;[18] it was launched by political and technological revolutions of the 1860s and early 1870s; a subsequent phase of European imperialism lasted until the First World War. Nation states then became the norm, especially after 1945 with the collapse of European empires. The social organization of money is unravelling fast.[19]

The 1860s saw a transport and communications revolution (steamships, continental railways and the telegraph) that decisively opened up the world economy. A series of political revolutions gave the leading powers of the next century the institutional means of organizing industrial capitalism. These included the American Civil War, the abolition of serfdom in Russia, Italy's Risorgimento and Japan's Meiji Restoration. Queen Victoria became Empress of India after a decade of democratic reforms at home. German unification led to the Franco-Prussian War, the Paris Commune and the French Third Republic. Karl Marx published *Capital* in 1867 and the First International was formed in 1864. Despite the appearance of global integration then, international trade still accounted for under 1 per cent of most national economies.[20]

Capitalism has always rested on an unequal contract between owners of money and those who make and buy their products. This contract depends on an effective threat of punishment if workers withhold their labour or buyers fail to pay up. The owners cannot make that threat alone: they need the support of governments, laws, prisons, police, even armies. By the mid-nineteenth century, the machine revolution was pulling unprecedented numbers of people into the cities, where they added a new dimension to problems of crowd control. The political revolutions of the 1860s were based on an explicit alliance between capitalists and the military landlord class to form states capable of managing industrial workforces and taming criminal gangs who controlled large swathes of the main cities.[21]

---

18. G.W.F. Hegel, *The Philosophy of Right* (1821).

19. Hart, Appendix 2000a, 2015f.

20. W.A. Lewis, *The Evolution of the International Economic Order* (1978).

21. Martin Scorsese's film (2002) takes its name and the 1863 setting from H. Asbury, *Gangs of New York* (1927).

After the Second World War, a world revolution installed developmental states in Western industrial democracies, the Soviet Bloc and newly independent countries. These aimed to reduce inequality by expanding public services and workers' incomes, while controlling capital flows. Ronald Reagan and Margaret Thatcher inaugurated a counter-revolution against all this whose main purpose was to replace political controls by 'free markets' that were only free for capital. This market fundamentalism has now spawned two variants.[22] The globalism of the transnational corporations confronts xenophobic nationalism, autocracy and protectionism.

National capitalism failed because money escaped from the political controls imposed after 1945. The causes include neoliberal policies and ideology; the reduced powers and legitimacy of nation states; the lawless global money circuit; the breakdown of the post-war international order; the replacement of citizenship by identity politics; financial imperialism; escalating inequality; debt and austerity; the rise of the corporations; the digital revolution and globalization; autocratic rulers and xenophobic nationalism. Humanity is sleepwalking into a disaster.

I don't have solutions for this mess, but I hope, through my example of lifelong learning, to help some readers become more aware of their own place in our current human predicament.

---

22. Hart, Appendix 2018a. See Chapters 14 and 15.

Part I

ANCESTORS

Chapter 1

WRITING THE SELF

A Genealogy

Michel de Montaigne's Self-Portrait

Montaigne and Shakespeare have often been identified as the first modern writers. All literature since them has explored their basic theme, the sense of being unsure of who you are.[1] Michel de Montaigne (1533–92) was a noble-man who lived in south-west France and sometimes held public office. He had the idea of writing about himself as 'a mirror in which other people recognize their own humanity'. He became the first modern writer. Montaigne wrote 107 essays of varying length, each on a named topic. These addressed big questions – his was a time of religious war. His book depicts an individual character, himself, his everyday life and deepest personal questions. Most writers, like me, are concerned with mental questions, but not Montaigne. We learn in detail about his bodily functions. After all, everyone has a body. The essays are a treatise on universal human nature told through disconnected fragments. In form they are not a treatise at all. Montaigne's *Essays* are not an autobiography, but a self-portrait.[2] There is no overall narrative or retrospec-tive view of his career as a whole, just parts. We learn nothing of his sixteen years as a jurist or of his four years as Bordeaux's mayor.

---

1. S. Bakewell, *How to Live: A Life of Montaigne* (2010).
2. C. Brush, *From the Perspective of the Self: Montaigne's Self-Portrait* (1994).

What I chiefly portray is my cogitations, a shapeless subject that does not lend itself to expression in actions. . . My actions would tell more about fortune than about me. They bear witness to their own part, not to mine, unless it be by conjecture and without certainty.[3]

Philippe Desan believes that Montaigne's persona as someone who has retreated into domestic life is misleading.[4] He shows him as a politician finely attuned to the conflicts of his day, arguing that in the *Essays* he concealed his real intentions behind the façade of a humanist litterateur. I disagree. Montaigne was sometimes a politician and they often lack a private life. That is a good reason for him to explore his private life. In any case, this is the most personal book of philosophy ever written.

Montaigne claimed that his 'was the only book of its kind in the world. Authors communicate with the people by some special extrinsic mark; I am the first to do so by my entire being, as Michel de Montaigne, not as a grammarian or a poet or a jurist'.[5] As Craig Brush puts it, 'His book raises the paean to the self, and suggests that becoming an essayist is the surest way to fulfil the potentiality innate in each self'.[6]

Montaigne always placed himself in the foreground and the *Essays* do reflect a coherent view of his self. But the man and his book are not the same. Each chapter has two levels: its ostensible topic and the author. The reader is a third party. Montaigne knew that once he let go of his book, readers would do with it whatever they liked. He embraced that possibility in his style and organization. Montaigne often addresses readers by the familiar *tu*. His tone is friendly and he is not a name dropper. Most of the public personages he mentions are anonymous.

Montaigne, apparently a modest humanist philosopher, set his personal observations and reflections against his reading of classical authors such as Plutarch. He relies heavily on anecdotes taken from ancient Greece and Rome. We read about great figures like Caesar and Pompey, but with no hint of hero worship. Montaigne treats them as equals, his familiars. This too reduces the gap between author and reader and encourages us to treat his book as a personal resource. He banks on us accepting his honesty and good faith. Rousseau thought the *Essays* were pioneering, but he 'laughed at the false naivety of Montaigne who, while pretending to confess his faults, is very careful to give himself only loveable ones'. Brush takes Rousseau's side here: 'He does admit again and again to having been foolish, but his book is so

---

3. M. de Montaigne, *Essays* (1957 [1580–95]: 274).

4. P. Desan, *Montaigne: Une biographie politique* (2014).

5. Montaigne (ibid.: 278).

6. Brush (ibid.: 263).

far from being foolish that we find it somewhat hard to believe.'[7] Rousseau's reactionary opponents, starting with Voltaire, often focus on his faults. Montaigne seems to have escaped scot-free.

The *Essays* were long banned on the Continent, but the English were enthusiastic. Shakespeare was a contemporary who knew their first translator into English, Florio. Many have looked for Montaigne's influence in his plays, the favourite being *Hamlet*. Shakespeare's plays could allocate his contradictions to different characters and set them in action on the stage. The poet Alexander Pope noted of the *Essays* in his copy:

> This is (in my Opinion) the very best Book for Information of Manners that has been writ; This Author says nothing but what everyone feels at the Heart.[8]

William Hazlitt based his own approach to writing essays on Montaigne. He and his sons made sure that the Victorians had access to him:

> [Essayists], says Hazlitt, capture things as they really are rather than as they should be. Montaigne allowed everything to be what it was, including himself, and he knew how to look at things. An ideal essay. . . plays the whole game of human life over before us, and enables us to become agents [who] have to perform a part.[9]

Nietzsche based his *Gay Science* on Montaigne's approach.[10] The *Essays'* fans include Diderot, Voltaire, Gibbon, Sand, Emerson and many others.

The affinity between the *Essays* and ethnography is obvious. But today's anthropologists lack Montaigne's vision of humanity. I side with Montaigne more than Rousseau and Brush on self-revelation. I prefer to teach students what pleases me. But I have included unflattering episodes here. My core ideas and practices have one source in a life that always involves reading a lot. My method is more historical than ethnographic. This book, I hope, is honestly written in good faith with my readers.

Jean-Jacques Rousseau's Two Exercises in Autobiography

Rousseau (1712–78)[11] had a purple patch in the early 1760s when he published books on politics, sexuality and education. All hell broke loose with

---

7. J.-J. Rousseau, Preamble to *The Confessions* (1782); Brush (ibid.: 245).

8. M. Novak (ed.), *English Literature in the Age of Disguise* (1982: 225).

9. Bakewell (ibid.: 283).

10. F. Nietzsche, *The Gay Science* (1882).

11. See Chapter 2 for Rousseau as a founder of modern anthropology.

the publication of the last one, *Emile: On Education*. Rousseau took refuge in Neuchatel, Switzerland. Its governor, George Keith, with David Hume's help, found him a safe house in England. He wrote most of *The Confessions* there. It was published after his death.

> I have entered upon a performance that is without example, whose accomplishment will have no imitator. I mean to present my fellow-mortals with a man in all the integrity of nature; and this man shall be myself. . . I have concealed no crimes, added no virtues.[12]

We each have a big voice and a little voice. The first tells us that we are a hero, star, genius; the second says, you're a fraud and they will soon find you out. This second voice keeps us sane, but without the first we would never attempt great things. Rousseau lacked a little voice here and was borderline mad. The English sojourn ended badly. He blamed Hume for a satirical letter published in France and England and signed by the 'King of Prussia'. Horace Walpole later admitted to having been its author. The English demonized Rousseau as the author of the French Revolution.

He was allowed back to Paris if he never wrote about politics or religion. He made a poor living there from copying music scores. He was the first object of celebrity tourism and wrote one more beautiful book, *Reveries of The Solitary Walker*.[13] This collection of ten essays has little of the strident egotism of *The Confessions*. They reveal deep self-knowledge, acute observation and even irony. The sixth walk deserves a place in the pantheon of discourse on the gift. On a regular weekend stroll, a crippled little boy addresses Rousseau by name and, touched, he gives him a sweet. The same thing happens next time and again. . . The spontaneous gift is by now expected and a burden. Jean-Jacques changes his favourite walk to avoid the boy. The seventh walk takes him to an Alpine wilderness:

> I compared myself to those great explorers who discover a desert island, and said complacently to myself: 'Doubtless I am the first mortal to set foot in this place.'. . . While I was preening myself on this notion, I heard not far off a certain clicking noise which sounded familiar. . . Surprised and intrigued, I got up, pushed through a thicket of undergrowth in the direction of the noise, and in a hollow twenty yards from the very place where I had thought to be the first person to tread, I saw a stocking mill.[14]

The little voice (and sanity) returns here. *Emile* reveals its author and has much more to teach us than *The Confessions*.[15] The *Reveries* is a delightful book,

---

12. J.-J. Rousseau, *Confessions* (2008 [1782]: 1).

13. J.-J. Rousseau, *Reveries of a Solitary Walker* (1782).

14. Rousseau (ibid.: 118).

15. See Chapter 2.

a low-key memoir in essay form. It belongs with Montaigne's *Essays* in style, content and humanity.[16] But Rousseau shows his quirky side, as Montaigne does not.

Benjamin Franklin's Autobiography

Benjamin Franklin (1706–90)[17] was celebrated as 'the greatest man in the world' during his lifetime. He was the youngest son of a Boston soap and candle maker with almost no formal education. He taught himself to read and write very well. At 17 he ran away to Philadelphia. There he became a successful tradesman, printer and journalist. He retired at 42 with a fortune large enough to support 'Leisure during the rest of my life for Philosophical Studies and Amusements'.[18] He entered public service and co-wrote the Declaration of Independence. He was lionized in Paris as American minister to France and took part in the Constitutional Convention of 1787.

Franklin unusually attributed his business success to his love of reading and writing.[19] He was a prolific inventor. He synthesized electricity out of the fragments available then. He wrote on 'agriculture, chess, military strategy, literary style, silkworms, pickled sturgeon, ice boats, mastodon teeth, garters and the balance of trade'.[20] To call him a polymath doesn't capture it. He was noted for his wit. Franklin travelled a lot as the revolution's foreign spokesman.

The *Autobiography* was written in instalments at home and abroad: the first section in England when he was 65, the second in France thirteen years later, the third and fourth in Philadelphia when he was over 80; but the book breaks off before his illustrious career in politics began. The Parisians said he looked like a peasant and admired him anyway. His book too is written without regard for appearance. He emphasizes his Puritan family background, with little style or emotion showing. His readers already knew him; he had no need of boasting.

Franklin's is an understated account of his public legend. It is a just-so story about what he valued and thought he personified of the American Dream: material success, moral regeneration and social progress. Millions

16. The all-time winner for self-effacing humanity in an autobiography is David Hume's *My Own Life* (1777). It was written on his deathbed in Edinburgh and is only three thousand words.

17. B. Franklin, *The Autobiography* (1790).

18. https://theobjectivestandard.com/2018/04/benjamin-franklin-the-enlightenment-personified/ (accessed 8 July 2021).

19. Warren Buffett, the legendary investor, also tells aspiring entrepreneurs to read two hundred books a year.

20. K. Silverman, 'Introduction', *Benjamin Franklin's Autobiography and Other Writings* (1986: 2).

who identify with America find their beliefs confirmed there. Its detractors find 'a national creed of capitalist avarice, sexual repression and bourgeois comfort'.[21] The author presents himself as being guided by reason, moderation and virtue. He offers few glimpses of the complex human being he was. Franklin seems to know nothing of Rousseau's struggles with contradiction.

Edward Gibbon's Memoirs of My Life and Writings

Edward Gibbon's (1737–94) *History of the Decline and Fall of the Roman Empire* was published in six volumes late in his life.[22] He was the only English member of the eighteenth-century European Enlightenment. He also wrote memoirs.[23] They combine truth with irony, confidence with modesty. Like all his work they are beautifully written. He spent a dozen years at the beginning and end of his adult life in Lausanne, Switzerland. My wife's clan lives at opposite ends of Lac Léman.

Gibbon's genealogy includes Pliny, Petrarch, Augustine, Erasmus, Montaigne, Cellini and Rousseau. Echoing Montaigne, he writes to please himself. Readers will find here as lucid an account of one mind as anywhere. It starts in a conflict with his father. A disastrous interlude at Oxford and a short-lived conversion to Catholicism follow. He then spends five years coming of age (16–21) in Lausanne. His account of living in a foreign place and language would be duplicated by many ethnographers. His transition from a lazy upper-class English twit into a top-drawer European intellectual is remarkable. Gibbon learned to think and write in French. He corresponded with leading thinkers. He had much help from a self-effacing Swiss tutor.

Gibbon's alienation from this one-horse town rings a bell too. But it encouraged self-learning. 'Every man who rises above the common level has received two educations: the first from his teachers; the second, more personal and important, from himself'.[24] He read the Latin writers, inventing a rigorous programme of language-learning:

> I breathed the spirit I translated, for instance, an epistle of Cicero into French; and later re-translated my French into such Latin as I could find; and then compared each sentence with the original. I persevered till I had acquired the knowledge of both idioms, and the command at least of a correct style.[25]

21. Silverman (ibid.).

22. E. Gibbon, *The History of the Decline and Fall of the Roman Empire* (six volumes, 1776–89).

23. E. Gibbon, *Memoirs of my Life and Writings* (1796).

24. Gibbon (ibid.: 46).

25. Gibbon (ibid.: 232).

Gibbon fell in love with a young local woman, Suzanne Curchod, a pastor's daughter whose wit, beauty and erudition he found compelling. Their engagement was cut short when his father, on whom he depended financially, opposed the match. 'I sighed as a lover, I obeyed as a son. Whatsoever have been the fruits of my education, they must be ascribed to the fortunate banishment which placed me at Lausanne'.[26]

Suzanne wasn't fazed by losing her English intellectual. She left for Paris, went shopping and realized she had to marry to survive there. She hooked Jacques Necker, a Geneva banker. Before long she ran a literary salon and helped found the Necker children's hospital. Her husband was Louis XVI's chief minister. His sacking by the King provoked the storming of the Bastille. They returned to Switzerland after the revolution wiped out a serious chunk of Necker's fortune. Their daughter, Germaine de Staël,[27] became Europe's leading woman intellectual and a vigorous opponent of Napoleon. She organized a literary circle at Coppet between Geneva and Lausanne. It included her lover, Benjamin Constant, her father, Humboldt, Byron, Sismondi, Chateaubriand and Schlegel.[28]

Suzanne Curchod's achievements, like George Keith's, are less well known than the famous people they nurtured. If I could have another life, I would use it to write their biographies. Gibbon maintained friendly relations with the Necker family. He returned in old age to live in Lausanne and wrote the last three volumes of *Decline and Fall* there. His first book had been an essay in French on its literature, published in London. Unsurprisingly, it flopped. He soon found his vocation as a historian, launching two projects on European democracy. The first was 'The History of the Liberty of the Swiss'. How could 'a poor warlike and virtuous republic' defeat the leading powers of the day and 'emerge into glory and freedom'? The Swiss abolished feudalism without bloodshed and repelled invasions by Austria, France and Burgundy. Unfortunately,

> . . . the materials of this history are inaccessible to me, fast locked in the obscurity of an old barbarous German dialect, of which I am totally ignorant, and which I cannot resolve to learn for this sole and peculiar purpose.[29]

The second was 'The History of the Republic of Florence under the House of the Medicis'. 'A commonwealth, soft, opulent, and corrupt, is precipitated by a chain of revolutions from the abuse to the loss of her liberty in a period of

---

26. Gibbon (ibid.: 11).

27. https://en.wikipedia.org/wiki/Germaine_de_Sta%C3%ABl (accessed 8 September 2021).

28. https://en.wikipedia.org/wiki/Coppet_group (accessed 8 September 2021).

29. Gibbon (ibid.: 133).

150 years'.[30] The Florence book also bit the dust. But Gibbon's reflections on Rome's decay led him to the writing project that made him immortal. 'My youthful habits of the language and manners of France left in my mind an ardent desire of revisiting the Continent on a larger and more liberal plan'.[31]

Criticisms of Christianity in *Decline and Fall*'s first volume provoked a storm of public controversy. Gibbon corresponded with David Hume, who told him that publishing his book in French was crazy. Hume's observations echo my own feelings about Brexit England and Trump's America:

> I own that if I had not had previously the happiness of your personal acquaintance, such a performance from an Englishman in our age would have given me some surprise . . . Your countrymen, for almost a whole generation, have given themselves up to barbarous and absurd faction, and have totally neglected all polite letters. I no longer expected any valuable production to come from them. . . The prevalence of superstition in England prognosticates the fall of philosophy and the decay of taste.[32]

Florence's descent from democracy seems particularly apt for our times. We leave Gibbon and his memoirs in an elegiac mood.

> The first and indispensable requisite of happiness is a clear conscience, unsullied by the reproach or remembrance of an unworthy action. The freedom of my writings has indeed provoked an implacable tribe; but an author cannot be indifferent to the fair testimonies of private and public esteem.[33]

Wordsworth's Prelude

> The mind of Man is framed even like the breath
> And harmony of music. There is a dark
> Invisible workmanship that reconciles
> Discordant elements, and makes them move
> In one society.
>
> —William Wordsworth, *The Prelude*

William Wordsworth (1770–1850) was not always an establishment poet who celebrated daffodils. He went from north-west England to St John's College, Cambridge[34] just before the French Revolution. He then spent 1791–93 in France and embraced Republican ideas. He had a child with Annette

---

30. Gibbon (ibid.: 122).

31. Gibbon (ibid.: 135).

32. Cited in Gibbon (ibid.: 91).

33. Gibbon (ibid.: 116).

34. The Wordsworth Room in my college is a place for meetings and private banquets. I held my first wedding reception there.

Vallon, but political and financial problems made him return to England. He immediately published his first poems. In 1802, he wrote a poem, 'To Toussaint L'Ouverture',[35] then dying in a French prison:

TOUSSAINT, the most unhappy of men!
Whether the whistling Rustic tend his plough
Within thy hearing, or thy head be now
Pillowed in some deep dungeon's earless den;
O miserable Chieftain! where and when
Wilt thou find patience? Yet die not; do thou
Wear rather in thy bonds a cheerful brow:
Though fallen thyself, never to rise again,
Live, and take comfort. Thou hast left behind
Powers that will work for thee; air, earth, and skies;
There's not a breathing of the common wind
That will forget thee; thou hast great allies;
Thy friends are exultations, agonies,
And love, and man's unconquerable mind.

In 1798, he wrote the first version of an epic poem that is 'the most sustained self-examination in English poetry',[36] about the growth of his mind from childhood. He reworked it all his life, producing more texts in 1799, 1805 and 1850 soon after his death, when it was published as *The Prelude*. In the evenings, he read out passages to his family. The 1805 version runs to thirteen books and 240 pages.[37] It reads like an English translation of Virgil.

My last and favourite aspiration—then
I yearn towards some philosophic song
Of truth that cherishes our daily life,
With meditations passionate from deep
Recesses in man's heart, immortal verse. . .[38]

But who shall parcel out
His intellect by geometric rules,
Split like a province into round and square?
Who knows the individual hour in which
His habits were first sown even as a seed
Who that shall point as with a wand, and say
'This portion of the river of my mind
Came from yon fountain'?[39]

---

35. W. Wordsworth, 'To Toussaint L'Ouverture' (1802). See C.L.R. James in Chapters 3 and 9.

36. S. Gill, *William Wordsworth: A Life* (1989: 13).

37. W. Wordsworth, *The Prelude: The Four Texts* (1995).

38. Wordsworth (ibid.: 1, lines 231–35).

39. Wordsworth (ibid.: 2, lines 243–49).

And:

> Meanwhile, my hope has been that I might fetch
> Invigorating thoughts from former years,
> Might fix the wavering balance of my mind,
> And haply meet reproaches, too, whose power
> May spur me on, in manhood now mature,
> To honourable toil.[40]

The Education of Henry Adams

Henry Adams (1838–1918) was descended from two American presidents. His maternal grandfather was a Boston plutocrat. He died at the end of the Great War and his autobiography, *The Education of Henry Adams*, came out the next year. It won the Pulitzer Prize. The Modern Library ranked it first in the last century's best non-fiction. His nine-volume *History of the United States during the Administrations of Thomas Jefferson and James Madison* (1801–17) is also very well written.[41]

Adams was a student at Harvard, where he was 'barred from philosophy and bored by facts'. He hated the education there as both student and teacher. One student told him that a Harvard degree was worth money in Chicago. In Adams's circle a Harvard degree was a drawback for a young man of his class. In the 1860s he was private secretary to his father as Lincoln's ambassador to London. John Stuart Mill confirmed his belief that the intellectual elite could take the lead in a democracy. He retired from Harvard at 39 and wrote history, journalism and the occasional novel, anonymously in the main.

Adams was a serious globetrotter and valued his close friends. He kept up a passionate friendship with a senator's wife. His wife suffered from depression and committed suicide. The years 1872–92, when all this happened, were left out of his memoir. The book begins with homage to Rousseau's *Confessions*, although *Emile* is about self-education. Like Kant, Adams claims that his own education was useless a century later. His world was in permanent revolution driven by technology. Adams refers to himself throughout in the third person. Objects had triumphed over subjectivity.

The Enlightenment followed self-realization as a path to making a new world. But industrial capitalism undermined that possibility and the forms of knowledge followed suit. Adams chose as the key symbol of his times the elec-

---

40. Wordsworth (ibid.: 1, lines 450–55).

41. H. Adams, *The Education of Henry Adams* (1918) and *History of the United States, 1801–1817* (1889–91).

tric 'dynamo', then replacing the steam engine as the motor of industry.[42] He bitterly regretted his lack of maths and science; and his understanding of science was weak. He says he got his education from varied experience, friendship and reading. His language relies more on scientific metaphors than knowledge:

> Education should try to lessen the obstacles, diminish the friction, invigorate the energy, and should train minds to react, not at haphazard, but by choice, on the lines of force that attract their world.[43]

Henry Adams had no time for the common culture that Alexis de Tocqueville saw as the cornerstone of the early American democracy.[44] Hereditary privilege required him to lead society, but not to question his class's role in subverting democracy. Yet his writing has broad human appeal. Midway between us and the eighteenth century, he kept alive self-learning as a theme for autobiography.

Vladimir Nabokov's *Speak, Memory*

The escalating power of industry in the nineteenth century introduced a rift between individuals and society. This grew wider in the impersonal societies of the last century. Scientific modernism – quantum (Planck) and relativity (Einstein) – sought to unify extremes of scale. But this outlook never penetrated the social sciences. Recent approaches to complexity use non-linear equations to investigate chaos, order and phase transitions – as when fast-moving water molecules become fixed as ice. Chaos is itself determinate. James P. Crutchfield, an American mathematician and physicist, asks 'What lies between order and chaos? The answer now seems remarkably simple: human innovation'.[45] The middle ground is where life and creativity grow. As Vladimir Nabokov (1899–1977) puts it,

> There is, it would seem, in the dimensional scale of the world a kind of delicate meeting place of imagination and knowledge, a point, arrived at by diminishing large things and enlarging small ones that is intrinsically artistic.[46]

How do we bridge the gap between a puny self and a vast universe? As Nabokov says, we need to scale the world down and scale up the self, so that

---

42. The Cambridge physicist James Clerk Maxwell aired a thought experiment in thermodynamics around 1870. A demon ('Maxwell's demon') regulates the flow of gas molecules between two chambers. Adams gets the idea wrong.

43. Adams, *Education*: 163.

44. A. de Tocqueville, *Democracy in America* (1840). See Chapter 10.

45. J. Crutchfield, 'What Lies between Order and Chaos?' (2002).

46. V. Nabokov, *Speak, Memory: An Autobiography Revisited* (2000 [1951]: 197).

the two can meet. This is not just about individuals and society, but the time and space coordinates we find ourselves in – bridging the big things and the little things that make up our lives. Ritual and prayer once connected people to an object world personified as God. Works of fiction – plays, novels, movies – now perform a similar role. The world or history is reduced in scale to a stage, paperback or screen, allowing us to enter it subjectively on any terms. Sophocles and Shakespeare are pre-eminent social thinkers because their plays bridge the personal and impersonal dimensions of existence. The digital revolution has collapsed this opposition.[47] But Western societies are still trapped in the world they made in the nineteenth century.

Vladimir Nabokov's noble Russian family fled the revolution in 1917. He became a student at Cambridge University (1919–22). His family moved to Berlin. He married a Russian-Jewish woman and they left Germany in 1937. In May 1940 he left France for the US in the face of Nazi violence. He stayed for two decades before moving back to France and Switzerland. Nabokov wrote a score of novels. The best-known is *Lolita*. His autobiography *Speak, Memory* covers only four decades, from his birth in St Petersburg to boarding ship in Le Havre. He is one of the great prose stylists. When first writing the memoir, he had no access to documents. This placed a great burden on his memory.[48] Later, he revised it to take account of written sources. The original version was *Speak, Mnemosyne*, the Greek goddess of memory. But 'little old ladies wouldn't like to ask for a book whose title they can't pronounce'.[49]

Speak, Memory is a collation of essays written at different times. The first, 'Mademoiselle O', was published in French in 1936. Its evocative and polished prose is a delight, but Nabokov's Swiss tutor is revealed in sensuous detail with no storyline. Nabokov tests his memory by recalling concrete visual images in great detail. We learn a lot about him and those he watches, but it is hard to follow what is going on. He had a condition known as synaesthesia, where people link something to a sense not normally associated with it. His version was 'colour hearing': each letter had a specific colour. Moreover, he 'heard' them in different languages – Russian, French and English. This explains a lot.

Chinua Achebe as a British-Protected Child

Turning and turning in the widening gyre / The falcon cannot hear the falconer; / Things fall apart; the centre cannot hold; / Mere anarchy is loosed upon the world.[50]

—W.B. Yeats, 'The Second Coming'

47. See Chapter 14.
48. See Chapter 20.
49 50. Foreword, loc.64, Kindle edition.
50. W.B. Yeats 'The Second Coming' (1920).

In 2003 I spent a term teaching at Northwestern University in Evanston, Illinois. The Iraq war was being launched. I compiled an auto-ethnography of that moment and later assembled my observations as 'Notes on the Counter-Revolution'[51]

> I had been to a meeting at the University of Chicago to protest the Iraq war and now had to take the Red Line to Howard and onto Evanston. I was reading Chinua Achebe's *Things Fall Apart* for a class. The title is taken from W.B. Yeats' poem 'The second coming' and that of his second novel, *No Longer at Ease* from T.S. Eliot's 'The journey of the magi'. These reflect awareness of a decline foreseen in *Things Fall Apart*. *No Longer at Ease* ends not with a machete swing but a gavel's tap.[52]
>
> I once read a book by Stephen Toulmin called *Cosmopolis*.[53] There he merges two poems by John Donne and Yeats, including this one. He claims that both poets were radical conservatives who, disgusted with contemporary society, would renew it in the name of a value taken from the past. One wanted to restore nobility based on kinship, the other the Irish peasantry, the fairies. . . Donne and Yeats are my two favourite poets, so what does that make me? Ever since, I have thought of myself as a radical conservative. Witness the fact that I prefer to read old books. The past value I want to revive is the eighteenth-century Enlightenment and its democratic revolutions. This idea now underpins my Human Economy project.
>
> The Chicago Transit Authority train made halting progress towards Howard (the nearest source of booze and sex for the inmates of the dry Methodist town where I worked). It came to me, not an original thought, but new to me. We are living in fascism now. I recalled a book about the US between the wars, *The Aspirin Age*, when fascism was a major theme – Huey Long, Father Coughlin etc.[54] I realized that the Bush clique continued this line, now with the state-within-a-state in tow (the Pentagon fuelled by two-thirds of American taxes), the most irresponsible American corporations and fundamentalist Christianity as a vision for fixing the world. I felt more sympathy for my depressed American friends. The United States has come under the control of fascists.[55]

Chinua Achebe (1930–2013) was a leading figure in the writers' movement that helped to advance the democratic revolution in Africa. I find him inspiring, not just for the humane lucidity of his prose, but as a passionate advocate for Africa. I first read *Things Fall Apart*[56] in Accra's slums and wept – he could say more in a page than I would in all my PhD thesis. He later published an

---

51. Hart, Appendix 2003d.
52. T.S. Eliot: 'The World Ends Not with a Bang, but with a Whimper', *The Hollow Men* (1925).
53. S. Toulmin, *Cosmopolis: The Hidden Agenda of Modernity* (1990).
54. I. Leighton (ed), *The Aspirin Age, 1919–1941* (1965).
55. The movie *Vice* (2018) brings it all back.
56. C. Achebe, *Things Fall Apart* (1958).

unusual autobiography – short essays written at various stages of his life. The collection takes its title from the lead essay.[57] I heard the original speech in Cambridge in 1993 and befriended his son, the archaeologist Ike Achebe.

> It is a gross crime for anyone to impose himself on another, to seize his land and history, and then to make out that the victim is a minor requiring protection. . .[58] What misfortune does [the middle ground] fence out? Fanaticism. . . It is the home of doubt and indecision, of make-believe[59] [T]he great thing about being human is our ability to face adversity down by refusing to be defined by it. . . The middle ground [is] where the human spirit resists an abridgement of its humanity.[60]

The ancient Greeks knew Achebe's 'middle ground' as 'the golden mean'.[61] This meant nothing in excess, the desirable middle between two extremes, excess and deficiency. In other words, don't perch on one pole of a dialectical pair.[62] Every one of the authors introduced here was a humanist in that sense.

---

57. C. Achebe, *The Education of a British-Protected Child* (2011).

58. 60. Ibid.: 7.

59. 59. Ibid.: 5-6.

60. 61. Ibid.: 22–23.

61. *Aurea mediocritas* in Latin.

62. See Chapters 15 and 20.

Chapter 2

ANTHROPOLOGY'S FORGOTTEN FOUNDERS

Many teachers and students of anthropology today identify its modern origins with racist colonial empire and now with the academic bureaucracy they are trapped in. Professionals trace their 'discipline' to great Victorian synthesizers, such as Morgan, Tylor and Frazer,[1] whose labours prepared the way for the ethnographic revolution and academic seclusion of the last century. For them, 'conjectural history' was a mistake linked to discredited empires. As a result, anthropology privileges a passive and narrow localism that has lost the nineteenth century's aspiration to understand human history as a whole.

My aim here is to revive modern anthropology's origins in the democratic revolutions of the eighteenth century, to show that there was a progressive anthropology before colonial empire and bureaucratic capitalism, a tradition that has survived as a minority undercurrent that I call 'the anthropology of unequal society' and that could inform our attempts to break out of the dead end we have reached. Giambattista Vico, Jean-Jacques Rousseau and Immanuel Kant were the pioneers of anthropology as a central plank of the drive to replace unequal societies. They hoped to unify humanity's two sides, the individual and society, in a new theory of human nature. The Victorians knew that society was global and human history far from finished. Imperialism was eventually undermined from within – by Marx's class contradictions, Freud's psychological discoveries and the growing voices of excluded classes such as

---

1. E.B. Tylor, *Primitive Culture* (1871); L.H. Morgan, *Ancient Society* (1877); J.G. Frazer, *The Golden Bough* (1890).

women. Racism provoked revolt in the colonies. The First World War was the midwife of a new paradigm, fieldwork-based ethnography. But this approach ended up serving national bureaucracy.

I select two figures from the early twentieth century as positive examples for us today: the English psychologist and anthropologist W.H.R. Rivers and the French sociologist and ethnologist Marcel Mauss. Some leading anthropologists of the last century sustained the critique of unequal society begun by Rousseau: Claude Lévi-Strauss, Marshall Sahlins, Eric Wolf and Jack Goody, to whom David Graeber offers a bridge to our century.[2] In Chapter 3, I argue that the anti-colonial revolution of the mid-century produced a rich vein of intellectuals who still have a lot to teach us.

Giambattista Vico (1668–1744)

We need to understand better how we build the infrastructures of collective existence. How do meanings come to be shared and memory to transcend the minutiae of personal experience? Giambattista Vico was a Neapolitan philosopher trained in jurisprudence whose life spanned the seventeenth century's scientific revolution and the eighteenth's Enlightenment. He was a nearer contemporary to Isaac Newton (1642–1726) than to Rousseau and Kant. After writing some important books, including the first autobiography by a philosopher, he published in 1725 his *Scienza Nuova*, 'The New Science' (or 'Knowledge'), a revised version of which came out in 1744.[3]

Vico justifiably believed that he was breaking new ground. His masterpiece had some influence on the German Romantics, but was only read widely in the nineteenth century, mainly thanks to the French historian Jules Michelet and the English poet Samuel Taylor Coleridge. Vico's influence has grown steadily since, but not much among anthropologists.[4] He has made a mark on modern philosophy, history, cultural studies, education, literary criticism, psychology and sociology. Vico in his autobiography claims he has been a 'teacher of himself'.

Beginnings, for him, mattered more than the ends (*telos*) of Aristotelian philosophy. The origin of nations, their birth (for nations are by definition

---

2. C. Lévi-Strauss, *The Elementary Structures of Kinship* (1949); M. Sahlins, *Social Stratification in Polynesia* (1958); E. Wolf, *Europe and the Peoples Without History* (1982); J. Goody, *Production and Reproduction* (1976); D. Graeber, *Debt: The First 5,000 Years* (2011); Hart, Appendix 2012b, 2014a.

3. G. Vico, *The Autobiography of Giambattista Vico* (1725); *New Science of Giambattista Vico* (1984 [1744]).

4. T. Costelloe, 'Giambattista Vico' (1995); I. Berlin, *Vico and Herder* (1976); P. Burke, *Vico* (1985).

born), was made by poetry, drawing selectively on what went before. In their maturity they came to depend more on reason, replacing the creative imagination of children and artists with the rationality and routines of adulthood. Societies became sclerotic and eventually died, bequeathing some elements to the next cultural synthesis. Vico developed a distinction between ideas and language. Philosophy aims to discover the principles of universal history, while philology discovers new principles of poetry which emerged naturally in the first nations. There is

> an ideal eternal history. . . traversed in time by the particular histories of the nations, each with its rise, development, acme, decline and fall.[5]

Vico intended his approach to knowledge to refute Descartes's hypothetico-deductive method, which treated phenomena as illusions if they could not be expressed logically or mathematically. For him, full knowledge of anything involves discovering how human action made it. Human beings are above all social: 'man makes himself the measure of all things'.[6] People judge distant and unknown things by what is familiar and at hand. Phenomena can only be known through their origins and causes. Wisdom comes from 'the science of making such use of things as their nature dictates'. Vico distinguishes between 'the true' (vero) and 'the certain' (certo); the first is the universal and eternal object of knowledge and the product of reason; whereas consciousness is particular and individual, the result of human choice. These two disciplines combine in a 'new critical art'. Philosophy articulates what makes experience intelligible; philology addresses the empirical consequences of human choice: language, custom and civic behaviour. Knowledge of facts requires us to grasp both the necessity of common human affairs and the contingency and causes of events.

The origin of nations has two distinct features, each part of human nature: 'the age of gods and heroes' results from memory and creative acts of imagination; while 'the age of men' is based on reflection. Institutions arise first from sense-experience – feelings and the childlike human capacity to imitate and anthropomorphize the world around them. Since 'in the world's childhood men were by nature sublime poets', nations must be 'poetic in their beginnings', so that their history can be discovered by recreating or remembering the 'poetic' or 'metaphysical' truth that underpins them.

Vico's vision of history is both linear and cyclical. Civilization's progress is human nature made actual; but history in individual instances consists in cycles that link particular histories to general patterns of invention and diffusion. Centuries before modern scholars studied the making of oral poetry

---

5. Vico, *Autobiography*: 167–69.
6. Protagoras of Abdera (c.490–c.420 BCE) cited by Plato.

in the contemporary Balkans, Vico brought astonishing insight to the role of great poets in forming ancient civilizations. 'Homer', he decided, cannot be the creative act of a single individual.[7] Homeric poetry rather represents the imaginative universals of the Greek people themselves, their models and ideals. The historical Homer was

> . . . quite simply a man of the people. . . a purely ideal poet who never existed in the world of nature . . . but was an idea of Grecian men insofar as they told their histories in song.[8]

Around 2000, I published a book on how the internet was transforming money.[9] My historical investigations brought 'the age of gods and heroes' and 'the age of men' into striking proximity. The word 'money' comes from Juno Moneta, the Roman goddess of memory, whose temple was the mint. A core meaning of the verb *monere* is to recall. Money is a kind of memory bank and one of its prime functions is remembering. Vico's thoughts on memory are brilliant. He points out that in the heyday of the Roman Republic, the Latin word *memoria* meant not only remembering, but also imagination.[10] Then, with the coming of the Empire, a new word, *fantasia*, was invented by intellectuals and entertainers who made things up without benefit of collective memory, thereby breaking the link between *memoria*'s two meanings.

Vico asks us to recall the vivid memories of childhood, when compared with adult memory (David Hume called ideas 'pale sensations'). Children bring lived experiences to mind and reshape them. This process owes nothing to reasoning. Only later do we learn to rationalize. We remember the rules we have been taught to abide by and these supersede the act of remembering. We outsource remembering to external machines detached from lived experience. We pay entertainers to imagine for us. Money may give expression to the child in each of us, by giving vent to our desires; but it is also the main way adults participate in normal society.[11] Vico's analogy between civilizations and the human life cycle is not just a metaphor.

---

7. Milman Parry found analogies with Homer in oral performance in the Balkans. Albert Lord later produced *The Singer of Tales* (1960).

8. Vico, *New Science*, 'The True Homer': 323.

9. K. Hart, *The Memory Bank* (2000), republished as *Money in an Unequal World* (2001); Appendix, Hart 2000a.

10. Vico, *New Science*: 264.

11. See Chapter 19.

Jean-Jacques Rousseau (1712–78)

Jean-Jacques Rousseau launched anthropology's more progressive currents. Lévi-Strauss made this point repeatedly.[12] Rousseau's *Discourse on Inequality*[13] brings revolutionary politics to the critique of unequal society. In the next decade, he transformed Western understanding of politics, education, sexuality and the self in *The Social Contract, Julie, Emile* and *The Confessions.*[14] But the 'fake news' of counter-revolutionaries has discouraged many anglophones from reading him.

Rousseau, son of a Geneva watchmaker, ran away to France at sixteen and converted to Catholicism. He became the lover of a noble woman, but his partner of four decades was a chambermaid when they met.[15] In 1750 he entered an essay competition for the Dijon prize. The question was, Have the arts and sciences improved morals? Walking out one day, the answer came to him in a flash. The arts and sciences have caused the moral degeneration of men who are by nature good. His essay won and Rousseau became famous overnight.

He later entered the same competition again. This time the question concerned inequality.

> Rousseau summons men to hear for the first time their history as a species. Man was born free, equal, self-sufficient, unprejudiced, and whole; now, at the end of history, he is in chains (ruled by other men or by laws he did not make), defined by relations of inequality (rich or poor, noble or commoner, master or slave), dependent, full of false opinions or superstitions, and divided between his inclinations and his duties.[16]

Rousseau was not concerned with individual variations in natural endowments, but with conventional inequalities of wealth, honour and the capacity to command obedience that can be changed. He imagines a pre-social state of nature, a phase of human evolution where men were solitary, but healthy, happy and above all free and equal. This freedom was metaphysical, anarchic

---

12. C. Lévi-Strauss, 'Rousseau, Father of Anthropology', *Structural Anthropology* Vol. 2 (1976); T. Luhrman, 'Lévi-Strauss's Debt to Rousseau' (1990); H. Kwon, 'Anthropology and World Peace', *Hau* (2020).

13. J.-J. Rousseau, *A Discourse on the Origin and Foundation of Inequality among Mankind* (1754), *A Discourse on Inequality* (1984). See also Chapter 3.

14. The first three were published in 1761–62; the last was written in the late 1760s and published posthumously.

15. The life partners of Friedrich Engels were also working-class women (see the Preface).

16. A. Bloom, 'The Education of Democratic Man: Emile' (1978: 344).

and personal. Original human beings had free will, they were not subject to rules and they had no superiors. They made the transition to what Rousseau calls 'nascent society', a prolonged period based on hunter-gathering with huts. This represents his ideal of life in society close to nature.

The rot set in with the invention of agriculture. Rousseau claimed that Hobbes's 'war of all against all' was the result of social development, not an original condition. Cultivation led to incipient property institutions. These led eventually to entrenched inequality. Political society with its new social contract was probably arrived at by consensus, but it was fraudulent. The rich gained legal sanction for transmitting unequal property rights in perpetuity. Political society then usually moved, via revolutions, through three stages:

> The establishment of law and the right of property was the first stage, the institution of magistrates the second and the transformation of legitimate into arbitrary power the third and last stage. The status of rich and poor was authorized by the first epoch, that of strong and weak by the second and by the third that of master and slave, which is the last degree of inequality.[17]

With one-man-rule 'all individuals become equal again because they are nothing, where subjects have no longer any law but the will of the master'.[18] New revolutions dissolve the government altogether and bring it back to legitimacy.

Rousseau published three masterpieces in 1761–62. The first was *Julie or The New Heloïse* ('Letters from two lovers, living in a small town at the foot of the Alps'). A *Bildungsroman*, it kicked off the Romantic movement. *Julie* cast new light on the duality of human existence. Its exploration of 'sensitive' themes prefigured the novel's later efflorescence. Rousseau examined the competing claims of reason and emotion, order and freedom. *Julie* was the biggest bestseller of the eighteenth century. Demand was so overwhelming that its publishers rented out copies by the day. In the *Social Contract*, Rousseau claimed that the aristocratic order was ripe for revolution. He saw that the balance of power might shift from the people to government; small-city states were best suited to democracy. This tract did not disturb the authorities unduly. That honour was reserved for *Emile: On Education*. For Immanuel Kant, its publication, with the French Revolution, were the two most important events of his lifetime.

Emile is fiction, but not a novel. Plato's philosopher-king is replaced here by the governor of a boy aristocrat. The book claims that church education damages the mind. Its goal is a passive citizenry, as is schooling today. The book's style is vivid, aphoristic and contrarian. 'I hate books. They only teach

17. Rousseau, *Inequality*: 131.
18. Rousseau (ibid.: 134).

one to talk about what one does not know.'[19] Kant was excited by Rousseau's attempt to reconcile nature and history, reason and emotion, human selfishness and civic duty. He wanted to integrate the private and public that John Locke kept separate.[20]

The schools taught only a repressed conformity. The upper and middle classes did their best to speed up their children's maturation. They preferred pseudo-adults to real children. Any fool can train his 5-year-old son to entertain guests with a violin sonata after dinner, but only by sacrificing most things a child of that age should do. Adults think that time is scarce. But children have plenty of time and wasting it is how they grow at their own pace. Their facility at learning ruins children:

> Their brain, smooth and polished, returns, like a mirror, the objects presented to it. But nothing remains; nothing penetrates. [The instructor] should remember that his business is not so much to teach all that is knowable, as to raise in [the child] a love and esteem of knowledge; and to put him in the right way of knowing and improving himself.[21]

There are three sources of education – nature, people and things. The other two should serve the first. An education of 'nature' is the internal development of faculties and organs. Learning how to use them is the province of teachers. Experience of the object world is the education of things. Each stage of maturation offers different opportunities for living a full life. All should be indulged.

The obstacle to a free and equal society was no longer the old regime, which was on its last legs, but the embodiment of English political science, whom Rousseau named 'bourgeois', a low type who privileged reason in the education of even young children. He argues that the capacity for reasoning comes late and is difficult to cultivate. If we push it too early, as Locke recommended,[22] the child grows used to manipulating half-understood forms, but can't engage fully with the substance.

> Each advances more or less according to his genius, his tastes, his needs, his talents, his zeal, and the occasions he has to devote himself to them. . . We do not know what our nature permits us to be. . . . The lessons pupils get from one another in the schoolyard are a hundred times more useful to them than everything they will be told in class.[23]

---

19. Rousseau, *Emile*: 184.

20. Locke, *Two Treatises of Government* (1690), *Some Thoughts Concerning Education* (1693).

21. Rousseau (ibid.: 107).

22. Locke, *Education*.

23. Rousseau (ibid.: 62).

The Archbishop of Paris issued a fatwa after *Emile*'s publication. Anyone who killed Rousseau would receive the benediction of the church. The hit squads multiplied and Jean-Jacques had to run for his life. He made it to Neuchatel in Switzerland, a Prussian dependency whose governor, George Keith, was a Jacobite exile whom Jean-Jacques met when he was Frederick the Great's ambassador in Paris. Keith arranged a safe house for Rousseau in England through David Hume, where he wrote *The Confessions*. Things came to a sticky end with the publication of a letter in Paris and London, purporting to be from 'the King of Prussia' and offering Rousseau refuge. He took the joke badly and fell out with Hume as a result. The letter's author was Horace Walpole, an English politician and Gothic novelist.[24]

Rousseau now sued to return to Paris and was accepted, as long as he wrote nothing on religion or politics. He wrote *Reveries of a Solitary Walker* there and made a modest living copying music scores. He became the first object of celebrity tourism and would empty his pisspot on gawping German admirers. He died of apoplexy in his weekend retreat. Germaine de Staël[25] believed he took his own life.

Immanuel Kant (1724–1804)

In man, as the only rational creature on earth, those natural faculties which aim at the use of reason shall be fully developed in the species, not in the individual.
—Immanuel Kant, 'The Idea of a Universal History with a Cosmopolitan Purpose'

The distinctive feature of our age is that mankind as a whole is on the way to becoming fully conscious of itself.

—C.L.R. James, *The Black Jacobins*

Humanity is that part of the world through which the world as a whole can think about itself.
—Roy Rappaport, *Ritual and Religion in the Making of Humanity*

We don't need to share one undifferentiated brain to think for the world as a species. We just have to improve how we find, store, retrieve, collate and share knowledge. Kant probably had libraries and newspapers in mind, James global political movements and radio, Rappaport advances in ecology and television. All three saw their moment of history as a great leap forward in

---

24. https://www.marxists.org/history/france/grimm/hume-rousseau.htm (accessed 9 September 2021).

25. See Edward Gibbon in Chapter 1.

human connection and consciousness. The internet went public three decades ago. It now takes the form of smartphones in our pockets and handbags, at once small, personal and mobile. We believe that we are alone in the universe. But we have only begun to explore our capacities as a species. We have as little chance of communicating with extraterrestrials as the ants do with us. We must develop our self-knowledge as individuals and as a species. The relationship between the two is important. What interests me is how each of us relates to the whole. How social divisions mediate that relationship is secondary.

Immanuel Kant lived in Königsberg, East Prussia all his life.[26] He was a university teacher, writer and philosopher. His was as remarkable an example of lifelong learning as Benjamin Franklin's.[27] The pursuit of liberal democracy entailed radical reappraisal of self in the world. Kant took that project further than anyone. He studied nature and history, life and ideas, individuals and society, morals and politics, past and future, local and global. His thinking was always original.

After Kant's first degree, he became a private tutor and hated it. His doctorate led to a university lectureship. Later he became professor of mathematics, physics and philosophy. He taught between 1755 and 1796.

> He gave courses on Logic 54 times, Metaphysics 49 and Physical Geography 46. Next come Moral Philosophy 28, Anthropology 24, Theoretical Physics 20 and Mathematics 16. Kant taught Natural Right 12 times, Encyclopaedia of Philosophy 11 and others, including Education, less often.[28]

He made an important breakthrough in astronomy and published some remarkable essays. His three great *Critiques* – of *Pure Reason, Practical Reason* and *Judgement* – came out between 1781 and 1790. Later he wrote an essay on universal history, *The Metaphysics of Morals, Perpetual Peace* (a philosophical sketch) and *Anthropology from a Pragmatic Point of View*. Kant's lecture notes on education (*Pedagogy*) were published shortly before his death.[29]

Throughout, Kant 'emphasized the education of the individual. Not in his solitude, but as a man, as a citizen, and as a member of a kingdom of ethical ends [as a cosmopolitan]'.[30] He was not just concerned with how individuals reconcile personal inclinations with social duties or the transition from agriculture and monarchy to capitalism and modern government. He states that our human capacity for reason will only reach its potential at the species level,

---

26. Hart, Appendix 2010b.
27. See Chapter 1.
28. E. Buchner, *The Educational Theory of Immanuel Kant* (1904: 13).
29. A. Churton (ed.), *Kant on Education* (1900 [1803]).
30. Buchner (ibid.: 22).

not the individual. Humanity's last task is the equal administration of justice everywhere. War as an inducement to peace is the catalyst for this. Kant interviewed sailors to find out how they managed conflict resolution beyond the reach of state laws.

Immanuel Kant's assumptions in *Anthropology from a Pragmatic Point of View* (1798, after he retired from teaching) are light years from what modern academic anthropology has become.[31] He believed that education should prepare students for a world quite unlike the one they knew. His book provided a template for organizing future experience. Whereas Rousseau would perfect the natural man in each of us, Kant saw moral idealism as the key to human progress. We need both intelligence and social obligation to overcome instincts that are often untrustworthy. Kant, like Thomas Hobbes, focused on reform of the universities as an educational priority, not on child-rearing.

> It was no longer how does the world get into the mind? But how does it get out of the mind?. . . Education is no longer world-appropriation, but world-building. Each man, by his own mental processes, builds up his own world. The question is, how is this done?[32]

In a world of wars, Kant asked how humanity might construct a 'perpetual peace' without state boundaries, based on principles that all humans share.[33] This 'cosmopolitan' society was a bridge to exercising reason at the species level. His anthropology studied the cognitive, aesthetic and ethical universals on which human unity might be founded. The categorical imperative to be good provided a moral link between individuals and this emergent order.

Copernicus solved the problem of the movement of the heavenly bodies. The spectator revolves while they are at rest, rather than the opposite. Kant extended this achievement to metaphysics. In the *Critique of Pure Reason*, he writes: 'Hitherto it has been assumed that all our knowledge must conform to objects. . . but what if we suppose that objects must conform to our knowledge?'[34] Society can be found inside us all, not just as a collective force. We must combine these poles as subjective individuals who share the object world in common. Kant held that knowledge of society must be personal and moral before being imposed on us from above.

Kant's *Anthropology* was based on lectures. He held that 'cosmopolitan right', the basic right of all world citizens, should rest on conditions of universal hospitality. A stranger should not be treated with hostility when they arrive on someone else's territory. We should be free to go wherever we like

31. I. Kant, *Anthropology* (2006 [1798]); Hart, Appendix 2010e.

32. Buchner (ibid.: 29).

33. I. Kant, *Perpetual Peace* (1795).

34. I. Kant, Preface to *The Critique of Pure Reason* (1781).

in the world, since it belongs to us all equally.[35] He died in the year of Haiti's independence. He summarized 'philosophy in the cosmopolitan sense of the word' as four questions:

> What can I know?
> What should I do?
> What may I hope for?
> What is a human being?
> The first question is answered by *metaphysics*, the second by *morals*, the third by *religion* and the fourth by *anthropology*.[36]

The first three questions might be subsumed under anthropology.

Kant conceived of it as an empirical discipline; but it was also a source of moral and cultural improvement. The book offers a bridge from the everyday to horizon thinking. It moves between vivid anecdotes and Kant's sublime vision. He concentrated on pragmatic anthropology – 'what the human being as a free actor can and should make of himself'. This combined observation with the construction of moral rules. Anthropology is the practical arm of moral philosophy. Its province is interaction between human agents. It is 'pragmatic' in several senses: 'everything that pertains to the practical', popular (not academic) and moral, focusing on people's motives for action. Kant recommends 'world history, biographies and even plays and novels'. They are inventions, but use close observation of real behaviour. The first print run of two thousand copies sold out in two years.

Kant wanted to understand emergent world society. He conceived of anthropology as a form of education. His 'pragmatic' approach implied a personal programme of lifelong learning with the aim of gaining practical knowledge of the world. World history is indispensable to any anthropology worthy of the name. Biography is well suited to the anthropological study of self and society.

W.H.R. Rivers (1864–1922)

William Rivers[37] joined the 1898 Cambridge anthropological expedition to Torres Strait as an experimental psychologist.[38] He then kept self and world

---

35. See Chapter 14.

36. Kant, *Anthropology*: 8.

37. Hart, Appendix 1998, 2003a, 2019a.

38. Pat Barker's *Regeneration* trilogy (*Regeneration*, *The Eye in the Door* and *The Ghost Road*) was published as a set in 2014. The novels focus on Rivers in the First World War. See also Richard Slobodin, *W.H.R. Rivers* (1978).

apart as psychology and anthropology.[39] His war experience launched a short career as a public intellectual. He found that he combined self and society in his own personality; psychology and anthropology shared a method.

The functionalist ethnographers combined fieldwork and theory in one person, two roles that the Victorians kept separate. They also bucked the modernist trend for compartmentalization. Their vivid analytical descriptions compensate for a lack of transparency in method. They had to span two poles: social isolation as fieldworkers in exotic places and the academic guild back home. The Cambridge expedition invented modern anthropology's most distinctive feature: making up stories about humanity based on living with real people. Bronislaw Malinowski and A.R. Radcliffe-Brown divided the nation state between them. One contributed the idea of society as a *nation*, the other the *state* as guarantor of social order.[40] Today's anthropologists are not free of this dualism. Functionalist ethnography is now decomposing along with the nation state. My focus here is on the transition from nineteenth- to twentieth-century anthropology and Rivers's place in it.[41]

British social anthropology in its prime comprised the following:

Ethnography: writing about one people circumscribed in time and space;
Fieldwork: observation and analysis of live activities where they take place;
Ideas from life: abstract generalizations built from concrete descriptions;
Kinship: especially the use of genealogies for formal modelling ('kinship algebra')'
Social structure: society (not culture or psychology) as a coherent system of rules;
Comparative method: sometimes based on regional surveys;
Professional jargon: close specification of concepts, as opposed to popular usage;
Functional integrity: the whole expressed as institutional patterns in the here and now;
Culture contact: social change addressed through practical anthropology;
Science of society: social anthropology as the sociology of primitive societies.

What did Rivers contribute to this project? *The Todas* (1906) was then considered to be a pioneering example of the new ethnography. But Malinowski's monographs are much better written. Fieldwork was the great message of the Cambridge expedition. Rivers later argued for long-term immersion by

---

39. He divided social anthropology into sociology and ethnology (the study of historical diffusion).

40. G.W.F. Hegel, *Philosophy of Right* (1821).

41. George Stocking's *After Tylor: British Social Anthropology, 1888–1951* (1995) sticks to the official story and has little affection for Rivers.

a single fieldworker.[42] Rivers developed the genealogical method of studying kinship for the Cambridge expedition. He mapped kinship relations in a community on a network diagram based on many informants.[43] Radcliffe-Brown downplayed his teacher's influence. He turned Rivers's dynamic genealogical method into the formalism for which the British school became (in)famous.[44]

Rivers separated the study of social structure from psychology. He studied regional variations as historical interaction. The evolutionists and functionalists constructed abstract taxonomies. Rivers used concepts as needed for scientific exploration. He acknowledged the functional integrity of place: how else could he have developed a notion of social structure? But he emphasized the wider historical context. Rivers and his Cambridge colleague Alfred Haddon were disturbed by the damage done to local societies by colonial empire. The functionalists denigrated their legacy as 'conjectural history'.[45] Radcliffe-Brown mastered the rhetoric of science, but Rivers pioneered its practice. Social anthropology occupied a no man's land between science and literature. Rivers believed he was building two or more impersonal scientific communities. The First World War took him in a more engaged direction.

William Rivers started out as a physiologist.[46] He established the first two experimental psychology laboratories in England before joining the Cambridge expedition. He contributed to the latter studies of perception and kinship. He later undertook neurological experiments with Henry Head. They developed a two-stage model of nerve regeneration, the *protopathic* and the *epicritic*.[47] Rivers was drawn to German historicism and wilder forms of global speculation. As a psychoanalyst he followed Freud with some reservations. Treating shell-shock victims led him to a new version of social psychology. Afterwards, he became a socialist politician and friend of progressive literary men. This required a personality transplant. He had been a conservative recluse with a stammer. Now he was the very model of an outgoing public intellectual and stood for parliament.

Rivers built up psychology and anthropology as a practitioner. He sought to separate the study of society from that of individuals, for sure. In a general

---

42. Rivers, 'Methodology', *Notes and Queries in Anthropology* (1912).

43. Berger, *Picasso* (1965) shows how the diagram is the central figure of cubism, mediating the abstract and the concrete.

44. Meyer Fortes, *Kinship and the Social Order* (1969); Ian Langham, *The Building of British Social Anthropology: W.H.R. Rivers and His Cambridge Disciples* (1981). Malinowski called it all 'kinship algebra'.

45. http://www.anthrobase.com/Dic/eng/pers/radcliffe-brown_alfred_r.htm (accessed 9 September 2021).

46. Richard Slobodin's (1978) is the only biography of Rivers. Paul Whittle's (1997) memoir places Rivers as psychologist in his social context.

47. See Note 38.

social crisis, he discovered that he combined these within himself. In his last five years, Rivers produced some forty works of varying quality and length, while keeping up a punishing regime of professional and public engagement. He probably wrote a lot of these works off the top of his head. His method became more self-reflexive. He and Head believed that scientists were the best informants when they carried out research on themselves. He now sought to comprehend, synthesize and influence individuals' experience of society. The boundaries between disciplines became blurred.

In his posthumous book *Conflict and Dream*, Rivers recalls a dream he named 'Hidden sources'.[48] Overwork as an army psychiatrist prevented him from replying to American critics of his kinship theories. A conflict existed between psychology and anthropology. Rivers then concludes that the dream reveals the harmony between psychoanalysis and ethnology.[49] They are both based on the excavation of hidden sources. Both help us to understand the complex history of human personality and culture.

Armed with this integrated vision of self and society, Rivers was ready to change the world, not just to understand it. Radcliffe-Brown and Malinowski both sat out the war. They, not Rivers, forged an academic discipline attuned to the needs of the corporate state in mid-century Britain. Exploring relations between the new ethnography and psychoanalysis was fashionable in the 1920s.[50] Malinowski engaged with Freudian ideas until the exchange went badly for him. But the trend was towards divorce, not marriage. The name of the game was division of the professional pie. Rivers's death allowed the two chief functionalists to reinvent themselves as the only begetters of British social anthropology. This foundation myth is bad history.

Marcel Mauss (1872–1950)

Marcel Mauss was a French sociologist whose reputation has grown markedly in recent decades, perhaps because his vision of economy and society contrasted starkly with today's market fundamentalism. This vision is often conflated with the bourgeois opposition between gift and market that Mauss wished to refute. He contributed to the confusion by maintaining a firewall between his academic and political writings.[51] Mauss left a few essays of which *The Gift* has become a classic.[52] These were edited as a collection in

---

48. W. Rivers, *Conflict and Dream* (1923).

49. A methodological parallel noted by M. Foucault, *The Order of Things* (1970).

50. See Note 41.

51. D. Graeber, *Toward an Anthropological Theory of Value* (2001); K. Hart, 'David Graeber: Obituary', *Anthropology Today* (2020).

52. M. Mauss, *The Gift* (expanded edition) (2016 [1925]).

French by Claude Lévi-Strauss,[53] but are dispersed in English translation. Mauss was a prolific pamphleteer and journalist, but this output, along with three volumes of occasional writings[54] is only available in French.[55] In consequence, he is cited often, but not read closely by many who cite him. The key to his message is the man himself, especially his commitment to living as an integrated whole.[56]

Mauss's uncle, Émile Durkheim, took firm charge of their partnership in building up sociology as an academic discipline; he assembled a team of researchers in Paris around the journal *L'Année Sociologique*. Mauss wrote a vast number of reviews for the journal. He held a chair in the religion of primitive peoples, but did not complete his doctoral thesis on prayer.[57] Durkheim thought he spent too much time on politics. Mauss was a cooperative socialist who maintained strong relations with British anthropologists and political activists, and spent 1914–18 in the trenches as a translator for British and Australian troops. His party, the French Section of the Workers International (SFIO), was anti-capitalist, but embraced the social market and was opposed to Marxism. Mauss advocated an economic movement from below that would combine professional associations, mutual insurance and cooperatives.

This political engagement peaked in 1920–25, after Durkheim's death during the war, when Mauss assumed leadership of the *Année Sociologique* group, temporarily revived the journal and published *The Gift*. But in the late 1920s, he withdrew from politics and devoted himself to teaching France's first generation of ethnographers. He suffered from the Nazi occupation as a Jew, but was not deported.

Mauss's essay on the gift is a continuation of Durkheim's first book, *The Division of Labour in Society*.[58] This argued, against English utilitarianism, that contractual exchanges are based on a 'non-contractual element in the contract'. This consists of shared history, state institutions, laws and customs and is largely hidden from view by a legal focus on the contracting parties. Durkheim wanted to make the social market visible. Mauss did too. He saw both gifts and market contracts as belonging to the family of exchange relations. Ethnographies of archaic gift-exchange reveal submerged aspects of

---

53. M. Mauss, *Essais de sociologie* (1950); M. Fournier, *Marcel Mauss* (2006); K. Hart and W. James (eds), *Journal of Classical Sociology* special issue (2014).t

54. M. Mauss, *Œuvres* (1968). Mauss's writing is thought to be sparse; but these three volumes add up to two-thousand pages.

55. M. Mauss, *Écrits politiques* (1994).

56. Since finishing *Self in the World*, I have started a biography, *Marcel Mauss: An Anthropological Vision for the 21ˢᵗ Century*. See Hart, Appendix 2007b, 2014b.

57. M. Mauss, *On Prayer* (2003 [1909]).

58. E. Durkheim, *The Division of Labour in Society* (1893).

capitalist economies. These are not just Christmas and wedding presents, but key contracts with a time element – like wages, rent and loans – that cannot be understood if market exchange is conceived of only as immediate cash payments. For Mauss, the gift opens up the non-contractual element in the contract; his ethnographic examples showed the potential of markets to be solidary, humane and generous.

He stressed the interdependence of aesthetic, legal, economic, political and religious dimensions of social life. This was captured in synthetic events that he called 'total social facts'. He wanted the economic movement from below to grow, inspired by how archaic gift-exchange exposed repressed possibilities in French capitalist society. He debunked the bourgeois idea that market and gift principles reflect the opposition between self-interested individual contracts and altruistic gifts. The gift is often coercive and unequal, but it also has a generous side. Gift-exchange and markets both extend society from the local to the foreign. Their combination is hard to see in capitalist societies. Mauss did not have a paradigm of 'the gift'.[59] The Brazilian anthropologist Lygia Sigaud has a brilliant essay on how *The Gift* has been misinterpreted.[60] But the history of interpretive error rolls on.

Mauss departed from his uncle's approach in three important ways. First, he abandoned Durkheim's sociological reductionism, seeking rather to identify social phenomena as wholes – a dynamic assemblage of persons, networks, groups, things and ideas – more readily revealed through ethnography than by specialist disciplines. The generosity of the archaic gift does not point to a non-market alternative, as Malinowski insisted,[61] but rather to the humanity inherent in markets that remain to be liberated from capitalism. Second, Durkheim oversimplified the contrast between primitive and modern societies: he exaggerated the homogeneous and static nature of the former and downplayed this aspect of industrial nations. Mauss held that all economies are plural; the basic human economic arrangements coexist in any society.[62] Economic change does not require a radical replacement of one set of institutions by another. It is enough to give their combination a new direction and emphasis, while focusing on their human qualities.

Third, Mauss saw human history as a movement towards increasing inclusiveness as the boundaries of local societies are pushed outwards. After the war, he began two book projects on socialism and the nation. Fascism forced a rethink of these projects. Markets and money, in many different forms, are universal, since no society was ever materially self-sufficient, so that all had to trade

---

59. Hart, Appendix 2014b.

60. L. Sigaud, 'The Vicissitudes of *The Gift*' (2002).

61. B. Malinowski, 'Primitive Economics of the Trobriand Islanders' (1921).

62. This position was later held by Karl Polanyi in 'Economy as Instituted Process' (1957).

with outsiders. Gift-exchange was in some ways like the 'free market', in that the human expansiveness and trust made visible there sustained markets everywhere. The Bolshevik revolution's violent repression of markets was a disaster.

Why did Mauss separate his academic and political writing? One aimed to stimulate reflection in individual readers, the other collective action. The symbolic power of his concrete descriptions of exotic phenomena were food for personal thought, not prescriptions. Mauss wanted his readers to find their own true beliefs in his academic works, knowing that they would be more likely to act politically than if authors, teachers or leaders told them to think that way.

In the 1930s he gave well-attended public lectures at Paris's Institut d'ethnologie. A trio of Surrealist philosophers, led by André Breton, could not agree on their meaning. As an experiment, they proceeded to take notes separately and compared them later. They were quite different. The Surrealists then asked Mauss if he cared about getting his message across to 'the audience'. He replied, 'It was never my intention to impose my thoughts on you, gentlemen. I hoped to help you discover your own.' He knew that each of us only takes something to heart[63] if it is already there inside us, perhaps incoherent until given form dialectically. Others help us to find something that is intrinsically ours. When that happens, we should use it to do something – like join a political movement. This is how religion instils beliefs that should inform individual actions that are also collective. Mauss was the team's specialist in religion after all. He was a 'concrete dialectician'[64] who wanted to stimulate original thinking in receptive readers.

Between Then and Now

It sometimes feels like we are living in the climax of a horror story lasting two centuries, a story made by industrial capitalism and Western empires. The eighteenth century capped three centuries of exploration (1500–1800) that yielded advances in knowledge and global reach. But Europeans could not yet conquer the world. The Enlightenment's vision of human possibility has not yet been realized. They harnessed thinking about education, anthropology and 'self in the world' to the drive for democratic revolution.

Our great transformation began around 1800. The liberal philosophers knew they had come to the end of something. The King and his aristocracy had no credible claim to authority. The church endorsed monarchy as God's will. They understood reasoning and morality to distinguish us from the

---

63. 'Belief' means beloved, something held dear, in Old English.
64. I am grateful to Nicolas Adell for this insight.

animals; but human beings are born without either. Education should teach us to combine personal freedom with social duty. A good citizen is an autonomous person. The right balance between individuals and society was hard to achieve, even in these small societies; but they aimed for their integration. We retain the words for their concepts, but they are empty of meaning.

European society expanded in force and scale during the nineteenth century. The Industrial Revolution spawned unprecedented urbanization, a demographic explosion in Europe, huge political and commercial organizations, massive global inequality and the division of the world between empires. Hegel announced that Kant's philosophy was the last dying gasp of bourgeois individualism and was unsuited to this new stage of society. His political recipe – what I call 'national capitalism' – retains a fragile hold over societies whose power dwarfs the agency of individual citizens. Social science was the result. Hegel, with Auguste Comte and David Ricardo, launched a new social science combining German politics, French sociology and English economics.[65]

Impersonal society was no longer an extension of individual personality. It was at odds with it. The 'sentimental education' provided by novels partly bridged the gap. Private property now belonged mainly to businesses and governments. The last century's horrors were the result. Licenced professionals were trained to replace families in social reproduction. The humanities lost their human impulse. Corporate universities have now finished off this process. We must widen our horizons without losing sight of how each of us lives.

Anthropology is the only field of thought whose range covers the human predicament as a whole. Humanity's next great project is to construct a democratic world society capable of acting as a responsible steward of all life on earth. We need to synthesize anthropology's methods of the last three centuries: critical humanism, world history and ethnography.[66] Higher education today is wholly inadequate for this task. It should be replaced by commitment to lifelong learning through personal experience and mediated by digital technology.[67] Biography – of self and others – should be part of anthropology conceived of as lifelong learning.[68] My three passions are for music, numbers and money – in that order. What they share is fluent movement back and forth between life's extremes. We must find new ways of moving like that. Some of them could be developed through new intellectual configurations including anthropology – or whatever it comes to be called.

---

65. D. Ricardo, *Principles of Political Economy* (1817); G.W.F. Hegel, *Philosophy of Right* (1821); A. Comte, *Positive Philosophy* (1830–42).

66. C. Hann and K. Hart, *Economic Anthropology* (2011).

67. See Chapter 14.

68. See Chapter 1.

Chapter 3

THE ANTI-COLONIAL INTELLECTUALS

Thinking New Worlds

You couldn't miss the dissolution of colonial empire in the 1950s and 1960s. By 1970, the prevailing attitude among students was that Western societies were decadent. We chanted the names of Mao Tse Tung, Fidel Castro, Kwame Nkrumah and Ho Chi Minh, while burning the American flag. My time in Ghana was an eye-opener. I would naively admit, when asked, that I was supported by Cambridge University's Smuts Memorial Fund.[1] I soon learned better. Even admitting to the label 'anthropologist' won no friends there. We were agents of colonialism. 'Sociologist' was more acceptable. Anthropologists of Africa then gravitated to Marxist history rather than traditional ethnography. My first book, on West African history, gave space to the evils of the Atlantic slave trade and European colonial rule.[2] But its main thrust was a critique of postcolonial states.

Thanks to my classics training, my head was full of the Western literary canon. The anthropology I was taught celebrated how Western investigations of isolated peoples supported generalizations about the unity and variety of the human species. A two-year stay in Jamaica during the late 1980s stimulated a late-flowering personal synthesis.[3] I now saw that my anthropological education had been biased towards 'our' side of the main political event of the last century, the anti-colonial revolution. Its political leaders were often

---

1. Named for a South African soldier and politician.
2. K. Hart, *The Political Economy of West African Agriculture* (1982).
3. See Chapter 9.

intellectuals too. Their writings are a reservoir of inspiration for understanding how to build a better world. Many of them fed on the Marxist tradition and theirs was truly a world revolution. I have a bookcase in Durban with the complete works of Lenin and Gandhi. These two – with Rousseau, Kant, Marx, Mauss, James and Fanon – are my guides to making a better world.

Rethinking the World

What does it take to rethink the world? The circuit of money today is global and lawless. Politics is still national, but cannot handle global finance. Not long ago several models of humanity and society circulated together, but now there is only one made by and for money. We need to refresh our thinking. The colonies' leading thinkers not only had to imagine a new kind of world and persuade the masses to fight for it. Each follower had to educate themselves to participate in that world. The Pan-African movement was the largest and most inclusive organization for change in the early twentieth century. Black intellectuals like W.E.B. Du Bois, C.L.R. James and Frantz Fanon offered a vision of the world to replace racial empire. M. K. Gandhi developed the most original version of this strategy as India's inspirational leader. He has the most to offer.[4]

The Vietnam War felt like the end of imperialism. But the social anthropology syllabus still reflected the spirit of Radcliffe-Brown. I became a Ghana specialist, but only found out in the late 1980s that President Kwame Nkrumah was a protégé of the London-based Trinidadian Marxists George Padmore and C.L.R James. The latter wrote a devastating critique of his protégé's postcolonial politics.[5]

Resisting Alienation

We can only be fully human if self and society reinforce each other. Achieving this is a real, but largely unconscious need for most people. Profound obstacles stand in its way. Jean-Jacques Rousseau, Karl Marx and Frantz Fanon each grappled with the problem. They lived in the eighteenth, nineteenth and twentieth centuries respectively. All three believed that unequal society corrupts human nature. Yet human beings have the potential for redemption. We can become whole again by tackling the root causes of inequality together. For Rousseau, it meant abolishing the arbitrary class divisions of

---

4. Hart, Appendix 2015c compares Gandhi as a global thinker with the three Pan-Africanists.
5. C.L.R. James, *Nkrumah and the Ghana Revolution* (1977).

agrarian civilization, for Marx the class structure of industrial capitalism, and for Fanon the racism of colonial empires. All of these made people only part-human. Most were denied the chance to be whole persons in society.

I have summarized Rousseau's *Discourse on Inequality* in Chapter 2. Alienation means separation from something that belongs to us (land, personal integrity). It could mean the attribution of agency to forces beyond our control (the gods, the weather or just 'them'). Madness is the extreme form of alienation from oneself. In different degrees, the unity of self and society is weakened. The Enlightenment challenged religious alienation by overcoming inhibitions imposed by spiritual beings, or rather by their mediators. Instead of banking on redemption in the afterlife, they focused attention on here and now – 'life, liberty and the pursuit of happiness'.[6] Karl Marx captured the essence of Victorian capitalism in *Capital*.[7]

'The fetishism of commodities and the secret thereof' is his deepest reflection on alienation there. In capitalist society most people must work under conditions imposed by the owners.[8] They are estranged from their own humanity. To be human is to realize our intentions by producing objects with social value. But capitalism makes that impossible. In a system of private property, a worker is a tool, not a person. Products are designed neither by workers nor consumers, but by capitalists who keep most of the market sales. Work consists of repetitive, often meaningless acts. Religious alienation is hard to resist since spirits are our own mental fabrications. But capitalist production is material; we can do something about that. Workers overcome their servitude by understanding the causes of their alienation. Revolution restores the unity of self and society we have lost. It brings money, machines and the workplace under social management.

Frantz Fanon joined the Algerian War of Independence and became a leading figure in the Pan-African movement. He approached damaged humanity through the critique of racism.[9] The last chapter of *The Wretched of the Earth* reports on Fanon's psychiatric work with patients in the war.[10] His case studies include two 12-year-old Algerian boys who killed a European schoolmate. A young French soldier was driven mad by memories of torturing insurgents. Fanon concludes that, for the victims and victimizers on both sides, violence is impossible to live with. His death from cancer at 36 was induced by working for both sides in that genocidal war.

---

6. See 'the struggle for happiness' in Chapter 9.

7. K. Marx, *Capital* (Volume 1, 1867).

8. D. McNeill, *Fetishism and the Value Form* (2020) argues that 'fetishism' is the key to Marx's theory of value.

9. See Fanon's early writings in *Alienation and Freedom* (2017).

10. F. Fanon, *The Wretched of the Earth* (1961, English translation 1963).

Race defined two unequal and separate worlds in colonial society. Dehumanization as an inferior race under capitalism was an explosive combination. Fanon used psychiatry to rehabilitate individuals. But he believed that oppressed peoples could win emancipation. This is important. Many assume that the passivity of subordinate classes perpetuates alienation. Fanon thought colonized people possessed a drive for freedom. Resistance to alienation would defeat alienation itself. Classes whose humanity was denied by colonial racism offered proof of the drive for self-emancipation. How do we overcome alienation? This question underpins my book.

Humanity needs to develop social forms that secure our survival as a species. But we often feel disabled and lost. We are parts, not wholes. Saul of Tarsus put it this way:

> Charity never faileth: but whether there be prophecies, they shall fail; whether there be tongues, they shall cease; whether there be knowledge, it shall vanish away. For we know in part and we prophesy in part. But when that which is perfect is come, then that which is in part shall be done away. When I was a child, I spake as a child, I understood as a child, I thought as a child: but when I became a man, I put away childish things. Now *we see through a glass, darkly*; but then face to face: now I know in part; but then shall I know even as also I am known. And now abideth faith, hope, charity, these three; but the greatest of these is charity (my italics).[11]

'Charity' in Christian theology is love directed toward God but also toward oneself and others as objects of God's love. It is love of humanity. Paul says that we make do with knowing little about people and guess the rest. It's usually wrong. We don't understand ourselves and we project our dark side onto others. One day, when we meet face to face, not through the distortions of identity politics, we will recognize the humanity in everyone. Humanity is a historical project for our species. How will we find it? Through belief, hope and love.

This message is universally human. It is also an ethnographer's charter: when we interact with others, we want to see and be seen as we really are, not as a dissembling crook or white oppressor. Perhaps we will all find our way to humanity; but now we are only part-human.

Pan-Africanism: Du Bois, James and Fanon

The Pan-African Federation was founded in Manchester in 1944 by African and Coloured peoples. Delegates came from Kenya, Sierra Leone, the Gold Coast and other colonies. Its aims were

---

11. 1 Corinthians 13: 8–13, *The New Testament* (King James Version).

to promote the well-being and unity of African peoples and peoples of African descent throughout the world; to demand self-determination and independence of African peoples and other subject races; to secure equality of civil rights for African peoples and an end to racial discrimination; and cooperation between African peoples and others who share our aspirations.[12]

The Fifth Pan-African Congress was held in Manchester in October 1945. It was organized by George Padmore. The ninety delegates included Jomo Kenyatta, W.E.B. Du Bois, Obafemi Awolowo and Hastings Banda. There were thirty-three delegates from the Caribbean. The British media ignored the event. Why Manchester? Associations (friendly societies, the cooperative movement) flourished there in and after the Industrial Revolution. Manchester was central to the international campaign to end the slave trade. Lancashire suffered a cotton famine in the 1860s because of the American Civil War. Workers held demonstrations for free labour. Marx and Engels based their revolutionary vision on their experience of Manchester.[13] In the pandemic of 2020, Manchester's mayor led criticism of the government and a United footballer campaigned for free schoolchildren's meals and won.

Africa succumbed to the last phase of the European land grab. The Pan-African movement aimed to restore control to Africans. Its main intellectual drivers came from the New World. Du Bois, James and Fanon each provided visions of a democratic world order.

W.E.B. Du Bois (1868–1963) was of mixed ancestry. He grew up in Massachusetts without much experience of racial discrimination. University in Tennessee changed all that. He went to Berlin University and was the first black American to receive a PhD from Harvard. His first books were a history of the slave trade, a sociological monograph and an anthropological masterpiece.[14] He helped to found the National Association for the Advancement of Coloured Peoples (NAACP). At first, he wanted to build bridges to the white majority. But he later came into conflict with his government. He settled in Ghana when invited by President Nkrumah to work on an *Encyclopaedia Africana*. He died in 1963. When I arrived there shortly afterwards, his widow Shirley was the head of Ghana's television service.

Du Bois's speech to the First Pan-African Congress in London (1900) is famous.

The problem of the twentieth century is the problem of the colour line. How far will differences of race be made the basis of denying to over half the world the right of sharing the opportunities and privileges of modern civilization?. . .

---

12. https://en.wikipedia.org/wiki/Pan-African_Federation (accessed 9 September 2021).

13. See Chapter 10.

14. *The Suppression of the African Slave Trade* (1896); *The Philadelphia Negro* (1899); *The Souls of Black Folk* (1903).

[If] Negroes and other dark men [are given] the largest and broadest opportunity for education and self-development, [it] is bound to have a beneficial effect upon the world and hasten human progress. But if, by reason of carelessness, prejudice, greed and injustice, the black world is to be exploited and ravished and degraded, the results must be deplorable, if not fatal.

Let the world take no backward step in that slow but sure progress which has successively refused to let the spirit of class, of caste, of privilege, or of birth, debar from life, liberty and the pursuit of happiness a striving human soul. Let not the natives of Africa be sacrificed to the greed of gold, their liberties taken away, their family life debauched, their just aspirations repressed, and avenues of advancement and culture taken from them . . . .We appeal with boldness and confidence to the Great Powers of the civilized world, trusting in the wide spirit of humanity, and the deep sense of justice and of our age, for a generous recognition of the righteousness of our cause.[15]

The Souls of Black Folk is an extraordinary collection of essays.[16] Topics range from a polemic against the leading black politician, through a survey of Georgia sharecroppers to the death of Du Bois's young son. Du Bois aimed to touch his readers' hearts and minds. Negro spirituals, which he calls 'sorrow songs', head each chapter. Black music was the one thing of beauty produced by American society. It expressed the common soul of black folk and reached out to wider notions of soul. Du Bois sought recognition of his own human worth. Disappointment led him to adopt a strategy of separation. 'Soul' is the non-material, immortal part of each of us. It is our core, most integral, vital part, and the sensitive component of personality.[17] A religious meaning of soul could link blacks and whites in a Christian nation. Soul is a component of individuals, shared by peoples and by humanity as a whole.

Black people are seen first as black and then perhaps as themselves. This is a strategic resource for them, an opportunity. Du Bois writes 'through, inside, outside and above the veil'. The veil makes blacks unseen, but they are visible. One may be unseen but not veiled, veiled but visible. But the great prize is to be seen as oneself. The cracked mirror of race prevents us from seeing and being seen as we are. Knowledge of ourselves and others is always partial. All black people in the US are victims of 'double consciousness'. They aspire to be full members of society, but they never will be. Du Bois did not pursue white recognition for long. In *Darkwater: Voices from Within the Veil*, he was a fully fledged separatist.[18]

---

15. The full speech is at https://www.blackpast.org/african-american-history/1900-w-e-b-du-bois-nations-world/ (accessed 3 October 2021).

16. Du Bois, *Souls* (1903).

17. Introduction, Ibid.

18. W.E.B. Du Bois, *Darkwater: Voices from Within the Veil* (1999 [1920]).

C.L.R. James (1901–89),[19] like Du Bois, was an intellectual of extraordinary range and impact who lived for almost ninety years. His Trinidad was a more benign place to be black and middle class than Reconstruction in the US. He chose to stay at home to write fiction and sports journalism rather than train as a doctor or lawyer in London. James arrived there at 32. In six years he published a political history of labour in Trinidad and the first Caribbean novel of urban low life, ghosted a cricket autobiography, and wrote the first global history of the Trotskyist movement, a pamphlet advocating West Indian self-government, a play about the Haitian revolution's leader starring Paul Robeson, the definitive history of Haiti's slave revolution and a survey of black revolt in the Atlantic world.[20] He became the outstanding far-left political figure in Britain, organized the International African Service Bureau with George Padmore (formerly Stalin's global coordinator of black affairs) and wrote and spoke brilliantly in the media available.

James's masterpiece is *The Black Jacobins: Toussaint L'Ouverture and the San Domingo Revolution*. He showed there that Haiti's slave revolution changed the world as much as the American and French revolutions. Yet it was now forgotten. The leading powers sent large armies to defeat the insurgents and lost comprehensively. The British Prime Minister, William Pitt, switched the British Empire's focus from the New World to India as a result.[21] James saw here the inspiration for an anti-colonial revolution in Africa. Black revolt in the Atlantic region had now shifted from the New World to Africa itself.

The sugar plantations were the most advanced sector of machine production in the world. Their racism was appalling. Racism and advanced capitalism together provoked the revolution. Something similar is occurring in Africa now. Gold Coast dock workers, Johannesburg gold miners and East Nigerian women palm-oil producers were gestating an anti-colonial revolution that would erupt soon. No-one, from African politicians and European Marxists to colonial officials, thought this was likely. But James was right and they were wrong.

James's case for African unity drew on his vision of history. He was a practicing revolutionary and world history was his teacher. His second masterpiece, *Beyond a Boundary*, is a magnificent sports book (on cricket) and a political autobiography. James criticized the media for writing only about the field of play and ignoring society, present as the crowd. He spent fifteen

---

19. See Chapters 9 and 10.

20. *The Life of Captain Cipriani* (1932) and *Minty Alley* (1936), both written in Trinidad; L. Constantine, *Cricket and I* (1933); *The Case for West Indian Self Government* (1933); *Toussaint L'Ouverture* (1936); *World Revolution* (1936); *The Black Jacobins* (1938); *The History of Negro Revolt* (1938).

21. See Chapter 10.

years in the United States from 1938, forming the Johnson-Forest Tendency with Raya Dunayevskaya and Grace Lee. Letters James wrote to New York colleagues from Nevada while seeking a divorce were published as *Notes on Dialectics*.[22] He considered this his most significant contribution. But the world does not yet endorse that judgement. *American Civilization* stands with the other two classics as his supreme achievement.[23]

Frantz Fanon (1925–61) was a psychiatrist who moved to France from Martinique. He was taught in secondary school by the great Pan-African poet Aimé Césaire. He denied being black, preferring 'doctor, French and Communist'. He married the daughter of a white trade union leader. *Black Skin, White Masks* was an anti-racist critique of the successor ruling class back home.[24] The Algerian War turned the Marxist psychiatrist of the 1950s into the Pan-Africanist author of *The Wretched of the Earth*.

Fanon worked first in a French military hospital and then joined the FLN insurgency.[25] *The Wretched of the Earth* has a Preface by Jean-Paul Sartre. Fanon argues there that colonial society is racist and can only be overcome by force. But he was a consummate writer and this was not the book's only message. As we have seen, the final chapter shows how work with his patients led him to conclude that extreme violence is humanly impossible to live with. The longest chapter is a polemic against the weakness of the nationalist bourgeoisie in Africa. They will break up Pan-African unity, he says. Few African countries had then won independence. Yet national politics were also important for him.

Fanon's Pan-Africanism frames a holistic class analysis of the war for independence. Small urban elites were tied to the metropolis. They despised the rural masses and their chiefs. But persecution by the colonial power forced them to take refuge in the countryside. The two sides then exchanged political education for practical lessons in overcoming adversity. Their resulting partnership launched the national revolutionary movement for independence.

Gandhi's World Vision

Mohandas K. Gandhi (1869–1948)[26] grew up in the ancient Indian Ocean port of Porbandar in Gujarat. This was a cosmopolitan place. He borrowed

---

22. C.L.R. James, *Notes on Dialectics: Hegel, Marx, Lenin* (1948).

23. A 1950 manuscript edited by Anna Grimshaw and me as *American Civilization* (1993). See Chapter 9.

24. F. Fanon, *Black Skin, White Masks* (1952).

25. The National Liberation Front.

26. Hart, Appendix 2015c.

money to study law in London and then went to South Africa to advise on a dispute between Indian traders in Durban. He stayed there for over two decades (1893–1915), eventually becoming the country's most prominent civil rights activist. At first, he was concerned only with Indian politics; but in Johannesburg he led a non-white coalition. He worked through the British Empire, the world's largest political entity, in order to subvert it. He signed up as a stretcher-bearer in the First World War.[27] When he returned to India, he led the campaign for home rule. He was assassinated soon after India's independence.

Gandhi's critique of the modern state was devastating.[28] It disabled citizens, subjecting mind and body to the control of professional experts. A civilization should enhance its members' self-reliance. Instead, we are patients, students, taxpayers and prisoners under doctors, teachers, bureaucrats and jailers. Home rule started with personal realization of the self. Self-rule was *swaraj*,[29] focusing on political decentralization. Nearer independence in 1947, Gandhi was sidelined by politicians like Nehru, Jinnah and Ambedkar. Some say he was a religious figure and less effective as a politician.[30] He was once considered a saint, but it is now fashionable in India and South Africa to denigrate his achievements. Gandhi's ideal of bottom-up organization lives on through work organizations, voluntary associations and NGOs.

His method for achieving self-rule was *satyagraha*, 'insistence on truth'.[31] His autobiography, *The Story of My Experiments with Truth*,[32] is a revealing source for his politics and ethics. The pursuit of truth is related to non-violence (*ahimsa*). The political arts by themselves cannot mobilize the masses to fight for a new society. The Pan-Africanists combined religious thinking and secular politics, with early Du Bois at one extreme and James at the other. The idea of soul was central for Gandhi and at first for Du Bois. They moved between personal and global expressions of soul.

Gandhi's religious politics were humanist. Each of us is a unique personality and belongs to humanity as a whole. Many divisions, categories and associations mediate these extremes. We each feel small, isolated and vulnerable in a meaningless world governed by remote impersonal forces known only to experts. Yet modern cultures tell us that we are personalities with significance. How do we bridge the gap? The catalyst for anti-colonial revolution was world war and depression. But, like Rousseau, Gandhi knew

---

27. A. Desai and G. Vahed, *The South African Gandhi* (2015).

28. B. Parekh, *Gandhi's Political Philosophy* (1989).

29. https://en.wikipedia.org/wiki/Swaraj (accessed 9 September 2021).

30. P. Anderson, 'Gandhi Centre Stage' (2012).

31. https://simple.wikipedia.org/wiki/Satyagraha (accessed 9 September 2021).

32. M.K. Gandhi, *An Autobiography* (1927).

that mass society could overwhelm human agency. He chose the village as the site of India's renaissance because of its scale and because most Indians lived there. His philosophy aimed to build up the spiritual resources of individuals. He synthesized Victorian romanticism – Thoreau, Tolstoy and Ruskin – and Buddhist economics. Ajit Dasgupta shows Gandhi's debt to the Buddha as well as to Ruskin and Co. 'For the purpose of gaining understanding of Gandhi's social and economic thought, I would regard Buddha as his most significant predecessor'.[33] There is a strong affinity between Protestantism and Buddhism: both are middle class in origin. How do human beings span the chasm between self and world? Do divisions of race, class, nationality, religion, gender, time and place mediate the poles or exaggerate them? What size and type of society enables rather than disables its members?

Two examples show how Gandhi set about scaling up the self and scaling down the world.[34] In London to study the law, he joined the Vegetarian Society. When he left, London had a dozen more vegetarian restaurants. A large strike broke out in the industrial city of Ahmedabad. Gandhi sat down on a street corner there. The strike soon hinged around him. His method was not just for himself. Independence would succeed only if millions of Indians emulated him – and they did.

Traditional religion helps devotees to make a meaningful connection between self and world. Society's rulers once acknowledged its public role. This provided a bridge between men of power and the masses. It was fraudulent, but civilizations relied on it. The link has been broken in leading modern societies. The rhetoric and practice of science have replaced the humanities and religion as a guide. We need to synthesize these poles somehow.[35] All three offer pathways to truth. Great literature, formalized as Immanuel Kant's revolution in metaphysics, generates larger truths from subjective judgement exercised on closely observed details. The classical means for uniting self and world was prayer. Marcel Mauss, whose speciality was comparative religion, chose to study prayer because 'speech is the unity of thought and action'.[36] Religion links something personal inside us to the impersonal world of objects that we all share.[37] Many still bridge the gap between self and world by talking to God. But for two centuries, works of fiction – plays, novels and movies – have been where subject and object meet on more equal terms.

---

33. A. Dasgupta, *Gandhi's Economic Thought* (1994: 164).

34. Gandhi (ibid.: 24, 209–27).

35. See Chapter 20.

36. M. Mauss, *Prayer* (2003).

37. Hart, Appendix 2021.

Anthropological Visions of World Society

Humanity as a whole consists of individual personalities. How can anthropology help us to make a world society fit for all? We must learn how to make possible worlds out of actual experience. Contemplating little things makes it easier to think about the big things.[38] The anti-colonial movement invented a new and inspiring form of cosmopolitanism. They wanted the best achievements of Western civilization to be extended to humanity without racial exclusion. World society is still racist, but we can learn from them. The last century elevated impersonal society above the person. Our social science cannot connect the human predicament today with the eighteenth century. The digital revolution offers us new solutions, however. It spawns new kinds of person in a society whose time and space parameters are collapsing.

Truth is always local, but we must each extend our reach to grasp a world driven by power relations, whereas our common humanity is moral. Morality is the ability to act on personal judgements about our own and others' behaviour. Works of fiction allow us to span actual and possible worlds. They help us to resist alienation. How can we be at home in the restless turbulence of our world? Face-to-face relations make us feel at home. The digital revolution aims to make relations at distance as nearly like face-to-face experience as possible.[39] The drive to overcome alienation is more powerful than alienation itself. We now have universal communications to make world society in the image of our own humanity.

The anti-colonial intellectuals renewed the liberal Enlightenment by reviving its metaphysics. These have been hijacked by powers bent on imperialism and class warfare. Most people now rightly view the language of liberalism with suspicion. We need to rediscover the human truth of liberal revolution in language carrying fresh conviction. This is why I read the philosophers of democratic revolution and came round to the other side's perspective in the struggle for independence from colonial empire.

---

38. See Nabokov in Chapter 1.
39. See Chapter 14.

Part II

SELF

Chapter 4

I Come from Manchester

I never thought I was growing up in a culture. I found that in books about other people. Where I lived was a wasteland, scarred by bombsites. Manchester's industries were in free fall. The penury of post-war austerity was stifling.[1] The weather was all dark clouds, rain and fog. The few trees were grey with coal dust. I couldn't wait to get out. And then I saw Terence Davies's 1988 film, *Distant Voices, Still Lives*, about a Liverpool family. I found many echoes of how I grew up. Ritual was everywhere (the pub, the church, smoking in cinemas), above all singing (hymns, pop and folk). BBC radio marked social time with the shipping and weather forecasts. Weekends were the Saturday football results and a Sunday lunchtime sequence of record requests, band show and comedy. I was in a culture all right.

There was much local pride. Self-organized music-making was vibrant. There were church choirs, brass bands, fife and drum bands and operatic societies. All classes thought of the Hallé orchestra as theirs. The local culture, with a flat accent matching our open egalitarian nature, was described by Victorian novelists.[2] The DJ Dave Haslam picked up this connection in his book on the city's self-reinvention in the 1980s and 90s as 'Madchester'.[3]

1. Hart, Appendix 2018b.

2. Elizabeth Gaskell, *Cranford* (1851), *North and South* (1854), *Wives and Daughters* (1865) and *The Life of Charlotte Bronte* (1857).

3. Dave Haslam, *Manchester, England* (1999).

Manchester suffered a terrible economic defeat after the war. The national economy has changed a lot since then. The changes mainly favour London and south-east England; the rest have been left behind. But Manchester, at least its centre, is a net beneficiary of these developments. Some abandoned textile mills are now shopping malls, entertainment centres and apartment buildings. The heyday of the Hacienda club, ecstasy and Oasis is gone. But Manchester is booming as Britain's second city in the information services economy. I sometimes ask, 'What do Manchester and Philadelphia have in common?' They were both once industrial cities and the largest employer is now the university.

The Harts of Old Trafford

Trafford Park was a deer park, part of a manorial estate belonging to the de Trafford family since the Norman Conquest. In the 1890s it became the world's first industrial estate; it is still the largest in Europe. In the Second World War, it manufactured Spitfire fighter planes and Lancaster bombers. It was a German target then – and so were we next door. Old Trafford is a working-class dormitory area near the city centre. It contains Manchester United's football stadium and an international cricket ground.[4] Twice a day a 'buzzer' summoned the men to work and announced their leaving it. The roars of fifty thousand men on Saturdays reminded the women and children of collective male power.

As a baby I offered some diversion for adults trapped overnight in bomb shelters. Later I played football on a bomb site ('croft') with a floor of cinders, broken bricks and shattered glass. Anyone who fell over cut his knee. A gang controlled access to the site. My mother preferred us to play in the local park, a patch known as the 'rec' (recreation ground). Normally, we played in the street. The bomb damage was only made good in the late 1950s.

We lived in a small terraced house opposite my father's mother and his two unmarried sisters. Ours boasted small symbols of gentrification – a bay window with a tiny front garden and privet hedge. The backyard housed a bomb shelter, outside toilet, tool shed, dustbin and a few struggling plants. There were three rooms up and down and a cellar. The master bedroom was at the front, the children's bedrooms behind. A small toilet and bathroom were later carved out of them. Downstairs, the 'front room' had a fireplace, piano and brown lounge suite. We entertained visitors there. The main room ('kitchen') had a coal fire with two ovens, a dining table, chairs and a rack for drying clothes. The 'scullery' lacked floor covering, heating and electricity. It

---

4. See the Preface.

was for washing dishes and clothes, cleaning equipment and food cupboards. The cellar received coal through a hole and stored anything immune to coal dust. The dust was everywhere. Mum wiped all surfaces three times a day.

My great-grandfather, James Hart, came to Manchester from Belfast around 1870. He was a junior son of a landed family and bought a pub in Hulme. James married Elizabeth Bowes, a Manchester native. They had seven children of whom my grandfather David was the oldest. I have inherited a silver fob watch inscribed in 1837 to David Bowes, Elizabeth's grandfather. He received it on retirement as secretary of the Manchester Unity of the Independent Order of Odd Fellows. It provided welfare to members and their communities. The Manchester lodge launched a spin-off in Baltimore. The largest fraternal association in nineteenth-century America grew from that.

All James and Elizabeth's children received a private education. My grand-father became a craftsman, an upholsterer.[5] He married Harriet Harrop from Altrincham in Cheshire. Their four children were born between 1912 and 1924. The family was downwardly mobile in my father's generation. Grandpa had chronic bronchitis between the wars and worked intermittently. He died in 1941, the year my parents were married. Grandma carried the family and Dad left school at 14 to earn a wage. She and her sisters – Bertha, Harriet and Maud – were inseparable.

Grandma was an 'angel in marble', a working-class Tory who considered herself superior because she came from Cheshire.[6] But she knew that Manchester's money, even without much, beat the feudalism she came from. She rejected Labour's welfare state. It resembled the gift economy her family had escaped, where the landlord offered his tied workers a chicken at Christmas to cancel out all he took from them. 'My money is as good as anyone's', she would say. 'If you can't pay, don't go'. She didn't take advantage of the free library – she didn't read much anyway – and would not order spectacles through the National Health Service.

Dad visited her often after we moved from Old Trafford, but one day she didn't reply when he called. He found her, at 84, on a stepladder hanging wallpaper in her bedroom. She was packed off to her daughters far away. I loved her more than anyone then or since. I credit her with some attitudes to money, which equalizes as it divides. Three children bounced back into the middle class. Norman, Dad's brother, was never interested.

Uncle Norman was a sweet person – soft-spoken and uncompetitive. He trained as a carpenter and worked in the St John's Ambulance after he was demobbed. He made me a box of child-size wooden tools lined with baize.

---

5. Someone who covers furniture.

6. 'Angels in marble' was coined by a Victorian writer, but it is often attributed to Benjamin Disraeli, then leader of the Conservative Party

I can't remember using them, but cherished his present. Then he became a postman. He and Auntie Hilda rented council housing and never had a car.

Norman bought expensive furniture on instalment plans. He dispensed alcoholic drinks lavishly, but didn't drink himself. Their lifestyle seemed more affluent than ours, because they were not hooked on accumulation through saving. Norman and Hilda gave generously. Their Christmas and birthday presents were more expensive than our parents'. Mum couldn't stand this. She wanted to put a ceiling on presents to us, but didn't succeed. Norman retired to the north-east and had a fatal heart attack after eating fish and chips late one night.

Auntie Muriel was my favourite and I hers. She left school after two years of repeated surgery for osteomyelitis. She managed nevertheless to become a dressmaker. At 20, during the war, she took a year's training in aeronautics and joined Metropolitan Vickers in Trafford Park, where she became the first woman production line inspector for Lancaster bombers. She also produced the drama society's lunchtime shows, learned to drive a car and had a good time. Once, when I was 12, she told me, 'We were working nights, Keith, with all those lovely married men. There was a war on and I wasn't going to die wondering.' I knew this was dangerous talk, but didn't quite get it then. Muriel was egalitarian and subversive of normal family life. She was my hero and friend. I was a pageboy when she married Albert Coldwell, a Salford accountant whose solidity complemented her mercurial nature. He was a great pianist and Muriel, with her sister Gladys, sang in a world-famous choir. She died at 98 years old, three decades after Albert. They had no children. She left me and four cousins £100,000 each.

Gladys was pretty and smart, a lawyer's secretary who made her social life elsewhere than our neighbourhood. She married Tom Wibberley, an air force master sergeant. They lived in Germany before buying a cottage in North Yorkshire where Tom grew strawberries. He took a motorized sailing boat through the French rivers and canals to the Costa Blanca, where they built their main home. She died, much diminished, in 2021. Grandma, Dad, Muriel and Gladys all made it into the nineties.

Alice Wrigley, my mother, was the middle of three children. These were born in quick succession (1916–19) to Harold Wrigley and Mary Short. Harold was a distant, severe man and Mary died young of cardiac failure. We called her successor Ethel or 'Nannie'. Harold came from deep Lancashire. Mum knew this dialect and often spoke in proverbs. I discovered that this was not normal English at grammar school. Grandpa Wrigley had a background in mill engineering. He became chief sanitary engineer for Stretford (now Trafford). On Mum's advice, he retired to the Blackpool coast. He soon had a septic toe and his gangrenous leg was cut off in hospital. He died from the shock.

The Wrigleys had a large semi-detached house and a Ford car. Alice and her brother Harold both went to grammar school. Their sister, Marion, went to a school for the deaf. Harold lost a leg at Dunkirk, married twice, became a secondary school headmaster and had five children. Marion married Geoffrey from her school. Both their sons became deaf as young children. Mum took great care of this tragic family.

Visits at the weekend involved two related nuclear families. Tea consisted of sandwiches in neat triangles and salad items served individually without dressing; desert was tinned fruit, cake and scones. Mum was a leading organizer of this hospitality circuit. She worried about leakage of funds earmarked for upward mobility.

Mum and Dad

Philip Larkin wrote 'They fuck you up, your mum and dad'[7] I always thought I was the author of my own destiny, a self-made man. I was not; but the attitude dies slowly. At 15, I drank a lot, smoked cigarettes and bet on the horses. My parents only cautioned me. The breadwinner/housewife model ruled in the 1950s. I was the social climber they wanted. They gave me unstinting support and were proud of me.

The Harts said I owed my brains to my Dad. His sisters sometimes called him, with mixed sarcasm and respect, 'Saint Stanley'. After the General Strike of 1926, at 14, he took a job with an electric cable manufacturer. For seven years he attended night classes in electrical engineering at Manchester Technical College. His Higher National Certificate became a degree when 'the Tech' achieved university status. He then joined the General Post Office (GPO) telephones branch. There he got stuck in the manual grades for two decades. His was a 'reserved occupation' in the war. He won promotion in the mid-1950s and then shot up the hierarchy. When he retired in 1972, he coordinated plant planning for the North-west region. His long retirement was comfortable and fulfilling.

Dad loved numbers and science and hired out as a solo singer for church choirs and opera societies. He was a great dancer, Mum said. He played tennis and badminton at 60 and was the oldest active member of his golf club later. He taught himself to play the flute and the piano, took up Spanish and loved Alexandre Dumas's novels. In retirement, he studied the stars through a powerful telescope. A map of the world at night was pinned on their bedroom wall. He brewed beer and wine and kept detailed records. He believed the world is open to each of us and we should never accept being excluded from

---

7. P. Larkin, 'This Be the Verse' (2007).

any part. Anyone can enjoy doing anything without having to be expert. I was slow to learn this lesson. He taught me that life is a game we should learn to play well.

Mum became the personal secretary to one of the executives in Manchester's main post office. My parents met at church. In a five-year engagement they accumulated what furniture they needed – buying a house was out of the question. They rented upmarket accommodation in a suburb after getting married. Mum gave up her job, as was usual. She soon got pregnant and wanted the baby in the Stretford hospital where she was born. Grandma told them of a vacancy opposite her and they moved in for eighteen years.

This was a fateful decision. Dad wanted to keep an eye on his mother and sisters, but they were at best polite with Mum. She was marooned in a low-class neighbourhood with no job, two kids and a husband going nowhere. Dad wouldn't let her earn money since it diminished his status and exposed their children to maternal deprivation. He gave her housekeeping money and paid for everything else himself. She never had access to his bank account. They were poor and practised minute economies. Then money became more plentiful at last. Mum's first significant income was a state pension at sixty. She became a revolutionary then. She watched the world open up for her daughter and daughter-in-law whom she considered to be less deserving than her. 'I have wasted my life on a selfish man and two ungrateful children'.

She used her pension for driving lessons, since Dad wouldn't teach her. She passed on the fourth attempt. He agreed to take her out once a month, but couldn't or wouldn't. She died at 70 when a minor operation on her urethra revealed defunct kidneys for the first time. At the funeral I felt an incoherent desire to avenge her. Mum helped me with my homework. They once studied German for their first foreign holiday. Grandma was visiting us and Dad said,

D: Guess what mark I got in German, mother, 80 per cent.
G: You always were a clever boy, Stanley.
D: Ask Alice what mark she got.
G: What did you get, Alice?
M: 85 per cent.
G: How could you let her do that? Oops (hand to mouth).

I had several 'mothers' in Old Trafford, including elderly widows. Mum hit me often. I took refuge across the street for emotional compensation. Both my parents were puritans who accepted great personal sacrifices to give us the best start in life. According to Dad, 'We take responsibility for you until you are 18. After that you are on your own. And don't worry about us later; your responsibility is to your family.' His protective attitude towards his mother and sisters contradicted this. At the last he went to a retirement home. He never got over the demented screams of old ladies at night and died.

This was the worst period of my life, when Sophie and I had a new baby in Paris, her father was dying in Geneva and we both had a long commute to work. My sister Janice had already died of a cerebral haemorrhage, so I had to cope with Dad alone. It was a relief when he died – I have not mourned him properly since. Writing this helps me to appreciate him, to love what they both did for me.

My Sister Janice

My companion from 2 years old was my sister, Janice. She claimed that I ruined her life. I hoped to make amends later. We were friendly as adults, but lived far apart. I looked forward to when we would be each other's closest relative. She died without warning at 52, leaving a hole in me that I can never fill. We spent so much time together as children. We were bored and squabbled often, but played games of great variety. We both became expert card players. Janice knew that if she yelled 'He hit me!', Mum would slap me. It mattered little if my crime was physical or verbal. We argued over food at the dining table – it was scarce during austerity.[8] We worked out some Jack Sprat deals:

> Jack Sprat could eat no fat. His wife could eat no lean. And so between the two of them They licked the platter clean.

For example, Janice liked the whites of fried eggs and I spread runny yoke on toast.

Our temperaments were different. Janice was placid and kind; I oscillated between hyperactivity and abstraction. Mum attributed this to our innate personalities. Mothers take refuge in genetic fundamentalism; my theory is *in utero* socialization. I was her first and she was nervous. She was an experienced mother for Janice and calmer. Mum thought her brother and sister both got more love and attention. But she favoured me. I have a photograph of me and Janice at 10 and 8 years old, in front of a castle, beaming with legs crossed. That's how I want to remember us.

When our daughter Louise arrived,[9] Mum and I discussed breast- versus bottle-feeding. She gave us a 2 a.m. breastfeed until we were 2 years old. The age gap was two years and two months. This knowledge cast our relations in a new light. I delighted in subverting my mother's rules at home. Janice always

---

8. T. Rakopoulos, *The Global Life of Austerity* (2018).

9. See Chapter 12.

said I treated her as a non-person. It was hard no longer being the only child and grandchild.

Janice went to a girls' grammar school. Our parents had long refused to buy a television set since it would distract me from my homework. When I won a Cambridge scholarship, they bought one. Janice asked, 'What about my homework?' She was certainly a victim of discrimination; but, as a small child, I couldn't engineer the conditions all by myself. Janice never wanted children of her own. Larkin would have approved. After Newcastle University, Janice joined IBM as a computer analyst. They made her a 'trouble-shooter', driven around the country in a taxi to solve local computing problems. She had a small white sports car. Then she married a divorced mill engineer, John Pollitt, twenty years older with two grown sons. John claimed that he and she were exploited as wage slaves. They opened a boarding house on the coast and later speculated in real estate.

I bought her a personal computer, but she didn't open the box: 'I can't unlearn what I knew of the mainframes. All I care about now is budgerigars, carnations and the *Daily Telegraph* crossword'. Once I asked, 'Guess what my favourite Beethoven symphonies are now?' 'I know what they are'. 'But they are not the same. . . OK, what are they?' 'The 4th and 7th'. 'How did you know?' 'Because the 1st, the 2nd and the 8th are too slight and the 3rd, 5th, 6th and 9th are too well known'. That is the sister I lost. Actually, those two symphonies are upbeat and brilliant. That's why I like them now.

Janice was visiting her husband in hospital. One day she had a severe headache. Her local hospital gave her no treatment and an appointment for Saturday. She found that the clinic was in Blackpool. The Saturday morning traffic was heavy. She had difficulty parking, to be told that the clinic was where she had come from. She stopped to see an old lady she shopped for at weekends and drove off again. She parked the car and keeled over dead from a cerebral haemorrhage on the spot. She had no previous history of cardiovascular problems, but her mother, aunt and grandmother did.

Memories of My First Decade

At 3 I was allowed to go out to the street alone. I entered primary school at 5 and passed exams to three grammar schools at 10. Other fragments of memory lack context. One has me holding Mum's hand above my head. We are in a butcher's shop with sawdust on the floor. It is a time of rationing. Mum wants the fat old butcher to give us above our usual ration (a few ounces of meat each week). I feel the shame travelling down her arm. She was young, pretty and shy. I later discovered that I am sensitive to the energies that people exchange.

I had a nightmare when I was 4. Mum and Dad woke up to my screams; I was staring at the wall catatonically. They were both being killed by 'cowboys and Indians'. I have been blind in one eye since birth and have poor visualization. William Rivers claimed that he lost his ability to visualize from being molested at 5.[10] After that frightening dream, did I shut down my visual imagination?

I received three pence a week spending money.[11] Money's source was unknown to me and it passed quickly through my hands. I soon spent it on sweets, always at Mrs Hewitt's shop. She reserved my favourites and sometimes gave me extra. When she sold the shop, she introduced me to the new owner as a regular customer. 'This is Keith and he likes wine gums, pear drops and liquorice all-sorts'. Rationing entitled everyone to the same meagre share. With my three pence, I handed over a coupon entitling me to two ounces of sweets. When I was 5, Mum announced that sugar rationing was over. We could buy as many sweets as we liked. I rushed to Mrs Hewitt's and ordered three bags of two ounces each.

MH: That will be nine pence, please.
K: But I only have three pence. They said you could have as much as you like.
MH: Well, you need the money too.

Money is a rationing device. Markets are democratic; all you need is the money. Why some have more than they need and most of us hardly any should remain a deep mystery.[12]

At 9 I was admitted to a children's hospital to have my tonsils removed. I had a huge bribe – two ounce packets of my favourites. I was anaesthetized and woke up with a raging thirst, aware that my throat had been got at. I turned to my bedside cabinet for consolation and found that my sweets had gone! I shouted for the nurses and one came eventually. She couldn't understand that I worried more about my property than pain. It was hospital policy to pool patients' goodies. Didn't it feel good that poor boys and girls, many with more serious problems, could enjoy my sweets? I was incandescent. They had drugged me to steal my sweets. I demanded restitution. The nurse brought some inferior sweets back.

I missed my sweets more than my tonsils. Ah, the NHS in its heyday, how decent it all was then. Recall that my mentor was a working-class Tory and a snob. Sweets played an enormous part in the reward-and-punishment game of my life then. The lady next door kept a jar on a high shelf. One day, I tried

10. See Chapter 2.
11. Hart, Appendix 2000a: Chapter 5.
12. See Chapter 19, however.

to talk my way into some. Janice just stared at the jar; she got one 'for not asking'.

The breadwinner-housewife model had been re-established after the war. Mum didn't need much persuading to give up her job. But understanding later what she had signed up for made her less compliant. I grew up believing that gender inequality was the most bitter of class struggles. In the 1970s I chaired the women's studies programme at Yale for a year.[13] Mum took me one afternoon to see *Showboat,* a movie featuring Paul Robeson's song 'Ol' Man River'. She could not leave me unsupervised. I was petrified in case Dad found out. In the darkness I became aware of Mum feeling something I would rather avoid. I made an excuse for us to leave early.

The three of us (Dad was working) visited Auntie Muriel near Bedford. We caught a bus and Mum was soon sick. We descended and waited for the next one. The journey was a revelation, all that greenery of middle England hour after hour! I couldn't wait to get out and embrace it. In my aunt's village it was still a bright afternoon and the hedgerows were verdant. Wearing summer clothes, I threw myself into the nearest grassy bank. It was a bed of nettles. I spent a week in bed with a body rash.

There was an outing to Cambridge University. I asked, 'Why do they have so many churches here?' and was told, 'They are schools, not churches'. 'When I grow up, I want to go to a school that looks like a church'. This became enshrined in family lore as 'Keith wants to go to Cambridge University'. I soon became a skilled examination-passer.[14] At 10, I won admission to Manchester Grammar School. I was the first from my district to do so. It was on the front page of our local newspaper. Dad kept the cutting.

---

13. See Chapter 8.
14. See Chapter 5.

THE ESCALATOR

Grammar School and Cambridge

I have only once been single-minded about my future and that was as a teenager. I would ride the escalator to social recognition through Cambridge University. That meant passing examinations. I wasn't sure what I would find there; but I would do whatever it took to have that chance. I felt later that I wasted my youth and remembered only the pain and sacrifice. But there was more to it than exams. I found religion, consumed lots of fiction and music and was active in sports as spectator and performer. I made some money by betting on the horses. I acquired adult vices like drinking and smoking. My sexual education was deferred indefinitely; but I had a number of male friends. These lent humanity to life outside the classroom, examination hall and homework. But the main goal set strict limits on their indulgence.

Manchester Grammar School

Children were then assigned at 11 between 'grammar' and 'secondary modern' schools. Entry to the former was by competitive examination, with the prospect of non-manual employment. The latter had no intellectual aspirations for pupils, who would leave early for a manual job, if they were lucky. Manchester Grammar School was founded in 1515. It was classified as 'independent' along with exclusive establishments for rich children known confusingly as 'public schools'. It was a leading producer of scholarships to Oxford and Cambridge ('Oxbridge'). I took the entrance exam at 9 and failed. Admission to the exam within a forty-mile radius depended on a primary school headmaster's recommendation. Ten thousand boys entered each year and were reduced to two thousand on the first round. The second selected two hundred winners. The odds were fifty to one against and thousands to one in the population. Private schools trained pupils for this exam. Winners and losers were separated by residence, as in apartheid.[1]

On the second try, I passed. I chose the classics side and entered 1β. We were tested in each subject every two weeks. Many boys discovered that they were only mediocre or worse in that company. Given the resulting negativity, we all pretended not to work, caring little for our scores. I next entered 2α and stayed near the top of the top class from then on.

Once schools bought closed scholarships in Oxbridge. MGS had the grain milling monopoly in central Manchester until the nineteenth century, so it could buy many. Now only one was left, the Patchett scholarship in classics at St John's College, Cambridge, and I was nominated for it. This guaranteed a place if I reached the scholarship standard. There were major and minor scholarships, with different prestige and financial rewards. The telegram said: CONGRATULATIONS YOU HAVE WON A MANOR SCHOLARSHIP. I am a glass-half-full person, so I interpreted this as 'major', but 'minor' was always more likely. I soon got over the disappointment. I was in!

The cultural capital that I laid down as a teenager has supported me ever since. But I could not guess how much work was necessary. I lived a monastic life. Most days I got home around 4.30 p.m., went for a twenty-five-mile time trial on my racing bike and did four hours of homework every Monday to Thursday. At weekends I took off one period of the seven available. I could watch a movie or a soccer game, but not both. It came to forty hours of homework a week. If I left my seat, it might be an hour before I returned. I played pop music on Radio Luxemburg non-stop. If my attention broke, it would pick up the music and soon return to my homework. I am on social media a lot and people ask, 'Where do you find the time, Keith?' It keeps me at my work station, the same laptop for both activities. If my writing is stuck, I move into email, surfing and reading newspapers. Then an idea pops up and I return to my writing.

Confessions of an Examination-Passer

I wore the school uniform through a rough area every day. Unemployed teenagers hung around, so I made myself a difficult target, assuming the air of a street fighter. That combative expression never left me. When I was 17, my mother asked why I never brought friends home from school. I blurted out,

---

1. See Chapter 13.

'Because I am ashamed'. She burst into tears. I wasn't ashamed of the home she made, but of the area I had to bring them through. We soon moved to a semi-detached house in the Cheshire suburbs.

The examination process bugged me. I couldn't bear risking all that work and native ability in an impersonal system. I built up an image of the examiner: someone in his fifties with a backlog of scripts after midnight. He was on his fourth whiskey and desperate for sleep. I knew I would be good enough; but what if he skipped some scripts? He could give me a B without reading. How to get his attention, slow him down, make him want to read? I first studied calligraphy. Forward-sloping is extravert, backward-sloping is introvert and big loops are psychotic. I settled on upright, legible and medium-size handwriting, pleasant to read with some low-key mannerisms. But I needed more. I started inserting a joke on the first page. Either he liked it or he didn't, but he was reading. This didn't seem peculiar then, but it amazes me now. Ever since, my passion has been to make a personal connection with impersonal society.

I am a sentimental moviegoer and tear up easily. Once I watched *Billy Elliot* (2000). Billy is a Durham coalminer's son during the 1984–85 strike. He wants to be a ballet dancer. Imagine how that goes down with his family and friends. He tries for a place in the Royal Ballet School, then waits for the buff envelope, looking every day. But his father finds it first. Billy won't open it and storms out of the room. I broke into racking sobs. Billy wants it so much, he would rather not know the result than face rejection. He gets in, of course. This is a movie after all.

I read everything available in Greek and Latin, covering the most significant authors. My favourites were the Greek tragedians (Aeschylus) and Latin lyric poetry (Catullus). As a technical linguist I focused on formal accuracy, not content. I might be given some Victorian bombast to translate into fourth-century Greek prose. 'We must not sacrifice our principles on the altar of expediency'. Greek had a fraction of modern English's vocabulary and preferred verb to noun forms. I had to grasp the basic meaning of the sentence, keep the metaphor if I could and throw in a phrase from Demosthenes.

This training has stood me well as a writer and editor later. Reading for technical language slows you down and requires concentration. If I am blocked in my writing, I fiddle around with the text I have and this sends me back with renewed interest. Writers have to remain enthusiastic about stuff they have been working on for ages. Technical editing does that job for me.

Religion, Culture and Sport

Something had to give and it did. I found religion. Dad was the lay official of our church. I was chief choirboy. At 13 I was told that my mature voice, a light baritone, was mediocre and gave up singing. I forgot Dad's principle of doing what interests you. I refused to take communion at 12. Then I learned to read the Greek New Testament. This synthesized religion and intellectual life for me. At 14 I signed up with a different church. At 16 I won a competition for translation and commentary on the Greek New Testament. The Gospel of St John and Acts were both written in Greek. They made more sense. I could accept 'In the beginning was *loghos*', universal reason, rather than 'the word'. 'Faith, hope and *kharitas*', or 'love', beat 'charity'. I embraced the idea that we should love all humanity.[2] We should recognize the human being in those we meet. I later lived in an African slum. I had to get beyond the binaries of race, class and power that divided me from my neighbours. I learned how to make human connection across unequal divisions.

In the suburbs, I asked Dad why we didn't go to church any more. 'St Brides was politics; if I didn't take on the warden job, a rival family would.' His voting Conservative in the late 1950s was as shocking. 'When I earned less than average, I voted Labour because they were on my side. Now that I earn more than average, I want to keep it.' I joined the Christadelphians, Bible fundamentalists who didn't believe in the Trinity or the immortal soul. For them, Archbishop Ussher had correctly calculated the world's origin as 4004 BC. The Bible said so. It was a joke; but they were nice people who knew how to party. I went on Sundays. In Cambridge, I found a girlfriend at the local Christadelphian church. Religion soon faded out of my life. God supported me in my MGS years. Once I arrived, religious belief vanished and has never returned – not conventional religion. Its general meaning for me now is bridging what we know and the unknown, making the unknown known.

When I was 16, I decided that we must be Sephardic Jews posing as Northern Irish Protestants. They share Hart as a surname. Jews were the custodians of local high culture. The conductor of the Hallé Orchestra was a Jew. Jewish kids at MGS were richer and more civilized than me. I posed as a Left Bank Jewish intellectual, with black polo-neck sweater, gold-rimmed spectacles and a cigarette. But the Jesuits were right; the Protestants got to me early. This became clearer in middle age.

My human side was also sustained by fiction, music and sport. I accepted that 'analysis' and 'story' were contradictory. One was compulsory and secured professional success; the other gave me existential freedom and social connection. English literature was an unexamined subject at MGS. We had some great teachers. One became an Oxford don specializing in Dickens and Trollope; another had been the head of BBC North radio drama! I always had a passion for fiction. But I didn't mix my main interests then. That has come with old age.

---

2. See Chapter 3.

Shakespeare was obsessed with my dilemma. How to be yourself and part of impersonal society? How can someone be a king and a man?[3] His patrons were aristocrats, but working out this problem in the late tragedies pushed him to explore democracy. Plays make social contradictions personal. At 17 my favourite novels were *Crime and Punishment, A Passage to India* and *Jude the Obscure.*[4] In *Crime and Punishment* I first encountered a mind as complex as my own. Raskolnikov was my hero, a student who lost sight of himself in society. The police detective plays him like a fish. 'I read an interesting article where you say if someone would do something new, he must be a criminal. Do you still believe that?' I pumped the air with my fist and shouted 'YES!' I always thought that rules were there to hold me down. Two decades after Poe invented murder mysteries, Dostoevsky made one in reverse – not a who-dunit, but waiting for the murderer we know to crack.[5] Forster lit in me an abiding passion for India.[6] I was impressed by Hardy then, but now I find his vision cruel and repellent.

I once asked Dad why he had been so rough when teaching me cribbage from the age of three.[7] He said, 'I wanted you to be my friend' – his own father refused to play cards with children. Stanley and his mate Vernon developed an agonistic friendship and that was his model for me. Guessing the classical music on breakfast radio worked better. Janice learned to play the piano well and had a fine appreciation of classical music. But she stayed out of that competition.

Rock 'n' roll was invented just for me.[8] At 14, I preferred black singers coming out of rhythm 'n' blues to Elvis Presley and the white pop stars. At 16 I found Miles Davis's *Kind of Blue*; it hooked me for life. At the millennium I was in a car going to a beach in Brazil. The century's top hundred pop songs were on the radio. I was singing along when the driver said, 'He knows all the words!' I did, at least for the 1950s to the 1970s. One daughter kept me in touch with the 1980s and the other with now. I feel blessed that my teens were when rock 'n' roll was born. We owed nothing to older generations.

My other diversion was sport. I was a cricket fan. I saw every ball of the 1956 Manchester test against the Aussies when Jim Laker took nineteen wickets. Manchester United's run ended in February 1958 when half the team died in the Munich air crash. Mum was an avid cricket follower and

---

3. A theme explored in K. Hart, *The Hit Man's Dilemma* (2005).

4. Fyodor Dostoevsky, *Crime and Punishment* (1864); E.M. Forster, *A Passage to India* (1924); Thomas Hardy, *Jude the Obscure* (1895).

5. See Chapter 20.

6. See Chapter 11.

7. See Chapter 20.

8. See the Preface.

captained her ladies' crown green bowls team. Dad played tennis and badminton. I signed up for lacrosse at MGS, but entry to school teams was too competitive. I took up tennis and golf in my late teens. I was a keen racing cyclist. At a nearby velodrome, the final race was a 'devil take the hindmost'. The last in each lap dropped out. At 17 I cycled to Auntie Muriel's in Essex – 350 miles in two days. I lay on the couch with the curtains drawn, watching the Rome Olympics for three weeks. She never forgave me for that.

I earned wages in the holidays, nights at a bread factory and at a haberdashery emporium. This involved working with mature women. Most of the emporium's customers and employees were women too. I made friends there and learned more about wool, buttons, zips and the rest than I cared to. From the age of 15, I drank and smoked a lot. I sometimes delayed buying a new pack of cigarettes for abstinence's sake. These vices took over from rule-breaking in primary school. I was one of the boys, not just a swot.

The poles of my teenage years were passing exams and betting. When I was 12, the last thing I wanted was a job like my dad's. He would vent his frustration at meals, while Janice and I stared at our plates. The threat of unemployment gripped me even then. What if I failed my exams? How do you make money without working? I could only think of betting on the horses. I set out to learn about horse racing. Every day I borrowed grandma's *Daily Express*. I made notional bets in a notebook. After three years I was making a regular profit on paper. I now had some money – from a newspaper round and fiddling my daily expenses for food and travel. I made small cash bets. Whenever I earned wages, my betting expanded. What I lacked in capital, I made up for in deep knowledge. I scraped by. It was mostly about gaining experience. I was still deeply afraid of being tied down to one job and place.

I needed to get off the escalator sometimes to meet my human needs. My recreations helped me to cope with being enslaved to a dehumanizing system. I was never wholly focused on academic advancement. I made human connection through religion, fiction, music, sport, gambling and drinking. There was more to life than social mobility.

Cambridge Student

I 'went up' to Cambridge in 1961. The gap between college and home was huge. I moved between them three times a year, while trying to preserve an identity. My student years were very happy. I love Cambridge University.[9] But I must begin with its strangeness. I spent four years as an undergraduate –

---

9. See Chapter 10.

two as a classicist and two reading social anthropology. Anthropology was part of the solution. Cambridge would get me into the wider world.

Cambridge was still a backwater in the early 1960s, beautiful but retarded. Social relations were feudal. St John's College has buildings from the sixteenth to twentieth centuries, with a world-famous choir and a school for the choir-boys. The dining room and chapel are the main meeting places. The small college bar was next to the dining hall. If we spent too much on credit, we had to see the Dean. My room overlooked the river. Across it was a Victorian monstrosity, New Court. From behind it looked like a workhouse. But the front was a 'wedding cake' tower and façade, providing an ornamental view from the Backs; but internal space was cramped. Another court was added in the 1960s.[10]

Social Life

I had a licensed independence there. The college took care of me and I fell back on my parents' home during the vacations. Even so, I had to manage on my grant and scholarship in three instalments, £420 a year (£8,700 today). At first, I listed everything I bought in a heavy ledger. This lasted for two weeks. The big question was how to use my bursary windfall. A bed-maker tidied up my room daily. Although I was used to exploiting Mum, I was not prepared for Mrs Pleasance. She called me sir, but combined wary circumspection with patronizing familiarity. I encountered it often in that town.

Many students had to live in lodgings. I found my future room-mate, Robin Devenish, through a friend who lived on my staircase. He was a maths student whose family had been Caribbean landed aristocracy, but were now upper middle class. In England the main indicator of class is accent. The Beat-les made regional accents fashionable. BBC newscasters were now allowed to speak in their native voices. The post-war baby boom accelerated social mobility. Regional grammar school boys found their way into elite bastions of higher education. Cambridge's feudal working class were immune. A woman once said of me, 'Oo, doan' 'e talk fanny!' A student asked me, 'Are they all like you where you come from?' 'Yes, but they don't all win scholarships to Cambridge'. I exaggerated my regional accent. Like John Lennon, I was another lower-middle-class grammar school boy pretending to be a 'working class hero'.[11]

10. With Ricardo Leizaola, *Keith Hart's Improvised Cambridge Tour* https://thememorybank .co.uk/keith-harts-improvised-cambridge-tour-in-7-webisodes/ (accessed 10 September 2021).

11. https://www.youtube.com/watch?v=iMewtlmkV6c (accessed 10 September 2021).

The anthropologist Sir Edmund Leach once asked me, 'Do you think you are different from the rest, Keith?' I nodded yes. He shook his head. 'You don't think the aristocracy and the high bourgeoisie have the brains between them to keep a place like Cambridge University going, do you? No, they have to scour the country for bright lower-class boys like you. We then teach them how to speak and behave as if they grew up here. I am different – I had wealth and power to start with! You may choose to speak here as you do at home, but you are the norm here'. He liked me.

I met the Oxford philosopher A.J. Ayer at a Cambridge cocktail party. He was in his seventies and had just published his memoirs.[12] He said he was only interested in his first fourteen years, since everything afterwards was entailed in what he had become by then. His memories of childhood were vivid and plentiful; mine weren't. Like most people, I peer through the fog of my youth for clues to what I became.

Joining In

I was not a rebel at Cambridge; idiosyncratic maybe, but committed to rubbing along. I did my best to learn the customs of the place. At my first college feast, I watched carefully what others did with all the cutlery, plates and glasses. But I relaxed too soon. A large silver dish containing water, ice cubes and rose petals appeared on my blind side. I tipped some of the water into a glass. You were supposed to dip your napkin in the cold water and wipe your brow.

The main melting pot was the college bar. The big division was between 'aesthetes' and 'hearties', literary types and sportsmen. I preferred to hang out with the latter; but I enjoyed talking about books, art and music too. Some friends decided to join the boat club's novices eight and they needed a cox. My classics tutor told me to do it six days a week. Our college boat club fielded a dozen boats and was always a contender for first place in the races. I soon made it to second boat cox and then coxed a boat at the Henley Regatta merged from two other colleges. I stuck it out for another year and then quit. I captained our college occasional cricket team. We played village sides at the weekend and drank in the local pub. I sometimes captained the college darts team against pub sides. I took up squash and even played as a hooker in the fourth rugby team, mixing it up in the front row.

I was not a full member of a working-class bar clique who wore football scarves and drank Newcastle Brown Ale. I got on fine with the aristocrats. Our mutual enemies were the bank managers' sons from Surrey. No-one

---

12. A.J. Ayer, *Part of My Life: Memoirs of a Philosopher* (1977).

doubted that I was a prole because of my accent. We shared an interest in betting on horses and playing cards for money. I played bridge with them and three-card brag with the Northerners. The toffs threw parties at unusual hours, sometimes when students were on their way to lectures in the morning (épater les bourgeois).[13] Their preferred drinks were 'black velvet' and 'champagne cocktails'. The first was a mixture of champagne and Guinness ('the best wine and the best beer'). The middle classes wouldn't mix dear with cheap. The second mixed champagne with Remy-Martin five-star cognac, similarly anomalous. I loved black velvet and won enough at cards to pay my share of party expenses.

This makes me sound like a chameleon. I suppose I was, but I never pretended to be anyone else than myself. I couldn't feel at home in that strange society. Occasional dates with a girl from the town courted social disaster. I settled for sport and male bonding in the bar.

Academic Work

I had read more classics than most students and translated fluently in both directions. Our classics lecturers – on Roman history, the pre-Socratic philosophers, Greek tragedy and ancient philosophy – were global stars.[14] But I generally coasted on lectures and coursework.[15] I spent my time drinking, betting on the horses, playing cards, reading novels, watching movies, playing college sports and sleeping in.

I soon figured out that classics didn't offer good prospects for an academic career. There were many bright students and most worked a lot harder. Worse, academic jobs for classics were drying up. That was the push side, but social sciences were then enjoying a boom at Cambridge. I thought of sociology, but it was part of the Economics Faculty and that put me off. My rowing coach, a geographer from Turin, spent the winters in Sicily and Lebanon studying how the goats make deserts. He returned to Cambridge in time for the Mays. It looked like a good plan to me. Social anthropology was sociology with travel thrown in.

I sometimes drank with Jack Goody, our college's social anthropologist. He was running a seminar on clientship. I offered to talk on Roman clientship and then forgot about it. He reminded me two days beforehand. There was no time to mug up on the Latin writers. I could only consult secondary

---

13. 'To impress the middle class'.

14. Dennis Page (Greek tragedy), A.H.M. Jones (Roman history), Kirk and Raven (pre-Socratic philosophers), W.K.C. Guthrie (philosophy).

15. Chapter 20 discusses how I learned as an academic.

sources in English. Any classics tutor would have thrown my essay out. My talk went down well. I thought, 'These people have no intellectual standards'. Anthropologists could study anything in the world. The only knowledge rule was 'I have been there and you haven't'. I signed up. My reasoning was callow and uninformed, of course. Perhaps I glimpsed the mind-expanding potential of anthropology; but that mostly came later.

That summer I burnt all the writing I had kept in the incinerator of my parents' new suburban garden: notes, essays, exam cribs, letters. I resented working so hard as a teenager. I never wanted to go back there and destroyed the tangible remains. I am still a hard worker, but nowhere near what I did as a teenager. Now I am grateful to him for what I learned then.

My Apprenticeship in Betting

I now had capital in Cambridge. Six years spent grubbing around the bottom end of the betting market paid off.[16] I knew a lot about the horses. I realized that bets made on a hunch could ruin me. I needed to make a science of it. Three variables matter most: the total fund available, the risk of losing it all and the size and speed of making bets. Most punters try to win a lot with a little occasionally. They lose. You need a large reserve and to bet small amounts often. This is the key to capital growth. I didn't know that then.

I doubled up on losing bets made with a 50 per cent probability of winning, like a coin toss. The binomial theorem says the chance of losing such bets ten times in a row is one in 512 (2 to the powers 0–9). By placing bets worth a five hundredth of my stake on horses starting around evens, I had an 0.2 per cent chance of losing the lot. My compendious knowledge of horse racing reduced the risk. With a fund of £100 (£2,000 now), my initial bet should be four shillings (£4). How to make these bets fast enough? I bet on all favourites starting between evens and two to one against. This covered betting tax on winnings. Odds-on bets were too risky. Favourites in Britain win one in three races on average. I made bets mechanically until I reached four consecutive losses. The fifth bet in a losing sequence required roughly sixteen times the original stake to cover my losses. I then slowed down and picked my bets. In four years, my longest losing sequence was seven bets; the seventh bet cost over sixty times the original stake. It wasn't pleasant. My hands shook and I was sweating. But this happened only a couple of times in my student career.

Operating this system wasn't the problem. Gatekeepers (bookmakers, casinos) have the right to refuse anyone a bet. They will do so if they believe

---

16. Hart, Appendix 2013a. See Chapter 19.

someone is using a scientific system – card counting at blackjack or betting on horses in a regular way. I made an average 8 per cent on turnover. I disguised this by spreading my custom between three betting shops and varying how much I won or lost. I came across as a high-volume punter who didn't cost them much. I stopped keeping records after a while. I knew now that I couldn't lose.

I had an ally, a Cockney who worked in the college kitchen. We shared an interest in horse-race betting. Once he told me that three horses from a Newmarket stable would win at Yarmouth that day. They would start at short odds, so I should bet on them as a treble. I put £5 on it (£100 now). The first horse won at evens, the second at six to four on. The third drifted out in the betting to eight to one. . . and won! The treble paid off at thirty to one: £150 (a term's grant then or £3,000 today).

My friend introduced me to the Cambridge underworld. It met in a large mobile home that doubled as a strip club. The main currency of crime was food. College staff supplied Cypriot restaurateurs. Students paid for college meals in advance, but sometimes ate in restaurants. An incipient Italian mafia dealt in cement, construction and pizza. The strip club's regulars included bent cops and touts from Newmarket.

I always played for money in Cambridge, often for high stakes. From cards and betting, I roughly doubled my income. I never worked for a wage and took no money from my parents. I had enough for drinking bills, books and cinema tickets and long summer holidays in the Aegean. Jack Goody suggested Newmarket horse racing as a suitable topic for doctoral research. But I didn't fancy ending up under a truck on the Newmarket Road. I went to Ghana instead, which I laughably thought would be safer.[17] Two years in Ghana ruined my British betting career and made me dependent on odd jobs. I lost track of the horse-racing form and no longer had a regular grant. My new wife had no income.[18] It made more sense to write up my PhD and get an academic job. This involved more work than before.

Two Civilizations

I never got over that primal scene of moving between Manchester and Cambridge. They seemed to be two completely different civilizations: South vs North, feudalism vs industrial capitalism, fenland town vs big city. It took me a long while to figure out what my Ghanaian research was about. Migrants with demeaning urban jobs took pride in their home ties. Dual affiliation did

17. See Chapter 6.
18. See Chapter 7.

not make them anxious. They knew who they were. By studying my negation there, I was learning how to become whole, not part-human.

Cambridge's social structure was an inverted hierarchy. College 'servants' and figures of authority in the town (porters, shopkeepers and policemen) were older. Students treated them as social inferiors. The little lords addressed grown men by their first name or surname only and were addressed as 'mister' and 'sir'. This turned relations between the generations at home upside down. Yet deference often came with a surly undertone, even heavy sarcasm. 'That wasn't very clever, was it, sir?' Privacy in college was at a premium, the opposite of Old Trafford, where the front door had to be kept open for casual visitors. Privacy undermined our main collective weapon – solidarity against the bosses. In Cambridge, if you wanted to shut out unwelcome visitors, you locked your outer door ('sport the oak').

Perhaps I exaggerate the contrast. If the two societies were so opposite, why did I enjoy college life? Was I really integrated in Manchester? It took me a long time to get beyond Raskolnikov's dilemma. Perhaps I never did.

Chapter 6

AN AFRICAN APPRENTICESHIP

This is a freewheeling account of the most formative experience of my life, the two years I spent in a West African slum when researching a Cambridge PhD in social anthropology. I squeezed a doctorate out of this, but was never able to write up a monograph from it. My form of adaptation to the badlands on Accra's outskirts was to become an apprentice to a small-time Ghanaian crook. I tried to play it from the middle, but soon realized that I would have to join the criminal side of the law if I was to survive. I was principally a receiver of stolen goods, then a money lender. I recount some chastening moments and some stories of life on the fringes of the postcolonial economy. I end by reflecting on how hard it was in those pre-postmodern times to make an academic career out of this material without lying.

I've got Africa on my mind. Not an old sweet song, more a beat: *tá-tá ti-ti tá-ti-tá*. It takes me back to those times I spent in Atinga's gin bar, tapping out the rhythm on a beer bottle while the guy sang to a one-string guitar. I don't know when or how Africa first got into my mind. Dad was keen on Rider Haggard and Edgar Rice Burroughs when he was young, but he didn't pass on that enthusiasm to me. Nothing in my background prepared me for a world society based on racial inequality. I grew up in a part of Manchester that was still fighting the Battle of the Boyne,[1] after which my Scottish Presbyterian ancestors settled in Northern Ireland as crowd control, long before my great-grandfather moved from Belfast to Manchester and bought a pub. I

---

1. See Chapter 17.

learned much later that the Irish were sent as slaves to the sugar islands, before their health problems led to them being replaced by Africans.

Early Days

As soon as I arrived in Accra, I headed to the university to meet an American professor who knew Jack Goody. I expected him to be interested in my research, but he just wanted to know whether I had hard currency. The official exchange rate was 1:1, a Ghanaian pound for one pound sterling, but he said he could get me an exchange rate of 1.5:1. I left it vague and asked around the town. The unofficial exchange rate was 3:1! This was the first of several culture shocks in those early days, usually involving economic transactions. I couldn't believe that a senior academic would cheat a graduate student, newly arrived in a foreign country. I soon realized, however, that I was the cultural dope. I had swallowed the idea that academics were an aristocracy of intellect who valued money less than ideas. This was not the last time my assumptions about money and morality were challenged there.

I went to Accra with my head full of notions about rural–urban migrants learning to be active citizens through voluntary associations, politics and public propaganda. We did that kind of thing in the 1960s. I actually believed then that African independence from colonial rule had launched political experiments from which the whole world could learn. It was my first trip outside Europe; I was 22 years old. Audrey Richards wrote to Jack, 'God knows what Keith is going to do, because he doesn't.' I was to hook up with him in a small town 500 km north of Accra. The driver had a girlfriend near the Volta River ferry, so we spent the night there in the bus being eaten alive by mosquitoes. I reached Bole the next day in the early afternoon. It was very hot, but I found Goody's living quarters out of town. There was no response to my knocking and shouts, so I went indoors and found the whole family sleeping naked in water on the bathroom floor. This wasn't the only primal scene this place had in store for me.

It was decided that, since my topic was migration, I should stay a few days in the strangers' quarter (*zongo*) with an army sergeant major's family. I was given a small room with an unmade floor where I unpacked my Safari camp bed and mosquito net, with some clothes and writing materials on a small table. In those days I wore knee-length black leather boots that a colonial outfitter in Manchester had persuaded me to buy. I looked ridiculous. The one reason white men visited the *zongo* was for sex and the only available female in the house was the sergeant major's sister, a trader twice my age. Needless to say, communications were difficult; but I got the message that she thought we could be an item. One night, as I was sleeping under my net naked, she came into my room. I was terrified and this got through to her, since she withdrew and left something on the floor. In the morning I discovered it was a papaya – the inside is thought to resemble you know what. I felt the least I could do was to eat it for breakfast. When I cut it open, the inside was seething with maggots. I have never eaten one since.

My third surprise, the day we were leaving town, was that Jack told me I was to have one of their cooks, a thin, middle-aged man with a moustache who, it turned out, had been given no more notice of this arrangement than me. I thought it was a crazy colonial anachronism, but was told that I didn't have the time to shop, cook and clean and they only needed one cook in future. Salifu was with me for more than two years, a man of considerable dignity except when he was drunk. He told me later that he had served British army officers and normally wouldn't put up with treatment like that, but he decided that I needed looking after. . . When we returned to Accra, I set about looking for a place where Northern migrants lived.

Nima

Nima in the 1950s had been a thinly populated cattle camp and refuge for criminals on the outskirts of Accra. Then it started filling up with cheap housing for the flood of low-skilled migrants from the remote interior. The original Hausa-speaking leadership remained in place and the police treated it as a no-go area, except for occasional raids with trucks, guns and dogs. I was told that lots of Northerners lived in Nima and I was offered rooms by a man I met one Sunday afternoon in a place that sold millet beer (*pito*). Asaa was a small-time crook then recovering from a short spell in prison that had left him broke, save for a house he had bought before he was locked up. He had just cleared out the previous tenants so that strangers could not spy on what he was up to. I wondered why he risked taking in a white youth like me. The likeliest reason is that, when he was a cook for a British official, he formed a lucrative partnership with the man's teenage son, filling their van with all kinds of bootleg stuff. It didn't take us long to make a similar relationship.

Colonial society was built on the premise that if one of us is harmed, we destroy three of your villages. That regime was still close enough in time to feed my sense of being untouchable. Compared with Nima's poor, black, illiterate and vulnerable inhabitants, I was rich, white, educated and powerful. I realized soon enough that, unless I broke out of that contradiction, I would socially dead, perhaps literally so. I had never been beyond the Med, I was young, culturally inept and desperately lacked human warmth, which my new neighbours had in abundance. I began to exchange what I had for what they had. I wrote letters, intervened with bureaucracy and gave them rides on my scooter, while they made me feel at home, gave me food and drink, conversed in pidgin English, let me play their games badly and laughed and smiled a lot. I played up the idea that I was a young, raw and poor student.

When I got to Ghana, I found no political activity worth investigating. It was a one-party police state and that side of things was all locked up. Nima's migrants found government to be predatory and remote. I soon found that no-one wanted to discuss politics with me. Casting around for another topic, I could not help noticing the vitality of street commerce, not just roadside vendors, but mobile dealers in everything from refrigerators to marijuana. I found that I was being drawn into local society through a variety of economic transactions – exchanging currency, shopping, paying rent and wages, making gifts, loans and bribes, gambling – all of which challenged my assumptions concerning what is normal. I embarked on the road to what became eventually the informal economy.[2] Nima fed my Manchester liberal side and temporarily modified the socialism of my youth.

A woman might come to me for money to help her sell sugar lumps outside her door. I would ask her about the selling price – four lumps for a penny. A quick calculation showed that a profit could still be made if she sold them for five a penny and she would undercut the competition. Yes, she said, but the other women would beat me up. That's how I learned. But I was ignorant of the history that might help me to account for my market savvy. Ghanaians wore cloth from my home town, but I had little idea why or how.

I soon realized that, if I wanted to enter deeply into my fieldwork situation, I would have to learn an indigenous language, and there were plenty of those around. Hausa was a *lingua franca*, but most people spoke their own language at home. I decided to pick a group that had been studied intensively in the countryside, and it did not take long to choose the Tallensi (now Frafra), whose ethnographer was Meyer Fortes.[3] These migrants combined mundane urban occupations with strong attachment to their traditional roots. They easily contained what seemed a contradiction to me. I explored their networks throughout Ghana. In two years, I spent time in Ghana's second city, Kumasi, and in mining areas, in their homeland's administrative centre and the village where Fortes had stayed. I shadowed translocal society, spanning town and countryside.

I was captivated by what seemed a paradox: on the one hand the banal individualism of a Dickensian mob of water carriers, bread sellers, shit shovelers, taxi drivers, pickpockets and bartenders; on the other the communal spirit of hill tribesmen who expected to end their days as custodians of ances-

2. See Chapter 7. Hart, Appendix 1973, 2006c.
3. See Chapter 9; Hart, Appendix 2018d.

tral shrines. I was impressed by the energy and ingenuity of their efforts to improve their economic situation and by the inevitable failure of all but a few. It seemed as if the economy was being made, unmade and remade from day to day. The central task for everyone was to find a durable basis for livelihood and perhaps for accumulation. That was why even a poorly paid job was valued, as an island in a sea of ephemeral opportunities. I came to think of this as the search for form, for regularity in a world constituted by flux, emergence and informality. Eventually I followed up their relations with home, 800 km away in the West African savannah. I traced the contours of what I took to be the migrants' translocal society, bridging rural and urban areas.

I kept two rooms in Nima, one for sleeping and working, one for eating and storage. There was no running water, electricity or sanitation. We used buckets and kerosene lamps. I designed a complex questionnaire asking respondents to rank local notables. No-one would answer it. 'We are small people; we can't talk about big men'. I dropped that idea. I hired a language teacher for formal instruction, but didn't get far. Then I fell ill with hepatitis B and on my way into hospital collected the three biggest paperbacks I could find in the university bookshop. These included T.E. Lawrence of Arabia's *Seven Pillars of Wisdom* (1926). At one point he asks, 'How can a white man with limited language skills pass for an Arab?' His answer was to talk fluently and mistakes will be attributed to being from the wrong side of the dune. When I recovered, I abandoned lessons, notes and vocabulary lists and set out to learn my adopted language orally like a child, with fluency my motto. One visitor told me he had never heard an anthropologist speak an African language so fluently. . . with a Manchester accent.

Crossing the Line

Nima was a tough place. The first night I slept there, a corpse hung from the tree outside in the morning. It was not suicide. When the police made raids, neighbours would try to guess the informant. I was the usual suspect. My presence interested the authorities. The Special Branch was on my case, six of them. Their leader once asked me, 'Do you understand "code", Mr Hart?' I nodded. 'We have to know six languages and none of us knows the one you are learning. Are you sending coded messages to the exiled opposition?' They harassed people I spoke to. I feared deportation. I asked the head of the university's sociology department for a letter saying that I was not a CIA spy. 'How do I know you are not?' was his reasonable reply. Later he told me he had seen my name on a list for deportation and thought I was a lost cause.

I could see my career going up in smoke. But the military coup against Kwame Nkrumah's government in February 1966 saved me. The president's palace was nearby. We could hear the bullets pinging off our zinc roofs below. Next day a small patrol came to fetch me. A corporal pushed his Kalashnikov into my stomach and made me raise my hands.

C: You escaped from the President's palace. We believe you are a Russian sub-
   version agent.
K: I don't look Russian, do I?
C: Yes, you do – you have a beard.
K: I don't talk like a Russian.
C: You Russians are very good at learning languages.
K: I have a British passport.
C: You Russians are good at forging those things.
K: The local police know I am a research student.
C: Our police are very corrupt. You must have bribed them.

A crowd had gathered. A friend made signs past the corporal's shoulder and I smiled weakly. 'You think we are funny, do you?' He jabbed the gun into me and my legs gave way. They took me off to a police station for interrogation. They beat me up badly, but all I could think of was saving my career. I never imagined that I could end up dead. After the weekend a British-trained army officer told me to get lost. My fieldwork took off after that.

The crisis made me rethink my relationship to the law. I couldn't stay in limbo. I would have to leave or cross the line, sharing the locals' risks and vulnerability. My landlord was often short of money. Sometimes he would borrow cash to pay off a thief. We became partners, not just in crime, but in a series of enterprises. I put up the money, Asaa supplied the expertise and networks, I got the field notes and we split the profits fifty-fifty. We had two gangs, 'night people' (burglars) and 'day people' (pickpockets). I went out with them. One identified the mark and provided interference; the other was the pick. The first would point to the mark while rubbing his nose. I asked about this. Their biggest fear was a mark who can summon help. Locals look at the ground; strangers walk with their noses in the air. I forged receipts for stolen goods and fenced drugs seized by the police. Apart from a few Lebanese traders downtown, I knew the difference between hard and soft currencies.

We tried 'legitimate' speculation, such as hoarding maize against seasonal price fluctuations. Every year the price doubled in six months after harvest time. We found hidden expenses and worse. First, a porters' ring took a cut for lifting each bag onto the ground. The bags had to be turned out to avoid rot and we bought insecticide against the weevils. When the price had doubled, American PL 480 aid flooded the country with maize[4] and the price reverted to what we had paid. To recover our costs, we sold the bags on credit with more hassle. There is more to trade than the headline rate of profit.

I financed myself after my first-year grant ran out. This success became an embarrassment. I tried giving the money away. I employed seven research assistants, hosted sheep, rice and beer parties and gave old people blankets and sandals. But this only increased my standing as a big man. The migrant community was a sea of young men anchored to a few married elders whose houses were islands of stability. I moved from one class to the other. I managed to get rid of my surplus before I left. It took effort.

I was arrested four times, twice by the army for espionage and twice by the police for receiving. I came home one day to a noisy crowd. Its focus was our house and police dogs kept onlookers at bay. Asaa said, 'They have got the radio, but it's alright, they only want a bribe'. It was a Grundig Satellit. I had fenced and then sold it to Mallam Hamidu, a Muslim priest. He later pawned it back as security for a loan. I gave him a false receipt. I used the names of expatriates who recently left the country. I also filed off the number from the radio. Now I had no documents and the radio was on their list.

The Assistant Superintendent of Police (ASP) is there to handle bribes. It is no good throwing money at everyone. You pay off someone senior enough to control the small fry, but not too expensive. That's the ASP. You don't say, 'OK, I did it. Who do I need to pay?' We sat around his swimming pool, sipping gin and tonic, proclaiming my innocence.

A Ghanaian lawyer told me, 'I don't mind our police being corrupt. What offends me is that they are so cheap!' 'I know that you are a man of integrity', the ASP said. 'But the police force is full of bad men who will make trouble for you unless I persuade them with money.' We agreed on a sum of £135 (almost two years' rent). The desk sergeant made life difficult. Corrupt policemen need a legitimate story. Ours was that I had a receipt from Hamidu. An Arabic signature was invalid without the signer's presence. I had to bring the Mallam in. But he had gone missing.

Hamidu was on a money-doubling expedition in Accra's hinterland. He would turn up, resplendent in white robes and red fez, and offer to double any money placed overnight in his suitcase. The villagers are suspicious, but someone tries depositing five pounds. Next morning it has become ten and everyone piles in. The Mallam then does a moonlight flit with the full suitcase. Hamidu was being held in custody. I had a friend in the drugs trade, only in his twenties, but a pious Muslim with good Arabic. When I asked him to come to the police station as Hamidu, he refused. Subtle threats changed

---

4. US Public Law 480 of 1954 was an aid programme known as 'food for peace'.

his mind. The sergeant gave me the radio. I later sold it to a regional military governor. What could be cleaner than a white man's goods offloaded when his time ended?

Money in My Ghana Fieldwork

I have mentioned above that monetary transactions were often a learning device for me in Ghana. I soon entered the field in a more professional way.[5]

I checked exchange rates in the British newspapers. Many clients did not understand hard and soft currencies. One midnight soon after the coup, an army truck turned up with armed and excited soldiers. They had found many boxes of Egyptian pounds in the bedroom of Kwame Nkrumah's wife. They wanted us to buy them. I pointed out that she could spend the money when she went home. But it had no foreign exchange value. What do you say to a disappointed soldier with a Kalashnikov? It was a relief when they left.

A lot of the business was small change. But one evening Asaa was over the moon. 'We're rich', he shouted. He had bought US $1650 for a bit more than £50. I thought it must be counterfeit and told him so. The dollars were in four notes: $1000 + $500 + $100 + $50. Only later did I notice that the banknotes were issued by the Confederate States in America's civil war. They were 'greybacks', not 'greenbacks'. It was 1967, more than a hundred years after their issue.[6] I gave Asaa his £50 – he accepted the ups and downs of our shared life – and kept the Confederate currency as a memento. They are in a box of field notes somewhere. They sell on eBay. Each note was particular. Some have the value of rare stamps.

Receiving segued into moneylending. The moral, ethical and economic landscape here is even more confusing. I already made small loans in my household. Atinga often borrowed from me for his impoverished gin bar (see below). One day, he had lent on money I had loaned him. I was pretty mad. People often pursued him for repayment of loans and he could now send them after his debtor! I now lent money to strangers. We read about astronomical interest rates in informal finance, say 50 per cent a month. But what matters is the default rate. No moneylender would admit to bad loans, saying they do not allow default. A middle-aged beer brewer was considered to be the richest Frafra woman. She sold beer on credit and often lacked the cash to start a new brewing cycle. She was rich in young male debtors. They were useful for casual tasks, such as heavy lifting and sharing her bed. Money-changing and lending expanded my network of thieves, debtors and

---

5. From K. Hart, 'Greybacks' (2017).

6. They were never legal tender.

confidants. Money is a means of communication. I could not have managed without it.

Some Enterprising Friends in Nima

'Family business' has many meanings. 'Family' is a metaphor for people you are stuck with. Love and friendship can sometimes be the glue. Personal relations are still important for the economy. By the 1960s the Frafras had spread throughout Ghana. They worked as domestic servants, soldiers, petty traders and general labourers, but were known as thieves. Their networks spanned cities and their villages. The economy was made, unmade and remade daily.

I settled on studying small and quite big entrepreneurs.[7] Most that I studied had a portfolio of part-time investments. About half earned wages or had recently had jobs. Investment vehicles included rentals, trade, bars, construction, machinery for hire and usury. A third owned commercial transport, the riskiest and potentially most lucrative business. Many activities were illegal. There were more Muslims and Christians than average. I thought of them as individuals, never as a class.

Atinga was discharged from the army. He had been in the South for a decade and lived with his wife and nephew. He had £10 from his last pay packet and set up as a retailer of crude gin (*akpeteshi*). This meant converting his room into a bar by hanging a cloth down the centre and piling his possessions on both sides. Chairs and a table occupied the public section. Atinga then bought a four-gallon drum of *akpeteshi*. He gave his remaining cash to his wife for food and borrowed from me to pay the rent. His business opened on New Year's Eve. The retail price of gin was 6s. a bottle. Receipts for a drum should come to £8, twice its cost. Customers were poor and improvident. He could only keep up sales by offering generous credit. But he needed to replenish his stock and feed his family. He also tried to diversify. But his wife's sugar lump trade foundered. A Coca-Cola business failed for lack of a cooler.

Atinga soon faced a major crisis. Credit accounted for a third of turnover. This kept daily turnover at one gallon. Some customers took advantage of his ignorance. Others had no money. His gin ran out before payday. He survived by borrowing again. Otherwise, his clients would leave without paying their debts. He insisted on cash payment more and some paid off their debts. This slowed down turnover. He kept a small, regular clientele of homeboys who drank whatever the gin's quality.

---

7. Hart, Appendix 2000a. See Chapter 3.

Atinga needed a job. His wife was pregnant. He tried to get back into the army. His landlord's wives helped out with food. A backlog of rent was his biggest debt. Turnover steadied out at four drums a month – yielding him more than the unskilled wage which was eventually realized as cash. The bar's fortunes declined, but not Atinga's income. He worked as a watchman, leaving his wife to tend the bar. Turnover slowed to a trickle and his wife consumed the gin. Trade was sometimes boosted by a once-off enterprise, like making meat and soup with a stray dog. Then the bar did great business. Usually it was empty at night because he had no gin, his customers no money or both.

Atinga's wife gave birth to a son. Two months later the army got round to paying him an advance on his gratuity (£40). The bar took on a new lease of life; £20 went on wood for a counter, partition, door and shelves, and he even bought a license. He did not pay off any debts. For a while his capital sustained an artificial rate of business. But he was soon back in the vicious circle of credit and turnover. He lost his job as a watchman, but entered training as an escort policeman (a colonial hangover with red fez and khaki puttees). He could only visit his family at weekends. His landlord suspected him as the informer behind a police raid and seized the room and its fittings in part compensation for £32 owed in rent. Atinga left Nima with his family. His landlord's wife took over the bar, but offered no credit, so nothing came of it. Being 'unemployed' did not lead Atinga to destitution or dependence on others. He was rather unimaginative, but he showed some enterprise in adversity.

Atia had been hawking his camera around. His customers would not wait for a full film and business was often slow. He bribed the principal of a girls' secondary school to let him photograph the students at weekends. The girls wanted to send photos to their boyfriends and families. Some asked to be shot nude. He worked on the basis of mutual trust and relied on goodwill. If a girl did not like her photos and tore them up, he did another set for free. Good photos fetched whatever he asked for. The profits from two films in a weekend, although variable, were more than a domestic servant's weekly wage.[8]

Atibila allowed me to tape long interviews. He was an army sergeant in Accra and his father had been a soldier too. He knew great hardship as a youth. But he had accumulated two houses, a minibus, a corn mill and other assets. He lived as a monogamous Christian with his wife, a trader. His five children attended missionary schools. He stayed aloof from other migrants. He had not been back north for twenty years; he wanted nothing to do with Frafras. He only aimed to provide for his nuclear family's security through his own endeavours. He rejected traditional religion – 'you cannot vote for two

---

8. For a fuller account see Hart, Appendix 1988a and 2000: 97–114.

parties at the same time'. He was indifferent to cooperation between kinsmen. He also avoided mutual aid societies and funeral parties; both promoted ethnic solidarity in the city. He was a model of rationality, monogamy and asceticism.

Atibila had not been reading Max Weber at evening classes. There was enough fact to make his story credible. But the account was one-sided. He was much involved with kinsmen and other Frafras. He visited home often. He wanted his children to keep their ethnic identity. As a lineage elder back home, his attitude towards traditional religion was synthetic.

Anaba was 40, the second son of a poor farmer. He was now a staff sergeant in charge of army meat supplies in Accra. The scope for personal profit was substantial. He owned five houses and nine commercial vehicles. These, with many other trading and investment activities, brought in an annual income of around £20,000. He had eleven wives and seventeen children, a household of eighty people and scores more clients and dependents.

Transport is high-risk enterprise. You can drive a commercial vehicle yourself, hire a driver or sell to a driver on 'work and pay'. No driver-owner can accumulate. Naive operators opt for hiring a driver. The prospective profit is greater and the wages are poor. They often fail for this reason. An employee has no incentive to maintain the vehicle or to be honest with the takings. Owners can make a driver pay a daily sum; but he has no interest in maintaining the vehicle. He could arrange with a fitter to supply inflated repair bills, but a better method is for the driver to be responsible for his truck's maintenance while buying it on an instalment plan. Lebanese traders pioneered this method in Ghana.

Anaba would buy driving licenses for young men from his home village, many of whom lived with him. They then served an apprenticeship on someone else's taxi. When he was satisfied, he bought a vehicle and wrote up a contract, adding £1,000 to the purchase price. The driver repaid him £10 a day. He could seize the vehicle if the driver missed three days' payments. The latter was responsible for maintenance. If he lacked the money, Anaba would pay for the repairs and add it to the bill. This minimized how long a vehicle lay idle. Most drivers took eighteen months to buy their bus or taxi.

Anaba stayed aloof from the transport system run by Muslims of Northern Nigerian origin. He relied on self-reinforcing agreements and legal contracts more than on kinship or trust. He was not a trusting man, unlike Atia. Most impersonal written contracts were worthless at this end of society. But personal relationships develop over time and are a learning process. People find out by trial and error what works for them. They often lose.[9]

---

9. Hart, Appendix 1988a.

Some Afterthoughts

Why am I telling you all this now? It can't be to ingratiate myself with these confessions. It's because how I represented what I learned then as a professional academic was a lie. Imagine what it was like in those pre-postmodern times, trying to conjure a doctoral thesis out of this material. I had to convert all my stories into the third person. I gave a talk in Chicago in 1983, where I revealed some of it, and I was told to shut the hell up or I would compromise Anthropology Inc. as well as myself. This was the general attitude I started out with, so I joined the development industry afterwards and saw the world another way. I have given the impression here that I got by in Ghana as a sort of social chameleon. But I was sometimes forced to recognize that I was an overeducated young prick who thought he knew more about the world than the poor Africans he met.

I once visited a remote village in the northern savannah, 800 km from the coast. Land shortage had pushed people to settle too close to the Volta River. They were now dying from river blindness. It had stopped raining when I arrived; but the thatched roofs were wet and the air was hot and humid. I saw no-one. It felt like the end of the earth. I imagined that I was bringing the outside world into these villagers' drab lives. It was 1967 and I was 23 years old. I found the chief under an awning, wearing only a jockstrap. A woman and child played a bead game. He invited me to play with them and I won. He agreed to talk. I was quite fluent by then. After a while he asked,

Chief: What do you think of Vietnam?
KH (surprised): How do you know about Vietnam?
Chief: My son is at secondary school and listens to the BBC World Service. Which side is going to win?
KH: The Americans of course, they have all the money, weapons, machines. . .
Chief (shaking his head): I don't think so – too many trees. The people will hide behind the trees.
KH: How do you know about the trees?
Chief: I fought the Japanese in Burma with the British army. We did better than them in the jungle.

My bubble burst. Most of my news came from *Time* magazine. This guy had seen more of the world than I had. But he wouldn't let me go yet:

Chief: You know how long it took you British to get us out of our hills when all we had were bows, arrows and jockstraps? Twenty-five years! In the end, they brought up heavy artillery to get us out. I don't think the Americans will stay in Vietnam for twenty-five years, do you?

My host, as was customary, gave me a live guinea fowl to strap onto my scooter handlebars and I left, much chastened. Ghana taught me that, for all my democratic pretensions, I was a snob. Global and local are not separate.[10] We all live in the world and have our points of local anchorage. Some of my academic colleagues are the most parochial people I know. The working-class autodidacts I have met would put them to shame.

Ghana was the last time that I did extensive ethnographic research. I found it impossible to convert my thesis into a monograph. A decade later, I published a literature review on West African agriculture, something I knew nothing about. This set me on a course than I have only rarely abandoned since. I read books in order to write about them and I file stories from my own experience in my memory. But that time in Ghana shaped me more than any other and still does half a century later. Africa will always be on my mind, a song to light up my darkness, like the Hoagy Carmichael tune made famous by Ray Charles.

10. See Chapter 15.

Chapter 7

THE DEVELOPMENT INDUSTRY

After completing my PhD thesis, I joined the development industry to learn more about the world's political organization. I worked full-time in universities during the 1970s in Britain and North America. But I also moonlighted as a high-level development consultant and as a writer for *The Economist*. I played a major part in the discovery of the 'informal sector'.

Anthropology and Development

When I came back to Cambridge, Jack Goody introduced me to the Chicago sociologist Edward Shils, who greeted me with 'Ah! the Mayhew of Accra'. I soon found out about Henry Mayhew thanks to him.[1] Meyer Fortes offered me a fellowship to work with him on Northern Ghana. I might get the next available lectureship to teach 'primitive and peasant economics, like Raymond Firth'. I declined the offer.

I married almost as soon as I returned from Ghana. Nicky Tahany was a research assistant to Esther Goody, later her PhD student. She transferred her degree to Norwich when I got a job there. While I taught at Manchester University, she worked as a county planner before landing a sociology lectureship at Salford University, in Manchester's twin city. We then moved to a Manchester suburb and soon had a daughter, Louise. The story of this dif-

---

1. Henry Mayhew, *London Labour and the London Poor* (1851).

ficult period is told in Chapter 12. A year later, I was appointed to a tenured position at Yale University, Nicky moved to Essex University and, after nearly a decade of marriage, we split up. We bought five large houses and sold four at a time of housing price inflation.

When I joined the job market, I understood Accra's street economy as well as its denizens. But, like them, I couldn't explain the events that had shaken Ghana a decade after independence. The collapse of the world cocoa price wrecked the national economy. Then an army coup overthrew Nkrumah, pushing politics to the right. I felt at home in the lawless trade of Accra's slums. Rather than just record what people told me, I challenged them as an actor. I knew nothing of the region's history. I now set out to learn about colonialism and its successor, 'development'. I wanted to enter the world of governments and international organizations.

I joined an academic consultancy organization at the University of East Anglia.[2] In the next decade, I carried out a multi-sited ethnography of the global development industry. At Norwich I debated Third World urban unemployment with economists and consulted on development policy in the Cayman Islands. I later found similar elevated employment in Papua New Guinea, Hong Kong and West Africa. I failed to write up my doctoral research as a monograph. A book on West African agriculture started out as a report to USAID.[3]

My Norwich job combined a teaching salary with paid consultancies. My first lecture was on Marx and Weber. I decided to improvise since I felt comfortable with the topic. The room was a rectangle of tables, whereas in Cambridge I lectured from a raised podium. It was almost full when I arrived and I had to squeeze in among some forty students. My wife and her mother attended. After fifteen minutes, I dried up. A graduate student asked a question. I spun out an answer for four minutes and stalled again. I wound up the lecture and left the room. I handwrote my lectures for twenty years after that.

Most of my colleagues were development economists. I had to talk to them. Our exchanges went something like this:[4]

> Econ: Is the marginal productivity of agricultural labour zero in Northern Ghana?
> K: What do you mean?
> E: Arthur Lewis has a dualistic theory of labour migration between rural and urban areas.[5] He assumes that people can leave the countryside without reducing output there.

---

2. The Overseas Development Group in what became a School of Development Studies.

3. The United States Agency for International Development.

4. Hart, Appendix 2007a.

5. W.A. Lewis, 'Economic Development with Unlimited Supplies of Labour' (1954).

K: Does their income from working in agriculture make a difference?

E: What do you mean?

K: Young men do the farm work, but their elders control the product and they get very little. If they leave, they keep their earnings.

E: What do you call that organization?

K: Unilineal descent groups. Pierre-Philippe Rey calls it the 'lineage mode of production'.[6]

E: And you say economists like jargon! There is a new version of the Lewis model. Migration hinges on rural-urban income expectations.[7]

Both: Let's write an article. 'The lineage mode of distribution: a reflection on the Lewis model'.

It would have been easy to become a broker from anthropology to economics and back again. But I wanted to synthesize them. I set out to learn the economists' language, since they dominated the field.

'The Informal Sector'

My Norwich conversations had an unexpected outcome. I became the contested founder of a major concept in development studies – 'the informal sector', later known as 'the informal economy' and eventually as 'informality'. The context was the world crisis of the early 1970s. The Vietnam War led to the dollar's detachment from gold in 1971. Money market futures and the collapse of the post-war exchange rate system soon followed. An oil price hike triggered a global depression. Then a glut of petrodollar loans ended up as the Third World debt crisis of the 1980s.[8] 'Stagflation' – high unemployment with inflation – helped Thatcher and Reagan to take power.

The development model in the 1960s was 'modernization'. Poor countries would become rich by emulating the West. Gloomier scenarios emerged around 1970, feeding theories of 'dependency', 'underdevelopment' and 'the world system'.[9] This crystallized as fear of 'Third World urban unemployment'. Cities were growing fast, but without 'jobs' provided by governments and corporations. The few liberal economists did not influence policy then. Keynesians and Marxists held that only the state could manage growth and development. How could 'we' – the bureaucracy and its academic advisers –

---

6. P.-P. Rey, *Les alliances des classes* (1973); 'Class Contradictions in Lineage Societies' (1979).

7. John Harris and Michael Todaro, 'Migration, Unemployment and Development: A Two-Sector Analysis' (1970).

8. Hart, Appendix 2000a: 142–45.

9. F.H. Cardoso, *Dependency and Development in Latin America* (1969); A.G. Frank, *The Underdevelopment of Development* (1974); I. Wallerstein, *The Modern World System* (1974).

create the jobs, public health and housing that people needed? And what if we didn't? The spectre of riots and revolution raised its head. Some advocated sending the urban mob back to the countryside. The term 'unemployment' evoked images of the Great Depression.

This story didn't square with my fieldwork experience. The people I lived with in Accra were working, often for low and erratic returns, but they weren't unemployed. In 1971 I wrote a paper for a conference on 'Urban unemployment in Africa' at the Institute of Development Studies, Sussex. I called it 'Informal Income Opportunities and Urban Employment in Ghana'.[10] I meant my ethnography to persuade development economists to abandon the 'unemployment' model. More was going on in the grassroots economy than they imagined. I first offered a vivid description of what I had seen. Then I tried to engage their interest in development theory, using jargon picked up from Norwich colleagues.

I had no ambition to coin a concept. I just wanted to insert a vision of irregular economic activity into development debates. This was a classic move in the genre of 'realism', making visible what had been invisible. I left it open whether these activities contributed much to development. My audience greeted these arguments with enthusiasm. But the organizers – two famous economists, Richard Jolly and Hans Singer – were sceptical. They promised a book of the conference and we all went home.

A year later, a team led by Singer and Jolly published a report on Kenya for the International Labour Office, Employment, Incomes and Equality. The Third World economic crisis needed 'growth with redistribution'. The report's central theme was 'the informal sector'. This was a sphere of small-scale, self-employed, non-mechanized economic activities. It could redress the unemployment problem. By adding to the urban poor's resources, it would promote significant bottom-up development. I was not mentioned. Then they cancelled the book of the conference.

This caused a minor scandal. Several people mentioned in print that 'the informal sector was Keith Hart's idea'. This was only partially true. The term 'sector' suggests that formal and informal activities were separate, like agriculture and manufacturing. For me they were inseparable dimensions of the modern economy. I drew attention to unremarked aspects of economic life, but did not demarcate a separate field of study. Informality would not solve the development problem. Yet I became more closely identified with the concept.

A colleague urged me to publish a reader on the informal sector with Penguin Books. 'This could be your most important contribution'. If it is, I said, I would rather give up now. I had recently taken up Marxism and they

10. Appendix 1973, 2006c, 2015d.

had their own label.[11] The Sussex team then published a 450-page Penguin reader on the employment problem.[12] It included the second half of my conference paper without the ethnography. One reviewer wrote, 'the essence of the author's thesis is blunted considerably in Hart's article on the informal sector in Ghana'.[13] The editor of the *Journal of Modern African Studies* offered to publish my article fast. It is now usually cited as the original source for a new field of study.

I returned to Manchester in 1971 as a lecturer. We lived outside the city, mostly in the Rossendale Valley. This was a purer version of working-class culture than I had known before. Economic life there was highly diversified. I did some fieldwork and read about local history. This gave me a clearer understanding of the class system that I grew up in.[14] By the time I arrived, the Manchester School of social anthropology was almost over.[15] Max Gluckman was in Israel and he died there in 1975. Sociology had separated from his department. Emrys Peters brought in four outsiders including me. John Comaroff and Ken Brown became friends for life. My task was to teach urban anthropology. The Manchester School had moved on.

The Manchester job soon followed Norwich. After a year in Manchester, Nicky found a research post in regional government. We thought nothing of using two cars to work in separate places while living in a third. The energy crisis of 1973 blew up that idea. Nicky then joined Salford University as a sociology lecturer. She became pregnant soon after, so we made our fourth move in five years, to Manchester. We accumulated capital by taking out mortgages we couldn't afford, recouping our debts in an inflationary housing market.

Moonlighting: The Caymans and *The Economist*

My closest friend at Norwich was the economist John Bryden. I later joined him as a research fellow in Aberdeen where we wrote a book on rural development together.[16] He knew the Caribbean development scene well and arranged for me to undertake a 'manpower survey' of the Cayman Islands. Nicky and I spent three months in Grand Cayman. We shared the research and I wrote up the report. The place was setting out as a criminal centre for money laundering, tax evasion, gambling and tourism.

---

11. 'Petty commodity production'.
12. R. Jolly et al. (eds), *Third World Employment: Problems and Strategy* (1973).
13. H. Rempel, 'Review of Jolly et al., *Third World Employment*' (1974).
14. See Chapter 4 and below.
15. T. Evens and D. Handelman (eds), *The Manchester School* (2006).
16. J. Bryden and K. Hart, *A New Approach to Rural Development* (2004).

The beach hotel was idyllic; but the society was obnoxious. Racist white crooks from North America joined British refugees from Africa's anti-colonial revolution there. The natives were mixed descendants of British pirates and believed they were 'white'. The newcomers thought otherwise. Workers in the hotels, banks, construction and public services mainly came from Jamaica next door. They were 'black' and would soon become a majority. The British Development Division appointed us to address this problem. Our report argued that planning permission for new banks and hotels should be cut if the island was to stay Caymanian. An immigration quota on Jamaicans was abhorrent and would generate wage inflation. Soon after, Holiday Inns received permission to build a hotel that added a third to Grand Cayman's tourist capacity. A racist quota was imposed on Jamaicans.

Ulf Hannerz from Stockholm was carrying out fieldwork in Grand Cayman.[17] He chose to stay with the natives. We met again in London at an anthropologists' conference. A group went out drinking and Ulf left at 9 p.m. to prepare his presentation for the next day. He intended to avoid the anthropologists' norm of poor conference performance. He was a hit and later joined a panel of worthies to sum up. I took his lesson to heart and soon joined the Manchester department.

Meyer Fortes was once asked if anyone else had studied the Tallensi. There was someone, he said, but he gave it up to work on tourism in the West Indies.[18] I made two more excursions into the high politics of development – co-writing the development programme for Papua New Guinea's independence and a clandestine enquiry into Hong Kong's labour relations. Both advanced my understanding of development elites.

The Economist Intelligent Unit asked me to write reviews of some West African countries.[19] They were to be written in *The Economist*'s style. This was a high-priced product, sold to embassies, governments, banks, corporations and researchers with grants. I wrote five reviews a year for three years. EIU staffers sent me envelopes stuffed with newspaper clippings and reports. I used them to compile something that might seem worth the money. I learned to write 'economese' – how to sound like an economist without formal training. Authors were anonymous and opinionated. *The Economist* cultivates an air of omniscience. After sending off a report, I would bin the source material and move on with my life. This habit got me into serious trouble.

The government of Sierra Leone wanted to nationalize its iron mines. I read somewhere that these were stockpiling iron ore to keep up the asking price. I knew from Papua New Guinea that mining companies' figures were

---

17. U. Hannerz, *Caymanian Politics* (1974).

18. See Chapter 9, 'Cambridge Mentors in Retrospect'.

19. Ghana, Sierra Leone, Liberia and the Gambia.

opaque. I wrote a paragraph based on this 'intelligence'. My editor received a threatening letter from the corporation that owned the mines. They denied my assertions. She replied that my scholarship was impeccable and I could supply the sources. But I had thrown them away! I knew I had not made it up. My editor bluffed it out and that was it. They probably didn't fancy a confrontation with *The Economist*'s owner.

Papua New Guinea

I joined a team recruited by East Anglia to draw up a development programme for Papua New Guinea's independence.[20] Mike Faber, a general economist, was its leader. The other three members were an agricultural economist, an industrial economist and me. My remit was employment, labour relations, education, health, women, social policy and local government. We spent three months in Australia and PNG and wrote a preliminary report. Faber and I returned for discussions with the new government. The other two experts disputed our policy line and resigned.

In Australia, Liberal/Country Party rule was about to give way to Gough Whitlam's Labor Party. The department of External Territories was a Country Party fiefdom. We had a whistle-stop tour around PNG. The country was much less populated and commercial than West Africa. But I thought East Africa could be a fruitful comparison. I had in mind a rural socialist government aiming at national self-sufficiency, like Julius Nyerere's Tanzania.

We ran into opposition all round. The World Bank's representative had a first-class ticket with Pan-Am to carry his golf clubs on board. He could head for the local elite's watering holes without delay. He thought the Bank's mission was to maximize the profits of transnational corporations. Faber and I emphasized the need for grassroots rural development generating income to nationals. The government should license a few foreign extractive projects and collect the highest possible revenues from them. A central fund would distribute these for regional development. The Bank's man called this a 'racist' deviation from the free market's mission to maximize economic growth regardless of its beneficiaries.

The Australian government and National University were generally hostile. Bureaucrats and academics resented our interference with their arrangements for stitching up PNG. The colonial administration was even worse. There were three secessionist movements in outlying districts. It felt like the Congo to me. Foreign powers colluded in Katanga's independence to save Union Minière from a left-wing national government. The Australians, however,

---

20. This and the next section were first published in Hart, Appendix 2002b.

threatened to close down the operator's Queensland nickel mines if they fostered rebellion in Bougainville.

A subsidiary of Rio Tinto Zinc ran a copper mine there that was then the world's largest gold producer. After Nixon took the US dollar off gold, its price increased eightfold in a decade. The colonial government had signed a giveaway contract, including a tax holiday encouraging the company to speed up extraction. We proposed scrapping this deal. Mike Faber had pioneered the 51 per cent nationalization of Anglo American's copper mines in Zambia. The Bank man believed that a contract was a contract. All the rest treated our proposal as the end of the world. In this climate of confrontation, we found ourselves reduced to two.

Canberra saw more of the same. I walked into the hotel's glass doors, smashed my spectacles and had to use shades. Moving between air-conditioned offices and the steamy tropics gave me bronchitis. I sounded and looked like Don Corleone. It was rough going. But the top official in the Commonwealth Treasury joined me in the bar one evening. 'You're doing a great job, Keith. Let me buy you a drink.' He told me that PNG siphoned A$500 million a year from taxpayers to Australian interest groups: trading companies, civil servants and farmers who dumped subsidized rice and dairy products there. We were advocating increased national autonomy and this would reduce the Australian aid needed. The bureaucracy was split by Labor's electoral prospects.

Returning to Australia, Mike Faber and I stopped over in Singapore and I went shopping. I lost my passport, wallet, travellers' cheques and air tickets. I thought I had left them at a shop selling pens. But no luck. I drew a blank everywhere. It was 5 p.m. on Friday. The British High Commission were closing for the weekend. They recommended relying on the Australian government to bail me out. I went to the airport. A Qantas official pulled out my missing valuables from under the counter. 'Is this what you are looking for?' The Chinese owner of the pen shop discovered that his assistants had my stuff. His honour was at stake. He looked at my air ticket and drove out to the airport. I asked how I could thank him. I could write a letter to the *Straits Times* mentioning Thomas Ong. I did that.

Whitlam did win the election. The Pangu Party was elected as the first indigenous PNG government. It used our development policies in its campaign. The prime minister, Michael Somare,[21] told us, 'Before you came, we knew only one model of development. Now we know there are at least two.' The Bank guy and the head of the colony's planning office claimed to have had our ideas before us. They hoped to manage the government's development programme. Mike and I drank champagne on the return flight.[22]

---

21. Pangu's 'eight points of development' were inspired by our draft report.

22. See J. Conroy, *The Informal Economy in Development* (2020).

Outsiders think of large bureaucracies as monolithic. But they are often fragmented and incoherent. Department heads tended to defend the status quo, but their subordinates saw chances for advancement and some supported us. You can sometimes run an idea through a bureaucracy and win. A report would normally be seen as legitimating if it reflected its employers' plans. Or it went straight into the bin. In PNG we made a difference. I was never employed by the same development agency twice. In time I was struck by my social power in Ghana and PNG as a young white ignoramus. What anthropologists learn depends more on local politics than on ideas we stuff our heads with before.

Hong Kong

One day in 1976 Bert Turner, professor of industrial economics at Cambridge, phoned me up at Yale. 'I need someone who can bullshit about Third World cities', he said, 'and I thought of you'. James Callaghan's Labour government was under pressure to do something about Hong Kong. A Victorian capitalist colony was exploiting cheap Asian labour and undercutting British clothing factories. Callaghan promised a commission of enquiry into labour relations there. The Foreign Office hit the roof. For the PRC's sake Britain pretended that Hong Kong was a municipal authority, not a colonial state. A parliamentary commission would imply three Chinas. They proposed a secret academic enquiry, its report delayed until the political heat subsided. I briefly considered the ethical dilemmas, but overcame my doubts.

Hong Kong was then enjoying rapid economic growth, mainly because of different local and global inflation rates. The latter was running at 15 per cent, whereas Hong Kong's internal rate was 1 per cent, mostly rent. The PRC supplied most wage goods (water, food, clothing, etc.) at national market prices. Hong Kong's export firms distributed the inflation bonus between profits and wages. The Cultural Revolution was recent, so bosses wanted to keep organized labour happy.

I had to investigate the 'free labour market'. Milton Friedman made a TV documentary where HK was described as the best example of a free market economy. Employers told us they could not control wages since factory workers shopped around in their high-rise buildings at lunchtime. I didn't believe this; but evidence was hard to find. For lunch and flattery, I advised businessmen on whether to send their daughters to Oxbridge or the Ivy League ('Oxbridge for undergraduates, Ivy League for graduate school'). They included the Director of Human Resources in a top-three Hong Kong firm. We met for drinks at his golf club. Dinner and bridge followed. His wife was an English aristocrat. They had a rural mansion in middle England. If I passed the cultural test, I might receive confidences.

During bridge my host said, 'You were a classicist once, Keith. I like to read the *Oxford Book of Greek Verse* in bed. Here is my favourite poem.' My Greek was being tested, fourteen years after I gave it up. My heart sank when he opened it at Pindar, the most obscure poet. But he was a bluffer with only schoolboy Greek. The passage was easy to translate and I congratulated him on his taste.

Afterwards, I was asked to stay behind for brandy. 'This is how the labour market works here.' The top dozen Hong Kong firms meet every Wednesday lunchtime. They fill in a huge questionnaire, setting the price for every job. This goes to the government's Labour Office who publish it as their own survey. Everyone else negotiates from that. The Shanghainese cotton spinners meet in a tea house on Tuesday afternoons. My report undermined Hong Kong's *laissez faire* capitalist image. Its workers needed no help from the British government. But, as predicted, the issue was by now a dead duck. A book came out some years later.[23] I had little to do with it. I now knew about dealing with criminal elites, their slum counterparts and development practitioners.

I stayed at the university on Victoria Island, but most of my work was in Kowloon, so I had to take the Star Ferry. The taxi drivers claimed not to understand English. They took me on joy rides round the island. I complained to some Japanese visitors at dinner. They told me, 'Say you want "the end of Kotewall Road" in Cantonese'. They taught me: *yaw waw doo meh*. Next day, I hailed a taxi and said my piece. He looked at me blankly and, in perfect English, asked, 'What are you speaking Japanese for?'

West African Agriculture

USAID offered me a contract to write what became the substitute for a monograph on my Accra research. They wanted a handbook for rural field officers in West Africa. They would pay me $10,000. I spent a month reading in Cambridge University library, assisted by Victoria Ebin. What followed was manic. I compiled a book-length manuscript in three weeks. One Sunday, in fifteen hours, I wrote a fourteen-thousand-word chapter on the state's role.

I took a long historical view – sixteen countries, four colonial traditions, three centuries and more, four million square kilometres, 150 million people. I enjoyed challenging conventional wisdom.

---

23. H.A. Turner et al., *The Last Colony – but Whose?* (1980).

The Sudanic civilizations of Ghana and Mali were rich and powerful by any standards. An Arab geographer reports seeing in 951 a bill of credit made out to a trader from Ghana for 42,000 dinars, a sum unheard of in the Muslim world at the time. When Mansa Musa, the King of Mali, went on a pilgrimage to Mecca in 1324, he spent so much gold in Egypt as to cause runaway inflation there for several decades.[24]

I thought of this as 'doing anthropology from a Boeing 747' – there were no people in sight. I knew nothing about agriculture and too much about urban lowlife. My development experience helped me to understand how West Africa's rural civilizations had shaped the cities there. This contradicted 'modernization' theory's emphasis on cities as transforming agents. I knew that countryside and city were a single universe in the lives of Frafra migrants.[25] My literature review showed that the colonial presence in the region had been slight. Africans had built, provisioned and organized large coastal cities. Urban and rural areas in the region were complementary, not contradictory. Unlike in Central, East and Southern Africa, these cities extended the reach of societies that still controlled their homelands. Postcolonial nations were, however, founded on a ruinous contradiction. Large modern states depended on small-scale, low-productivity agriculture. Some economic sectors would have to add significant machine production or these states would devolve to a level consistent with peasant agriculture.

The rich countries abandoned development as a goal after the neoliberal counter-revolution. Then the Third World debt crisis made the 1980s a 'lost decade' for many. The World Bank and IMF freed up the flow of global capital. 'Structural adjustment' made governments marginal to their own economies. Many African states were bankrupted; some succumbed to civil war; others 'failed'. The 'political kingdom' did not unlock the door to prosperity. The first fifty years after independence saw economic regression in most African countries. The informal economy filled the gap between promise and reality.[26]

Jack Goody published my USAID report in a Cambridge University Press series as *The Political Economy of West African Agriculture*. I asked Meyer Fortes why anthropologists always made their first book a fieldwork-based monograph. I couldn't write one, but this literature review had been easy. He said, 'Anthropologists are peasants, Keith. They like digging holes. But they need someone to tell them where to dig. That's where you come in.'

---

24. K. Hart, *West Africa* (1982: 20).
25. See Chapter 6.
26. See above and Chapter 15.

Chapter 8

LEARNING TO FLY IN AMERICA

A fight in the Manchester department spilled over into our family life. Peters promoted one of the new recruits to a senior lectureship. Our little clique soon split up. I wrote to the Vice Chancellor accusing our head of nepotism and corruption. I didn't get a reply. I wrote to anthropology departments at Harvard, Yale, Chicago and Northwestern. To my amazement, Yale and Chicago offered me interviews. Yale was first. They said they were unsure whether to offer me Associate Professor with or without tenure. In my ignorance, I told them I would not come without tenure and they agreed.

I had friends at Chicago, like Marshall Sahlins and Raymond Smith. I came later to love the city above all others, but intellectual life there was cut-throat, with graduate students competing as proxies for rival professors. At seminars, the article to be discussed was thrown onto the table like red meat to be worried by the hounds. You only scored points by being negative. I spent four delightful visits there later, but I don't think I made the wrong choice for my first American job.

Nicky didn't want me to go – we had a young family, a beautiful house and two secure jobs in the same city. I was booked to spend next year at the Centre for Advanced Study in the Behavioral Sciences in Palo Alto, California. She proposed that we go there and apply together for positions in the US. Yale sounded out a position for her in sociology. She had a good book out – on marriage and divorce.[1] I was 32 without a book. I felt compelled

---

1. N. Hart, *When Marriage Ends: A Study in Status Passage* (1976).

to go, the strongest compulsion I had known. I blame Dvořák's New World symphony.[2] Ever since the birth of rock 'n' roll I felt American, certainly not English. The stalemate dragged on. I decided to trust my unconscious mind, the way I had resolved my ambivalence about giving up cigarettes. Eventually I wrote two letters, one saying yes, the other no, put them in their envelopes each with a stamp. I posted one and tore up the other. I had accepted the job.

Yale

I felt confined in Britain, held back. The Americans told me: 'Run with your stuff, big boy.' I experienced a surge of liberation when I arrived at Yale. It taught four-field anthropology (cultural, biological, linguistic and archaeological). Cambridge produced confident ignoramuses with fast mouths. American scholars accumulated filing cabinets stuffed with documents. I was a French structuralist Marxist by then.[3] Yale anthropology was not friendly to the social sciences. The university administration liked my affinity with economics. I founded a new graduate programme with Fred Jameson and David Apter, the Council for the Comparative Study of Culture and Society. It allowed famous humanities professors to teach outside their own department. Less eminent social scientists got to rub shoulders with them. Umberto Eco was our first visiting fellow. The university awarded anthropology two new chairs linked to the social sciences. We appointed M. G. Smith, a Jamaican political anthropologist. But our cultural anthropologists balked at adding another.

I was a card-carrying feminist and found myself appointed as acting chair of the Women's Studies Program. I would step down whenever a qualified woman candidate appeared. Structuralist Marxism went down well with them. I argued that class struggles based on work, race and gender were homologous. I had a minder, Catharine McKinnon. She was doing a PhD in political science and was a trainee lawyer. She is now a legal scholar and activist, famous for her work on affirmative action. Catharine and I got on well. The following year I was replaced with no hard feelings.

My first apartment was small, noisy and smelly. Nicky was turned down by the sociology department. We looked for a pile in Connecticut, but found none we liked. I then moved to West Haven, a working-class area known for its seafood restaurant. I bought a Ford Torino for $2,000 with a 302 cubic inch (five litres) straight-eight engine.[4] It did nine miles to the gallon. My

---

2. See Chapter 4.

3. D. Seddon (ed.), *Relations of Production* (1978).

4. A downmarket version of Clint Eastwood's *Gran Torino* (2008).

landlady was a Lebanese matriarch. I loved it. Then Nicky took a job in Essex University. I knew now that my American sojourn was unsustainable.

I soon got drawn into a labour dispute. A young thug in big boots collected my waste bin one day; an elderly black lady did this. When accosted, he ran away. Yale's contract with unskilled workers came up every three years. It took some months to settle. The conflict traditionally focused on the power station supplying the prestigious scientific experiments. In 1971 students lay down before the fuel delivery trucks. In 1974 the teamsters' union refused to deliver the oil. In 1977, the students complained about not getting their breakfast. The union leader was an Italian American, currently being prosecuted in California. The teamsters showed no interest. I was the only professor to join the cause. I went on local TV to dispute the Provost's story. It was a lockout, not a strike. The union colluded with Yale to save them some money. I learned a lot, but it was a waste of time.

I participated in a 1970s Yale seminar on 'The Left in Europe' for tenured social science professors and visitors from State, CIA and Pentagon. The assumption was that north-west Europe was sewn up; the problem lay with the 'Mediterranean promontories', Iberia, Italy and Greece. These areas were politically unstable and the Soviet Black Sea fleet could support insurrection there. I had never heard talk like this before. We did one country a week starting with Lech Walesa's Poland. A political scientist updated us on the Italian Communist Party. 'We own its top forty members, but the party is being upstaged by far-left groups who have just occupied our Singer factory'. He floated this idea: the sixth fleet could simulate an invasion of the Bay of Naples. The CP, primed by us, would then emerge as stout defenders of the nation against American imperialism.

One old professor asked me why I used words like 'state' and 'working class' (instead of 'government' and 'workers') – 'you got a theory of history or something?' Despite this, I was impressed by the vision, seriousness and scope of global research in Washington. I applied to join the CIA. I wanted to get my hands on their computers. I imagined being able to find anything there, like how many sheep are there in Morocco? I was not accepted. Washington's top civil servants impressed me greatly; their private discourse never appeared in public. Soon after the Lehmann crash, I attended a Chicago conference with the likes of James Galbraith and Eugene Fama. I was the only speaker who referred to economies outside the US. This is empire. My countrymen inhabit the shadow without the reality of empire.

I made many friends, mostly students and young academics, since I was single too. Yale transformed my outlook. My students wanted to discuss anthropology's future direction. Columbia University took an evolutionary line ('cultural ecology'). Lévi-Strauss's structuralism was popular at Chicago. One day a voice spoke to me in the shower: 'Why read Marvin Harris when you haven't read Immanuel Kant?' I am bipolar, not schizophrenic. I listened to it. The bubble burst soon enough. My marriage failed and I had two mental breakdowns in short order, the first of ten over fifteen years.[5]

Gun for Hire, Will Travel

I resigned from Yale for a one-year appointment at the University of Michigan, Ann Arbor, brokered by my friend, Skip Rappaport. I hired a U-Haul van, towing my car behind. My possessions were few: a reclining armchair, a television, a large number of books, clothes and kitchen utensils. I had brought from England a thick Bakhtiari rug. I bought it from a Dutch hustler in Manchester. He told me: 'The Bakhtiars are Iranian nomads – at least they were before the Shah put them in factories to make these carpets'. I kept climbing from Pennsylvania to Ohio and never came down. The Great Lakes are on a high plateau.

I liked Ann Arbor. Unlike the Ivy League, the University of Michigan was not obsessed with status. It had one of the biggest libraries and ranked first nationally in anthropology, history and political science. It had introduced to America a democratic version of the German seminar system. They called it 'the Athens of the Midwest', which was a stretch. It also featured Big Ten college sports. Detroit with its rock music and fabulous Arab food was only forty miles away. The Museum used two half-assistant curator posts to appoint me. I like archaeologists – they take a longer view than ethnographers. I ran a seminar course on ancient Mediterranean society. Professors of Roman history, economics and Assyriology attended it. I found the time to write the report on West African agriculture.[6] My social life was more relaxed than at Yale.

Skip was writing his big book on religion and we discussed it often. We had met in Manchester when he gave a seminar paper there. I was so impressed with his opening line – 'Like Durkheim, I will tread the thin line between profundity and banality' – that I drove him to Cambridge. I was even more impressed that he had once owned a hotel in the Berkshires frequented by the New Jersey Mafia. Only when he died did I realize how much he meant to me. He was the older brother I never had.

Peter Yates was a photographer from Preston, Lancashire, a stringer for UPI.[7] At 17, he entered the US illegally from Canada as a John Coltrane groupie in the 1960s. He ended up in the Ann Arbor of Students for Democratic Socialism and the Weather Underground. Eventually an amnesty was

5. See Chapter 12.
6. See Chapter 7.
7. United Press International.

offered to anyone who could prove continuous residence. His mother had kept his letters, so he passed. Peter lent me an assistant's card and an empty Nikon. I squatted on the basketball touchline while Isaiah Thomas of Indiana dribbled past.

Sarah Cahill was an English student and the girlfriend of Skip's godson, Neil Gordon, who was then away. Sarah had been a teenage concert pianist in San Francisco. She made Beethoven's most difficult sonata (Opus 109) her own and played Debussy's longest piano piece, *L'isle joyeuse*, in a recital. Sarah loved poetry. Ours was a romantic but chaste friendship. It opened up the first cracks in the wall of my grief. I had another breakdown while I was there.

My daughter Louise, now 7, was visiting from England. She asked me if a pink spot on her leg was poison ivy. 'It looks as if your leg will have to come off, Louise.' 'Daddy loves me, he isn't upset, so this is another of his silly jokes.' She said 'Oh Daddy!' and stalked off. An old lady nearby couldn't resist. 'That is the most disgusting thing I have heard in my life. You lied to your daughter! A father always speaks the truth to his children.' Many Americans believe that children should be protected from the ugliness of adulthood for as long as possible. In Manchester we agree on the first point, but prepare children by making them choose between contradictory versions of events. Is an aversion to contradiction in child-rearing more common in the US than in Europe? There's a clue to Franklin's autobiography there.[8]

My attempts to study agrarian civilization in India or Egypt failed for lack of funding. President Sadat was having trouble with big landlords in the South. I hitched onto a research project there and learned Egyptian colloquial Arabic for two years. Then Sadat was assassinated and it fell through. I once drove through a heavy storm on the plains. The radio news started with 'A rebellion in Luzon has cut rice supplies from the Philippines. Wheat supplies from Southern Egypt have been held up.' These farmers are better informed about world politics than anyone.

I was renewed for a second year and applied for untenured associate at Harvard's Institute for International Development. I got the job. Harvard's anthropologists wanted it re-advertised as a full professorship. I won the position again. After a long delay I had a phone call from an outsider on the committee. 'I'm sorry, Keith, you are not getting the job, but it's not your fault'. The anthropologists had shown me off at a conference. Its head now claimed they never offered me the post. I saw a temporary position at McGill University in Montreal and settled it with a phone call. The grapevine later leaked the Harvard story. One referee approached by the senate wrote that I was a communist and a maniac. HIID wanted to go ahead, but Anthropology pulled out.

---

8. See Chapter 1.

I was very fond of Skip Rappaport and his family. When I moved from Cambridge to Paris, he wrote saying that he had lymphatic cancer and would not live long. Thinking of his unfinished masterpiece on religion, I jumped on a plane to Detroit. Skip was in reasonable shape, but his manuscript could have been compiled by a psychotic typist. We agreed on a new title and chapter order and, after more visits, reached a full text a year later. Skip died soon afterwards. I acted for the author in publication. I also co-wrote Skip's obituary for *American Anthropologist*.[9] His book provides an exhaustive treatment of ritual. It is the most important anthropological study of religion since Émile Durkheim's *The Elementary Forms of Religious Life*.[10] Its final chapters outline an ecological basis for a new world religion.

Skip's death came as a huge blow and I didn't understand why. It left a big hole, like Janice's death not long before. He wrote

> I dedicate this book to four anthropologists who have very much influenced the ideas expressed in it and who have been otherwise important in my life and career. In the order in which they entered my life, they are: Robert Levy, Eric Wolf, Mervyn Meggitt, Keith Hart. All of them have acted like elder brothers to me, even Keith who is many years my junior.

I was much moved, but I still didn't understand. Skip said that he learned most from Gregory Bateson and me. The day that he brought us together was a disaster. I blame contrasts of generation, region, class, accent and manners. Skip had been a surrogate kinsman to whom I deferred *as a junior*. We learned a lot from each other, as intellectual friends do; we started out unequal in age, status, knowledge and wealth. Most social relations start from inequality and later establish greater equality, if they are lucky.

Did Skip endorse my intellectual ambitions? He co-authored my existence at a vulnerable time, following God's analogous role when I was a teenager. He was always my religious expert. I had fallen for religion as an anthropology student. Later I told myself that economics – the religion of capitalist societies – was a temporary diversion. But I never left it and the study of money filled that vacancy in my mind.

Shortly afterwards, I drove to Montreal's Esplanade facing Mount Royal. Leonard Cohen lived four doors down. Two anthropology students, Eric Worby and Louise Sperling, greeted me. They became close friends. It had been a Jewish quarter and the street behind figured in a famous novel.[11] The

---

9. R. Rappaport, *Ritual and Religion in the Making of Humanity* (1999); K. Hart and C. Kottack, 'Obituary: Roy A. Rappaport' (1999).

10. K. Hart, Foreword to Rappaport (ibid.); E. Durkheim, *The Elementary Forms of Religious Life* (1912).

11. M. Richler, *St. Urbain's Horseman* (1971).

Boulevard St Laurent had wonderful food shops and the finest cooked meats at Schwartz's. The ethnic neighbourhoods opened up new secrets to walkers. My landlady was a feisty Southern Dutch Catholic. I held Thursday soirées for students with wine and snacks.

I had the happiest moment of my life in Montreal and knew it then. I was walking with a companion near the port and saw a cardboard sign 'to the beach'. A tug boat was anchored in a huge derelict loading bay with some sand scattered in front. The great ships of the St Lawrence Seaway passed at the open end. The boat had pretty young women in low-cut blouses serving beer to Cajun rock music. The sky was blue and the sun shone. I felt completely happy there. Why? The blackened girders and empty loading bays echoed Lancashire's post-war decline. But here the joys of life were vibrantly asserted against industrial decay. It opened up to the world's oceans. The boat offered a mix of beer, sex, music, irony and sunshine – all with a French slant. My stay in Montreal was not all sunshine, however.

Refuge (A Lazy Neurotic)

All day I lay
in a self-imposed twilight,
Longing for night,
Resisting the day.

The clock strode through time
with lengthening paces.
Its digital clicks covered vast arid spaces,
Deserts whose emptiness fathered this rhyme.

At first I imagined the heat of my brain
was building a fire and Forging the iron
To cauterize festering sources of pain.

But the tumbling streams
of my guilt-ridden fears
Reduced fiery ideas
To the dark stuff of dreams.

In the greyness of those hours
I recalled how the brilliant
moments of dalliance
live in the memory, vivid as flowers.

Then the black hole
of vulnerability
Filled me with pity,
Enveloped my soul.

And so I slept,
A dried-up husk,
And never wept. [12]

In Montreal and then Chicago I read about writing screenplays – Joseph Campbell, William Goldman, etc.[13] I wrote a three-part TV drama based on Rousseau's *Confessions*, but did nothing with it. Louise Sperling and I wrote a long treatise on East African herders as a template for comparative economic anthropology. The publisher's reader rejected it because he didn't get a 'whiff of the camp fire smoke' from our text.

Chicago wanted someone to teach three courses on economic anthropology for a year. I jumped at the chance. The city caught my imagination. I loved its panorama of skyscrapers seen from Lake Shore Drive. My interest was sparked by the symbiotic evolution of its financial markets and the agriculture of the Great West.[14] I had another mental breakdown as soon as I got there and that ruled out a permanent job. I enjoyed teaching fieldwork methods at the Chicago Mercantile Exchange, where money derivatives were invented in 1972. Agricultural markets are the most volatile of all. After the dollar left gold, exchange rate uncertainty destabilized Midwestern farmers. When they sold pork bellies to German supermarkets, they could not predict how much they would get months later. The CME met their needs. This was partly Milton Friedman's doing, just to snub the Keynesians. I had a $25,000 gambling fund in case of unemployment. I used it now to trade dollar/deutschmark exchange rate futures.

My friendship circle in Chicago was large and warm. I coincided there with John and Jean Comaroff, and John Peel was visiting with his family. Marshall Sahlins and I went way back.[15] Hyde Park was an island of privilege in the world's biggest black ghetto. I was told not to go beyond Fiftieth St at night. But sometimes I went as far north as Elijah Mohammed's temple on Thirtieth. I found small bars where old men just up from the Mississippi Delta sang the blues. I always had a friendly welcome.

One day I came across a Scientologist handing out a quiz in a supermarket. I like quizzes and my cousin Richard Wrigley had been L. Ron Hubbard's

---

12. In Charles Baudelaire's poem, '*Mon cœur mis à nu*' ['My heart laid bare'], he describes himself as a *paresseux nerveux*: 'As a child I had two contradictory feelings in my heart, the horror and the ecstasy of life. This is the mark of a lazy neurotic' (my translation).

13. J. Campbell, *The Hero with a Thousand Faces* (1949); W. Goldman, *Adventures in the Screen Trade* (1983).

14. W. Cronon, *Nature's Metropolis: Chicago and the Great West* (1991).

15. Marshall died at 90 in 2021. It was not unexpected, but was still a great loss to me and many others. See K. Hart, 'Obituary: Marshall David Sahlins, 1930–2021' (2021).

assistant before they fell out.[16] I filled it in and handed it over. Next week he gave me the results: 'Your energy level is off the charts, but so is your depression score'. My psychiatrist told me later that he wanted to give me my money back because he had misdiagnosed my condition. My energy level misled him over how depressed I was. I told him that I didn't expect him to understand me anyway. 'Watch it, smartass. When did you ever hear of a Chicago shrink offering you money?'

I threw a party for my fortieth birthday. I made *pasta al pesto* and *salade Niçoise* with strawberries and Spanish *cava* bubbly. The cooking pots came from Fernando and Julie's commune. It was a happy occasion. I had long contemplated leaving academia. I could be a journalist, businessman, politician. . . But at that party I asked, 'Who are you kidding, Keithy? You have been in school all your life. If you were ever going to get out, it would have been before now.' This released a tremendous surge of freedom in me. Accepting my academic vocation opened up so many possibilities.

---

16. L. Ron Hubbard, *Dianetics: The Modern Science of Mental Health* (1950).

Chapter 9

BACK TO CAMBRIDGE

Caribbean Interlude

I stood on a street corner in Chicago, with the wind whistling up my arse. It felt like there was no-one in a thousand miles who knew or cared much for me. Despite the disasters, I had found liberty in America. I had a chance to spread my wings. The idea of freedom runs deep in the United States and is synonymous with movement.[1] I would never have grasped the meaning and sources of 'freedom' if I had stayed in the Old World, where the past weighs so heavily. Conformity is the complement of American freedom. Culture builds ties that a fragmented society cannot. I embraced aspects of the common life, especially sports. But I didn't know what made those strange people tick or how I could become one of them.

I now found myself alone, overstretched and without prospects. When I was going crazy in Ann Arbor, I called up Skip near midnight and told him that my skull was bursting. I didn't think I would make it through the night. He said, 'Thanks for letting me know, Keith. Call me again whenever you like. We are academics and always borderline crazy. We are afraid of madness and don't know what to do about it. If we can, we avoid it, in others and ourselves.'

Apart from enjoying some freedom and suffering its consequences, I read the great philosophers. In this context I found an essay by William Hazlitt.

---

1. See Chapter 13.

Our romantic and itinerant character is not to be domesticated. . . In fact the time we have spent abroad appears to be cut out of our substantial, downright existence. We are not the same, but another, and perhaps more enviable individual: 'Out of my country and myself I go'. . . [But] we can be said only to fulfil our destiny in the place that gave us birth.[2]

I knew what he meant: expatriate life offers freedom from social obligation. To insert oneself in the conditions of our formation is hard; but it is a more reliable way of getting to know oneself. I had to go home; but where was that? Manchester or Cambridge? I had spent half my life in Manchester aiming for Cambridge. I was an intellectual more than a football supporter. My betting stake had grown to $30,000 thanks to money derivatives. I would go to Cambridge without a job and see what turned up.

Back to Cambridge

Cambridge Mentors in Retrospect

I was now ready to revise the idea that I owed nothing to my seniors. Jack Goody and Meyer Fortes were both mentors to me, but in very different ways. Jack was a shambolic teacher and Meyer cultivated a superior aloofness. I found out later how much Jack had moulded my intellectual trajectory. He told his students to find a question and follow it wherever it leads. He placed local studies in a comparative historical framework. In a short preface to his first volume of world anthropology, he laid out his mature approach to anthropology:

It is time we tried to fit the numerous detailed investigations of social life in different parts of the world with the larger speculations on the development of human culture.[3]

I agreed with all his main points. Jack had taught me by example, not by instruction! I later published several review articles on his work.[4] They were my homage to him as my teacher.

My relationship with Meyer Fortes was more complicated. In 1968, a small student uprising occupied the department coffee room. Fortes asked us what we wanted. We proposed writing our own examination questions and letters of reference. 'Alright', he said, 'I'll sit at your feet!' He worried that

2. W. Hazlitt, 'On Going a Journey' (1822).

3. J. Goody, *Production and Reproduction* (1976: 1–2).

4. Hart, Appendix 2006b, 2011a, 2014a.

Jack would merge social anthropology with sociology and political science. In Ghana I announced that I would restudy the Tallensi. Meyer thought Jack set me up to undermine him. I wrote five letters without reply. When I went up north, he sent voluminous letters with detailed questions for fieldwork.

I let him down. He was upset that I didn't accept his postdoc offer and concluded that I chose development studies for the money. He encouraged me to write up a family of earth priests who were entrepreneurs. In 'Cashing in on Kinship', I argued that they were not representative. I got back a seven-page handwritten *cri de coeur*. 'I have always known that you are a Bentham-ite with hedonistic tendencies. But I had not grasped before how foreign the idea of filial piety is to you.' It went downhill from there.

Over coffee at lunch one day some years later, he asked me, 'What do you mean by "time"?' I was soon floundering. But I had been promoted from the class of young ignoramuses. Meyer Fortes was a labour organizer *manqué*. I once told him he needn't worry about paying me for a lecture. 'You working-class aristocrats will be the death of me. I had to struggle to get my staff paid for outside teaching; and now you tell me to keep my money.'

All of this fuelled my respect for him. I still rank him first among the anthropologists I have known. I have begun to publish short assessments of his best work. The first instalment looks at his scientific and political work in the 1940s.[5] I earlier published a paper on Tallensi economic history.[6] In 1983, while I was teaching in Chicago, I received a postcard from Meyer. He had just read this article and recognized its originality. He had been wrong to think that I was an opportunist. My work on development was serious. The postcard came from the grave. By the time it reached me, he had died in hospital.

The Nadir

The years 1983–86 saw me at my lowest ebb. I felt humiliated and could not muster the concentration to write. Apart from periodic breakdowns, daily life was a struggle with severe mood swings. Equilibrium was unattainable and I could barely write for half an hour. I worried that my mental condition would prevent me from publishing in my middle years, when I should be at my peak. I was lonely and angry. My daughter Louise, now 10, lived not far away and stayed with me on alternate weekends. She was too young to allay my self-pity and grief; but with her around, love was not banished from my life. I felt bitter and frustrated that I was so handicapped. But, thanks to three

5. Hart, Appendix 2018d.

6. K. Hart, 'The Economic Basis of Tallensi Social History in the Early Twentieth Century' (1978).

excellent doctors, I came to terms with my mental illness, which lasted fifteen years from my first breakdowns in Yale.[7]

I spent the first year back in a motel. Two junior posts were advertised in the Department of Social Anthropology, fixed-term assistant lectureships. I didn't think of applying for a moment. But one day an American graduate student urged me to consider the possibility.[8] Jack Goody, in his last year as head of department, was against it. He thought these posts should be reserved for first-time appointments. I was now 40; he had helped me get the jobs at Manchester and Yale. I worried about my *amour propre*, but decided that I would give them what they were paying for and take other part-time jobs. The term in development circles is 'pluriactivity', which was my normal MO anyway.

Ernest Gellner joined the interview panel, having been just appointed as Jack's successor. I got one of the jobs, Chris Hann the other. Jack told me that I performed as if on Valium and owed the job to Ernest Gellner. I believed that for a long time. Gellner wanted me to be 'Mr Development'. I did not come to Cambridge for that; if I wanted to focus on that, I would have gone somewhere that took it seriously. I was appointed department secretary, administrative assistant to the head. Gellner told me that I must support him in meetings. He had me typecast as a Marxist, not his favourite category after having fought the Red Army in Prague. When I left for Jamaica, he asked me if I had thought about becoming unemployed. There were three assistant lecturers and I was the one most likely to find another job; he would not support me for tenure while I was away. Two decades later, I mentioned Jack's story about my interview to an anthropologist colleague. He said my performance had been so outstanding that the committee was unanimous; someone else told me that my references from Rappaport and Sahlins were good enough to be in a museum.

I could not swallow the demotion of being on the bottom rung. Cambridge is a status-conscious place. I bought a house. Jack was against that idea also. It was in a terraced street, once working class and now gentrified. My parents saw it was exactly the same as ours in Old Trafford. I now recognized features like the step where I once cleaned my shoes. I used my savings as a deposit on the house and for some furniture. I thought of myself as the 'Kant of Cambridge' – not on intellectual grounds, but because I wasn't going anywhere. My neighbour, Graham Pledger, was a college gardener. He made good the gaps in my householder skills. He was always there for me as a friend.

7. See Chapter 12.
8. Thanks, Parker Shipton.

Caribbean Interlude

I spent two years in Jamaica helping to set up a graduate school for the social sciences in the English-speaking Caribbean. I knew then that this was a life-transforming experience and it launched my mature perspective. I could now place my movement through the North Atlantic slave trade in a vision that I call 'cubist'. After an epiphany on a beach, I wrote a long fan letter to the writer and revolutionary C.L.R. James, comparing our respective journeys through this space. This led to co-editing his majestic *American Civilization*, with its reflections on the 'struggle for happiness and democracy.'

Jamaica 1986–88

The sun was already high when I drove my Japanese car round the last bend before the junction. It looked as if a pile of rags had been left in the road. Rather than run over them, I stopped. It was a very thin man, a beggar with tangled dreadlocks, apparently asleep. I got out and tried to rouse him. It wasn't easy.

'Hey! Get to the side of the road. You'll be run over here.' 'It's warmer in the middle than the side.' (In desperation) 'What's your name?' A beautiful smile lit up his face. 'Alvin. No-one has asked me my name for twenty years.'

'OK, Alvin. How about moving to the side?' He moved. 'Have you had anything to eat today?' 'No.' 'Here, take this and get some patties down at Liguanea.' I gave him a small banknote which he put straight in his mouth. He began to eat it pensively. I ran to the car and drove away as fast as I could. As Dr Johnson says, 'Smile with the wise, eat with the rich'.[9]

I knew Ray Smith from Chicago and we shared places like Manchester, Cambridge and Ghana. He asked me to replace him as Professor in the new Consortium Graduate School for Social Sciences. It was based at the University of the West Indies (UWI) near Kingston. Being an assistant lecturer in Cambridge had already worn thin for me and I dreaded a tenure review. Jamaica seemed like a good place to sit it out. I left convinced that I was not coming back. I had been invited to the University of Cape Town in South Africa. I asked a Ghanaian friend, a senior official at the Commonwealth Secretariat, if it was OK to go to South Africa, given the embargo. He said it wasn't meant to keep people like me away. When I arrived at UWI and mentioned that I might be going to South Africa, they looked at me aghast. Jamaicans were watching white cops shooting rebellious black youths in Soweto on television.

The British Empire abolished slavery in 1833, but the land for the former slaves was too small to sustain them; they had to return to the sugar planta-

---

9. Hart, Appendix 2000a.

tions as 'free' wage labour. They rose up more than once, but were defeated. Many left, first to build the Panama Canal, then to the fruit farms of Central America and Florida, lately to London, Toronto and other northern cities. They had received 'independence' from colonial empire in the 1960s, but knew that emancipation was far away. They saw the South African struggle with Pan-African eyes. If the apartheid regime was defeated, it would be a universal victory for blacks everywhere and could bring their own freedom nearer. They told me that I should not come back if I went to South Africa. I stayed.

I had not yet made sense of my voyages through the North Atlantic, seeing each leg of my journey separately. The gap between America and Europe was huge. West Africa was familiar, an old society, like Britain, where people knew who they were. America was new, but I had not figured what that meant for me. The Caribbean was the other three combined. Like the US, it was created from scratch by adventurers, the aboriginal population destroyed. But Africa and Europe remained a conservative force there that the Americans had broken with decisively. Sometimes Jamaica seemed frozen in the eighteenth century. This was the last leg of the quadrilateral made by the slave trade. The Caribbean helped me to integrate where I had lived in the North Atlantic.

A new relationship with James and his assistant, Anna Grimshaw, was a catalyst for that synthesis. In shadowing the African diaspora, I had absorbed their perspective on history as dispersion and movement. The Paris avant-garde,[10] at a time of unparalleled movement around the world, abandoned traditional perspective and placed the viewer inside the picture at different points. According to John Berger, the key figure was the diagram, a method for making abstraction concrete.[11] The Middle Passage of the Atlantic slave trade spawned the first modern people, formed by dislocation and dreams of emancipation, who held perspectives from several places at once. I placed myself imaginatively where I had been and the world changed too. The triad of Cape Town, Cambridge and Kingston triggered this revelation.

Epiphany on a Beach

I was reading a collection of James's writings on cricket on a beach in North Jamaica.[12] The place had once belonged to Errol Flynn. My daughter Louise, now 12, was playing in the shallows of a turquoise sea. James was a cricket correspondent for the *Manchester Guardian* in the 1930s. I found myself

---

10. R. Shattuck, *The Banquet Years: The Avant Garde in France, 1885–1914* (1955).

11. J. Berger, *Picasso* (1965). See Rivers in Chapter 2.

12. C.L.R. James, *Cricket* (ed. Anna Grimshaw, 1986).

reading about my Dad's heroes in the Lancashire cricket team as if it was today's news. I devoured everything I could get by James in Jamaica. In Britain, he left London to join Learie Constantine, the Caribbean's best cricketer, in Lancashire.[13] We had been to the same regions at different times – the Caribbean, Britain, the US and West Africa. Our trajectories were very different. Now I watched my daughter play on that exotic beach, with my father's stories coming alive. The gap between me and that old man was erased by the immediacy of James's prose. Generation and racial difference collapsed in an epiphany of timeless connection. I felt compelled to meet him and wrote my first and only fan letter.[14]

Dear Mr. James,

Like you I have lived in Britain, the United States, Africa and now the Caribbean. I started out from Lancashire. In the last few months, I have read many of your writings, as well as a large number of West Indian novels (mostly Trinidadian). I feel energized by the experience and would very much like to talk with you when I return to England in August. I would not place the scope of my life on a par with yours; but there are numerous parallels that give me insight into your writings and allow them to speak directly to me.

I was born and raised in Old Trafford, Manchester, so that first-class spectator sport was a convenience I took for granted. I learned to play most games with enthusiasm, discipline and varying degrees of skill. I went to Manchester Grammar School and won a scholarship in classics to St. John's College, Cambridge. My favourite ancient authors were Aeschylus and Catullus; I consumed Russian, French and English novels voraciously. I captained my college's occasional cricket team and sometimes played bridge with Mike Brearley [later captain of the England cricket team]. I switched to social anthropology and spent over two years in the slums of Accra. I dreamed of writing a novel like *Minty Alley*, but wrote a PhD thesis instead. My academic work focused on migration, urban economy and ethnicity, without knowing that I was exploring my own migration from the streets of Old Trafford to Cambridge.

I returned to teach at Manchester University and lived in Rossendale, where I found a purer form of Lancashire working class culture than any my background provided. About this time, I began to read Marxist philosophy seriously. My politics have always been broad left. I wrote the development program for Papua New Guinea on the eve of its independence. I also worked as a part-time journalist for *The Economist*. Eight years of teaching at Yale, Michigan, McGill and Chicago followed. America has made a more profound and disturbing impact on my life than Africa. (Jamaica is having a similar effect in a much shorter time.) After some fairly shattering experiences, I returned to Cambridge. Now I have taken up a two-year secondment as visiting professor at UWI to help start a new research school in the social sciences. The work is

---

13. James ghosted Learie Constantine's autobiography.

14. The letter was stored by Jim Murray in New York via Anna Grimshaw.

demanding, often frustrating; but I share your vision of the potential of West Indian intellectuals and culture; and so I bat on.

I am particularly interested in your experience of the United States, perhaps because I have read less of your writing from that period. In the Melville book [*Mariners, Renegades and Castaways*] you refer to an intention to write about 'American civilization'. I can understand that you never found the time to sit down and write that book. But your comments on baseball and American culture in general make me wonder if you have a manuscript tucked away; and this was confirmed by a brief reference Anna Grimshaw made to such a manuscript [in the *Cricket* book]. I am sure that I will be drawn back to America before long. The idea of coming to terms with that great society, with all its contradictions and reasons for hope, is more powerful than the seductive insularity of Cambridge.

I am teaching a course on society and culture this term which rests heavily on your work. Caribbean students must somehow find their own vocabulary for addressing the universals of modern social history. A masters' student here is doing a thesis (with heavy reference to Gramsci) on West Indian cricket and politics. This is a receptive moment for your work. More to the point, you have set off incalculable reverberations inside me. It would be more than an honour to meet you. In some ways for me it is a necessity.

I got back a letter from Anna Grimshaw in Brixton, London; and I arranged to meet them both in August. On the way there I stopped for a job interview in the anthropology department at Washington University, St. Louis. I received the best job offer I ever had. It was full professor, a high salary, half-time teaching, fellow of Douglass North's Institute of Political Economy, one semester a year minimum residence and a say in five new appointments in anthropology and political economy. I said I would let them know when I returned to Jamaica.

My visit to Brixton was very successful. C.L.R. ('Nello' to his friends, but not to me) was in his late eighties and frail, but intellectually lively when he was awake. Anna Grimshaw was from Lancashire and had been Edmund Leach's last PhD student at Cambridge. She worked in a Ladakh nunnery and wrote a wonderful book about it, *Servants of the Buddha*.[15] She took a job in Manchester with Granada TV, but the old man persuaded her to work with him. We discussed pooling our resources in future. Anna was committed to the old man. When I returned to Kingston, I phoned St. Louis to turn down their offer.

I returned to my job in Cambridge after two years and spent 1988–89 in and around Brixton. Anna and I edited James's *American Civilization*.[16] He died, precipitating an ugly dispute with his literary executor. We founded the

15. A. Grimshaw, *Servants of the Buddha* (1994).
16. C.L.R. James, *American Civilization* (1993).

Prickly Pear series of pamphlets. A dozen were later preserved online.[17] Anna joined me in Cambridge and trained as a documentary film-maker, then took a lectureship in visual anthropology at Manchester University and moved to Emory University in Atlanta where she remains.

Snapshots of My Life in the Caribbean

I had a romantic conversion in Jamaica: hated society, loved nature. I took photographs of flora, vegetation, sea and skies with no people in them. The country people were hospitable, but Kingston was tough. I took a luxury apartment in the foothills of the Blue Mountains. The situation was beautiful, but the society ugly. One title for the poem below is 'Ishmael at the Masthead'. For James, Ishmael, narrator of *Moby Dick*, is the perfect compromised intellectual.[18]

View from a Balcony, Kingston

I
The evening sky parades its wonders just for me:
Here towering columns, residue of rainclouds,
Boiling black smoke, hellfire of blast furnaces;
There thin purple islands, feathered archipelago
Floating in an unmapped, turquoise lake.
Encircling hills, reduced to pristine dormant shapes,
Stretch out familiar fingers to the golden sea.
A forest city spreads its winking lights beneath my feet.
This surge of elevated power intoxicates,
Brings on wild fantasies of flight,
Makes all things possible from here.

II
We clasp cold Red Stripe in the still warm air,
Hands slipping on the bottles' icy dew,
Our senses captive to the evanescent spell
of sunset's lurid melodrama,
Brief recapitulation, daytime's curtain call.
But Herman was uneasy. 'It isn't right
to be up here when they are all down there.'
The godlike seeming was dissolved
and cooling beer now mixed with clammy sweat.

---

17. https://thememorybank.co.uk/prickly-pear-pamphlets/ (accessed 13 October 2021).

18. C.L.R. James, *Mariners, Renegades and Castaways: The Story of Herman Melville and the World We Live in* (1953).

III
My home's a hillside fastness, garden paradise,
Container walls like fortress ramparts,
Far more lovely, twice as safe as any bank.
Here yelping curs outnumber people,
Harass dark strangers night and day.
White mansions show the world a surly shuttered face.
Grim burglar bars, sham rococo,
Cannot disguise the prisons that they make.
Guns guard the inmates, rich inviolate,
From unseen dangers, bleak reminder of their wealth.

IV
The restful cool of breezy night
is shattered by rounds of canine choirs,
Redundant drone of air conditioners
and TV movies broadcast for the world to hear.
Then daylight brings the peaceful sun
to light this magical profusion —
Royal palms, wild ferns and clinging vines,
Banana's crazy leaves, cascading banks of flowers—
and then at last to lull abandoned dogs to sleep.

V
Each morning sleek new German cars,
Evading potholes and debris of rainstorms,
Carry the masters down the winding, unkempt road,
Past servants trudging slowly up that steep incline,
Eyes averted from their rulers and the sun,
Their unpaid journey almost done,
An hour or more from Kingston slum
to bright, fantastic cages on the hill

VI
For all their fortifying bulk
this colony's foundations are not firm.
The fluid earth escapes the shoring walls
and leaks away in swift corrosive streams.
The race threat grasps them by the throat.
The sound of distant jungle drums
Drifts up to fill the owners' restless dreams
of dread invasions, crime and death.
Subversive nightmares are transformed
In frantic talk of hurricanes and landslides,
Elemental cataclysms, nature's revolutions,

Displaced symbols of a deeper terror,
Monstrous fear of fellow men.

VII
This fragile platform on the edge of empty space
Suspends me over chasms of despair,
Until the evening sky parades its wonders once again
and idle torment shifts to fantasies of flight
Where contradiction's black and white,
Made gaudy by the dying sun's strange light,
Fade into nothing and the night.

I became obsessed with dogs. A vertical cartoon strip in the *Daily Gleaner* showed a boss beating up on his worker; the worker beating up on his wife; the wife beating up on their kid; the kid beating up on their dog; and the dog beating up on a beggar with dreads. I started collecting material for an unfinished book called *A Whole Other Story*. 'Of course, dogs eat the same things as people, so this affects the population/food ratio. But to go further into this would be a whole other story'.[19]

I read a lot in Jamaica. I gave up on local history, social science and anthropology because of the poor quality. During my stay I read fifty Caribbean novels, a more reliable source. Most Western first novels concern a young man's self-exploration. But here several, like George Lamming's *In the Castle of Their Skin* and Jamaica Kincaid's *Annie John*, had children as narrators.[20] These drew on the parent/child metaphor of colonial rule and children's estrangement from adult society. Half the novels came from Trinidad, including the Beacon Circle that C.L.R. James once belonged to. I was hooked on V. S. Naipaul. I published in a Trinidad literary review on 'Naming in Earl Lovelace's *The Dragon Can't Dance*', using my knowledge of Greek mythology.[21]

I listened to music a lot, especially to romantic operas – *Der Rosenkavalier*, *Madama Butterfly* and *La Traviata*. I consumed African American novels. One weekend I read three of them with Debussy's piano music on continuous playback. They all featured black men's struggles with the Communist Party.[22]

I was building up to another breakdown. One day I was listening to Cyndi Lauper's 'True Colours' while driving. The colours outside the car began to

---

19. Book not found.

20. G. Lamming, *In the Castle of my Skin* (1953); J. Kincaid, *Annie John* (1985). See also G. Gbadamosi, *Vauxhall* (2013) and C. Achebe, *Education* (2011) in Chapter 1.

21. E. Lovelace, *The Dragon Can't Dance* (1979).

22. R. Wright, *Native Son* (1940); C. Himes, *Lonely Crusade* (1950); R. Ellison, *Invisible Man* (1952).

move in kaleidoscopic patterns. Something chemically unusual was happening to my brain. I drove to a friend's house. She had a barbecue going with beef and chicken. Digesting meat and alcohol uses up a lot of energy and makes us drowsy. I often drink beer or wine at lunchtime to slow me down. I ate a huge amount of meat and drank half a bottle of rum. It slowed me down all right. I fell asleep for two hours.

The reputation of Jamaican mental hospitals was scary. I called Anna in London.

A: Who is your best friend?
K: Ronnie Salter, an Irish woman.'
A: Ask her to buy you the first available British Airways ticket to London. I'll wait for you at Heathrow and we'll take a taxi to the Maudsley hospital.

Anna looked after me for a week while I attended hospital as an outpatient. By then I was over it. This was the only breakdown where I avoided being sectioned.[23] I was back in Jamaica three weeks later.

I made many friends at the UWI Mona campus, especially Don Robotham, a Chicago anthropologist (student of Ray Smith), a leading figure in the Workers Party of Jamaica and Dean of Social Sciences, and Barry Chevannes, a specialist in Rastafarianism and a different sort of political activist who was head of Anthropology. For the first time since Yale, I found myself working with a network of feminist academics in the humanities and social sciences. We co-organized a conference on Caribbean women and a good book resulted.[24] My main watering hole was the staff bar, where I always found congenial company.

I visited Trinidad and St Lucia, but preferred the Jamaican countryside. In my second year, I made regular visits to St. Elizabeth in the far West. I went to four coves known as Treasure Beach near the Black River estuary. I was captivated by the place's history. Around 1900, Black River was the second biggest town in Jamaica and the island's wealthiest. Apart from sugar products, it was a major logging exporter – the first place electrified and to have cars, the very cutting edge of Caribbean modernity. Founded in the early seventeenth century, the parish was very large and is still known as 'the breadbasket of the nation'. By the 1980s, Black River was run down and isolated, picturesque but with hardly any public transport. I considered undertaking a long-term research project combining history and ethnography after I left. But I thought better of it. Why did Jamaica need foreign anthropologists when they had Don, Barry and their students? I would read about the places where I lived and as widely as possible, my old MO.

---

23. See Chapter 12.
24. K. Hart (ed.), *Women and the Sexual Division of Labour in the Caribbean* (1989).

Chapter 10

WHEN THE WORLD TURNED

I felt out of time and place for most of the 1960s. Self and the world did not fit. People said that a cultural revolution was going on. But I was a career academic who spent his spare time in cinemas and betting shops. This was a period of full employment and low inflation. Science gave us 'a man on the moon and colour TV'.[1] My upper-middle-class friends could indulge the fantasy that they were 'orphans' and drop out. A good job was waiting for them whenever they wanted it. Some became Trotskyite 'entryists', while I drove old ladies to vote Labour in elections.

It was no better in the 1970s when entryism for me meant moonlighting for the World Bank and *The Economist*. The world was changing, but not in a progressive way. The book of my Ghana fieldwork was stuck in the 1960s and I was riding with the punches in the 1970s. People sometimes hold onto the idea of an open future in their thirties. but their world is closing in because of decisions they have already made. Personal accumulation is everything: family, house, car, work, learning a trade. I had something to say about where the world was going, but I couldn't say it yet.

The neoliberal counter-revolution got the world moving – in the wrong political direction. I perked up, however, abandoned writing an urban eth-nography and published a literary digest on West African development. I only felt in sync with the world's movement from the late 1980s. The catalyst was my Jamaica trip and meeting C.L.R. James and Anna Grimshaw. I was already

---

1. P. Feyerabend, *Against Method* (1975).

moving, personally and politically, when the world turned with the end of the Cold War. I turned with it because I now had the means of connecting with it. There are intellectuals of structure and intellectuals of transition. For all his talk of revolution, Karl Marx nailed Victorian capitalism as a structure. Lenin was interested in how to get from A to B. I was with Lenin. The years from 1989 (the fall of the Berlin Wall) to 1994 (the diffusion of the World Wide Web) saw the most profound changes of my lifetime: the collapse of the Soviet bloc, one-world capitalism, the rise of India and China as capitalist powers, money's escape from politics and law, the internet going public.

I knew immediately that the digital revolution in communications would change everything.[2] Here I focus on my other preoccupations after I received tenure and returned to Cambridge in 1988, while spending time in London with Anna and C.L.R. (who died in 1989). I was Director of Cambridge University's African Studies Centre (1992–97) while lecturing in social anthropology. I left Cambridge for Paris in 1997–98; this has been my base for serious globetrotting ever since. I start with the work Anna Grimshaw and I did as editors of James's *American Civilization* in the years 1989–93. I began to understand something about revolutions.

James on America and the Revolutionary Struggle for Happiness and Democracy

C.L.R. James often said after 1968 that there were only two world revolutions left – the second Russian revolution and the second American revolution. In *American Civilization* he argued that the contradiction between totalitarian bureaucracy and the struggle to bring democracy into people's lives was strongest in the United States. He always believed that Americans would play their part in any future world revolution. I watched Tiananmen Square on television with him in April 1989. He was 88 years old and died soon afterwards. The students were protesting because of an international meeting there. The world was gripped by the spectacle, not least by a young man holding up a line of tanks.[3] James said the Chinese would put down this protest easily, but 'the Russians will find it hard to hold onto Eastern Europe after this'. The Berlin Wall came down six months later and the second Russian revolution began – or so we thought before Putin hijacked it.

Here are two occasional pieces by Lenin and James. In January 1917, Lenin gave a speech to Swiss socialists and said he did not expect revolution in his lifetime, but hoped that the younger comrades would fight in one. The

2. See Chapter 14.

3. Image used on the cover of Hart, Appendix 2003e.

Russian Revolution got going in February/March, when the workers' and soldiers' soviets took to the streets and the tsar abdicated; in September, Lenin wrote a letter explaining why he called for revolution then but not in July,[4] and by October the revolution was a done deal. Between July and September, two million Russian soldiers quit the Eastern front and returned home, many with their weapons. Trotsky's *History of the Russian Revolution* takes 1,300 pages to cover nine months in 1917.[5] It was the first Marxist book that James read, in Lancashire – he was lucky. He used Lenin, Trotsky and Stalin to organize the narrative of *The Black Jacobins*.[6]

James returned to Lenin's role in a 1981 speech to Berkeley students about the Guyanese academic-turned-revolutionary Walter Rodney, who was blown up in a car by an *agent provocateur*.[7] He tells them that they don't understand revolution and neither did Rodney. No revolutionary organization should have left its leader unprotected. James was the leading British Trotskyist in the 1930s, dodging the bullets of Stalinist assassins in Paris while researching the Haitian revolution; he had first-hand experience. Lenin once advocated a vanguard party; but he abandoned that idea when he arrived at the Finland station and found the soviets in the streets. Until then, he confessed, he was just another bourgeois politician with a line in extremist rhetoric. Revolutions change people. Lenin says in his letter that insurrection is an *art*, not a science. James summarizes from it three components of any revolution. The party has nothing to do with any of them.

> Firstly, there must be a clash, a revolutionary upsurge of the people. Then, secondly, there must be a turning point, when the activity of the advanced ranks is at its height; and thirdly, the enemy must be vacillating.

James then recalls a conversation with Trotsky in Mexico in 1938 when he asked:

> 'How come, time and again, the revolutionary party – this is the party, not the mass movement – was wrong in its analysis of the situation and Lenin turns out to be right and set it the correct way? How did that happen?' I expected him to tell me how Lenin knew philosophy, political analysis, psychology, or just knew the revolution. He did not. 'Lenin always had his eyes upon the mass

---

4. V.I. Lenin, 'Marxism and Insurrection' (1917): https://www.marxists.org/archive/lenin/works/1917/sep/13.htm (accessed 13 September 2021).

5. L. Trotsky, *A History of the Russian Revolution* (1932, 3 vols).

6. Toussaint, Christophe and Dessalines, respectively (James, *The Black Jacobins*, 1938). See Chapter 3.

7. C.L.R. James, 'Walter Rodney and the Question of Power' (1981): https://www.marxists.org/archive/james-clr/works/1981/01/rodney.htm (accessed 13 September 2021).

of the population, and when he saw the way they were going, he knew that tomorrow this was going to happen.'

Louis Antoine de Saint-Just brought the revolutionary principle of happiness from America to Paris: 'happiness is a new idea in Europe'.[8] It never really took root there. James drew heavily on this idea in *American Civilization*. Happiness appeared repeatedly in his writings, from asserting that Marx and Hegel 'believed that man is destined for freedom and happiness', to emphasizing the centrality of happiness to American society and culture, in contrast to Europeans' sense of the tragic. The notion of happiness lay too at the heart of his *Modern Politics*,[9] where he called it 'the good life'. Conventionally, happiness has been understood to be a moment of fleeting pleasure.[10] It now often means just material satisfaction. In the eighteenth century, however, the pursuit of happiness in this life was contrasted with religious passivity in the face of earthly suffering. James held happiness to be as essential as the desire for freedom and equality. It was the desire of the modern age, 'what people want', expressive of complex and deeply rooted needs of human beings for integration, to become whole, to live in harmony with others in society.

For James, then, happiness had two facets: the freedom to be a fully developed, creative, individual personality and a part of a community based on principles conducive to that end. This was the unity of private interest and public spirit that Alexis de Tocqueville found in the early American democracy,[11] which James believed was still the palpable goal of the American people. The integration of individuals in modern society requires a fundamental reorganization of how people experience work; and this is 'the struggle for happiness'. The US contributed the idea of happiness to our understanding of civilization itself. Today it has become a universal goal; and the peoples of the Global South are potent symbols of humanity's force in opposing oppression. Happiness is inseparable from the active struggle for its attainment.

Both Tocqueville and James visited the New World after the political landscape had been transformed by the French and Russian revolutions respectively.[12] Each thought that democracy was the moving force in modern history and that America played the leading role in that movement. Their faith was not based on laws and formal institutions, but on the common people, on their pragmatic political sense. They saw ordinary Americans' customs and attitudes to life as the safeguard of democracy's future. The structure of

8. From the editors' introduction to James, *American Civilization* (1993).

9. C.L.R. James, *Modern Politics* (1960).

10. See Montreal in Chapter 8.

11. A. de Tocqueville, *Democracy* (1840).

12. See also https://www.coronatimes.net/covid-19-pandemic-revolution/ (accessed 13 September 2021).

both *Democracy in America* and *American Civilization* reflects this premise. Each has two parts, the first dealing with the ideas and outward appearance of America's public institutions, the second with the inner life and social practices of the American people. Each contains a movement from form to content that mirrors the historical contrast between European civilization and its American successor.

James's study builds on Tocqueville's. In *American Civilization* he takes up the themes of liberty, equality and the forms of association, and examines their meaning when the pursuit of material wealth peaked in Henry Ford's system of mass production. For James the society's original ideals of freedom and equality had been sacrificed to an oppressive work regime that still allowed many to aspire to the means of achieving these goals. Whereas Tocqueville made equality central to the new democracy, James was preoccupied with freedom, or rather with awareness of its loss. Moreover, the worldwide struggle of popular forces against totalitarian bureaucracy had brought Tocqueville's prediction of rivalry between America and Russia to the nightmare conclusion of the Cold War. Thus, for both, the pursuit of happiness can only take root in a democratic society whose institutional forms and cultural content support the self-expression and free association of equal citizens.

Jamesian Enterprises

C.L.R. James was my fourth mentor, after my Cambridge teachers and Skip Rappaport. Anna Grimshaw came from Lancashire. After her Cambridge anthropology PhD and a spell in television, she worked with and for James in the 1980s. He lived in a bedsit with the *Race Today* collective. Anna organized his affairs to prepare for his legacy. Jim Murray founded the C.L.R. James Institute in New York. He was Anna's staunch ally. I had read James's published books and started reading the unpublished papers. The archive was larger and richer than his published output.[13] Jim died much too early in 2003.

My time with Anna and C.L.R. was amazing. He saw me as a rival and called me 'professor' (no deference intended). Our conversations about art, revolution and history were wonderful. He would send me out for refreshments as if he were gentry. 'Go to Selfridges and buy fine claret, wood pigeon and some Schubert.' After he died, Anna plunged into publishing collections of his work.[14] Later she updated the *Cricket* book.[15]

---

13. It is now stored at Columbia University, New York.

14. A. Grimshaw (ed.), *The C.L.R. James Reader* (1992); *Special Delivery: Letters from C.L.R. James to Constance Webb* (1995).

15. C.L.R. James, *Majestic Innings* (2006).

The most spectacular product of our collaboration, after editing *American Civilization*, was the *Prickly Pear Pamphlets*.[16] The idea was Anna's. Prickly pears are a cactus growing wild in semi-arid zones like Mexico and Sicily. They provide food and refreshment for the poor. We produced ten pamphlets in three years (1993–96). A jointly-authored essay, *Anthropology and the Crisis of the Intellectuals*, launched the series.[17] 'Somehow we must all devise ways of inserting ourselves meaningfully into the most inclusive versions of human history.' This book's theme goes back to then. Anna's spirit was very strong in our manifesto:

> The prickly pear is a humble fruit which grows abundantly in arid places. It may be spiky, but it is refreshing too. The inspiration for the series is the eighteenth-century pamphleteer. We emulate the passionate amateurs of history who circulated new and radical ideas to as wide an audience as possible; and we hope in the process to reinvent anthropology as a means of engaging with society. Essayists will be free of formal convention as they seek to give expression to the content of our world. The pamphlets will be provocative and entertaining, cheap and pocket-sized. Like the prickly pear, they will come in several colours – red, yellow, green and more besides.

I was chief editor and business manager. Patrick Verdon, the teenage son of a colleague, did everything technical. Salah Bander was our graphic designer. Later Ruth Van Velsen and Michael Ward helped with the administration. We sold seven thousand copies in three years, each pamphlet of ten with a print run of a thousand. We handed the enterprise over to younger colleagues for a while.[18] Then Matthew Engelke joined Marshall Sahlins in his Prickly Paradigm successor imprint. Justin Shaffner, a student at Virginia and later Cambridge, preserved the pamphlets online. He became steward of my website and a partner at the Open Anthropology Cooperative.

I became a teaching fellow at Girton College after Marilyn Strathern left for Manchester. It had been a women's college and was now co-ed. I decided to write an autobiography during sabbatical leave. I have used some of it here. I gave it to a friend who said, 'Don't ever show it to anyone else, Keith; it's too brutal'. I tried to revive my Ghana book, failed and had a breakdown.

I was the Anthropology Department's external relations specialist. I liaised with archaeologists and biological anthropologists, sociologists, African Studies and information technology. I chaired a university committee on using IT for research and teaching. I chaired a faculty committee to design a new first-year teaching syllabus. My partners were a paleoanthropologist and an archae-

16. https://thememorybank.co.uk/prickly-pear-pamphlets/ (accessed 13 October 2021).
17. Grimshaw and Hart, Appendix 2003a.
18. Matthew Engelke and Mark Harris. They added two pamphlets.

ologist.[19] We proposed a compulsory course each for archaeology, biological anthropology and social anthropology. For the fourth, students could choose between sociology and an interdisciplinary course, 'Becoming human'. It passed unanimously. In 1994, the university awarded teaching prizes for the first time. I won one for the humanities and social sciences.

Anti-Colonial Anthropology and African Studies

How could I give students access to the other side in the war against colonial empire?[20] The intellectuals in question were rarely anthropologists. They wrote novels, poetry, history and political tracts, made films. I put on a course, 'Voices from the Third World'. It began with a TV documentary featuring Edward Said, *The Idea of Empire*.[21] A Palestinian of high family brought up in Egypt, Said was a hybrid figure. He identified 'Orientalism', a distorted Western perspective on the East.[22] The film included some shocking footage of forced labour in the colonies (with musical backing by Elgar's Enigma Variations!). I chose three novels, one each from Africa, Latin America and Asia – Chinua Achebe's *Things Fall Apart* (1958), Gabriel García Márquez's *One Hundred Years of Solitude* (1970) and Salman Rushdie's *Midnight's Children* (1981); clips from Richard Attenborough's movie *Gandhi* (1982) and Jean Rouch's *Les maîtres fous* (1955); Frantz Fanon's *The Wretched of the Earth* (1963) and James's *History of Negro Revolt* (1938).

The students usually wrote essays based on ethnographies whose truth they did not challenge. They couldn't read novels or political works that were 'made up'. They wanted to check these fictions against 'what really happened'. My focus was on the global vision animating their art. The students didn't mind reading Evans-Pritchard's *The Nuer* as God's truth, even though the British were bombing them then.[23] *Writing Culture* was all the rage.[24] But that revolution had not reached Cambridge.

I determined that we would discuss how these works were made. What 'world' did each author create and how? What was the narrative voice, the organization of tense, the treatment of race, class, gender and generation? How was political authority portrayed? I also included two ethnographies by E-P (with Clifford Geertz's chapter on 'the anthropologist as author')[25] and

---

19. Robert Foley and Todd Whitelaw.
20. From Hart, Appendix 2018c.
21. BBC Two Arena, February 1993.
22. E. Said, *Orientalism* (1978).
23. E. Evans-Pritchard, *The Nuer* (1940).
24. J. Clifford and G. Marcus (eds), *Writing Culture* (1986).
25. C. Geertz, *Works and Lives* (1989).

Marjorie Shostak's biography of a !Kung woman.[26] Exploring magical and realist thinking in novels and ethnographies was fun. The course attracted a crowd of mixed discipline and region, as is usual in Cambridge.

When I took up the African Studies Centre, an offer came from Nigeria's head of state, a former general called Ibrahim Babangida. He proposed to fund a £1.5 million research fellowship on African women through the Centre. It would be named for his wife, Maryam.[27] He came to power in a bloodless coup and organized presidential elections only to have them annulled. He then resigned in favour of another general, a monster called Sani Abacha. Babangida had been rich before entering politics, allegedly through smuggling drugs. Others claimed that he just stole from the Nigerian people in the usual way. It seemed obvious that the fellowship offer was tainted. It could embarrass the university on several grounds – crimes against humanity, fraud and embezzlement, unconstitutional behaviour and drugs trafficking.

I was alone in taking this view. The Centre's management committee thought the offer too good to turn down. Feminists told me I would be a marked man if I refused a unique initiative in women's studies. Nigerian students accused me of double standards. 'The whole of Cambridge was built on dirty money', they said. 'What's wrong with black people's dirty money?' I began to doubt my judgement. A visiting Yoruba professor rescued me. 'Ask him why this award is coming to Cambridge', he said. 'An equal grant to a Nigerian university should be a condition for accepting the offer.' I wrote along these lines and that was the last I heard.

My judgement was political, not moral or ethical. Most academics will grab a free lump sum when offered one. Nigerian military rule and dictators' ill-gotten gains are offensive. But I felt obliged to protect my institution's good name. Elihu Yale, 'an English merchant and philanthropist', bought his university with loot gained as President of the East India Company in Madras. The college changed its name to his. 'Primitive accumulation'[28] ought not to be acceptable. Yet prestigious universities still rely on tainted money. There is something absolute about the prestige enjoyed by Cambridge or Yale. This is why so much dirty money flows into their coffers. But prestige is not immune to charges of malpractice. The Director of the London School of Economics resigned over a scandal involving Libya's Gaddafi family.[29]

An Italian associate came into my office: 'They are killing my friends in Angola. What are you going to do about it?' A thirty-years war had cost a million lives there. It started up again when Unita, led by Jonas Savimbi, attacked

26. M. Shostak, *Nisa* (1981).

27. K. Hart, 'On Not Accepting Money from African Dictators' (2011).

28. K. Marx, *Capital Vol. 1* (1867: Part 8).

29. https://en.wikipedia.org/wiki/LSE%E2%80%93Gaddafi_affair (accessed 13 September 2021).

a hospital with Italian doctors who supported the MPLA government. I wrote a letter, signed by over a hundred British academics and published in *The Independent*, in which Unita was described as a 'genocidal organization'. Later, the Angolan government suggested a conference in Cambridge. I persuaded Unita to come. The two sides had not appeared in public together for years. The conference, *Why Angola Matters*, brought together government representatives, Unita's foreign affairs spokesman, the British ambassador to Angola, academics and students, Angolan refugees, landmine activists, journalists, diplomats and businessmen. Discussion was heated.[30]

A poster of the Mines Advisory Group hung on my office wall. Barbed wire encircled the Earth. A warning triangle and gruesome pictures framed the edges. A student, Richard Moyes, was fascinated by this poster: MAG's base was his home town. After graduation, he went to Cambodia to save children who thought landmines were toys. He next formed an NGO, 'Article 36', to promote action against illegal weapons. In 2010 he drew up a sketch to get nuclear weapons banned by the United Nations. They would work around the nuclear powers, not with them. The International Campaign to Abolish Nuclear Weapons (ICAN) was formed. In 2017, 122 out of 193 UN member states accepted in principle a Treaty on the Prohibition of Nuclear Weapons. ICAN received the Nobel Peace Prize.[31]

In 1995 the Nigerian writer, television producer and environmental activist Ken Saro-Wiwa was hanged by Abacha's military.[32] He was an Ogoni from the Niger Delta. This was a war zone combining oil production, local resistance and military repression. I organized a conference with government spokesmen, Shell executives, Ogoni activists and others. Jack Gowon, a Northern general in the Biafra civil war and former president of Nigeria, chaired one session. A Shell official made an unconvincing defence of the company's policy. The mid-1990s also saw the Rwandan genocide and South Africa's post-apartheid election. I recruited professionals, activists, scholars and students for events. Cambridge University's name has enormous pulling power.

The Industrial Revolution in Lancashire

I knew more about West Africa than I did about Manchester's history. I set out to make good the omission. It was easier to write about African history,

---

30. K. Hart and J. Lewis (eds), *Why Angola Matters* (1995).

31. Richard Moyes (personal communication).

32. https://www.dw.com/en/why-nigerian-activist-ken-saro-wiwa-was-executed/a-1883 7442 (accessed 9 September 2021).

where the sources are scarce, than British history, where an army of historians could demonstrate my errors. I wanted to move beyond Africa as a regional object to its place in the Atlantic history of slavery, colonial empire and unequal development. I delved into the place of black people in the university. Most of this came after my Caribbean interlude, but its origin was feeling a historical ignoramus when writing my dissertation.

In the early 1970s, I found Engels's book on Manchester thrilling.[33] I took friends and visitors on an Engels tour of the inner city. I knew none of this when I was growing up. Ever since, I have run classical social theory through what I learned of Lancashire's factory system in the nineteenth century.

Marx and Engels thought that the industrial working class would overthrow capitalism.[34] Hegel found that capitalism, left to its own devices, generated abysmal poverty. He saw no way round its ability to generate wealth. Its contradictions could be contained by the state. A 'universal class' of university-trained bureaucrats would manage the process. Marx and Engels saw only one candidate for such a class. Industrial capitalism would render the state obsolete. But the factory system, by adding machines to human labour, was concentrating workers in new urban centres. There they could offset the power of the owners' money by organizing more effectively. The workers had no property save their labour power. But they had the potential of combination. Small proprietors and the 'dangerous classes' who lacked stable jobs formed separate classes. The workers would represent society as a whole.

A 'cotton famine' beset Lancashire in 1861–64 owing to the Union navy's blockade of Southern ports.[35] Supplies to the textile industry dried up, causing massive unemployment. The owners petitioned parliament to send battleships to relieve the blockade. The workers held demonstrations supporting the North in the Civil War and the freedom of labour. People died, but fewer than if workers had only their labour power to sell. What sustained them? Lancashire's workforce came from Ireland, western Scotland and North Wales. They were migrants from homelands that had largely avoided feudalism. Lancashire has a wild hilly landscape to set against its dark satanic mills. I once took a French Marxist onto the moors overlooking Oldham. He loved being above it all in that bracing wind. 'I never knew; they never told us', he said. The buoyancy that Marx and Engels noted in Lancashire's workers could have had several causes. Working in a factory was the least likely of them.

Beatrice Webb was a cooperative socialist who, with her husband Sidney, helped found a think tank, the Fabian Society. She reports her shock when she

33. F. Engels, *Working Class* (1845).

34. Hart, Appendix 2000b.

35. https://en.wikipedia.org/wiki/Lancashire_Cotton_Famine (accessed 13 September 2021).

left London to visit her northern relatives.[36] She found a new working-class civilization in the north. This stood, she writes, on three foundations made by the workers themselves: the chapel, union and co-op. Each addressed collective and individual interests. The congregation was offset by protestant individualism. Solidarity at work was based on private ownership of tools. Combination in the marketplace assumed private property.

Studies of the workplace must take in the institutions people devise for themselves outside it. The informal economy was a strategy of Lancashire's factory workers too. In Rossendale this included strip mining, quarries, transport, catering for pilgrims, hunting and keeping animals. These helped workers' families to survive downswings in the business cycle. Marx and Engels missed it all. They clung to a contrast between working-class collectivism and petty bourgeois individualism that was never there.

If being human requires us to be individual and social at once,[37] Marx and Engel's class analysis falls down immediately. The lines demarcating the proletariat, petty bourgeoisie and lumpenproletariat dissolve. When people can combine on their own terms, formal boundaries are never absolute. Napoleon was right. The British are a 'nation of shopkeepers', addicted to fairness and conformity. A huge population moves up and down between the upper-working and lower-middle classes. My own family offers much evidence of this over three or four generations.[38] This prefigured what I found in Ghana, once I abandoned the study of politics.

Cambridge University: Networks in History

Visitors to my soirées in Cambridge, graduate students from Africa, India and Southern Europe, were often depressed.

> Cambridge is so conservative, so heavy in its traditions, so establishment-oriented. They don't want to touch anything that is relevant in our world. They break us up socially and farm us out to highly specialized disciplines. They split us up into colleges with public schoolboys who just drink beer. We feel lonely. We are not getting what we want.

I would say:

> This place is full of people like you – progressive and engaged young people with extraordinary backgrounds. If you stick with a preconceived model of

---

36. B. Webb, *My Apprenticeship* (1926).
37. Durkheim's *homo duplex*.
38. See Chapter 4.

building a social world, you will see nothing else. Cambridge is decentralized. The departments, colleges and institutes are semi-autonomous. If you find one oppressive, you can move to another. There is no social structure to adapt to here.

In the 1990s I dug quite deeply into Cambridge's history with a view to excavating a more engaged vision of its intellectual politics.[39] Some monks split from Oxford and formed the first Cambridge college. They rejected a backward-looking and parochial orthodoxy. They sought universality, a wider sense of relevance and connection with the world. Each new college broke with the establishment and opened up to the world, then closed down again. This dialectic waxes and wanes over time.

Thomas Clarkson of St John's pioneered single-issue politics.[40] He led the abolitionist network that flourished in Cambridge around 1800. This crossed divisions between academic life, the town people and national politics. Anti-slavery is the matrix from which the international movement for human rights grew. Peter Peckard, Master of Magdalene College, was 70 when he became Vice Chancellor. He advocated religious freedom and human rights for Jews, Gypsies and Methodists. In 1784 he gave a sermon against slavery: 'Am I not a man and a brother?' This was the greatest preached in Cambridge since the Reformation. It galvanized everyone. Peckard also led a team of subscribers. They published the autobiography of Olaudah Equiano, an Igbo freed slave.[41] The book went into eight editions and sold thousands. In a revolutionary era, Peckard, an old academic churchman, organized and financed the leading black activist literature.

The movement to end slavery united people of disparate religious and political views. William Pitt and William Wilberforce went up to Cambridge together. Clarkson drew Wilberforce into the abolition movement. Pitt became Cambridge University's MP and Prime Minister at 24. He persuaded Wilberforce to become the parliamentary leader of the movement. Benjamin Flower owned the country's most radical political magazine, *The Cambridge Intelligencer*. He advocated slave emancipation by revolution.

Clarkson won an essay competition on slavery and devoted his life to its abolition.[42] He made fact-finding and publicity trips on horseback – five thousand miles over seven years. He was beaten up and thrown into the sea at Bristol and Liverpool. A large enthusiastic crowd greeted him in Manchester and signed his anti-slavery petition. What was his method of campaigning?

---

39. Hart, Appendix 2018c.

40. E. Wilson, *Thomas Clarkson: A Biography* (1989); Hart, Appendix 2020a.

41. O. Equiano, *An Interesting Narrative of the Life of Olaudah Equiano* (1789).

42. H. Brogan, https://www.oxforddnb.com/view/10.1093/ref:odnb/9780198614128.001 .0001/odnb-9780198614128-e-5545 (accessed 13 September 2021).

First, these were field trips; he insisted on going to see for himself. Second, he wanted evidence, but he also wanted to show it to people. He bought thumbscrews and whips and built up a portable chest to shock his audience. Clarkson wrote many pamphlets and threatened parliamentarians with deselection. He knew that someone needed to personify the movement. Cambridge, at that time and possibly always, was not detached from the world and national politics. It was not divided by an irreducible gap between town and gown. The university became a centre for training evangelical missionaries. It was a crucible for a new and distinctively British revolutionary ideology and movement. This combined anti-slavery, free trade, economic individualism and evangelical Christianity.[43]

World society is being formed in our times. Humanity is becoming unified for good or ill. We are all connected through a network for exchanging goods, services, information and money. We must find the forms of association that can put them to good use. Imagine what Clarkson would do with the internet and mobile phones! The man had to go charging around the countryside on a horse over bad roads. He risked being assaulted. He had to print and distribute books and pamphlets by hand. What do we do? We write trivia to mailing lists, tick likes on Facebook, put selfies on Instagram. A few use the internet to mobilize networks and knowledge. Ours is a new stage of human society. The 1990s were as pregnant with possibility as the 1790s, perhaps more so.

The Anthropological Cinema of Jean Rouch

While publishing several collections of James's writings, co-editing *American Civilization* and launching Prickly Pear Pamphlets, Anna Grimshaw enrolled as a student with the National Film and Television School at Beaconsfield. One outcome was *Mr. Wade* (2003), a year in the life of a pigeon racer in Lancashire's Rossendale Valley. A working-class man, Mr Wade belonged to a racing club whose organization was the democratic mirror image of work in the textile mills. Its members set the rules, judged disputes and generally exercised the collective freedom enjoyed by the pigeons and denied them by the owners at work.

In Cambridge, Anna began work on a book, *The Ethnographer's Eye*.[44] Watching with her the movies discussed there led me back to West Africa in mid-century, to movement and agency as anthropological themes and to French cinema through the extraordinary film-making of Jean Rouch (1917–2004). For two decades from 1941, he studied migration from the region's dry savannah interior (the Sahel), then colonized by the French, to the Gold

---

43. B. Hilton, *The Age of Atonement* (1986).

44. A. Grimshaw, *The Ethnographer's Eye* (2001).

Coast, which became the first post-colonial African state in 1957. These migrants drew on a glorious past that included medieval empires (Mali, Songhay) and before them the Empire of Ghana, whose name was taken by the leaders of Gold Coast independence. Rouch filmed this historical moment in 1954–60, eventually producing *Les maîtres fous* (Accra), *Jaguar* (migration to the Gold Coast), *Moi un noir* (Abidjan, Ivory Coast) and, back home in Paris, *Chroniques d'un été*, a pioneering example of *cinéma vérité*.

Before that, his output as a Paris-based researcher consisted mainly of conventional publications and many ethnographic short films.[45] *Migrations au Ghana*[46] was the most important point of reference for my own study of Northern migrants to Accra's markets a decade later. I met Jean Rouch after I moved to Paris. His book takes a bird's eye view, covering the history, geography and general structure of the migrations and the great markets of Kumasi and Accra. He then outlines the economic, social, religious and political organization of the migrants' lives. In conclusion, he mentions two films – '*The Mad Masters*' (1955) and *Jaguar* (1967, slang for a sharp young man). These are a blend of ethnography and fiction that fully reveals the social complexity and individuality of diverse migrant careers.

Les maîtres fous is an unsettling account of a spirit possession ritual where the migrants imitate their colonial masters in a countryside retreat. It is framed by the participants' working lives in Accra's teeming panorama and caused an uproar at the time, especially among African intellectuals and politicians. It is now widely acknowledged as a classic of modern cinema. The film's title leaves us wondering who is mad – the colonial rulers, their African imitators or both?

In *Jaguar*, three young men leave their interior village for the Gold Coast – a herder, a fisherman and a 'ladies' man' with some schooling.

> Rouch takes this defining moment in history, Europe's encounter with the exotic other, and inverts its key elements to undermine the very premises upon which anthropology, among other modern disciplines, has conventionally rested. The journey undertaken by Jaguar's African characters replicates that of the European explorers and ethnographers; but it is, crucially, the mirror opposite.[47]

> [Rouch's] work, pushing at the limits of both anthropology and cinema, may be understood as a counterpart to the fluidity in social and political structures which marked the collapse of European hegemony. . . [He] united the humanist impulse of anthropology with the transformative power of cinema.[48]

45. In the Centre national de la recherche scientifique (CNRS) and Musée de l'homme.
46. J. Rouch, *Migrations au Ghana* (1956).
47. Grimshaw, *The Ethnographer's Eye*: 108.
48. Ibid.: 118.

Chapter 11

RESTART IN PARIS AND DURBAN

Paris

In my youth Paris was the gateway to the ancient Mediterranean. We never stayed there for more than a day on our way south. Paris was the capital of European civilization, the most sophisticated city in the world. But I only knew it through literature. French was a dead language I had read since I was 15 – as a classicist, cineaste, West Africanist, Marxist, world historian and reader of novels. I sometimes review French books for possible publication in English translation. I thought I knew the language well.

Sophie spent two years as a postdoc in Cambridge. We hardly knew each other then. She was trained as a lawyer in Geneva and an anthropologist in Paris. In 1996 she wrote saying that if I was ever in Paris, she would give me a meal. I went there for dinner in February 1997. I remember that meal well. She served five courses: poached eggs with herbs, quails braised in brandy with raisins, salad, five cheeses and an ice cream cake. I thought I was getting special treatment. I discovered later that she goes over the top for any dinner guest.

I returned for a few days. She visited me in Cambridge and we had a holiday in Ireland together in July. In late August I moved to her Paris flat, while she was in Bulgaria. In April 1998 we moved into the ninth-arrondissement apartment that is still our home.[1] We married in 2001, and our daughter Constance was born the next year. I have not known such domestic conti-

---

1. See the Preface.

nuity since childhood. At my age, fatherhood is a huge blessing. Freed from mental illness, I took to writing and globetrotting. My anchors were my laptop and home life in Paris.

In two decades, I have worked part-time in a dozen universities. I have given public lectures in two dozen countries. I spend a lot of time online. I launched a website to promote the book I wrote in Paris.[2] I embraced social media with enthusiasm after 2000. A major illness in 2016 forced me to cut back on travel.[3]

Sophie showed me around on my first return visit. There were three epiphanies. The first was the great basin of Stalingrad. This was a docking area on the canal system linking Paris to the Seine. It has a lovely eighteenth-century customs house and arts cinemas on either side. Stalingrad is Paris's communist heartland. It was near twilight; the pink and blue sky was reflected in the still water. I felt profoundly at ease. The second was in the Beaubourg Café next to the Pompidou Centre. The customers in casual black uniform sat nursing their tiny cups of coffee while reading and smoking a cigarette – like a scene from a Woody Allen movie. The third was in the rue des Écoles next to the Sorbonne. I went into Présence africaine, bookshop of the legendary Pan-African journal. Its authors included Gide, Sartre, Camus, Leiris, Wright, Senghor and Césaire. Across the street was L'Harmattan, a left-wing publisher and bookshop with global reach.

Anyone who could introduce me to experiences like these was worth hanging onto. The weather held up in Ireland. I liked Yeats country in County Sligo ('I will arise and go now and go to Innisfree'). The most spectacular spot was Skellig Michael, a rocky outcrop on the tip of Kerry. It was once the westernmost place in Christendom and had a monastery for five hundred years. It was home to seals, puffins, cormorants and gulls aplenty. In the *Star Wars* movie, the last Jedi lived there.[4] Sophie announced that I now had a totem. Like the indigenous Australians, I was a puffin of Skellig with a postcard to prove it. This was brilliant symbolism. Puffins are Britain's favourite bird. In French they are called *macareux moine* (monk with a colourful badge). They are at once attractive and ridiculous when they jump into the sea. 'Puffin' has been her pet name for me ever since.

I used sabbatical leave to spend time with Sophie in Paris. I arrived on the day that Princess Diana died. I planned to be a freelance writer. But I couldn't hear or reproduce spoken French. I left everything I had in Cambridge. I had no job, institution or circle of friends, just the English language between my ears. Perhaps unconsciously I needed to preserve my only working asset. In

---

2. Hart, Appendix 2000a.
3. See Chapter 12.
4. *Episode VIII – The Last Jedi* (2017).

my twenties and thirties, I learned eight languages. But that was then – I was young and reaching out. The older I got, the more introspective I became. I get by in basic French for transport, shopping, restaurants and medical treatment. I have translated some articles and chapters from French to English since coming here.

I took to the food and drink, the Metro, three hundred movies every week, the buildings and walks, the palpable sense of a 'public' sphere. I live on the Amsterdam–Brussels–Paris–Geneva–Milan axis, a land of fast and reliable trains with multilingual conductors. As a transport hub to the world, Paris is hard to beat.

I have lived in Paris during an explosion of economic sociology.[5] The *Traité de sociologie économique* has fifteen masters, each with a chapter on what they know best. My closest collaborator has been Jean-Louis Laville. His familiarity with left-wing thinkers in Latin America and Europe has been an education. There is a lively network discussing alternative approaches to money. I helped to organize a conference on anthropology, economy and globalization. I joined the scientific committee of the *Journal des anthropologues* and advised on informal economy research for the Ministry of Culture. My time spent abroad expanded and Paris engagements became fewer.

Living in France opened me up to Marcel Mauss.[6] Alain Caillé welcomed me into his group and journal based on Mauss's concept of the gift.[7] He and I organized a large international conference in a Normandy chateau.[8] Mauss's political writings in French reveal him as an activist and financial journalist. My next book project after this is a biography of Mauss. The two books speak to each other. Soon after moving to Paris, I entered an important intellectual exchange with David Graeber, who shared some of my Paris networks. He died tragically early while I was finishing this book.[9]

My family's presence anchors my mind in reality while it roams free in abstract space. Family life, along with writing, world travel and the internet, make this by far the most productive period I have known. The suffering of my middle years humbled me. It also stored up unpublished experience that I draw on now. Since 2000, I have published 120 books, articles, papers and posts on money and economy alone.[10]

---

5. P. Steiner and F. Vatin (eds), *Traité de sociologie économique* (2012).

6. Hart, Appendix 2007b, 2014b. See Chapter 2.

7. MAUSS: *Mouvement Anti-Utilitaire en Sciences Sociales*.

8. Two collections came out of this conference: A. Caillé et al. (eds), 'Mauss vivant', in *Revue du MAUSS* (2010) and K. Hart and W. James (eds), 'The Living Mauss', in *Journal of Classical Sociology* (2014).

9. Hart, Appendix 2020b is an obituary.

10. Many are in the Appendix.

Around the millennium, Profile Books of London issued *The Memory Bank* as a trade book. When I sold the American rights for $50,000, I believed I had a future as a freelance writer. A New York literary agent offered to support me in the US while I gathered material for a book on changing patterns of movement and stability in the internet era. But Sophie and I married and had Constance.

A New Family

I felt married to Sophie well before we tied the knot. Continental Europeans have a stronger sense of descent. The property of spouses is more separate. My extended family of origin is almost extinct. Sophie belongs to a three-generation clan descended from one woman and her four daughters. They had eleven children and thirty grandchildren plus spouses. Sophie would like to engage with the English-speaking world. She was my passport to knowing the French at first hand. We share a protestant upbringing and raised our daughter for independence, not attachment. Living in France as Swiss and British citizens made moving with a child complicated, so we decided to make it formal. Our marriage was in two stages: a civil ceremony in May and a formal affair in July. My father was now in a Lancashire care home. I went to see him on the way to Geneva.

There was one plane a day to Geneva from Liverpool and I booked a taxi for the forty-mile ride. When we crossed the Mersey into Cheshire, I became quite vocal. The driver ignored me. He turned round at last, but I reached the departure desk too late. I called Sophie to tell her I would get a flight from Manchester the next day. I booked a ticket for 7 a.m. The wedding ceremony was at 3 p.m. I was at Manchester airport well in time. I opened my wallet, no passport. I must have left it when I missed the Liverpool flight. British Airways gave me an office to phone, but no luck. The Swiss are rigid about passports.

I called Sophie. 'Look, darling, I won't be there for our wedding today.' No expletives or recriminations. 'How long is it before your flight leaves? I have copies of all your certificates for the marriage license. I'll go to the airport.' Twenty minutes later BA learned that I could go. In Geneva the personnel had changed and they wouldn't let me in. Sophie harangued the guy and he gave in. I got married in the afternoon. Could they all be as tough as Sophie?

Sophie's family home is next to vineyards on the outskirts of Geneva. It has a lovely garden with a swimming pool. Our nuptial dinner was for seventy or eighty people. There were two huge tents supplied by a top catering firm. A massive thunderstorm broke out, so we needed them. The guests were entertained by its flashes and bangs. The first course was a huge mound of seafood on ice. The British guests thought this was it, so they piled up their plates and went back for more. The meal had five courses. Afterwards, I sat alone amid the detritus, with the moon shining bright, in awe of my new life.

I like the Swiss. When I meet someone at a party and tell them that I study money, it interests them. J.S.G. Boggs, an American artist, satirized modern money by drawing bank notes and selling them as art objects. In London he couldn't find buyers. In Basel, they saw the joke and the potential profit. He sold all his banknotes and launched his career.[11]

I felt put out on subsequent visits when Sophie discussed arrangements with her brothers, but not me. I was her husband! But husbands don't count for much in her family. This disturbed and liberated me: I could do what I liked there – read, write, watch movies. Sophie does most of the work at home. I supply drinks, set and clear the table. I tidy up the kitchen, make the bed, carry bottles from supermarkets and take out the rubbish. The kinship model suits me. But the couple stereotype lurks in my brain. The matrifocal family hinges on three types of relationship: mother–child, siblings and relations between any two women.[12] Men are marginal, except as sons and brothers. Swiss kinship traditionally added patriarchy, which accounts for how long it took women to get the federal vote. They get their own back at home. I was an expatriate male in a matrifocal household, at once marginal and free. With Sophie, I have enjoyed world travel and the freedom to write while being rooted in family life. That seems like a bargain.

After Constance's birth,[13] I noticed the unconditional loving care that Sophie lavished on our baby. She said it was 'normal'. The English keep some distance from their children. I am good with babies, dogs and madmen. They all want to stay in and get out of their predicament. My method is studied indifference. Childcare in France is organized by the PMI (Protection maternelle et infantile). The government wants a growing population. This means that women are encouraged both to work and have children. A ready supply of cheap and reliable childcare is the result. Fees are income-related; the top rate is very low compared with Britain and the US. Children can be dropped off and collected between 8.30 a.m. and 6 p.m. The service is Stalinist, but affordable by everyone. We found a middle-class Togolese lady to look after Constance. Her husband was a French colonial magistrate. Constance went to a Montessori crèche afterwards and at 3 to a Montessori kindergarten. Learning there focuses on handling objects. We were well pleased.

Another glimpse of the woman I married. We once landed from the US in Charles de Gaulle airport early one Sunday morning. The commuter train was

---

11. L. Weschler, *Boggs: A Comedy of Values* (2000).

12. R.T. Smith, *The Matrifocal Family* (1995).

13. See Chapter 12.

almost empty and I put my laptop bag in the rack. Two men walked by, casing the joint; but they passed us. Later one asked me for directions, while the other stepped on the seat for my laptop bag. Sophie yelled 'Oh no, you don't!' and grabbed him. He dropped the case and they both ran out of the train.

Durban

Vishnu Padayachee came to Cambridge as a visiting fellow. He checked out the African Studies Centre while I was still Director. We hit it off immediately. He was an economist from Durban, South Africa.[14] We chatted about Gandhi, cricket and the Indian Ocean trade. It was the beginning of a long working friendship. He was head of the School of Development Studies at the University of Kwazulu-Natal, had been an economic adviser to the ANC government and held diverse public appointments. He owned a bookshop – Ike's Books and Africana Collectables, a cultural landmark. Vishnu invited me to Durban, the largest Indian city outside India. They came there as indentured workers in the nineteenth century. The British installed a sugar industry in Natal after slave emancipation. I could connect with India there while remaining in Africa.[15]

It was risky to spend my sabbatical year with Sophie in Paris. I am a gambler, but also a Manchester man. I hedged my bets by organizing a trip to South Africa if she threw me out. She didn't, but I went to South Africa anyway. I spent a month in Durban and Cape Town, checking out African Studies there. I loved Durban with its mixed white, brown and black population. The Indian Ocean, port and beach appealed to me greatly. The atmosphere in Vishnu's school was very relaxed and amiable. The university was in a beautiful campus on a hill. I came back often.

Vishnu and I wrote a paper on Indian businessmen after apartheid; we cooperated in a book, *The Political Economy of Africa*, and later embarked on a history of South African capitalism seen in national and global perspective.[16] We took breakfast in a colonial hotel or sat on Ike's veranda sipping Sauvignon Blanc. We explored parallels in our personal histories.

In 2008 Vishnu told me he had seen a fantastic apartment on the beach. I decided to buy it. I retired as a British academic when the Lehmann crash occurred. Sterling lost 30 per cent in the first two weeks. Our flat in Paris is

---

14. Vishnu died unexpectedly in 2021. The quarter century that I have been visiting and living in Durban was only made possible by him.

15. See Forster, *Passage to India* in Chapter 4.

16. K. Hart and V. Padayachee, 'Indian Business in South Africa after Apartheid' (2000); Hart, Appendix 2010c, 2013b.

crowded and I wanted a place where I could express myself. The building was 1930s art deco, right on the beach. It had panoramic views, with a huge living room and eight smaller rooms. Cable television gave me English football and world cricket. I have become a connoisseur of local wines. The first night I slept there, I woke up to the sound of heavy traffic, but it was the ocean. I slept again soundly.

The first thing Durban meant to me was Gandhi. Of the two decades he spent in South Africa, one was in Durban. I have all of Gandhi's writings in my living room. His effort went into scaling up the self and scaling the world down.[17] He tried to unify the subcontinent against the British Empire's divisive politics. He needed to mobilize people. But they had to believe in their own ability to achieve great things.

In 2011 I set up the Human Economy Programme at Pretoria University with John Sharp.[18] Sophie switched her ethnographic interests to Durban. The three of us now spend the northern summer holidays there. Durban's winter (April to August) is delightful, 23–25 °C, blue skies and a breeze. *Lonely Planet* lists it in the world's top ten family beach resorts.

I like having more than one home. The main pairs have been Manchester and Cambridge, Ghana and Cambridge, Britain and North America. Jamaica showed me a plural strategy for living. Durban and Paris play a similar role now. I can't bear to be stuck in one place. The society that I belong to is global and I must have the freedom to move in it. If I don't like where I am, I complain and, if that doesn't work, I move on. This is why Cambridge University's institutional pluralism suited me so well.[19]

I was attracted to India as a teenager, but I ended up working in the North Atlantic. France and South Africa came into my life together. North America was the obvious alternative to Britain. My spirit is American. Americans have a music that is going somewhere. I am going somewhere and will not be stuck in one place. It's clear, if you compare Britain and the United States, which is the old society and which the new one. I found myself moving between them. Britain closed me down and America opened me up. England was more comfortable, however; people look after you there. American freedom soon became vulnerability. I felt exposed in that vast country. I wanted American possibility; but I was glad to return to where people knew and cared for me. I choose to live in two places with complementary features, each both positive and negative.

When I moved to France, I opened up South Africa as another new place. This pair repeats the previous model, but very differently. France is an old

---

17. See Chapter 3.

18. https://www.up.ac.za/human-economy-programme (accessed 13 September 2021).

19. See Chapter 10.

capitalist society, but it feels strange to me. I identify with black writers like Richard Wright and James Baldwin who took refuge from an unbearable society in Paris where they could write. But they were never integrated there, nor am I. South Africa is the old British Empire. It is only a century old. It has deep problems and people seem to be stuck in old patterns, as in Jamaica. South Africa is trapped in its past more than its neighbours whose history of racism was less strong.

Durban feels familiar to me. In Paris, I can't handle the practical nuances, but I can in South Africa. Whether dealing with Africans, Indians or British, I know how the infrastructure works. I get English soul food there – ginger beer and hot cross buns (all year round!). South Africa is reassuring and hopeful. It hasn't begun to explore its ultimate identity. It may crash, but the future will be better. England and France are depressing and depressive societies, wallowing in nostalgia for their imperial glory.

South Africa and France combine elements that were separate in Britain and the US. Paris is an old society but it's new to me, while South Africa is a new society, but it's old to me. In Paris I have the stability provided by my family. In South Africa I have British institutions. As an expatriate in both societies, I choose where and how to engage or detach myself. Together they provide a platform to enter the world more fully than before. They are linked by an eleven-hour flight in the same time zone. I can synthesize old and new, stability and movement, local and global. I renew myself while selecting from my past.

Durban society is the Zulus' home area; they dominate the city. South Africa is a magnet for Africans from everywhere and relations between Zulus and newcomers are tense. A third is Indian in origin. Natal is the first South African colony the British made. They pushed the Dutch out of the Cape and saw the possibility of transplanting Caribbean sugar production there. I find the triptych interesting: black, brown and white.

Durban's Indians mediate racial contrasts that are starker in Johannesburg and Cape Town. South Africa is the America of Africa. Each feels separate from the world. The two countries share a modern history of brutal capitalism and organized urban racism. It is different from slavery. America's blacks moved into the northern cities, while the Africans worked in the mines. Segregation followed – the colour line, Jim Crow, apartheid. Durban is South Africa's least polarized major city.

Durban is a port city too, the Marseille of Africa. A large harbour is around the corner. I watch the container ships coming and going. Port cities are always more mixed, open and dynamic. Paris is the main political centre, like London. I love Chicago because it is not Washington, DC. I like provincial industrial cities that do not live off taxes and rents from their subjects. I can see the horizon and an infinite expanse of sea and sky through eleven windows tight on the sea front. 'Horizon' is not a metaphor for me. Oceans open up the world from places that are often closed and inward-looking. I am at home and anchored there. I entertain my most ambitious and inclusive thoughts, stimulated by the ocean's restless expanse.

Ports generate red light districts. Behind me is a rather rundown area that once had more crime, drugs and prostitution than now. Since the container revolution the number of sailors coming to Durban has fallen dramatically. The strip clubs on Point Road (renamed Mahatma Gandhi Road!) have been reduced from nine to one. In front of me is a well-maintained international resort and at the back a neglected area for poor people. The first time I went to a supermarket there, I couldn't believe how cramped, noisy and vital it was, just like Nima.[20] All I saw were poor Africans, but the largest migrant groups were Congolese and Nigerians! Durban's beach front is a cross between Black-pool and Miami. It has many skyscraper hotels.

When I walk out at the back, I am revisiting my youth in Ghana's slums. The front evokes all the beaches I know from Santa Monica to Goa. A beautiful racecourse is nearby; it has the country's main race, the Durban July. I can pull together in Durban a patchwork from my life that combines its key parts. It takes the cubist vision I found in Jamaica to another level.[21]

In Durban I can watch English football all weekend. When I was a kid I could walk to United's and Lancashire's grounds in fifteen minutes. Manchester is the liberal, egalitarian, provincial city that formed me. Its industrial revolution changed the world. The cities I love, such as Chicago or Durban, have something of Manchester in them.

Paris is the opposite of Manchester, so I need to go somewhere else to tap into what Manchester means to me. That's Durban. Durban and the others are real cities with a sense of their own destiny. Vishnu belonged to a class that is almost medieval, a genuine bourgeoisie, a class of citizens who care for their city. This one knows its own power, does good works and builds museums. But it is also committed to fending off intrusive political power. National and city governments contest its power. So far it seems that the African politicians are winning.

A great city is in decline. Is it surprising that I feel at home there? The Manchester bourgeoisie was very strong in the nineteenth century. With the organized workers, they launched the free trade movement, liberal economics, the cooperative movement, anti-slavery and Chartism.[22] Then London pulled the plug. Manchester and Durban are inseparable in my imagination.

---

20. See Chapter 6.
21. See Chapter 9.
22. See Chapter 10.

Chicago is an industrial city, but it also organizes the agricultural commerce of the Great West.[23] The architecture is adventurous, beautiful and brave. A self-sufficient political class encouraged that. I love the sheer spirit of what they have made there.

My aim is to find the fullest self-expression and free association I can. This requires movement and combining activities in different places. It needs social structures conducive to it. Some places – several at once – support me in this goal more than others. We live in a world that is ever more interdependent and in great danger. We must all connect with this situation in shared ways. But the media fill us with the pap of national politicians and pretend that movements in stock prices are the best index of an economy's health. Rousseau knew that education in the Old Regime limited what individuals can become.[24] Colonial India did the same, as do France and South Africa now. What can we do?

This was the inspiration for the Pretoria Human Economy Programme.[25] We must win democracy from the expert classes. People often don't know much about what affects their lives most. We can't settle for less than making the world a better place, for our children's sake. But our dealings with the world must be grounded in what we do daily. It is no good believing in an ideology that has nothing to do with your actual life. That's symbolic politics. It is also the opposite of how Gandhi saw the world. I put on a course of improvised lectures in Pretoria on 'Africa in World History'.[26]

> What does world history look like from an African perspective? These lectures are not a survey, but each will examine one or more outstanding books addressing various aspects of this topic, arranged in historical sequence. Every book, many written by Africans and the African diaspora, has inspired me. This is lecturing for belief, not for knowledge. The lectures are a guide to reading and stimulus to personal research.

Watching Movies with My Daughters

When Louise was very young, she would visit me in America during the summer holidays. Every year there was a new blockbuster movie – Superman, Star Wars, Indiana Jones. She got to see them all before they appeared back

---

23. W. Cronon, *Nature's Metropolis* (1991).

24. See Chapter 15.

25. See Chapter 2.

26. https://soundcloud.com/soasradio/sets/africa-in-world-history-lectures-by-keith-hart (accessed 14 September 2021).

home in the autumn. There was a new generation of young Hollywood direc-
tors – Scorsese, Lucas, Spielberg, Coppola, Bogdanovic.[27] We made up plays
together starring her favourite soft-toy animal, Henri Hippeaux. I sent her
stories when we were apart. Most of them featured a young couple, Annie and
George. Each was set in a different time and place and hinged on a problem
that they solved with the help of non-human friends.[28] Later, when I returned
to England, Louise kept me in touch with 1980s pop music: Roxy Music,
Michael Jackson, Dire Straits, Eurythmics. After 2000 she worked for Sony
Pictures Entertainment in MGM's old Hollywood lot, where she played an
important part in the marketing and launch of Blu-ray.

Louise and I had to snatch our times together, but in Paris I have been
with Constance all the time she was growing up. When I first came to Paris,
I took advantage of the three hundred movies that were showing there every
week, sometimes taking in four a week. But family life soon took over and
we watched DVDs at home instead. An early favourite was (and still is) Walt
Disney's introduction to classical music, *Fantasia*. But our big breakthrough
came when Constance was 8 or 9. We saw all of Jane Austen's novels filmed
as television series and several of Elizabeth Gaskell's, including *Cranford* and
Wives and Daughters, about North Cheshire where my grandma's family came
from.[29] Constance was not up to reading nineteenth-century novels then, but
she loved these TV dramas. We would second-guess the plot: what would
happen to this woman? What will happen next? We didn't just consume the
movie, but thought about how the story was made.

In the last decade we have watched lots of movies together. Our favourite
director is Christopher Nolan, from the quirky *Memento* (2000) through
The Prestige (2006), the *Batman Trilogy* (2005–12), *Interstellar* (2014) and
Dunkirk (2017) to the disappointing *Tenet* (2020). But the winner by far is
Inception (2010), a complex fantasy about manipulating dreams. Hans Zim-
mer's music is a compelling feature of several. I hate movies being described
as a visual medium; they are a total medium, with music and story at least as
important as the cinematography. Constance and I share clips from YouTube
and, like her older sister before, she educates me in French pop music today.
I recall that when she was 6 or 7 we regularly watched a kids' talent show on
French TV called *Star Academy*. The performers were male and female, white
and black, singers and dancers, but they all shared a new hybrid pop music
combining French lyricism, hip hop and North African tonalities.

---

27. P. Biskind, *Easy Riders, Raging Bulls: How the Sex-Drugs-and Rock 'n' Roll Generation
Saved Hollywood* (1998).

28. For example, https://thememorybank.co.uk/other/stories-for-louise/ (accessed 14 September 2021).

29. See Chapter 4.

I am very lucky to have a Gen-Z daughter who is actively plugged into some of the most creative and progressive movements of our time. I am equally grateful for how Louise helped me through my dark middle years by plugging me into the contemporary music and movies of the 1970s and 1980s. Who says that children learn from their parents and not the other way round? I would have been lost without my daughters as companions and guides to new forms of shared life. As Jean Rouch showed us, cinema transforms us, allows us to grow.[30]

At Home in a New Quadrilateral

France and South Africa are now linked for me with Britain and Switzerland. The historical connections are more obscure than the quadrilateral formed by the Atlantic slave trade. My associations are now part-time, more specialized and globally distributed. Since leaving Cambridge, I have had three academic posts in Britain: a full-time research fellowship in rural development studies at Aberdeen; a half-time professorship in anthropology at Goldsmiths, London; and a 30 per cent centennial professorship in international development at the London School of Economics. Geneva has been a staple of our family life until now. After their parents' deaths, Sophie and her brothers decided to convert their family house into apartments.

This new quadrilateral embeds my personal network. Each place offers temporary anchorage for unprecedented global movement. My laptop is omnipresent,[31] my work station and constant companion on journeys. It provides continuity in movement (virtual social life). I believe that humanity's goal and destiny is to be at home in a world of movement.[32] The idea of a 'human economy' rests on this. The balance between home and away is never quite right – how could it be?

The disruptions of my middle years prepared me for this late flowering. I gained a lot more knowledge then, but could not produce it. My suffering made me humbler. When my mental illness cleared, I felt an urgent need to catch up for lost time. Life with Sophie has given me that chance. Since I moved to Paris, I now belong to one world community. This has made globetrotting easier and even functional. If this pattern were commonplace, we might become more conscious of people's humanity in other places. Money, markets, the internet and social media are not impediments to this. They enable it, if only we keep the image of human unity in mind.

---

30. See Chapter 10.
31. See Chapter 14.
32. See Chapter 13.

Chapter 12

HEALTH PROBLEMS

When I was nine months old, my mother noticed that I didn't see her when she approached from the right side. Today they test children's eyes at three months, and my condition is reversible then. Acute myopia involves the progressive transfer of muscular control from one eye to the other. For four years I shuffled my bottom on the Royal Eye Hospital's polished benches. Eventually the doctors concluded that they could do nothing for me. Dad refused to let this delay my training as a sportsman. From eighteen months he had me catching tennis balls in the back yard. Stereoscopic vision matters for close work, but not to assess the speed and direction of moving objects.

Since I wasn't interested in crafts and one eye was good enough for reading, playing and navigating, I forgot about it. When I took my driving test at 18, they only asked me to read a number plate at middle distance. They had machines to test eyesight in Ann Arbor, but I got through by twisting my head round. Driving in South Africa became so accident prone that I gave it up. Sophie took over.

At 30, I began to have second thoughts about smoking. It was dangerous, dirty and expensive. I loved smoking a cigarette with whiskey or leaning over a bridge at twilight. I often lit up when knocking at a strange door. After two years of dithering, I woke up one morning and knew that I would never smoke cigarettes again. I haven't. This was my first lesson in decision-making by the unconscious mind, ideal for choosing a life partner and, as I discovered at 50, for giving up cars. Again, the decision was both conscious and unconscious. Cars too are dirty, dangerous and expensive. I noticed that I was driving as fast as ever, but my reflexes were slowing down. But having a mechanized horse to take you directly from A to B is hard to give up.[1]

One day in Montreal I asked my friend if she wanted a coffee. She replied, 'No. I've had two already and with another I'd be as high as a kite.' 'What? You mean coffee is a stimulant?' I thought coffee was a soporific. Mum offered us kids a milky nightcap – Horlicks, Ovaltine, Bournvita or Camp coffee essence. This last was made from chicory. Even late at night, coffee makes no difference to me. When I am asked how I do it, I reply in an Eastwood drawl, 'My brain's so fast, coffee slows me down'. I stay off drugs other than booze because my brain is mind-bending enough already.

Concussions

I was concussed six times between the ages of 3 and 50. The MO differed: a metal dustbin lid in the forehead; a teenage bike crash in Manchester; falling on my head from railings in Cambridge; slipping on ice in the Midwest (twice); and being mugged in Cambridge. Only one of these was life-threatening. Concussion is a fear reaction. The brain shuts down when a blow threatens life. It records these events, so that each blow has a cumulative effect. Professionals exposed to major shocks, such as boxers and jump jockeys, in time suffer prolonged blackouts from even minor knocks. Something like that happened to me.

It was 1964, soon after the Easter holidays in Cambridge. I had been drinking with friends since 5.30. At 11 we went to an Indian restaurant. I was plastered. Soon after midnight I left the others mid-meal. The entrance to the college was closed; I had to climb over Chapel Court's twenty-foot railings. What happened next is a blur. I must have stood upright at the top and tipped forward onto the cobblestones below. Bikes in concrete blocks at the bottom broke my fall. I ended up wedged between two with my head on the ground and my legs in the air. Around 3 a.m. a porter heard me breathing in my blood and called for an ambulance. I had over twenty stitches on my head, with deep lacerations on my face. I woke up with the king of all hangovers.

I had to wear a cap made of bandages and was told to avoid mental work for three months. I didn't have to sit exams. My supervisor was from Sri Lanka – a replacement for Jack Goody who was in Ghana.[2] I told him that I couldn't read or use my brain. Years later, he said that, having heard tales about Cambridge student pranks, he wanted to yank the bandages off my

---

1. Only the privileged had a horse in medieval times; the rest walked. See Chapter 13.

2. Stanley Tambiah was one of my favourite Cambridge teachers. He ended up at Harvard.

head. College council knew that I could have been killed, so they changed the rules. Students could now come in through the porters' lodge after midnight. Many years later I relived that fateful scene. I stood with both feet on the railings, instead of putting one leg over. I looked up into a starry sky before tipping forward. One bike was completely wrecked.

I have been mugged once, never in Nima's badlands or when cruising the South Side ghetto at night. I told myself a story about this. In Jamaica, a student asked me why I felt it necessary to conduct a seminar like a street fight. My habit of projecting aggression came from my Old Trafford childhood, especially when I ran a gauntlet of mean streets between home and grammar school. Going out with the pickpockets in Accra taught me to walk as if I belonged to where I was. In the US I read about a survey of three thousand rapists and muggers in prison. They were given twenty photos of faces, half victims of rape and mugging and half who had avoided that experience. They picked out the first category with great accuracy. I thought I was protected by a mixture of evolved body language and *savoir faire*. Then it happened.

I was in Cambridge, walking past my college chapel at midnight. The streets were deserted. I was 50 years old. Two boys in their late teens walked towards me, loud and drunk. As they passed, one spoke to me and I ignored him. He yelled at me, turned round and came towards me while his mate stayed back; I noticed a beer bottle in his right hand. I slagged him off dismissively – wrong! He stepped up and while I watched his bottle, he caught me on the chin with a left uppercut and then kicked me in the stomach on the way down, like an under-18 kickbox champion. His fury was incandescent and I was his last chance to express it. If I had been a lamp post, he would have done the same. I passed out briefly; his friend dragged him away and apologized. I was depressed for some time afterwards – I had joined the old ladies as a suitable victim. But it never happened again.

Tropical Diseases

In Ghana, I got cocky and sometimes relaxed hygiene. Early on, I got drunk on crude gin and felt really ill afterwards. I had hepatitis B and spent two weeks in the university hospital. Then I was snatched soon after the coup.[3] I had a bayonet stuck in my lower leg and the soldiers amused themselves by tramping on our hands with their boots; I still bear the scars of both. I had the odd bout of malaria. Who doesn't? But the worst came near the end. I was staying in a government compound up north and my neighbour was a Polish doctor. He asked me if I was jaundiced – my eyes were yellow. He then asked

---

3. See Chapter 6.

if I had diarrhoea: about once a week, explicable by what I had eaten. He sent me for tests and I had amoebic dysentery. The amoebae spend nine months crawling from the colon to the liver, where they kill you. They were almost there. My time in hospital was incredibly painful, as the antidote (emetin) slugged it out with the amoebae. The drug won.

Childbirth Crisis in Manchester (but Not in Paris)

Nicky's pregnancy was straightforward. We supported the Natural Childbirth Trust's methods, but signed up at a university hospital. She had an epidural anaesthetic. We sat in the waiting room, a monitor registering the foetal heartbeat for company. The machine's pen started drawing jagged peaks and troughs. The baby was in distress. Nicky needed a caesarean section.

Mother and child were healthy. Twenty years of looking after my daughter stretched ahead. Parenthood is not always the fastest way of growing up, but it was for me. Three days later, when I reached their room, it was being fumigated. Nicky was in the main infirmary next door with a virulent genital infection. Louise was in the special care baby unit, having probably been infected while breastfeeding. I raced next door. Nicky's temperature was 116 °F (47 °C) and her pulse was 160. If the drip didn't bring these down in thirty minutes, she would die. The drip worked.

I now checked out Louise. She was squalling in a plastic box. A doctor updated me. The chance of her being infected was high; she would probably succumb to meningitis and die. They recommended a lumbar puncture for a more accurate diagnosis. This procedure was painful and risky. The decision was mine. I was in shock. The decision was impossible. I tried to reason it out: Louise could be ill or not and if she was, she would likely die. The lumbar puncture could do her harm and would be unnecessary if she wasn't infected. I said no. After I left her, I sat down on the back stairs and sobbed. It had been an hour from first seeing that room. I could hardly think, never mind feel. I crawled home. Louise was soon fit to leave hospital. Nicky's infection was from a hospital superbug combining streptococcus, staphylococcus and something unknown. She would be on penicillin for six weeks. No question of her seeing the baby. I was working and her mother was staying with us. I visited Nicky twice a day. I needed to sleep. I developed a routine. If Louise slept in the afternoon, we kept her awake in the evening. I organized a bedtime ritual: at 10 p.m. she had a bath and a full bottle feed. When she lay down, I ignored her crying unless it persisted. Something similar (without the bath) occurred when she woke up in the small hours. After five or six weeks, she was sleeping from 10 p.m. to 7 a.m. without a nocturnal feed.

Nicky was taken off penicillin. The bug had not been killed. The fever started again and she went through the whole cycle again. Now she took no interest in recovery and became morose and passive. She stopped asking about Louise. Three months after admission, she returned home 'cured' and depressed. She was very happy to be with her baby, but the depression persisted. We found some therapy by writing an article together.[4] Nicky later became a specialist in the sociology of health.

Twenty-eight years later, my second daughter was born in Paris. A scan told us that she was a *bébé dodu* ('chubby baby'), which I thought meant a boy. Sophie went into labour on 17 October, the same as Louise's birthday. I was 59 years old. The delivery proper began around midday. Then panic stations broke out. The baby was caught in the cord and could not descend. There had to be a caesarean section. It was like *Groundhog Day* – I burst into tears. Constance was born at 3 p.m. A midwife asked, 'Would you like to see the baby?' I would. We went to a trolley on wheels with a squalling infant inside. 'You don't know the baby's sex?' She opened the lid and whipped off the nappy. I had another girl, which suited me. Gender surfaced again when I filled in the forms. Sex had already been marked with a circle around female, with male heavily deleted!

Constance is an eighteenth-century French Protestant name, and English too. It connotes persistence and loyalty in both languages, but in French also determination to achieve one's goals. In the evening I found mother and baby sitting up in bed together. The scene is burnt into my brain. This time there was no awful sequel. Why would twins be born twenty-eight years apart? So that one could take charge of the other? In my projected magical-realist novel, following Rousseau, the younger twin would guide the older. The 'magical twins' label stuck.

I considered myself an expert on sleep. Babies sleep because they are exhausted. But they resist sleep because it feels like death and they are programmed to avoid that. They must be persuaded that when they let go, they will return to life. I was Hades, lord of the underworld and guarantor of life's renewal. I was there when Constance went to sleep and when she woke. It worked.

I worried about my age. How old would Constance be when I died? I wouldn't see her marriage or children. I developed a Zen approach. She should believe I was there when I wasn't. Beethoven's last piano sonata ends with lengthening spaces between the notes. Silence at the end feels like a continuation of the music. Constance's speed of development made life a blur and all this was redundant. I soon forgot my age, while trying to keep pace with her urgent desire to grow up. She and her sister are excellent friends.

---

4. 'Authority and Conflict in Relations between Hospital Doctors and Their Patients'.

Birthday Surprise in Cambridge

I was at home alone for my forty-ninth birthday. I had Indian food on Friday night and woke up with a stomach ache. The problem persisted. A GP told me to starve it by drinking only water. That took me through Saturday, but the pain was a lot worse. By Sunday morning I was doubled up on the floor. I called the emergency health services and was taken by ambulance to hospital. A young Italian doctor was very kind. 'Mr Hart, we are going to treat you as a differentiated patient.' 'What's that?' 'I am going to tell you the truth. There is something terrible down there, it is so inflamed. It could be your colon, pancreas, appendix or anything. Afterwards you may wake up with a colostomy bag.' He told me later it had been my appendix. I had about twenty minutes to live when he got to it. He couldn't understand how I had tolerated the pain for so long.

The next morning, I pushed my mobile drip feed to the bathroom. The sun was shining through the windows. I turned on a tap and let it splash over my hand. The water sparkled in the sunlight. Life was renewed. I liked watching the nurses make the beds together – their sturdy and graceful teamwork when flipping the sheets. They embodied the spirit of the NHS,[5] unlike the doctors – pompous bosses with their sycophants. It was a joy to lie there, propped up and taking it all in. Back home, I had to sit still for three months while I healed. I discovered that peritonitis is the fourth-largest cause of death among single men in their forties. They live alone and figure out too late how life-threatening a stomach ache can be.

Disaster at Yale

It was my third year at Yale, 1978. I had spent a summer with Nicky and Louise in our new Essex home. I hoped to repair the marriage, but I couldn't. Louise was 3 years old. The divorce was amicable. But I didn't have much interest in the outcome beyond securing our daughter's interests. Until then my will and ambition had never been seriously checked. I thought I could resolve any strains caused by the transatlantic move. The possibility that I had destroyed my family for career reasons was unthinkable. It tore me apart. I swallowed my grief; and that was my downfall.

Signs of breakdown multiplied. My apartment was a mess, my routines dissolved. One day I drove into the countryside for dinner with a friend. I followed the colours of the cars. Red, blue, white and black meant turn right or left, overtake or slow down. This brought me to a posh rural suburb. I was

---

5. National Health Service.

cruising past some houses with undivided front lawns. A piercing scream brought me to a jarring halt. A small child was with a large German shepherd. This was some latter-day Labours of Hercules. I had to take a white plastic baseball from under the dog's gaze. The kid disappeared indoors. The dog didn't move. I turned the ball in my hands, looking across a valley with a red flashing light opposite. Venus was alone in the twilight sky. I got it now. I was to make contact with aliens.

I came to a tavern, parked and stood by the pond. I looked for meaning in ducks' muddy imprints. I hallucinated a spaceship overhead and entered the pub. I sat down with three young women. I asked them if Nicky and Louise were coming. They complained to the barman who summoned the police. Two policemen took me to the men's room. They started beating me up. Maybe this thing was not good for me. I decided to fall on the floor. If it hurt, get out; if it didn't, go ahead. The space was narrow and one of them caught me. Good. Before long an ambulance took me to Yale New Haven hospital.

They pushed my wheelchair through a subway. It felt like the underworld. I was entering Dante's Inferno; but that wasn't bad. Human civilization had gone through innumerable cycles of boom and bust. These were supervised by guiding agencies – gods, aliens, whoever. From time to time they removed promising individuals and stored them underground. These would restart the process after Armageddon. Why had I been chosen and for what? I had two options. I could excavate a prehistoric fish from the Connecticut River. Humans come from fish, not apes. Or I would discover a new hormone in the liver. I saw a photo of my fish skeleton in a newspaper. How had I been stupid enough to wreck my marriage and lose my daughter? The sacrifice had to be worth it. Hence aliens, Dante, etc., the victory of abstraction over social reality.

They doped and 'sectioned' me for three weeks. One day I watched TV while moving my head like the infinity sign (∞). Chugging around the universe in boxes was absurd. We think we are alone because we are too primitive to communicate with more developed species. The ants think they are alone. When we get our act together as a species, we will take our planet to wherever we want – with help from the others.

When Tom Petty wrote: 'I'm learning to fly, but I ain't got wings / Coming down is the hardest thing', he must have been somewhere like me, or he was just referring to recreational drugs.[6] My variety of psychosis is attractive at first. The mind finds its own way out of an impossible situation. Then doubts creep in. What if this isn't a new life, but death, the final rupture with humanity? I began making empirical tests. I would slap my thigh. I felt the slap! A more elaborate feedback loop was to call someone and they answered; it was them. Bingo! The line between madness and reason was blurred and painful.

---

6. See the Preface.

One day I remembered the policemen: I would fall down and if it hurt, I was in the wrong place. I was in a wide corridor with a marble floor and no-one near. The shock was unbearable. I kept on screaming until they jabbed me. When I woke up, I was over the madness. They let me out a few days later.

I thought this episode was one of a kind and went back to work. The mechanics of divorce ground away. I did some self-harming things like renouncing my share of the conjugal property and resigning from Yale. I had second thoughts about my job, but the administration would not rescind my resignation. The shock triggered another breakdown. I was now frightened for my life. Two breakdowns in under a year suggested chronic insanity. I might never work again.

A lawyer from the American Civil Liberties Union (ACLU) contacted me. He could sue Yale for damages. I had been sick for a while. They had neglected their duty of care for me. If I sat on a beach in the Bahamas for a year or two, I would be a rich man. His special interest, however, was tenure law. Is tenure a medieval or modern contract? In one, a party gives and the other renounces unilaterally. In the other, both parties sign on entry and exit. I did not make a formal response when offered a job and they had not given me a written reply now. I didn't want to be a cause célèbre. I could stay until the end of the year with no obligation to teach. Then Skip Rappaport offered me a year at Michigan. I took this option, not the Bahamas.

The Long Haul Back

I had more manic episodes before leaving North America, one each in Ann Arbor and Chicago. They continued in Cambridge. The Jamaica episode ended unusually well for me, and in Paris I had a minor breakdown which I slept off in two days. Soon after returning to Cambridge, I had an interview that convinced me I was suffering from a long-term disease, but might, if lucky, recover in my fifties. I came out of the illness roughly on schedule. Not long afterwards I left for Paris.

The years 1983–86 were the worst in my life. Apart from breakdowns, daily life was a struggle, with peace unattainable. I could write for barely half an hour. I worried that my mental condition would prevent me from publishing in my peak middle years. I was lonely and angry. Louise brought love into my life. Bipolar types often question the objectivity of their condition and blame their medicine for feeling out of sorts. I was no exception. But the head of Cambridge psychiatric services, a Peruvian professor of psychiatry called German Berrios, gave me a two-hour interview that changed everything.

He set out to establish the reality of my 'disease'. My only hope was to take medicine seriously. I came of age in the 1960s, when the idea that mental illness had social, not medical causes was commonplace. R.D. Laing pushed this line in several books.[7] While pressing me to take my meds, Prof. Berrios also gave me hope of eventually escaping from my condition. His rhetorical method was epidemiology. Bipolar individuals of my type became ill in their late teens or mid-thirties. In the first case, there was no redemption; but in the second, one could regain sanity in one's fifties. Lithium had been around since 1960 and they didn't know how it affected this scenario. But psychosis usually became more frequent and slighter with age. The victim lives out his years in an eccentric buzz.

My specific form of bipolarity erupted when I was 35. Berrios said it was quite common in Britain and rare in the US. The British region with the highest incidence was the north-west. The typical body type was 'pyknic' – short and stocky with strong legs for climbing mountains. He asked about bipolarity and psoriasis in my family. I ticked every box he listed. I now knew that I had an identifiable disease. I would take my pills and hope to get over it in time.

I still needed medical help. For ten years it was a struggle to get by. I would get wound up and tranquillizers left me in a stupor the next morning. I had a wonderful GP in Roger Irons (brother of the famous actor); and I found a therapist who saved my life. Sedwell Diggle was a Freudian and Jungian psychotherapist. I didn't want psychoanalysis since it made me sad. I needed help to get through the days, which Sedwell provided. We discussed taking a bath with sweet-smelling oils rather than watching TV late at night. Her calm wisdom coped with my mood swings and tearful confessions. It was a privilege to talk to her once a week for eight years.[8]

I couldn't write much and long-distance travel was out – I risked forgetting my lithium. I had five more breakdowns in Cambridge. The restlessness vanished when I passed 50. My colleagues reacted to these episodes with kindness. But the run-up to mania was always self-destructive. Keeping a professional career through ten manic episodes could be a record. Because I couldn't write at any length, I made myself a first-class teacher. I hoped that the students would come to my rescue if I faced the sack.

Health Crisis in Paris

There were signs of the impending disaster from June 2016. Things came to a head in September. After hospital I could not leave Paris. In December I found out what had happened and why. Since Yale, I have suffered from a skin disease, psoriasis. In spring my back was covered with pink, scaly

7. R.D. Laing, *The Divided Self* (1960); *Sanity, Madness and the Family* (1964).

8. Sedwell married the Cambridge University orator, a classicist contemporary of mine from near Manchester; she died recently.

patches. My GP and I both knew the relationship between psoriasis and lithium. I began ultra-violet light treatment. A psychiatrist who specialized in medication said, 'You have taken lithium for forty years and have been mentally stable for twenty. Why tinker with the lithium? Psoriasis may be the cross you have to bear.' My hands began to shake a little, and this too could be due to lithium; but we left it at that.

In June I went to a conference in Rio de Janeiro. I behaved oddly there. I spent July with Sophie and Constance in our Durban beach apartment. I fell over in the street four times, landing on my face and once breaking my glasses. My GP now changed her diagnosis after an anomaly appeared in my prostate. I had had prostate cancer since 2010. It turned aggressive in 2013 and I opted for radiotherapy. I had a new job at LSE then. I was easily tired. The cancer cleared. Now the cancer might have revived with a more dangerous diagnosis. The shakes became much worse.

Things started speeding up when we returned to Paris. Blood tests showed low levels of lithium. Maybe I had missed my meds while travelling. My kidneys were not doing well. I made involuntary jerking movements. I couldn't eat or use my laptop. I kept spilling my coffee. Memory lapses were more frequent. I still fell over, this time in our home. Once I fell over and hit some furniture; I heard a roaring sound in my head. A scan detected an ischemia (stroke). It could be new or old, so I should book an MRI appointment. Another specialist recommended kidney and brain scans. An old neurologist venerated by my GP ordered more scans.

I lost the plot around then. I left my laptop in the street. I bought a replacement and installed a French keyboard by mistake. I met Louise in London and bought another laptop which I screwed up. I was a happy psychotic before. Now I became paranoid. I thought Sophie and her brother wanted me locked up to gain legal control of my assets. Constance seemed angry with me. I invented a long-lost twin sister who was on my side. Sophie and I saw my psychiatrist; he told me to pull myself together. He still thought a low lithium level was my problem, but didn't order new blood samples.

One day I took a tourist bus ride around Paris. I ended up in a bar drinking beer and watching football on TV. It was now dark. I could only vaguely tell Sophie and Louise where I was. I then found my way home somehow. We went straight to Emergency at Lariboisière. Now Paris's leading hospital, in the eighteenth century they called it 'the Versailles of the poor'. I don't remember what happened next. The doctors discovered very high lithium levels and cleaned me out with two rounds of dialysis. They halved my lithium dosage. I stayed in the emergency ward for a week and then for two more weeks in a general ward. My memory was awful. Parkinson's became the main focus of my treatment.

I had been diagnosed with prostate cancer, a stroke, kidney failure, Parkinson's and neurological dysfunction, not to mention psoriasis, mental breakdown and lithium poisoning. I had been treated by three hospitals, my GP, a psychiatrist, neurologist, ophthalmologist, nephrologist, cardiologist and a dermatology clinic. My folk theory of disease is Protestant. Germs are a metaphor for xenophobia. What matters is the brain's unconscious ability to mobilize the immune system. Now it seemed that I was overwhelmed by life-threatening diseases. This was system breakdown. My immune system, not to mention my confidence and will to live, collapsed. I had no resistance to whatever came next. I didn't expect to see Christmas.

After Lariboisière, lower lithium levels instantly solved the psoriasis and shakes. A nurse saw me daily. I was decrepit. My cardiologist did extensive tests and declared me very robust. Falling over was because the wrong hypertension pill caused occasional low blood pressure. I stopped falling over. Lariboisière now handled my neurological problems; Bichat hospital had the best kidneys unit. I had scans under huge machines. In mid-November I saw the neurologist in charge of my case. She was a specialist in senile Parkinson's, from the South of France. When I opened the door, she yelled, 'I can tell you, you don't have Parkinson's. It's all the lithium.' 'Are you sure?' 'Nothing is certain in medicine, but yes, I am sure.' My scans had shown nothing untoward, except for a small patch in my brain. I should get an MRI for that. I had never before met a medic who was so direct and positive. I walked out of her office on air. Weeks later, I had the MRI. The technician said, 'I can tell you that it is not new'. The 'stroke' was old, unknown to me.

I went for my all-day kidneys check-up. There were many blood and urine samples and an MRI for dessert. A doctor gave me an update. My kidneys had failed. Next time the *chef* would give me the bad news. What was my attitude to *invasive* treatment? 'Invasive' means anything that enters the body, dialysis and surgery. I thought of advertising for a transplant on Facebook. The numbers for my kidneys improved. Another working over the following year cleared me.

I only got the story of my health crisis in December. A non-malignant ball had grown in my prostate. It shut down my kidneys, leaving lithium to run amok in my brain and body. All the life-threatening diseases were effects of temporary and reversible lithium poisoning. By New Year, I believed I had a future again. But the idea that my time is up still lingers. Every memory lapse, hand tremor and clumsy movement triggers my sense of mortality. I was afraid that I wouldn't finish this book.

On Ageing

I worried about having a child at nearly 60. Constance's need to grow up fast put paid to those fears. She is a gifted student whose public high school (*lycée*) was the top-ranked in France. She specialized in languages and literature and aims for a career in art and design. She received a *mention très bien* in her Bac. I have a trust fund for her higher education. In 2021 she entered a three-year industrial design course at La Cambre School for the Visual Arts in Brussels. Both my daughters and Sophie are heiresses without me. Although I spend my savings liberally, my reserves have remained roughly the same in the last decade. I learn more about the world economy from playing the markets than from studying. My 2016 health crisis was also economic. I could not travel and all my income came[9] from outside France. I have given up most of my former globetrotting. I decided to write books that sell at home.

I have become more aware of my age than before – whether real or imagined, I don't know. I was hit by a car in Durban while crossing the road and that didn't help. I feel more vulnerable now. As long as I could travel freely, it didn't matter that my social life in Paris is weak. For the first time, I conform to the social stereotype of old people – isolated, unwanted and irrelevant. My laptop is a lifesaver. Giving up the nomadic life strengthens my commitment to my Paris family. I will spend more time on Durban beach.

My recovery seemed to be sudden and total – or nearly so. I came racing out of the blocks in 2017, boosted by the Lazarus effect and six months of not working. I almost finished a book on Africa. But I couldn't sell it as a trade book to publishers in London and New York. For them, my basic message (Africa is going up, Europe going down) was incomprehensible. I have three books I want to write in retirement: this one, the Africa and Europe book and *Futures: Who Killed Son Quick?* – a science fiction murder mystery that, like *Don Quixote*, is a pastiche of Western fiction.[10] I thought I had fully recovered, but I found that my publications before 2016 were usually better written, livelier than what I was capable of now. In January 2020, I suddenly felt myself again – more confident and well. My writing and memory operated again like before – sharper, faster, with a sense of totality and more unexpected connections. The synapses have been restored and seem to be working again. I was told that I must have suffered some brain damage from the lithium poisoning. Old age isn't a one-way street to the grave after all.

---

9. *Africa and Europe, 1800–2100: A History of the Future.*
10. See the Afterword.

Part III

WORLD

In 1800 the world's population was around one billion and under 3 per cent lived in cities. Animals and plants supplied the energy human beings produced and consumed. Now world population is headed for 8 billion; but for the first time in two centuries, the maximum total is being revised downwards. Half of us live in cities and that proportion is sure to grow. Most energy production and consumption now comes from inanimate sources. Machines convert these fossil fuels. Since 1800, the human population has grown on average at 1.5 per cent a year, cities at 2 per cent and energy production 3 per cent. As a result, many people live longer, work less and spend more than before. But the distribution of this extra energy is highly unequal. A third of humanity works in the fields with their hands. Americans consume four hundred times more energy per head than Ugandans.

This dash from the village to the city is driven by an engine of economic growth and inequality known as 'capitalism'. But several social forms have organized the process. They include empires, nation states, cities, business corporations, regional trade federations, international organizations, financial markets and telecommunications networks. Local self-organization is usually strong. But the need for global coordination is urgent. Progressives usually prefer self-organized groups and networks to large bureaucracies. Yet no society this century could dispense with the social forms that brought us to where we are now. Some states, cities and corporations must support citizens' efforts to build a more democratic world society.

Chapter 13

MOVEMENT AND THE GLOBALIZATION OF APARTHEID

Movement is:

The act of moving
changing places
tendency or trend
material flux or flow
political effort to a common goal
section of a musical composition
suggested motion of a design
evacuation of the bowels
military manoeuvre
mechanism of a watch
poetic rhythm or structure
emotion, a feeling of excitement
process, a series of actions with a result

The state is a state,
a fixed idea;
movement is life.

THE GREATEST POSSIBLE COMMERCE BETWEEN THE PEOPLES
OF THE WORLD THE LEAST POSSIBLE COMMERCE BETWEEN
THE GOVERNMENTS OF THE WORLD
—Richard Cobden, Frieze of the main auditorium,
Free Trade Hall, Manchester, 1856

I would tell my first-year students that animals and plants differ by moving or staying put. Animals go to where the food is, but plants expect it to come to them. For ten thousand years, societies were built on cultivating plants and raising herds nearby. Before that, human beings and their hominid ancestors moved around on foot to find their food. They knew no boundaries on earth. The Industrial Revolution began to pull people into cities, using machines for transport. But organized force was needed to control them there. Our lives today are an unstable compromise between agriculture and industry, fixture and mobility.

In David Lean's movie *Lawrence of Arabia* (1962), our hero crosses the desert with a guide to meet the Arab revolt. They stop at a well for water. The guide, whose eyesight is sharper, picks up a dark spot on the horizon. As it gets nearer, he realizes what it is, dashes for his camel and is shot dead at long range. The newcomer wears all black, with a bandolier draped over his chest and a rifle in the crook of his elbow. Lawrence berates him. How will the Arabs unite against the Turks while you indulge these barbaric habits? The reply: 'He knew it was our well'. Even desert nomads need fixed points. I search for my own combination of stability and movement; but by modern standards I am a nomad.

Watching Cricket in Lancashire

In the 1990s, I watched a Lancashire League cricket match in Rawtenstall. League cricket began a century ago with a dozen mill towns in east Lancashire. The mainstream game was concentrated in southern England. Posh amateurs were in charge there and some games took days to complete. League games lasted a day. Limited overs cricket is now dominant everywhere. Each side hired an international professional. C.L.R. James came to Nelson where the professional was Learie Constantine, the Caribbean's best cricketer.[1] A local baker paid for his trips to Paris to research *The Black Jacobins*. The spirit of these working-class communities was palpable.

The cricket that day was slow. I noticed there were no South Asians in the crowd nor players of colour in the home side. But the streets and parks were full of South Asian kids playing cricket. Racism in some Lancashire towns was beginning to attract attention. Whereas Manchester bounded back from its post-war economic defeat in the 1980s and 1990s, Lancashire's mill towns found little to replace textile production. The working-class people in north-east Lancashire once celebrated their mixed origin, coming originally from Ireland, west Scotland and North Wales. They bred dogs for hunting, but

---

1. See Chapter 3.

had no time for pedigrees. Like dogs, so their owners: 'we are mongrel folk', they said. The Brexit referendum was fuelled by anti-immigration feeling and resentment of economic decline; it was followed by significant right-wing gains in the 2019 national election. Blaming foreigners included leaving Europe. A region that had been a bastion of social citizenship a century earlier was now consumed with neoliberalism's identity politics.[2]

Later, I visited a smaller town to watch a game. There were seven South Asians in the home team. Masood and Mushtaq were cavalier opening batsmen from Pakistan. The mixed crowd adored 'Mas and Mush'. Why the difference? I discovered that in Rawtenstall public housing was segregated between white and coloured. Some regions and countries are often lumped together as hotbeds of anti-immigration hysteria. Local patterns are more variable. How general is the migration 'crisis' and what are its causes? How are movement and inequality related? World society today is organized by segregation in many forms. I call this 'the globalization of apartheid'.

Movement Subverts Unequal Society

Inequality is intrinsic to the modern economy. Rich and poor are kept apart in areas whose amenities differ greatly. Movement cannot be prevented between them. The rich need the poor to perform tasks for them on the spot. There are two methods for restricting movement: formal procedures (governments and laws) and informal prejudice (culture). Systems of classification perform this task. Racism is still the most important means of inclusion and exclusion in our world. We live in 'free' democracies whose principles are presumptively universal. Yet we grant some inferior rights. Functional economic inequalities would otherwise be undermined. Doublethink lies at the heart of the nation state.

The neoliberals' first aim was to dismantle the welfare states erected after 1945. They put downward pressure on wages and home unions by threatening to export capital to cheaper countries or to import cheap labour. Job insecurity and rising levels of poverty at home generated racist xenophobia. After 11 September 2001 the 'war on terror' curbed international movement, imposing various restrictions on passage through transport terminals. Immanuel Kant argued for the 'cosmopolitan right' of free movement everywhere around 1800.[3] Our world is the opposite of that. But crisis will eventually force world society to be reorganized.

---

2. See Chapter 17.
3. I. Kant, *Perpetual Peace: A Philosophical Sketch* (1795). See Chapter 2.

Movement requires some things to stay where they are. We build up durable attachments to particular places. These are hard to combine with movement across distance. Telecommunications can substitute for real movement and mitigate this contradiction. The digital revolution brings the world closer. It makes society at a distance possible without disturbing our commitment to particular places.[4] This revolution is comparable to the invention of agriculture ten thousand years ago. We must try to understand how they are related. Commerce (markets and money) and cultural exchange (language) are converging in the internet. Machines could promote human freedom while helping us to feel more at home in the world.

A new free trade campaign would aim to dismantle entrenched privilege. It would insist on movement as a human right. Then the rich would have to engage with the world outside their fortified enclaves. The world belongs to us all and we should be able to move in it as we wish. Global capital will only be checked when most people are free to move. The world is once more embracing national and regional trade protection. Transnational corporations and their home countries will resist this. Wars have begun for less.

Apartheid Is a Universal Social Principle

Maynard Keynes proposed a solution to the poverty and unemployment caused by the Great Depression: to raise the purchasing power of the masses.[5] The rich countries today are also cast adrift in a sea of human misery. Karl Marx claimed that capitalist markets could not organize machine production for the benefit of society.[6] Human development is held back today by a world of nation states. These block the emergence of new forms of economic life better suited to humanity's needs.

In *Annie Hall*,[7] Woody Allen says he doesn't feel like eating tonight because of the starving millions in the Third World. The audience laughs, uneasily. The gesture rings false: why tonight and not every night? How do people live with economic inequality? They don't, not if they can help it. We like to think of ourselves as good (Kant). This involves being compassionate towards others' suffering. We should not be held responsible for that suffering. Better explain it away as having some other cause. Maybe they deserve to suffer or are pretending to be poor. Better not to think about them at all. In the last resort, we define them as less human than ourselves.

---

4. See Chapter 14.

5. J.M. Keynes, *The General Theory of Employment, Interest and Money* (1936).

6. See Chapter 3.

7. Woody Allen (1977).

Distance – physical, social, emotional – moderates the conflict between compassion and inequality. We each engage in many acts distancing ourselves from the suffering of others.[8] But institutions perform this task more efficiently. An institution is a place to stand against the movement, flux and process of life. Institutions and agriculture go together. The main conflict today is between fixing society in the ground and reinventing it on the move. Keeping society unequal depends on controlling the movement of people. The poor should keep their proper distance. They should not invade protected zones of privilege. Better by far that they should know their place and stay there.

Formal organization (law enforcement) and informal custom (culture) do this job. Both separate and divide people in the interest of maintaining rule by the privileged. Classifying people is as old as language and society. It defines solidarity within and between groups. But labelling also weakens their combination on a wider scale. Modern ruling elites pigeonhole the masses in systems of classification. Academic and bureaucratic intellectuals devise and maintain these categories. Social science depends on this.

An important class of categories rests on visual signs, characteristics like skin colour and dress. Speech also sometimes indicates social identity. Modern states prefer identity cards with a photograph. They are now being replaced by facial and voice recognition. These sign systems stand for personal character – trustworthiness, ability and much besides. Personal destinies are decided on this arbitrary basis. People are included and excluded from society's benefits. Inequality is made legitimate and policed. The world is divided into segmented hierarchies of 'us' and 'them'. Monstrous crimes against humanity are committed.

In 1948 South Africa's National Party introduced a regime of 'separate development'.[9] Despite their close integration in the economy, the 'races' were segregated even more than before. The government allocated to 'blacks' rural homelands according to their 'tribal' origin. Unlike the whites, they needed a pass to live in cities. White, black, Indian and Coloured areas were separate and unequally endowed with resources. This required the use of force. Collaborators played a part. Internal resistance built up and the world expressed outrage through a boycott. Nelson Mandela's release in 1990 signalled a retreat from apartheid. African majority rule followed. But apartheid can't be abolished by the stroke of a pen.

The South African experiment was ugly, but it was not the most inhumane regime of the last century. Stalin and Hitler did much worse. While the ANC was being elected, a million people were killed in Rwanda. Bosnia showed that genocide was alive in Europe. Yet the Afrikaners were the main target

---

8. N. Geras, *The Contract of Human Indifference* (1998).

9. Hart, Appendix 2014e (with John Sharp and Vito Laterza).

for international opprobrium. What they did was obnoxious, but not exceptional. Their main crime was to be explicit, even boastful about their methods. Something similar operates everywhere, but is not publicly celebrated. The recent rise of authoritarian nationalists threatens to make xenophobia normal again; but not yet.

South Africa became an external symbol of a universal practice. Many around the world were already feeling uneasy about their own systems for managing inequality. It offered a limited target away from home. Rejecting apartheid was preferable to introspection. Opposing evil elsewhere displaces our ambivalence about inequality at home. Mandela became a universal hero. Meanwhile, so-called nations link cultural difference to birth and refuse citizens' rights to outsiders. National consciousness justifies unfair treatment of non-citizens. Most people are blind to humanity's common interests.

Apart from 'natural' signs, inferiors are also identified by ethnicity, religion and culture. But economic dualism comes from having to separate peoples whose life chances are grotesquely unequal. Friedrich Engels noticed this in Manchester during the Industrial Revolution's early stages.[10] Rich and poor lived together in medieval cities. Here, the rich lived in the suburbs and worked in the city centre. They rode to and from their businesses along wide avenues. A facade of shops concealed terrible housing conditions behind. Today, Johannesburg's rich white northern suburbs are protected by private security firms. Poor blacks crowd into monochrome townships nearby. The apartheid principle organizes local systems of discrimination everywhere. Israel, formed in the aftermath of a terrible racial attack, now applies South Africa's model to the Palestinians. After 11 September 2001, states everywhere followed the Americans' lead in instituting much closer controls over the movement of people at airports. That is what states do, given the opportunity.

Uneven Development

After 1945, 'development' referred to postcolonial relations between rich and poor countries. At first there was a semi-serious attempt to help the latter develop. Since 1980, development aid has been a sticking plaster for the victims of a stagnant world economy. It is also a self-serving tool of mercantilism. The peoples of rich and poor countries have long moved between them. Where does 'the immigration problem' come from? The West is losing the world economy it created. Impoverishment is intrinsic to an unequal world economy. Europe's 'refugee crisis' is caused by African poverty, Middle Eastern wars and the Soviet bloc's collapse. Xenophobic nationalism grows rapidly

---

10. F. Engels, *Working Class* (1845).

there. Africans drown in makeshift boats while crossing the Mediterranean. Donald Trump stirs up race divisions in the US.

The decades before the First World War saw mass migration of 50 million Europeans to temperate lands of new settlement. The same number of Asian 'coolies' moved to tropical colonies. Around 1900, capital unified the world economy as a racial hierarchy.[11] Machine industry encouraged a high-wage economy insulated from cheap colonial labour. Today the cheapest agricultural products come from Brazil, manufactures from China, information services from India, white migrant labour from Eastern Europe. Western workers face increased competition at home and abroad. Global capital now diffuses to new areas, especially to Asia. Separation of high- and low-wage labour streams has been a universal principle for a century. Treating apartheid as a South African problem obscures this.

Movement as a Human Right

How can anyone feel at home in the world today? What patterns of stability and movement are emerging now? How do sedentary and nomadic lifestyles alter the lives of individuals and families? In order to move we must hold some aspects of our lives constant. We can't fly without airports or take trains without stations.[12] New programmes need stability as much as movement. This dialectic goes to the root of personal identity today. Communications offer new means for resolving old contradictions.

The digital revolution allows us to join society at a distance without disturbing commitment to particular places. The middle-class revolution that launched modernity has stalled, even regressed. First it made an alliance with landed power. Then it adopted the state form of rule traditional for agrarian civilizations. No-one in the mid-nineteenth century imagined that the urban masses could be controlled by centralized states. Yet 150 years later, no other form of society is imaginable.

The institutions of agrarian civilization were developed with a passive rural workforce in mind. They are, in form if not in content, our institutions today.[13] Consider the wealth siphoned off by industrial states since the Second World War, the largest concentration of money in human history. It went on subsidizing food and armaments, the priorities of the bully throughout the ages. These were not the priorities of the urban consumers who paid the taxes. We unthinkingly reproduce the inhumanity of an unequal society built on

11. W.A. Lewis, *International Economic Order* (1978).

12. J. Urry, *Mobilities* (2007).

13. Hart, Appendix 2000b.

agriculture. Households, now as ages before, are thought to relate to society through their work rather than for self-improvement.

Civilization now depends on the information services that people perform for each other. The economy relies much less on material production. This shift evokes the lives of hunter-gatherers before humanity settled down. The agricultural roots of the first industrial revolution elevated producing things, thereby disguising the long-term implications of the machine revolution. Anthropologists who think about human history in the long run could throw light on all this.

Human beings once roamed around the world like the animals. Their nomadic counterparts today do not experience society and nature as contradictory. Their daily lives are infused with spirits that occupy the world around them. Their economy is based on sharing consumption. A society based on movement has fixed points that endure, but movement has been a central feature of society until now. The pandemic of 2020 and after brought unprecedented restrictions on movement. No human condition is permanent.

After settling down to produce food, society became wedded to place. Plants get their nourishment where they are rooted and farmers had to look after them. Domestication brought some animals under a similar regime. The world appeared to farmers as divided. There were now two zones. One was under precarious human control. The rest was 'the wild' – untamed thickets, fierce animals, human predators and vengeful spirits. This retrograde vision of a divided world is still ours, and it must go if humanity is to meet this century's challenges.

The world has never been more connected and unequal than now. The reason for both is capital's freedom to roam the world. The Victorian liberal state imposed free capital on those they enslaved and colonized. The neoliberal world economy imposes its own forms of coercion on all humanity. I have shown here that territorial states maintain inequality by restricting the movement of people from poor to rich areas. This dual economy of high- and low-paid labour took a universal form in the decades before the First World War. It persists as an unequal system expressed through the semiotics of race. Resistance to globalization would reinforce national boundaries against the predations of capital. But this plays into the hands of racists and fascists.

Africans were always at the bottom of that racial hierarchy. But their continent was under-populated and vulnerable to European imperialists. In 1900, Africa contained one in twelve human beings alive, whereas Europeans constituted more than one in three.[14] The UN predicts that Africa will house two in five human beings in 2100, Europe one in sixteen. The median age of Africans today is under 20 years. A massive transformation in the regional com-

---

14. See Chapter 16.

position of humanity is taking place. Asian exporters already expect Africa to be the most buoyant sector of world market demand. Racial stereotypes are in for a shake-up. After all, in the 1930s China was the world's main example of poverty and disorder. Africans could protect their growing economies by restricting movement through their territories. But when the British were the world's leading power, they encouraged free immigration. The US did the same for most of its history. Xenophobic nationalism is a mark of great societies in decline.

A new free trade campaign would dismantle the institutions of privilege by insisting on movement as a human right. Its motivation would be liberal – an attack on global divisions in the name of our common humanity. The world belongs to us all. An injury anywhere affects us all. Global capital will only be checked when popular forces are able to mobilize freely. The internet has increased this possibility. Removing state jurisdiction over international movement is as essential now as the repeal of the Corn Laws was to free trade 150 years ago.

Realists will dismiss this idea. The state system also makes international migration desirable or compelling. The citizens of rich countries rely on their state to use the force necessary to keep unwanted migrants out. But what if no such obstacles existed? Reducing international movement could take other forms. The rich countries could redistribute wealth to poor areas. The world would be less unequal and people might be encouraged to stay at home. If movement is a problem, we urgently need to redress the inequality that causes it. A Keynesian macroeconomic strategy for world society seems rather unlikely at present. But historical developments could justify one, as they did in the 1930s.

Georg Simmel wrote an essay about the changing character of liberalism. He pointed out that the early modern liberal revolutions were motivated by the need for freedom of movement. People needed to escape from the restrictions imposed on them by an agrarian civilization. But by 1900 in Europe, liberalism had become existential: 'The deepest problems of modern life derive from the claim of the individual to preserve the autonomy and individuality of his existence in the face of overwhelming social forces. . .'[15] What struck me about the US was that freedom is still more closely linked to movement than in Europe, even though identity politics now undermines the citizenship that emerged briefly during and after the Second World War. This chapter argues that freedom of movement, not a static concern with preservation of individual identity, should be reinstated as humanity's priority in the drive to make a viable world society.

---

15. G. Simmel, 'The Metropolis and Mental Life' (1903).

Chapter 14

AN ANTHROPOLOGIST
IN THE DIGITAL REVOLUTION

Computers have been with us for over seventy years, television for a bit longer and telephones for twice as long. These technologies converged in a world-wide network of communications, the internet. It is a conceptual unity like 'the world market'. Market transactions increasingly take place on the internet. The big innovation of the World Wide Web in 1994 was the move from words and numbers to visual images. Transmissions flow through an evolving network of satellites and cable grids.

The internet belonged for decades to a strategic complex of military, scientific and business interests in the US and Europe. These cliques lent the medium its style and content at first. It was technical, closed and clubby. When the internet went public in 1991, there were only three million users. In the next five years this increased to 100 million. This figure reached 5 billion in 2020, out of almost 8 billion.[1] No previous technology has diffused so fast.

Extrapolating from experience is useless. Guessing what happens next is a challenge to empiricism. Iron smelting was first discovered in the Eastern Mediterranean over three thousand years ago.[2] Small quantities were used for ornaments worn by the ruling class. Then iron weapons gave some groups a military advantage. Iron found its most general application some centuries later: in tools used by common people to produce food and manufactures. At

---

1. https://www.internetworldstats.com/stats.htm (accessed 14 September 2021).

2. I organized a Yale seminar, 'The Transition from Bronze to Iron in the Eastern Mediterranean, 1600–500 BC'.

first, iron was a symbolic and practical prop for the dominance of a military caste. Something similar could be said about the internet in the Cold War.

The digital revolution is driven by changes in the size, cost and speed of information-processing machines. Speed is now measured as millions of instructions per second (MIPS). The world's first modern computer, the Electronic Numerical Integrator and Computer (ENIAC), was built in the late 1940s. It cost millions of dollars, was fifty metres wide and three metres tall and processed five thousand instructions per second. Twenty-five years later, an Intel chip, 12 mm square, cost $200 and processed 0.06 MIPS. Pentium 4 chips processed ten thousand MIPS in 2003 and some chips passed fifty thousand MIPS in 2008. The fastest computing speed in 2019 was 148 petaFLOPS.[3] In 1980, copper wires transmitted information at a printed page a second. Now, hair-thin optical fibres carry over a million encyclopaedia volumes per second. Modems recently took an hour to download a five-minute video. Broadband technology now performs this task in a few seconds.

The World Revolution and Me

The new communications technologies blur the boundaries of academic disciplines. They transform the content of education and spawn new genres of research. They demand fresh intellectual strategies. The universities impede our ability to engage with all this. Anthropology has not yet grasped the potential of this new world. We should rethink who we wish to address, how and where.

We have launched a world revolution as far-reaching as the invention of agriculture. It is a machine revolution, of course. It is a social revolution, the formation of world society with universal means of communication. It is a financial revolution, the detachment of the virtual money circuit from production. It is an existential revolution, transforming what it means to be human – how individuals participate in humanity. Everything we have done before seems like its prehistory. Oswald Spengler said that the world historical moment you are born into will carry on with or without you. But he asked his readers, 'Do you have the courage to embrace it?'[4] So too with this revolution: you can jump in or hide from it. Everyone's path is unique, yet the revolution has discernible outlines.

I never warmed to the typewriter.[5] Whiting out mistakes was messy. I depended on fierce Scottish matrons to type up my handwritten manuscripts. We both knew where the power was. With word-processing in the early

---

3. A petaFLOPS is a quadrillion (million billion) floating point operations per second.

4. O. Spengler, *The Decline of the West* (1918).

5. Hart, Appendix 2009c.

1980s, I seized my chance for liberation. I was an artisan, designing layout and content. Email was an oral/written hybrid, between a letter and a phone call. I still love its fluency. I next produced beautiful pamphlets through desktop publishing. The roles of editor and publisher were added to my craft identity. Then I started a mailing list, the *amateur anthropology association (small-triple-a)*. It flourished for two years.[6]

Desktop publishing was alright, but the challenge was distribution. Waiting for someone to find a booklet on a shop shelf was old school. We considered reviving the eighteenth-century subscriber system with an online database. But I was committed to print publishing. The World Wide Web made the internet more visual, personal and interactive. I chaired a university committee exploring uses of IT for teaching and research. Some said that Cambridge had no place in this new world. The former polytechnics had more experience with online techniques. But Cambridge has treasures that could become an internet resource. The digital revolution is not linear. Everyone enters it with their own bundle of advantages and drawbacks. The technology evolves. Early users become over-adapted to older techniques. Latecomers use software needing less specialist knowledge. The machine revolution is a river. You cannot step into the same one twice.[7]

What could I give the young geeks who helped me find a toehold in this revolution? I settled on 'history': I was born in the war and have a vision of history that they don't. I developed as a network entrepreneur. My activities had no money or prestige. Participants needed to do something they couldn't do elsewhere. They might try out graphic design. I got an amateur product, but it was free. When they had to, they would leave. The value added by the group must be cool! I adapted online discoveries to normal academic practice. The two spheres fed each other.

After I moved to Paris, I wanted to sum up thirty years of teaching and point forward too. I asked what would interest future generations about us. Obviously, the digital revolution. What we do now will have consequences for them. I found an old lecture about money[8] and wrote *The Memory Bank*, about how the digital revolution was shaping money and exchange. I built a website to promote this book.[9] Without helpers I would be nowhere. But I now do far more for myself.

The social media revolution used the excess bandwidth left over from the dot com bust. This was my chance. I used Twitter to develop as an editor. I

---

6. See Chapter 10.

7. 'No man ever steps in the same river twice, for it's not the same river and he's not the same man' (Heraclitus).

8. Hart, Appendix 1986.

9. Hart, Appendix 2000a.

sent economic journalism from Europe to American traders, gold bugs and currency freaks. I met interesting anthropologists. I honed my subediting skills. Social bookmarking turns me on.[10] Knowledge before was classified by experts; each bit of information had its unique place in a folder. Tagging allows us to mark something we like or find useful. Software locates connections for you. We generate the categories now. Google's algorithms are already obsolete.

Facebook gave me a networking platform like no other. I published political and economic analysis. I wasn't interested in personal trivia. Readers expected interesting material from me. When the malfeasance of Zuckerberg's empire became obvious, I quit. Big Tech is ruining our ability to make society for ourselves. Convenience shouldn't beat working for the internet we want. Google and Amazon are next on my list. I have posted many papers on Academia.edu. I follow strangers there who show interest in my work.

The internet greatly increases my intellectual efficiency. I used to spend a day lifting heavy books in Cambridge University library to find references for an article. Now I get them online in seconds. I can translate an article from eight European languages in under a minute. Kindle is the biggest innovation for me since email and websites. I can highlight notes, send them to myself by email and transfer them directly to a document. Wikipedia is our library of Alexandria and universally accessible. My young friends are cutting edge and I am not. It's all a bloody miracle for me. I can't get enough of it. Bring on the virtual revolution!

Students, readers and those we study will expect us to engage them through the new media. We must move from monologue to dialogue, from guild disciplines for adolescents to lifetime self-learning. The universities lag behind students in media literacy; they will soon be known as 'late academia'.

Anthropology Online: Between Social Networks and Academia

Discussion about Open Access in contemporary anthropology is mostly American, where the contradictions are acute.[11] It involves resistance to privatization of the commons, an aspect of the intellectual property wars. A narrower issue is how to make research publications freely available without undermining their role as cultural capital in academic careers. Unemployed young researchers can't afford to pay for information and yet they hope to find academic employment someday. The contradiction is between the intellectual commons and owning ideas as private property.

---

10. D. Weinberger, *Everything is Miscellaneous* (2007).

11. Hart, Appendix 2012c.

The situation in American anthropology was made worse by the policy of the AAA to elevate private production for profit above sharing knowledge with the public.[12] I recall Marx's early polemics against restricting peasants' access to fallen wood in the Westphalian forests. OA activists today can't fight privatization with his intensity because they have already bought into an academic career as individual owners. American anthropologists rarely consider if the French, for example, have some interesting responses to this problem. Is OA an issue in Brazil or Scandinavia, in Japan or India? Language barriers also restrict public access. English is not universal. Now I have a German translator based on artificial intelligence feedback processes that is far superior to the algorithms of early social media.[13] This is the next stage of the revolution: an article in any of the major European languages translated readably in under a minute, with Mandarin and Arabic to come.

In May 2009, casual griping spread to Twitter, where a loose network of anthropologists had formed. Before long, there were quasi-revolutionary suggestions to start an open, less bureaucratic and more inclusive worldwide community of anthropologists. Twitter was ideal for this, but more space was needed if we were to build a global network of anthropologists. Justin Shaffner and I set up a forum on my website to find a name and purpose for this proposed collective. Participants brainstormed about two issues: 'structure' and 'function'. What would the organization look like and what would it do? One suggestion was that 'we should offer a structure that is open enough to become whatever it will. Every member should be able to take an initiative. There is no need to get bogged down in unnecessary voting; if something needs to get done and you can do it, then go for it'. We settled on the Open Anthropology Cooperative as its name.

We moved to the Ning platform and then tried to catch up with uncontrolled expansion. The OAC aspired to global scope and no hierarchy. Its model negated formal academia's typical malfunctions. This proved to be both liberating and stifling. We made a lot of mistakes and some of the founders left in a huff. The OAC's members came from over fifty countries. We hosted specialist groups in German, Norwegian, Italian, French, Russian, Georgian, Portuguese, Spanish and Turkish. Yet the trend was towards the online dominance of native English-speakers.

The OAC never settled on a 'brand', but there was no parallel in world anthropology for the interaction offered there. Fran Barone and I wrote a book chapter on our experience.[14] Building an open network brings com-

---

12. The American Anthropological Association has since made some moves towards open access.

13. DeepL Translator takes its name from AI deep learning with individual user feedback.

14. Hart, Appendix 2015h.

plications. Faced with an unexpected flood of enrolments, we never solved tough problems of organization and site navigation. We had to moderate admissions in order to control spammers and trolls. Any member could open up a discussion group, but many soon neglected what they began. The result was proliferating pages with no recognizable shape. We allowed too many decisions to be debated openly. We opted for a platform that allowed new-comers to get started without any preparation; and we conceded control to them.

Egalitarianism meant that we didn't pay enough attention to leadership. We mixed an academic network with social media without resolving the contradictions between them. Administrators were mainly graduate students writing a thesis. Anthropologists already find it hard to make their public presence felt. Newcomers were astonished by the vitality and diversity of the site, only to discover that finding your way around was hard and substantial areas seemed to be dead.

Professionals, students and outsiders interacted freely there without central direction. We accumulated a remarkable archive of spontaneous commen-tary, visual and literary artefacts, plus thousands of personal pages. We tried to establish a repository for research and teaching materials, but lacked the manpower. The OAC Press publishes working papers, classical texts and book reviews online; and we held successful interdisciplinary seminars lasting two weeks. They replicate the familiar academic model, but with more time for reading and reflection before commenting. We opened an OAC page on Face-book. Membership is more diverse and less academic there, much younger on average, especially from India. Posts are shorter, more suited to grabbing readers' passing attention. By 2019, OAC Facebook had fourteen thousand members and OAC Ning seemed stuck at eight thousand. I resigned from the admins team; Avi Khalil and Justin Shaffner moved the main site,[15] stored the Ning page as a static archive for 2009–19[16] and explored new experimental forms. OAC Facebook carried on as before.

Anthropology did not help us think through online problems theoretically and practically. We are meticulously documenting bits of the world and can't catch up with its movement. Its priority was never to change the world. We can't even solve issues that our grounded humanism should train us for. The fastest-growing sector of world trade is in cultural commodities – entertain-ment, education, media, information services – increasingly online. Every-where, sclerotic corporations are outsourcing to smaller flexible units or being replaced by them. The need for lifelong self-learning is met only by individual

15. http://openanthcoop.net/ (accessed 14 September 2021).

16. http://openanthcoop.net/archive/openanthcoop.ning.com/index.html#sthash.hSfPD Nri.dpbs (accessed 13 October 2021).

initiative; and anthropology's holistic approach ought to be well suited to it. With imagination and less dependence on the universities, anthropology could enter a golden age. But we still privilege research publications over teaching, the Faustian contract of last century.

With very few exceptions, such as Michael Wesch at Kansas State,[17] we don't ask what the people want or how to give it to them. The spirit of academic bureaucracy killed the OAC, even as we tried to escape from it. Luddite universities regard online activities as a hobby, not serious work.[18] The OAC proved that anthropologists cope well with virtual worlds. We were artisans, piecing together technologies for chatting, learning, teaching and sharing. We aspired to be transparent and encouraged informal discussion and formal debate. We were an anomaly in a tidy classification system, a compromised public island. We wanted to avoid the academy's formality; but most members worked in universities.

Intellectual snobbery and populist rhetoric blocked learning from the online stars.[19] Yet social media's preoccupation with followers and friends reflects an important development in society. When the Latins found being a disorganized rabble a handicap, they formed three named groups ('tribes'). These sacrificed a cow and 'dis*trib*uted' the meat among participants.[20] They made ad hoc alliances with neighbours and called them *socius*, the whole thing *societas*. Anyone under attack assumed leadership and the rest followed them. But this was transient and contingent, like the social media of today. Society as a bounded hierarchy with a centre was a medieval French idea. Anthropologists should reflect more on the fast-breaking features of society online.[21]

We are losing concepts like 'culture' and 'ethnography' to better-organized disciplines.[22] Anthropologists do have something to offer the public. We are just terrible at communicating it. Fear of 'branding' anthropology and 'looking like Facebook' undermined the OAC project on Ning. Our web-based activities came to resemble office politics. We suffered from the same prejudices that hobbled the universities. Creating new social forms is hard. Radical ideas are often subverted by unconsciously held older forms. The OAC was a new social form. It allowed Asian women graduate students to express themselves more freely than at home. We encouraged students to network with established academics. We gave outsiders access to information, discussions

---

17. See Hart, Appendix 2009c.

18. Luddism was a nineteenth-century movement resisting mechanization.

19. S. Godin, *Tribes* (2008).

20. Hart, Appendix 2003c.

21. G. Coleman, *Coding Freedom* (2013).

22. J. Breidenbach and A. Nyiri, *Seeing Culture Everywhere* (2009); Hart, Appendix 2011b.

and writing normally locked up behind university doors or paywalls. But we lacked a big idea and old social forms lurked beneath the surface. Invention and self-expression dwindled over time.

Even so, we contributed to public anthropology by providing a global medium for exploring anthropology's potential to change the world. That world is still searching for democracy. The OAC has been and still is part of that. We didn't draw on anthropology to fulfil the OAC's promise. Intellectual life is intrinsically individualistic. We may think of ourselves as social creatures, but they only hand out brains one at a time. Collaboration is strong in the hard sciences. Universities have always depended on informal cultural commons: teaching, seminars, conferences, sharing ideas, access to libraries and so on. Everyone wants personal recognition; but, until the 1950s, this came second to academic life as a community of scholars, teachers and their students.

The Cold War and the need to restore home food supplies after the war boosted research on armaments and agriculture. Public money was pumped into universities for research. Big Pharma funded research on chemicals. Student enrolments took off in the 1960s and universities became big business. The late-twentieth-century university was the state's main research arm and a mass production line for workers in bureaucracies. Academics, like monks, always ruled their own institutions; but this expansion gave power to administrators. Research now dominated. The humanities and social sciences didn't have much to offer, but they jumped onto the bandwagon.

The 1970s culminated in Reagan and Thatcher's neoliberal counter-revolution against post-war social democracy. Pseudo-markets now based academic assessment on 'objective' indicators like research publications. Bureaucracies became more interventionist. Wholesale corporatization of university cultures followed. What was left of academic community was destroyed by the growing gap between a few established professors who took leave often and a reserve army of precarious young teachers ('adjuncts').[23] The publishing oligopoly exhausted library budgets with their overpriced journals, while the academics competed to be published in them. Everyone agrees that the contents are worthless and mostly unread. Faced with the digital revolution, most academics zealously upheld a feudal private property system that subverted their places of work.

Even so, we are living through a genuine revolution in the production and dissemination of knowledge. The vast reserve army of graduate students well understands the freedom and opportunities afforded by digital commons; they accept in principle the system of private property and competitive markets, but maintain a critical attitude to them. The AAA is an endless source

---

23. See Chapter 17.

for such scepticism. Yet its critics are tied to the labour market it serves. At least the AAA is 100 per cent for the private property system.

Academics have been losing a class war for half a century. We are 'rebels without a clue'[24] and have no idea how we got into this situation or how to get out of it. This makes us easy pickings. Wedded to bourgeois ideology and ignorant of guides from Marcel Mauss to C.L.R. James, we can't preserve the social conditions for our individuality and have sold our commons for the illusion of personal advancement. Young researchers, desperate to gain a toehold in the academy, did not bring about this situation. Those of us who got in when the going was good acquiesced in the destruction of what we were given.

Our main strategy must be to take advantage of the social and technical possibilities afforded by the digital revolution. This will require other means of economic support. It makes no sense to bank on an academic job for life these days. But every serious online initiative I know was compromised by attitudes and habits formed in the academy. The main clients for any anthropological forum are graduate students and they want to conserve a status quo they hope to join – while nurturing half-hearted attitudes of rebellion.

I don't disparage academic work. I have devoted my life to it. But anthropology was born as part of a democratic project and the academy is now gripped by a coercive bureaucracy. I have a pseudo-Maoist slogan: walk on two legs (it's better than standing on one leg and falling over). By all means keep one foot in the academy, if you can, but don't settle for the status quo and keep the other foot in the market, moving forward while shifting your balance. 'What the people want' is the slogan of a genuine democracy. It is not something the privileged give to the needy, but we must find out what it is, if we aspire to be socially useful. It bears repeating that anthropology was originally a project to discover what human beings had in common in order to replace arbitrary inequality with a democratic constitution.[25]

The Rise of the Corporations

Neoliberal globalization undermined the strong version of national capitalism that prevailed after 1945. By the millennium, the nation state's detractors could argue that national governments are corrupt and ineffective; national laws are irrelevant and unenforceable; national citizens are lazy and disaffected. What other powers exist in our world? We must begin with the American Empire. The free-market idea is a rhetorical fig leaf for this empire.

---

24. Tom Petty, 'Into the Great Wide Open' (1991).

25. See Chapter 2.

Intellectuals on both sides of the Atlantic underestimate its strengths. Europeans play up every sign of American hubris, incompetence and malfeasance.

American global hegemony rests on world market share, weapons and bases, the world currency, intellectual property and Big Tech. The US invented and still dominates the internet, which supplies much of the world's hardware, software, content and giant firms.[26] The American Empire today rests on mercantilism, militarism, financial monopoly, private property in ideas and the digital revolution.

The second force is the move towards regional trade federations. The European Union is the largest, followed by ASEAN, Mercosul, NAFTA and the African Union. China and Russia challenge US hegemony. Transnational corporations, however, pose the main threat to nation states. To understand this, we must grasp the evolution of private property.[27]

We still think of private property as belonging to living persons and oppose private and public spheres on that basis. But what makes property private is holding exclusive rights against the world. Abstract entities like governments and corporations, as well as individuals, can thus hold private property. States and corporations have acquired the property rights of individuals. Private property in this form does not shore up liberal democracy. It favours totalitarian bureaucracy and always has. Personal identity is forced into categories devised by impersonal institutions. We are understandably confused by this, especially since the corporations' rise to public power rests on collapsing the difference between real and artificial persons in economic law. This constitutes an obstacle to the practice of democracy and to thinking about it. Sadly, many intellectuals obscure the distinction between living persons and social abstractions.[28]

Private property has not only evolved from personal ownership to corporate forms, but its main reference has shifted from 'real' to 'intellectual' property, that is from material objects to ideas. The digital revolution has led to the economic preponderance of information services whose reproduction and transmission is nearly costless. If I steal your cow, its loss is material, since only one of us can benefit from its milk. But if I copy a CD or DVD, I am denying no-one access to it. Yet corporate lobbyists depend on this misleading analogy to influence courts and legislators to treat duplication of their 'property' as 'theft' or even 'piracy'.

The term 'information feudalism' is apt for all this.[29] Human work not long ago was conceived of as collective physical energy, as 'hands'. The inter-

---

26. FAANG: Facebook, Apple, Amazon, Netflix, Google.

27. C.B. Macpherson (ed.), *Property* (1978).

28. Hart, Appendix 1988b.

29. P. Drahos and J. Braithwaite, *Information Feudalism* (2002).

net has raised the significance of intangible commodities. Labour is increasingly understood as individual creativity, as subjectivity. This shift has been captured by big money when claiming that 'intellectual property' must be regulated in its owner's interest. The fight is on to save the commons of human society, culture and ecology from the encroachments of corporate private property. This is not just about conserving the earth's natural resources or public services left to the mercies of privatized agencies. The large corporations now assert their exclusive ownership of what was shared culture to which all had free and equal access. Across the board, separate battles are being fought over music, movies, literature, software, GMOs, pharmaceuticals, the internet and the universities, with little awareness of the common cause they share.

Where did all this come from?[30] Investors were once personally responsible for a firm's debts. In 1580, Queen Elizabeth of England granted 'limited freedom from liability' to *The Golden Hind*, a ship owned by Sir Francis Drake. She was the largest shareholder. Investors were now liable to repay only the amount of their investment. Creditors had to absorb the losses. The returns were 5,000 per cent and the queen was well pleased. Drake was a national hero, but the world called him a pirate. The business model they invented underlies the modern corporation.

The Dutch then dominated world trade. In 1600 the queen granted a charter to the East India Company in the City of London. Its ties to national government were always close. The Company financed James Cook's explorations of the Pacific and controlled trade with the American colonies. By the 1770s it was almost bankrupt. Dutch traders and local smugglers sold cheaper tea to the Americans. The 1773 Tea Act exempted the Company from taxes on exports to America with a tax refund on 17 million pounds of unsold tea. It could now undercut retail prices in America, where resentment fuelled the Boston Tea Party.

Thomas Jefferson saw three main threats to democracy: governing elites, organized religion and commercial monopolies.[31] He called the last 'pseudoaristocrats' and 'monarchists'. He wanted freedom from monopoly in the Bill of Rights, but failed. Corporations then sought the constitutional rights of individual citizens, but were denied. After the Civil War the railroads tried again. The Fourteenth Amendment guaranteed former slaves equal protection under the laws. The railroads used this to sue local authorities when regulations singled them out. It created 'different classes of persons'. Corporate personhood was widely debated.

---

30. T. Hartmann, *Unequal Protection* (2002).
31. M. Hardt, 'Jefferson and Democracy' (2007).

The corporations finally won in the 1886 Supreme Court judgement on Santa Clara County vs the Southern Pacific Railroad. The latter was being sued for back taxes. It claimed it was a person entitled to equal rights under the Fourteenth Amendment. The Supreme Court's written judgement says:

> The defendant corporations are persons within the intent of the clause in section of the Fourteenth Amendment of the Constitution of the United States which forbids a State to deny to any person within its jurisdiction the equal protection of the laws.[32]

Many businesses took advantage of this ruling in the next few decades, but only a few former slaves did.

The world's three largest corporations today are Chinese banks. Finance dominates the top 150 transnational corporations. The top hundred non-financial corporations are over half (56) European. The United States (23), Japan (10) and China (5) follow. Australia, Brazil, Canada, Israel, Korea and Malaysia have one each. The drive for independence would have corporations the only citizens in world society. 'Shareholder value' is no longer the rationale for corporate behaviour. 'Corporate social responsibility' is taking its place.[33] National capitalism, they whisper in secluded places, is decadent and must be replaced. After structural adjustment policies dismantled restrictions on capital flows in the 1980s, the corporations turned to investment abroad. They want nation states to police international laws administered by international organizations.

Companies control the marketing of their brand, outsource production, logistics and much else. Why have state laws, when the world needs moral law? 'Corporate social responsibility' informs internal management practice. It also negotiates relations between firms and society.[34] This corporate drive for world domination is celebrated annually at the World Economic Forum in Davos. Celebrities pay homage there.

Intellectual Property

Private property today is mainly intellectual property.[35] The phrase was invented by Lysander Spooner.[36] He was an old-fashioned liberal philoso-

---

32. Hartmann (ibid.: 147).
33. D. Crowther and G. Aras, *Corporate Social Responsibility* (2008).
34. Ibid.
35. Hart, Appendix 2008c.
36. L. Spooner, *The Law of Intellectual Property* (1855).

pher of the mid-nineteenth century: individualist, anarchist, abolitionist, an American Proudhon. He was often broke. Spooner wanted to guarantee a living for mental workers. Property traditionally belonged to living persons. But holding exclusive rights makes property private. Private property has not only evolved from personal ownership to corporate and state forms, but its main reference has shifted from 'real' to 'intellectual' property, using Spooner's term for property in ideas. The corporations' rise to public power rests on collapsing the difference between real and artificial persons in economic law. Private property in this form does not shore up liberal democracy. It favours totalitarian bureaucracy and always has. The US was born in resistance to corporate monopoly. Now it promotes an intellectual property treaty that shores up corporate profits.[37]

Large corporations assert exclusive ownership of what was common culture to which all had free and equal access. The feudal barons of the music business contest our traditional right to share songs. The Hollywood studios spread propaganda claiming that DVD rents are real property. Corporate privatization forces people who never knew they had a common culture to defend it. The US, with more weapons than the rest together, imposes global compliance to its legal fictions. The corporations' antiquated methods of 'command and control' browbeat governments and consumers into obedience. This 'culture war' has only just begun and is universal. Classical slogans like 'free markets' and 'liberal democracy' were weapons in the war against feudalism. They now provide a fig leaf for corporate monopolists.

Living in society combines personal agency with its impersonal conditions. But the difference between them has collapsed. World society now resembles the Old Regime as a result.[38] Copyright once protected the interests of individual authors. Music, movie and software corporations now invoke it to justify monopolistic rent extraction. Liberal democracy has become its antithesis. We must resist this new enclosure of the commons. An impersonal public sphere is indispensable to living in society. But individuality, moral purpose and religion no longer have any place in our common affairs. We must learn again how to separate personal and impersonal aspects of social life and then combine them anew.[39]

37. Trade-related Aspects of Intellectual Property Rights, TRIPS (1989–2002).
38. Hart, Appendix 2002.
39. K. Hart, *The Hit Man's Dilemma* (2005).

Chapter 15

ECONOMIES CONNECTING
LOCAL AND GLOBAL HUMANITY

Only connect.
　—E.M. Forster, *Howards End*

Self and world, individual and society, personal and impersonal, local and global often seem to be far apart, even antagonistic, unreachable one from the other. These dualisms are useful and must not be abandoned, but they always form a single whole and overlap closely. Our task is to find what is universal in these pairs and constantly revise their connection in the light of experience. In my work and life, I have consistently addressed this dialectic in relation to economy. Reflecting on my Ghana fieldwork, I found the formal/informal pair to link the economic activities of poor migrants to government bureaucracy.[1] Much later, the internet led me to explore virtual reality. It seemed now that the informal economy had gone global through a combination of neoliberalism and the digital revolution.

Studying money and national capitalism revived my teenage compulsion to bring together personal and impersonal dimensions of social life while keeping the poles separate.[2] Corporate personality has collapsed the distinction between real and artificial persons in economic law, with profound consequences for democracy in thought and practice.[3] After the millennium

---

1. See Chapter 6.

2. K. Hart (ed.), *Money in a Human Economy* (2017).

3. K. Hart, *The Hit Man's Dilemma* (2005).

I searched for a way of bridging the gap between human actors on the ground and the sense we have of being one humanity. The idea of a human economy was the result.[4] I briefly sketch this sequence here.

How the Informal Economy Took over the World

Soon after the millennium I learned of an illegal trade that had grown up in the southern French ports of Marseille and Montpellier. It supplied stolen cars and car parts to Africa and was staffed mainly by North Africans. Some of them dreamed of reclaiming the Mediterranean for Islam and they all ignored official paperwork, relying on word-of-mouth agreements, mainly within a religious brotherhood. This traffic grew so big that industrial plant in the French car industry was drawn south to meet a demand from something absent from official records. An army of corrupt policemen and customs and tax officials were allegedly part of this remarkable machine. Russian and Latin American mafias became involved and the gang added Brussels and Hamburg as bases for their global strategy.

Mainstream French politics has its criminal side too. President Mitterand's office ran a slush fund supplied by petrol companies and licenced traders in Africa from which he illegally transferred election funds to Helmut Kohl in Germany. When Jacques Chirac ran for president against Jean-Marie Le Pen of the National Front, the schoolkids in our street marched with placards saying 'Vote for the crook, not the fascist!'[5] Chirac's prosecution for corruption from his days as Paris's mayor continued long after he left the Elysée Palace. Money scandals still beset the political class, ranging from tax evasion by the controller of the government budget to allegations of corruption against Christine Lagarde, when she was Minister of Finance, later head of the International Monetary Fund, now President of the European Central Bank. In 2021 former president Nicolas Sarkozy received three years imprisonment for bribery and suborning officials.

Meanwhile the Tuareg tradition of smuggling everything from smartphones to bazookas across the Sahara on camels was interrupted by a French military invasion in the name of the 'war on terror'. All of this pales into insignificance next to the City of London, which converted a failed colonial empire into a network of tax havens that would probably surpass even Swiss private banking, if either could be measured.[6] At the other end of the world,

---

4. https://www.theasa.org/publications/asaonline/articles/asaonline_0101.shtml (accessed 2 October 2021).

5. *Votez l'escroc, pas le fasho.*

6. N. Shaxson, *Treasure Islands* (2011).

in 2006 a major Japanese information technology corporation, NEC, discovered a parallel criminal company using the same name, accountancy methods, suppliers and customers, while paying no tax because it was off the books.[7] This is known as brand-jacking.

The idea of an informal economy was born when the post-war era of developmental states was drawing to a close.[8] The 1970s were a watershed between three decades of state management of the economy and the free market decades of one-world capitalism. The economy has now escaped from all attempts to make it publicly accountable. What are the forms of state that can regulate the lawless world of money? The informal economy started off as a way of talking about the Third World urban poor, living in the cracks of a rule system that could not reach down to them. Now the rule system itself is in question. Everyone ignores the rules, especially the people at the top – the politicians and bureaucrats, the corporations, the banks – and they routinely avoid being held responsible for their illegal actions.[9]

We need to analyse the contemporary world economic crisis at a number of levels. Above all, the core problem is not narrowly economic, but one of political failure, both national and international. Money and markets have escaped from public control and cannot be put back in that straitjacket. What democratically accountable structures might be capable of regulating the world economy and under what social conditions? An uneasy alliance of governments and corporations is now sometimes classified as the 'formal sector'. On the surface they share conformity to the rule of law and being subject to regulation. How might unregulated economic activities, 'the informal economy', relate to the formal order? I have identified four ways: *division, content, negation* and *residue*.

The moral economy of capitalist societies is based on an attempt to keep separate impersonal and personal spheres of social life. Money is the means whereby the two sides are brought together, so that their interaction is an endless process of separation and integration (*division*). The male/female pair is the master metaphor for this. For any rule to be translated into human action, something else must be brought into play, such as personal judgement. Informality is built into bureaucratic forms as unspecified *content*. Some activities break the law, through a breach of safety regulations, tax evasion, smuggling, child labour, selling without a licence, etc. Informal activities also relate to formal organization as *negation*. Some activities exist in parallel, as *residue*. They are separate from the bureaucracy. It is a stretch to include peasant economy, traditional institutions and domestic life in the

---

7. A. Johns, *Piracy: The Intellectual Property Wars from Gutenberg to Gates* (2009).

8. See Chapter 7.

9. Hart, Appendix 2015d.

'informal' category. Yet their social forms often organize informal economic practices.

The informal economy's improbable rise to global dominance is an outcome of the mania for deregulation since 1980. This is linked to the wholesale privatization of public goods and services and the capture of politics by high finance. Deregulation provided a fig leaf for corruption, rentier accumulation, tax evasion and public irresponsibility. Yet while the credit boom lasted, criticism was drowned by celebrations of unending prosperity. Even after the bust, the political ascendancy of finance has not been seriously challenged.

Apart from the main financial houses, the shadow banking system – hedge funds, money market funds and structured investment vehicles beyond state regulation – is literally out of control. Tax evasion is an international industry that dwarfs national budgets.[10] The criminal behaviour of transnational corporations is blatant.[11] Where to stop? The drug cartels from Mexico and Colombia to Russia, the illegal armaments industry, the global war over intellectual property ('piracy'), fake luxury goods, the invasion and looting of Iraq, the Congo scramble for minerals. The informal economy was always a way of labelling the unknowable, but all this defeats comprehension.

Online Worlds and Virtual Reality

The digital revolution is driven by a desire to replicate at distance or by means of computers experiences that we associate with face-to-face human encounters. All communication, whether the exchange of words or money, has a virtual aspect as long as symbols and their media of circulation stand for what people really do together. This usually involves the exercise of imagination, an ability to construct meanings across the gap between symbol and reality. The power of the book long depended on sustaining faith in the possibility of human connection.

In that sense, capitalism was always virtual. Marx's intellectual effort was devoted to revealing how the power of money was mystified through its appearance as things (coins, products, machinery) rather than as relations between living people. Both Marx and Weber were at pains to show how capitalists sought to detach their money-making activities from real conditions obstructing their purposes. Moneylending, the practice of charging interest on loans without production or exchange, is the oldest forms of capitalism. The idea of the money circuit becoming separated from reality is hardly new.

---

10. Shaxson (ibid.).
11. J. Perkins, *Confessions of an Economic Hit Man* (2004).

The point of 'virtualism'[12] is abstraction and this is a function of the shift to ever more inclusive levels of exchange, to the world market as principal point of reference for economic activity, rather than the nation state. But reliance on more abstract forms of communication carries the potential for real persons to be involved at distance in very concrete ways.

The idea of 'virtual reality' expresses this double movement: on the one hand, machines whose complexity their users cannot understand, and on the other, live experiences 'as good as' real. It is the same with money. Capitalism has become virtual in two main senses: the shift from material production (agriculture and manufacturing) to information services; and the detachment of money circulation from production and trade. This is the latest stage of the machine revolution.

Daniel Miller and Don Slater have good news for traditional ethnographers: the internet does not make any difference.[13] In their fieldwork-based monograph on Trinidad, they rightly argue that cyberspace should not be treated as a separate sphere; but, instead of exploring the dialectic of virtual and real experience, they reduce the former to the latter, claiming that the location of internet users in everyday life, to be studied by ethnographers, is all that matters. They ignore business-to-business exchange and approach e-commerce solely through business–customer interaction on websites. They assert the unity of Trinidadians as a national group in defiance of a century's debate about the race and class composition of creole society. Malinowski is alive and well in the insular Caribbean.

If we would make a better world, rather than just contemplate it, we need to think creatively in terms that reflect reality and reach out for imagined possibilities. This in turn depends on capturing what is essential about the world we live in, its movement and direction, not just its stable forms. The idea of *virtual reality* goes to the heart of the matter. It expresses the form of movement that interests me – *extension from the actual to the possible*. 'Virtual' means existing in the mind, but not in fact. When combined with 'reality', it means a product of the imagination that is not quite real. In technical terms, 'virtual reality' is a computer simulation enabling the effects of operations to be shown in real time. The word 'real' connotes something genuine, authentic, serious. In philosophy it means existing objectively in the world; in economics actual purchasing power; in law fixed, landed property; in optics an image formed by the convergence of light rays in space; and in mathematics, real numbers are, of course, not imaginary. 'Reality' is present, in both time and space ('seeing is believing'); and its opposite is imagined connection at distance, something as old as storytelling and books, but given new impetus

---

12. J. Carrier and D. Miller, *Virtualism: The New Political Economy* (1998).
13. D. Miller and D. Slater, *The Internet: An Ethnographic Approach* (2000).

by the internet. The experience of near synchrony at distance, the compression of time and space, is altering how we think of social relations, place and movement.

How does what we do offline influence what we do online and vice versa? For Martin Heidegger, 'world' was an abstract category that did not correspond to any objective reality. Between writing *Being and Time* in 1927 and coming out as a Nazi in 1933, he gave a lecture course at Freiburg on 'the fundamental concepts of metaphysics'.[14] Here he focused on three: solitude, world and finitude. 'Solitude' celebrated a fiction – the isolated individual. Every human being makes a subjective 'world' whose centre is the self. This egocentric universe opens up only when we recognize that we start from 'finitude', concretely when and where we live. 'World' is thus relative both to an abstract version of subjectivity (solitude) and to our particularity (finitude) – position and movement in time and space.[15] Although finite existence is primary, ideas about 'self in the world' influence what we do there.

The internet is often represented as a self-sufficient space with its own distinctive characteristics, as when Manuel Castells writes of 'the rise of the network society'.[16] The idea that each of us lives alone (solitude) in a world largely of our own making seems more real when we go online. But both terms are imagined as well as being reciprocal; they are equally abstract and untenable as an object of inquiry. We approach them relatively from where we actually live, as Miller and Slater say. The social forms of the internet include what people bring from their lives elsewhere. This social life of people offline is an invisible presence when they are online. It would be wrong, however, to deny any autonomy to 'virtual reality'. Would we dream of reducing literature to the circumstances of readers? And this too is Heidegger's point. 'World' and 'solitude' may be artificial abstractions, but they do affect how we behave in 'finitude'.

Money Is Always Personal and Impersonal

My starting point is a legendary remark made in a movie by a professional killer to his victim: 'Don't take this personal, it's just business.'[17] But according to my favourite American dictionary, a 'person' is 'a living human being', and what could be more personal than taking their life? Perhaps the hit man

---

14. M. Heidegger, *The Fundamental Concepts of Metaphysics* (1929).

15. Quantum mechanics showed that position and movement can't both be measured at the same time.

16. M. Castells, *The Rise of the Network Society* (2000).

17. Hart, Appendix 2005, 2007c.

is referring to his own attitude, not to the effect. Killing people is a matter of routine for him, a 'business'. Why should business be impersonal and, if it is, how can that be reconciled with the person who practices it?

Morality concerns the principles of good behaviour. Although we can express 'the good' abstractly as a rule – 'always be kind to children and animals' – morality can only be expected of persons who face the choice to be good or otherwise in complex situations that cannot be reduced to simple rules. What politics, law and business have in common is that they define 'the good' in a collective sense. A group must be protected from subversion, disorder or loss, and this more general good may require leaders to sacrifice personal morality to that impersonal end. It costs too much if people must always be forced to do what you want. It helps if they can be persuaded to do something because they believe it is right. Often that means believing that a leader is a good person; but authoritarians make do with terror. It is not easy to separate the impersonal ends of society from their personal instruments.

The crisis in *Company*, an Indian movie about organized crime in Mumbai,[18] comes when Mallik, the big boss, tries to limit his reliance on Chandu, a young lieutenant he raised from nowhere. He delegates a hit to Chandu, the assassination of a politician, that the former decides to abort for operational reasons. He tells Mallik: 'I am about to do what I think is right. If you suffer any losses, don't take it personally.' Mallik moves swiftly to have him killed; but, thanks to the friendship of their women and the mobile phone, he escapes and civil war breaks out, spreading as far as Nairobi. The resulting mayhem fragments the Company and lends strength to their enemies, including the police. Someone says, 'whatever's happening is the fault of the business, not one man'. But the business can only operate with one big boss, or it fragments into impotence, as here. Actually, Chandu was trying to salvage morality from the mess. The hit man's dilemma is between morality and politics. Chandu is a classic individualist, in a line of American westerns and gangster comic strips, the loner who doesn't believe in justice unless he does it himself. He thinks official society is as corrupt as he is, but less honest; in any case he is excluded from it.

Chandu meets his match in the clever and basically decent policeman, Sreenivasan. He knows the police can't be effective if they always stay within the law. The law doesn't measure up, but it is all we have to save us from rule by the mob. Morality is what we ought to do, the law is what we can get away with. The lines between official politics, law and crime are blurred in practice, but we the public prefer to believe that they are separate. One recurrent Hindi jingle chants, 'Yes, it stinks, but it's business'. Gangster movies allow us to see society from outside the self-protective cocoon that the middle classes

---

18. *Company* (2002), available online.

inhabit. By evoking normal capitalism, the gangster 'firm' offers a metaphor for capitalism's dark side. Tony Soprano crosses the thin line between hoodlum and suburbanite many times a day. Impersonal society in its official guise can be just as immoral as criminal enterprise, whereas thieves have personal lives and morality of a sort, but impersonal abstractions have no room for morality at all.

Every human being is a unique person who lives in society. Society is personal when it is lived by each of us in particular; it is impersonal when it takes the form of collective ideas. It is as damaging to insist on a radical separation of individuals and society (or of life and ideas) as it is to collapse the difference between them. Max Weber, writing in the full spate of a bureaucratic revolution powered by machine industry, saw no social force capable of resisting a highly centralized version of impersonal society.[19] For us, looking back at the last century, bureaucratic capitalism has evolved to a highly mobile form operating on a global scale, while national bureaucracy and its industrial base seem to be endangered species. Before public bureaucracy is killed off, we should ask how the hopes it embodied might be preserved, if only as an alternative to the transnational corporations now dominating world economy. For all my criticisms, I believe that some economic functions can best be performed by corporations and that capitalism's historical mission to bring cheap commodities to the masses is far from complete. Progressive capitalist firms can take part in dismantling the resuscitated old regime that we call 'neoliberalism'.

Society now operates at global, regional, national and local levels. We need new impersonal norms to guide our social interactions in this world, as long as individual personalities are recognized to be significant. The stage is set for a new humanism capable of uniting these poles. We are still primitives; but eventually we will make society on our own terms, if we master the means of its development – people, machines and money. We will encounter immense forces denying us genuine democracy. But there is more to this than class war.

In the last few decades, the idea of government has been replaced by talk of 'governance', acknowledging that social order is no longer the nation state's monopoly. 'Good governance' speaks to a desire to fill the gap between politics and morality left by impersonal society. The remarkable strength of religious feeling in America and its Islamic antithesis is not an anomalous hangover from the past, but evidence of the need for meaningful connection when the secular state's grip on society weakens. It was never strong in America. It seems that science has driven religion from the governance of modern societies, but the search is on now for new forms of religion capable of reconciling scientific laws with personal experience. Kant's cosmopolitan moral

---

19. M. Weber, *Economy and Society* (1922).

politics offer one vision of such a religious revival.[20] The hit man's dilemma contains the seeds of a general human crisis.

Manifesto for a Human Economy

A movement of economics students, calling itself 'post-autistic economics',[21] soon took the form of the *real-world economics review*. Legions of heterodox economists formed the interdisciplinary World Economics Association in 2011, soon acquiring fourteen thousand members. Their priorities are to reconnect the study of the economy to the real world; to make its findings more accessible to the public; and to place economic analysis within a framework that embraces humanity as a whole, the world we live in. A century ago, Alfred Marshall, in his synthesis of the marginalist revolution, defined economics as 'both a study of wealth and a branch of the study of man'.[22] Marshall was Keynes's teacher at Cambridge, a cooperative socialist like Marcel Mauss and the Webbs, who developed a Hegelian theory of the welfare state.

The 'human economy' approach shares these priorities.[23] It is not an exclusive concept or method, but an umbrella term for a conversation between people who draw on many intellectual and political precedents. We encourage work pitched in dialogue with related approaches such as moral economy, global commodity chains, health, and popular and informal economies.

We hope to launch many nodes of enquiry united by a desire to make economy more human than we currently find it. We do not aim for an exclusive monopoly ('our side'), but to build a plural, inclusive and decentralized network. The economy is not a remote object reported online and in the TV news. It concerns how people should manage their lives to get by or improve their lot. The economics tradition has a variable history of answers to this question historically.

World society now undermines the national vehicles for living that dominated the last century. Professional economic discourse seems increasingly impersonal and remote from daily life. The human economy approach seeks to bring together scholars, activists and practitioners for whom connecting what people do and human interests as a whole is of urgent concern. We trace our own origins to the 'alter-globalization'[24] movement launched by the

---

20. See Chapter 2.

21. J. Earle et al., *The Econocracy* (2016).

22. A. Marshall, *Principles of Economics* (1890).

23. K. Hart, 'The Human Economy' (2008); Hart, Appendix 2010a, 2015b, 2016a, 2016c, 2021; https://www.berghahnbooks.com/series/?pg=huma_econ (accessed 15 September 2021).

24. G. Pleyers, *Alter-globalization* (2011).

first World Social Forum held in Porto Alegre in 2001. Our aim is to build a conversation among ourselves and with other specialists, ultimately with the general public. This is based on empirical investigation and comparison as much as on developing a theoretical and methodological framework for planning research. Our basic method is inspired by the ethnographic revolution that launched social and cultural anthropology in the last century. The economy is always plural and people's experiences of it across time and space have more in common than the use of contrastive terms like 'capitalism' or 'socialism' would suggest. We focus on the multiple institutions that mediate experience of economic life. We promote economic democracy by helping people to organize and improve their own lives. Our findings should be presented to the public in a spirit of pragmatism and made understandable for readers' own use.

This is all compatible with a humanist perspective. It must be so, if the economy is to be returned from remote experts to the people most affected by it. But humanism is not enough. A human economy must be informed by a vision bridging the gap between everyday life (what people know) and humanity's common predicament, which is impersonal and lies beyond the actor's point of view (what they don't know). To this end a variety of ideas and methods could be drawn from philosophy, world history, literature and grand social theory.

We need to make a world society where all people can live together. Small may be beautiful and a preference for initiatives grounded in local social realities is unchallengeable; but large-scale bureaucracies, whether governments, business corporations or international organizations, are essential too if our world is to embrace economic democracy. This dialectic of small-scale humanism and large-scale impersonal institutions is illustrated in Chapters 3 and 19. Since we anchor economic strategies in people's everyday lives, local circumstances and hopes for wider connection, the movement should be one of *extension* from the local towards the global. We can't arrive instantly at a view of the whole, but we can engage more with the world that lies beyond local and national institutions.

Money and markets are intrinsic to our human potential, not anti-human as often depicted. They should take forms more conducive to economic democracy. It helps to recognize that money and markets span the social extremes of our lives. Human motivations for economic action are more holistic than the economists allow for, taking in well-being and the good life, for example. These have traditionally been shaped by organized religion. A human economy approach must revisit the complex interaction between religion, education and economy.

The principles of an 'economy', conceived of as a specific strategy, must be discovered, articulated and disseminated. Such an economy, to be useful, should be based on general guidelines for what people do. It is not just an ideology or a call for realism. The social and technical conditions of our era – urbanization, fast transport and universal media – should underpin any attempt to implement these principles of human economy. We do not assume that people know best, although they usually know their own minds better than those who presume to speak for them.

In origin, 'economy' privileged budgeting for domestic self-sufficiency; political economy promoted capitalist markets over military landlordism; national economy sought to equalize the chances of a citizen body. 'Human economy' could be a way of envisaging the next stage, linking unique human beings to humanity as a whole. It would bring together an extended sequence, house–market–city–nation–world, whose typical social units do not replace each other, but rather coexist.

The human economy idea may have its origins in small-scale informal activities and a humanist ideology, but effective resistance to a global corporate takeover will require alliances between self-organized initiatives on the ground and large-scale bureaucracies of the public and private kind. It will also require global social networks such as those we drew our own impetus from. For, as Albert Camus told us in *The Plague*, the human predicament is impersonal; there are powerful anti-humanist forces in our shared lives.[25] We must build bridges between local actors and the new human universal, world society. To be human is to depend on impersonal social conditions. In confronting the corporations, we must be sure that we are human and they are not. The drive for economic democracy will not be won until that confusion has been cleared up.

Some Forms of Economy and Their Principles

Domestic economy: budgeting for household self-sufficiency, anti-market;

Religious economy (Buddhist, Christian, Islamic, Hindu): city and country in God's natural plan, for commerce against usury;

Political economy: capitalist markets against military landlordism;

Urban economy: independent cities trading with the world;

National economy: moderating capitalist inequality in a citizen community (macroeconomics);

Market economy: rational individual choice in a free market (microeconomics);

Socialist economy: (cooperative, state, communist): control by the workers in a workers' state;

Capitalist economy: one-world capitalism, free flow of money, financial globalization;

Human economy: house–market–nation–world, human beings for all humanity, economic democracy.

---

25. A. Camus, *The Plague* (*La peste*) (1947).

Chapter 16

AFRICA (1800–2100)

Waiting for Emancipation

It is hard to recall what I was thinking when I set out for Accra in 1965 to do field research. Although I was a would-be career academic, I was influenced by the zeitgeist of the 1960s. Western youth rejected the authority of our parents' generation – unwisely as it turned out. We chanted the names of the heroes of the anti-colonial revolution – Ho Chi Minh, Fidel Castro, Che Guevara, Mao Tse Tung and the rest – and believed that the defeat of colonial empire had major implications for humanity as a whole (civil rights, the women's movement, the anti-nuclear campaign, even world politics). In the course of the 1970s, we saw this dream unravel. I then wrote a book on West Africa[1] to explain why postcolonial state formation had failed in societies that were still predominantly rural.

It was an angry book. I argued that modern states had been erected on the basis of backward agriculture. Either some sectors of the economy had to raise their productivity by adopting machine methods or the state would devolve to a level compatible with peasant economy. I called this 'Haitianization', after C.L.R. James's account of the slave revolution's aftermath in San Domingo.[2] This recognized the role of foreign financial pressures after independence; and it was prophetic, since the 1980s saw the Bretton Woods institutions pull the rug out from under African governments. Before long

---

1. K. Hart, *West Africa* (1982).
2. C.L.R. James, *The Black Jacobins* (1938).

failed states became commonplace in the region. Later I joined James himself and began a belated education in Pan-Africanism.

As someone (Hegel?) once wrote, an old man repeats the prayers he learned as a child, but now with the experience of a lifetime. Perhaps I want to prove here that my youthful aspirations were not wholly misguided. We should ask now whether the international and national bureaucracies that regulate the movement of people, goods and money around the world serve the interests of humanity or just a powerful few. Hernando De Soto is a controversial figure; but he had a point when he claimed that developing countries like Peru were once stuck in a colonial mercantile system and now are constrained by an international bureaucracy that works only for the developed countries (and their corporations). The West would never have developed in the first place if their infant capitalist economies had been similarly encumbered (see below).[3] Politics is still mainly national, but the economy is global and as over-regulated as under-regulated. Nowhere is this problem more urgent than in Africa.

Between Slavery and Freedom in West Africa

If Europeans in the eighteenth century could look back on three centuries of Europe's expansion into the world and forward to the replacement of agrarian civilization by an age of democracy, our century looks back on two centuries in which European and American empires made an unequal world society powered by machines – and then lost it. We need to reflect on these three unfinished centuries when trying to build a democratic world. By 2100, four out of five people will live in Asia and Africa. In contrast, the world population of 1900 was one third of European origin, and they controlled 80 per cent of the planet's land and people. The period 1800–2100 is a drama in three acts, of which the last has just begun. The main issue will be Africa's population explosion and what its political and economic consequences will be.[4]

The movement to abolish slavery in the nineteenth century was the dramatic expression of a universal desire to end an old regime founded on varieties of unfreedom.[5] West Africa supplied most victims of the Atlantic slave trade. Internal slavery there, however, was not based on a sharp contrast between free and unfree labour. Emancipation from slavery was contradic-

---

3. H. De Soto, *The Other Path* (1989); *The Mystery of Capital* (2000).

4. https://opendemocracy.net/keith-hart/waiting-for-emancipation-prospects-for-liberal-revolution-in-africa (accessed 15 September 2021); K. Hart, 'Afrique: en attendant l'émancipation' (2016).

5. See Chapter 10; Hart, Appendix 1998.

tory and delayed. The subsequent history of the region – colonial empire and postcolonial failure – gave West Africans little reason to celebrate abolition as a route to political freedom.

Concepts of slavery and freedom slide between a narrow, realist definition and broader metaphorical extensions. To be sold in auction with a rope round one's neck was once commonplace and is no longer. In that sense, slavery has been abolished. Freedom is more ambiguous, but every child knows the difference between self-expression and being prevented from it. The rhetoric of freedom is widespread today. We are told that the 'free' world lives by 'free' enterprise and 'freedom' of choice in a 'free' market employing 'free' citizens as 'free' wage labour. These extensions of the idea of freedom often mask endemic inequality, mass poverty, racial discrimination and arbitrary power. Critics talk of wage 'slavery'. The plight of citizens under dictators may also be likened to 'slavery'. West Africa requires us to keep both absolute and relative definitions in mind.

If the French Revolution marked a new era of modern politics, the abolition of slavery was the most powerful symbol of the drive for human freedom and it still is. Agriculture requires control over land, plants and animals and by extension control over people. Denying people freedom of movement separates agrarian societies from their more mobile predecessors and their contemporaries.[6] Archaic institutions today, notably states reinforced by machines, still try to restrain populations that have discovered universal connection and movement.

The New World system of slavery was as debased a form of human exploitation as any in history. Chattel slavery reduced slaves to things; but objects are usually preserved, not maltreated. Fear of slave revolt led the owners to institute a terror comparable to Hitler's and Stalin's. Since African slaves were distinguished by colour, racial discrimination became the essence of the system. South African apartheid was similar. The New World whites went to horrific extremes in their abuse of blacks. The opening chapters of James's *The Black Jacobins* ('The Property' and 'The Owners') provide vivid descriptions of this.

Abolition was linked to the movement to establish free wage labour as the norm. This came with evangelical Christianity, economic individualism and popular commitment to freedom, democracy and human rights. Industrial capitalism was central to this momentous shift from old to new society.[7] The question of indigenous slavery in West Africa is thus hardly an innocent one. Centuries of Western propaganda claiming that slavery was a civilizing influence on primitive Africans is countered by the devastation caused by the

---

6. See Chapter 13.

7. B. Hilton, *The Age of Atonement* (1988).

unthinking barbarity of Western predators in Africa. This ideological mine-field can explode at any time.

I was once in a panel at Wayne State University, Detroit, talking about relations between traders on the coast and the indigenous aristocracies who supplied many slaves. A large shaven-headed African American on the front row stood up and interrupted me:

> AA: Are you saying we slaved our own people, motherfucker? KH: Yes. AA: How do you know? KH: Oh, Portuguese, Dutch records. . . AA: Any Africans write them records? KH: Ah yes, a good point, no Africans.

Years later I was discussing Africa with a middle-class Jamaican woman who didn't like Nigerians.

> MCW: I shouldn't say this to you, dear; but TGFS. KH: What's that? MCW: Thank God for slavery. Got us out of the jungle, didn't it?

A minefield indeed.

In time I understood the deep historical roots of a system that denied black people their right to the political forms they need for freedom and prosper-ity. Race is still central to an unequal world economy that inflicts appalling indignities on humanity. This unfreedom restricts me and people like me, if not as harshly as most Africans. From living in Britain, Ghana, the United States, Canada, Jamaica, Brazil, France and South Africa, I have learned that the perspectives of the 'Black Atlantic' are largely mine also.[8]

Kinship and slavery were the dominant forms of labour in West Africa. One is a model of community and consensus, the other the epitome of dom-ination and coercion. They had much in common. Some would say that African slavery (particularly domestic) is benevolent, since slaves were often treated like kinsmen. But kin, especially women and young men, were often treated like slaves. Land was abundant and labour scarce; social organization emphasized control over human beings more than control over real proper-ty.[9] Societies founded on kinship may be relatively consensual, if vulnerable family members can leave; they may be tyrannical too. Nor is slavery the antithesis of kinship, but a natural outgrowth of its development, as Morgan, Engels and many others insisted.[10] Any concrete relationship may modulate between love and abuse; similarly, social structures vary between being con-sensual or coercive.

---

8. P. Gilroy, *The Black Atlantic* (1993). See Chapters 9 and 10.

9. J. Goody, *Production* (1976). See Chapter 9.

10. See 'the anthropology of unequal society' in Chapter 3.

West African kinship organized reproduction and coordinated production. No society on earth represents the parent–child bond as equal. Inequality is the cardinal value of West African kinship. Brothers differ in rank according to birth order. Relations between men and women are highly unequal. A society organized through kinship is fundamentally disunited; this makes an ideology of community and solidarity essential.[11] Westerners, who retain the idea without the substance of a society organized through kinship, project their own nostalgia onto the faction-ridden and anxiety-prone family life of African villages. The relationship between slavery and kinship in West Africa highlights the contested character of human existence today.

Africa exported slaves to the Mediterranean, Arabia and the Gulf at least from the first millennium BCE. In a world of high transport costs, any commodity that could walk (people and animals) was at a premium. West Africa's slave trade is very ancient. The region's centralized powers captured slaves by raiding their neighbours; the revenue enabled rulers to maintain an aristocratic lifestyle. Some extracted tribute in slaves from groups on their periphery. Their own citizens were enslaved through debt enforcement or fines. Africans came to be preferred for the Atlantic slave trade because of growing resistance to enslaving Christians in Europe, epidemiological factors and the ready supply made available by slave-raiding aristocracies.

Within the region, slaves were put to work as soldiers, as servants and in a variety of occupations. At times they controlled the state. Internal slavery can only be understood through differences in kinship structures. Social anthropologists made these comprehensible, but preferred to downplay their coercive aspects. Social scientists later focused on race, class and gender.

The Long Road to Emancipation in West Africa

The Haitian Revolution, following on from the American and French revolutions, severely dented the Atlantic slave trade around 1800. Britain officially abolished that trade in 1807 and sought to deter the West African traffic from a naval base in Sierra Leone. Slavery was abolished in the British Empire in 1833; the American Civil War ended it in 1865; Cuba was still importing slaves in the 1870s, Brazil until the 1880s. By 1900, forest products (rubber, oil palm and cocoa) drove West Africa's export economy; and European empires completed the scramble for Africa then. Slaves were sometimes put to work on plantations by Africans.[12] The consequences for West Africa of global emancipation were ambiguous.

---

11. Hart, Appendix 2018d.
12. K. Polanyi, *Dahomey and the Slave Trade* (1966).

West African supplies of slaves did not slow up as fast as the overseas demand for slaves. Slaves became more abundant within the region and their price fell.[13] Life was cheapened. Whereas a slave might once accompany a great king when he died, human sacrifice now became commonplace at the funerals of minor figures. Europeans made much of this when justifying their civilizing mission in Africa.

The industrialization of killing (gunboats and machine guns) now allowed Europeans to extend their control beyond a few coastal enclaves.[14] Africans had been equal partners in the Atlantic slave trade; but the industrial revolution generated a growing gap in the means available to the two sides. The turmoil and instability brought about by abolition in West Africa also helped the Europeans. Wars, massive dislocation and religious upheavals disorganized and reduced local populations.

The new colonial powers (mainly Britain and France) were committed to abolition within West Africa. Emancipation was declared a legal fact there. The reality was more complex, however. Colonial regimes were undermanned and they lacked the support afforded by mines and settlers further south. They instituted systems of 'indirect rule'. Alliances were made with indigenous authorities. These were often the remaining slaveholders. West Africa's progress towards emancipation was deferred.

Colonial empire lasted for only sixty years in most of West Africa. Establishing rule was its first preoccupation and anticipating its own demise the last. In the interwar period, when the colonial regimes were most secure, moves were made to end slavery. Even so, the League of Nations arraigned the Liberian government for organizing an international traffic in slaves. Later, Mauretania implausibly argued that its highly stratified society was no longer based on slavery. Many African economies regressed for a half-century after independence. Apartheid was defeated in South Africa around 1990, but three decades later the country is more unequal than before. Africans still await equal membership of world society. But they have never encountered more favourable conditions than in the coming century.

In an East Nigerian university not long ago, a professor accused the Vice Chancellor of being a 'slave' to his family and won the case. Domestic servants, including children, are often family; yet many endure extreme drudgery. These are country cousins of the urban elite, teenagers lacking education, money or social skills who perform unpaid labour under harsh conditions. There is more to freedom and unfreedom in social life than formal slavery. The forms of West African slavery lack the brutal logic of English law transplanted to the New World. Independence from colonial rule has not delivered to most

13. R. Law (ed.), *From Slave Trade to 'Legitimate' Commerce* (1995).
14. S. Lindqvist, *Exterminate All the Brutes* (1992).

Africans political freedom or freedom from poverty, illness and violence. It is convenient for the region's ruling elites to stress European responsibility for this; but the entourages of military dictators and kleptocratic presidents are as complicit in this misrule as were their predecessors in the Atlantic slave trade.

A welter of lies obscures the options facing humanity. Nationalists invent a past of shared blood and soil. Apologists for capitalism see 'freedom' in wage 'slavery'. Racists on all sides explain inequality by cultural fictions. We could revisit the universalism of the 1790s, when the French and Haitian revolutions promised an end to inequality that was permanently deferred. Abolition was progressive, for sure; but the underlying causes of human inequality persist and, on some counts, are becoming worse. African writers like Chinua Achebe have flourished since independence; but the influential traffic has mostly been one way, about Africans, rather than by them.

Africa's Urban Revolution in the Last Century

Africa is 'the land of the blacks'. It is also a continent separated from Eurasia by the Mediterranean and Red Seas. It has an African Union, some policy-discussion bodies and an African cup for national football teams whose best players work in Europe. Africa is divided into three disparate regions – North, South and Middle (West, Central and East Africa); but some convergence between them is now taking place, enhancing the prospects for greater union.[15] Africa's relative poverty has increased since independence; but urbanization there is fast approaching the global average.

In the last century, a population explosion was accompanied by a jump in Africa's urban share from under 2 per cent to between a third and a half.[16] This urban revolution was not just a proliferation of cities, but also involved the whole package of pre-industrial class society: states, urban elites, the city bazaar, intensification of agriculture and extraction of rural surpluses.[17] The anti-colonial revolution unleashed hopes for the transformation of an unequal world. Africa's new leaders thought they were building modern economies, but they were actually erecting fragile states based on small-scale agriculture. Significant mechanization did not occur and the democratic legitimacy of independence gave way to dependence on foreign powers ('neo-colonialism'). The international organizations switched off life support for Africa's nominal rulers after 1980. Many governments were bankrupt and some collapsed into civil war.[18]

---

15. See Chapter 3.
16. Hart, Appendix 2010d.
17. See Chapter 13.
18. Hart, *West African Agriculture*. See Chapter 7.

The growth of cities should lead to cumulative rural–urban exchange, as farmers supply food to city-dwellers and in turn buy the latter's manufactures and services. But this progressive division of labour requires a measure of protection from the big beasts in the world market. Development was stifled at birth in postcolonial Africa by dumping of subsidized food from the tax-rich West and later of cheap Asian manufactures. 'Structural adjustment programmes' imposed by the World Bank and IMF removed protection from Africa's fledgling national economies. Tax collection in Africa was never as regular as elsewhere; and governments there rely on what they can extract from mineral royalties and the import-export trade. Rents secured by political privilege are the chief source of wealth. This is the Old Regime's classical formula and increasingly that of Western capitalism today.

Thinking about Africa's future must start from its urban growth in the last century. Regional commerce has been approached so far mainly in terms of the 'informal economy'. Currently 70–90 per cent of African national economies are estimated to be 'informal', meaning that governments impose rules they cannot enforce and their people largely ignore. The rise of cities has spawned weak and venal states, dependent on foreign powers and content to leave the urban masses to their own devices. 'Africa' is a continental territory – Africans, Europeans, Indians, Chinese and Arabs alike. But the legacy of imperialism means that race and development are still linked in symbolic and practical terms; and, as Africans' share of world population climbs inexorably, their dreams of emancipation have global implications.

For the sake of brevity, I distinguish between three types of African social formation: 'egalitarian societies' based on kinship, not class; 'agrarian civilizations', where the state and class privilege confer urban control of the mass of rural labour; and 'national capitalism', where markets and money are regulated by central bureaucracies. Africa's traditional societies south of the Sahara generally conformed to the first type, allowing for the informal inequalities of kinship. Agrarian civilizations covered North Africa and most of Eurasia for five thousand years. National capitalism was the model of development imposed on Africa by international organizations; but it only took root in racist Southern Africa.

Middle Africa made a belated transition to agrarian civilization after 1945, while the West, the Soviet bloc and Asia embraced national capitalism on the way to neoliberal globalization. This brought North and Middle Africa closer together as pre-industrial class societies, while South Africa's post-apartheid government, having learned nothing from postcolonial failure elsewhere, increasingly resembles the African norm. The whole continent, fragmented into fifty-five weak nation states, now constitutes an Old Regime ripe for liberal revolution. There are well-documented historical examples that suggest what that could mean. Any strategy for African development must build on the social conditions of the last century.

The struggle for African independence assumed that changing ownership of the state would deliver economic development, regardless of conditions elsewhere. Frantz Fanon took a different view. In *The Wretched of the Earth*, written from Algeria's anti-colonial war, he predicted that the 'pitfalls of national consciousness' would undermine Africa's postcolonial states, mainly because of the weakness of the new middle class that led them:

> From the beginning the national bourgeoisie directs its efforts towards (economic) activities of the intermediary type. The basis of its strength is found in its aptitude for trade and small business enterprises, and for securing commissions. It is not its money that works, but its business acumen. It does not go in for investments and it cannot achieve that accumulation of capital necessary to the birth and blossoming of an authentic bourgeoisie.[19]

These elites inevitably concede power to foreign interests. They first relied on revenues from agricultural exports, then on dubious loans, finally on the financial monopoly that came from supervising their country's relations with global capitalism. But this bonanza was turned off in the 1980s, when foreign capital discovered that it could dispense with local state intermediaries and concentrated on collecting debts from them.

Hopes for African democracy soon disappeared, to be replaced by dictatorship, whether civil or military. Concentration of political power led to primate urbanization, with the expenditures of presidential kleptocracy the main motor of economic demand. A peasantry subjected to political extraction and violence at home could only stagnate or migrate to the main cities and abroad. The cities survived through spontaneous markets that recycled the money spent at the top. These somehow met the people's needs for food, shelter, clothing, transport and the rest.[20]

African Development in the Twenty-First Century

There have been three modern shifts in the composition of the world's population. The first was Europe's growth between the 1830s and 1930s. Its motor was industrial capitalism – better food, sanitation and living conditions, and eventually electrification. The second was Asia's after 1945, for similar reasons; but Asia already had the largest share of population and its rank order did not change. Europe was home to 25 per cent of the world's population in

---

19. F. Fanon, *The Wretched of the Earth* (2001 [1961]: 144).
20. See Chapter 15.

1900 (36 per cent if we include the lands of temperate zone new settlement). Africa had only 7.5 per cent, with a population density much lower than the other main regions. 'The scramble for Africa' from the 1880s was an unevenly matched contest. The continent's global share then doubled from 1900 to now. According to the middle UN projection, Africa will be home to 25 per cent of the world's people in 2050, and 40 per cent in 2100; Asia's share will be 42 per cent then (60 per cent now). All the rest (the Americas, Europe, Russia and Oceania) will have 18 per cent (25 per cent now). Europe's share will have shrunk to 6 per cent, less than Africa's in 1900.

This third epochal change in the regional balance of humanity is much larger than the other two. Its motor is Africa's annual population growth rate of 2.5 per cent, while fertility and mortality rates are collapsing everywhere else. The main reason for these bursts of population growth is birth rates staying high for a time while death rates fall thanks to material improvements. When people gradually become surer that they will keep their children, they invest their energies in fewer of them and birth rates fall. This is 'the demographic transition model'.[21] In the African case, death rates have fallen there too, but continuing precarity has not yet persuaded African women that they should count on having fewer children. The Asian manufacturing countries already recognize that Africa will soon be the fastest-growing market in the world; not so the West, which wallows in nostalgia for its nineteenth-century hegemony. This could provide an opportunity for Africans to play a stronger hand in international negotiations. If they succeed in standing up for themselves, it would be a world revolution – the end of the racist world order as we know it, no less.

The institutions of agrarian civilization are alive and well today, not just in postcolonial Africa.[22] The greatest riches are no longer acquired through selling manufactures cheaper than one's competitors; rents secured by political privilege keep the super-rich afloat today – Big Pharma's licenced income from patents, for example, monopoly profits from DVDs and CDs or banks ('too big to fail') being bailed out by tax revenues.

Clearly, trade and finance are not organized, in Africa or the world at large, with a view to liberating popular movements. Successful popular revolutions need allies with significant wealth and power. Africans will have to develop their own transnational associations to combat the huge coalitions that would deny them self-development. One strong political movement is the formation of large regional trading blocs in response to neoliberal globalization. A national framework for development never made sense in Africa and it makes even less today. The coming revolution could leapfrog many obstacles

21. J. Caldwell et al., *Demographic Transition Theory* (2006).
22. Hart, Appendix 2002b.

in its path, but not if African societies still wear the national straitjackets they inherited from colonial rule.

To speak of economic growth begs the question of what Africa's new urban populations could produce to bring about their own economic development. So far, African countries have relied on exporting raw materials, when they could. Minerals clearly have a promising future owing to scarce supplies and escalating demand; but the world market for food and other agricultural products is skewed by Western farm subsidies and prices are further depressed by the large number of poor farmers seeking entry. Conventionally, African governments have aspired to manufacturing exports as an alternative, but here they face intense competition from Asia. The world market for services, especially digital services, is booming and perhaps greater opportunities for supplying national, regional and global markets exist there.

There was a time when most services were performed personally on the spot; but today, thanks to the digital revolution, they increasingly link producers and consumers at distance. The fastest-growing sector of world trade is the production of culture: entertainment, education, media, software and information services. The future of the human economy, once material requirements are satisfied, lies in the infinite scope for us to do intangible things for each other – like singing songs or telling stories. The largest global television audiences are for sporting events like the World Cup or the Olympic Games. The US's three leading exports are movies, music and software; they have sponsored an intellectual property treaty (TRIPs) that shores up corporate profits on products reproduced digitally at little cost.[23] Any move to enter this market will encounter transnational corporations and their supporting governments. Nevertheless, there is more to play for here and the terrain is not as rigidly mapped out. It is also one where Africans are well placed to compete because global audiences like their music and plastic arts.

Why is Hollywood where it is? A century ago, East Coast film-makers struggled under Thomas Edison's monopolies. Some escaped to the far West and launched the movie industry there without much regulation. For his first Mickey Mouse cartoon, Walt Disney ripped off a Buster Keaton movie, 'Steamboat Willie'. Now the Disney Corporation sues Chinese cartoonists for illegal appropriation of the Mickey Mouse logo. The world's second largest producer of movies is now Lagos in Nigeria ('Nollywood'); most of its movies cost under $5,000. American popular culture is still that country's most successful export. It could be for Africans too.

Africa must escape soon from varieties of Old Regime that owe a lot to the legacy of slavery, colonialism and apartheid; but these alone should not be blamed for conditions today. Africa now leads the world in mobile money

---

23. See Chapter 14.

networks, notably Kenya's M-pesa;[24] and, after largely missing out on the steam and electricity phases of the machine revolution, Africans have taken to digital economy with great dynamism and imagination. Learning from earlier commercial revolutions, while using contemporary technology, could offer fresh solutions to Africa's underdevelopment. Its future economic growth lies in the cultural production of its cities, not rural extraction or the reactionary hope of reproducing capitalism's industrial phase. This will require a broad-based social revolution. Contributing elements might include the energy of youth and women; the religious revival; exploding modern arts; the digital revolution; and the African global diaspora since 1945. Any African revolutions will be shaped by the continent's own history; but the West's liberal revolutions provide important lessons too.[25]

Free Trade and Protection in the Early Modern Revolutions

The American, French and Italian revolutions all combined mass insurgency with an extended period of international warfare driven by the desire to remove fragmented sovereignty, unfair taxes and restrictions of movement and trade. German unification had a similar focus, but followed a different political trajectory. The British global free trade regime in the nineteenth century and its American revival today have obscured the historical interplay of freedom and protection first articulated by the Jacobite exile Sir James Steuart.[26] His argument was later reinforced by American and German nationalists.

The main task was to overcome divided sovereignty within and between states. Development depended on removing these barriers to trade. Then incipient free trade areas needed some protection, so that domestic agriculture and manufactures could benefit from an evolving rural–urban division of labour. The French Revolution is a striking example.

In 1793, the Terror was unleashed and the Bretons raised a 'Royal and Catholic Army', forcing the new Republic to fight what became the War of La Vendée.[27] Nantes, France's largest port, was heavily involved in slavery and trade with the Caribbean. It stood out for the Republic and was besieged by the Royalist army. This battle was decisive for the Revolution; the slave shippers financed the Republican army. Why did the Nantes bourgeoisie risk so much for the Revolution? France, a centralized monarchy, was also a patch-

---

24. See Chapter 19.

25. Non-western examples include Bolivar's Latin America in the 1820s and the Southeast Asian Tigers from the 1950s.

26. J. Steuart, *Principles of Political Economy* (1767).

27. The subject of Victor Hugo's last novel, *Ninety-Three*.

work of local fief-holders, each of whom exacted what they could from people and goods moving through their territory. The Republic would establish a regulated home market with national police protection for traders.[28] The Nantes bourgeoisie wanted to reduce the costs of moving their trade goods inland to home consumers, so they allied with the Republic.

In the United States, Dutch traders and American smugglers led resistance to the East India Company's tea monopoly and to British taxes offsetting the crown's global military costs.[29] The Italian Risorgimento too was backed financially by the industrialists of Milan and Turin, who wanted a unified national home market and access to world trade free of Austrian restrictions. In all three cases, the power of capital played a decisive part in the revolution.

Long before the European Common Market became the European Union, the Prussian *Zollverein* was launched in 1818 and culminated in the German Empire. In each case political unification was preceded by a customs union lasting half a century. The *Zollverein* was a piecemeal attempt to harmonize tariffs, measures and economic policy in scattered territories controlled by the Prussian ruling family. The Germans attributed their weakness to extreme political fragmentation (some forty states in 1815). Prussia aimed to consolidate its own empire by extending a protected zone of internal free trade from which the Austrians would be excluded. By the 1860s, most of what became modern Germany had joined the customs union. Their leading economist was a German American, Friedrich List, who proposed a 'national system'.[30] He emphasized the scope for innovation within an expanded free trade area protected from the world market. Similar proposals were made by Americans like Alexander Hamilton and Henry Clay.

Towards Greater Integration of African Trade

South Africa's President Thabo Mbeki proposed an 'African renaissance' led by his black majority government to end African countries being easy pickings for the great powers through political coordination between African states and their economic revival. His initiative targeted the very political class that had failed Africa since independence. Civil society movements were absent from this vision. Africa consists of a labyrinthine confusion of regional associations that do little to strengthen their members' bargaining power in world markets. Meanwhile, despite governments' attempts to force them into

---

28. The Roman Empire protected traders' private property too; J. Hicks, *A Theory of Economic History* (1968).

29. Hence the Boston Tea Party.

30 . F. List, *The National System of Political Economy* (1841).

national cages, Africans maintain patterns of long-distance movement and trade developed over centuries.

This is why so much of the African economy is held to be 'informal': state regulations are routinely ignored, so that half the people and most economic activity are criminalized and public effort is wasted on trying to apply unenforceable rules. Classical liberalism offers an answer to this chaos – the widest possible area of free trade and movement, with minimal regulation by the authorities.[31] Neoliberal globalization has done much to discredit this solution, since political initiatives, even in pursuit of free trade, are anathema. Yet the policy is inescapable: the boundaries of free commerce *and* of state intervention should be pushed beyond the limits of existing sovereignties.

The world powers actively interested in Africa are China, the United States, France and Japan. Western politicians claim that China aims to subvert national regimes for the purpose of extracting minerals from Africa. This is wrong. China has been Asia's leading exporter of manufactures for some time, at first using cheap labour moving to its cities from the countryside. But this strategy is vulnerable to swings in world market demand. Lenin presciently argued that durable economic growth depends on developing the home market for large-scale industry.[32] Arthur Lewis showed that the division between rich and poor countries in the last century required insulating high-wage from low-wage labour streams.[33] Neoliberal globalization put an end to that.

Shipping has reduced transport costs for material objects as radically as the digital revolution has for information. A car made in Shanghai costs roughly $5,000 to make and ship to Dar-es-Salaam. It costs another $4000 to transport it overland to Kampala, 1,500 kilometres away. The reason is the same as in pre-revolutionary France: local thugs (including police and soldiers licenced by the state) extract tribute at every point, while holding up all travellers, however poor. The African masses and China-sponsored traders each have a stake in curbing this larceny. It just needs regional trade organizations to find ways of controlling thugs protected by kleptocratic political elites. The second stage is to expand and protect regional home markets from global predators. China could have an interest in this too. The Chinese government aims to build up its home market to replace reliance on exports. If it succeeds, urban wages will rise there. Strengthened African trade federations, representing the fastest-growing world market demand, could lobby for assembly and similar plants to be relocated within their boundaries, allowing Chinese corporations to take advantage of Africa's cheaper labour. In time, Africa could enjoy the upward spiral of development identified by Steuart 250 years ago.

31. See the epigraph to Chapter 13.

32. V.I. Lenin, *The Development of Capitalism in Russia* (1899).

33. W.A. Lewis, *The Evolution of the International Economic Order* (1978).

China once occupied a similar slot in Western consciousness to Africa today. I was told as a child to eat my spinach because the Chinese were starving. In the 1930s, China was crippled by warlord violence, its peasants mired in terrible poverty. Less than a century later it is the coming superpower. This shift from West to East does not guarantee that Africa will soon cast off the stigma of racial inferiority; but North Atlantic dominance is perceptibly shifting; and change is easier to envisage now. Humanity is entering a new era of social possibility. Africans' drive for emancipation from internal and externally imposed inequality affects us all. Revolution in Africa would be a world revolution.

Part IV

LIFELONG LEARNING

A Short History of Knowledge

I

Her every mood was mine.
Each heartbeat – her blood, my blood –
echoed in the empty chambers
of my embryonic brain,
reverberated through my cramped, elastic frame,
taught me to believe that life goes on.
The jagged contours of her work and play
made me scale mountains.
Her sleep was a quiet valley.
She trained me for struggle and for rest,
a foetus floating outside time
in the red-black moon-tide of that ever-changing sea.

What did this being know?
I knew the music of her organism,
rhythmic, life-sustaining heart and lungs.
I knew that she and I were one,
the undivided we,
immune to strangeness and the self.

II

Bypassing birth, the story of my life:
My mouth outstripped a stunted body's growth.
I learned to cut and break with words;
the razor sliced, the hammer smashed.
The schoolmen smiled a monkish smile
to see so frantic an apprenticeship.

And now I scan a dusty, barren plain.
My stride devours the bounded space of earth,
a hermit seeking to bridge the unbridgeable,
pilgrim to paperback shrines of the founders,
calling on ancestors, self-searching explorers,
to show me the way to others and myself.

We need to know, but not like this,
endless, abstracted seeming of horizons,
sacrificing moments to the logic-choppers' ends.
Oh the lingering death of a modern education,
meaningless sense and mind without content,
sad cleavage of my desiccated soul.

III

The cure is obvious enough,
woman, mysterious keeper of the womb,
dark-bright complement to my sex,
a window on infinity in each exploring touch.
But every heaven-bent freedom flight till now
has brought me crashing, wounded down to earth.

In these green eyes sea, land and sky are one.
This red mouth – wet tongue, dry teeth, hot breath –
Stops up my wooden words with watery fire.
This rainbow coupling takes me back to timeless rhythms,
hurls me forward to my destiny,
anchors my being singular in you.

So, knowing is biblical after all?
Self-knowledge comes from the love-object,
The ineffable, renewing 'thou',
the ambiguous flash of union, fusion of elements,
a light to guide our march towards blind death.
Beginning is all, the end nothing.

Chapter 17

AFTER THE BRITISH EMPIRE

Politics and Education

Britain is not just any country. Its industrial revolution, with my city as its prime focus, launched the astonishing global growth of the last two centuries. Its empire, the biggest in history, dominated the nineteenth century. English is now the world language, thanks to its successor, the American Empire. America and Britain are two nations divided by a common language,[1] and by a rather brutal transition of power between them, misrepresented (by the British) as a 'special relationship'. Britain's resistance to Nazi Germany in the Second World War provided a heroic legend that compensated somewhat for the drastic forfeit of world leadership afterwards.

The loss of empire and its industrial lead made Britain ripe for transformation from the 1950s.[2] But it never came. Around 2000, I began writing about Britain's 'creeping constitutional crisis' and its consequences for national identity. I was by then an expatriate in France and South Africa. This did not prepare me for Brexit – Britain's separation from the European Union – a savage tragicomedy that blew up my dream of a united Europe and amplified nostalgia politics in Britain. Maybe I have a better story of Britain's institutional implosion, but I didn't predict its actual political course. I begin this reflection on my self-education with the painful history of Britain since the Second World War. This includes the origins of the empire that collapsed soon after I was born, an account of British higher education in my lifetime and a brief account of the current political crisis.

---

1. Attributed to several wags, notably George Bernard Shaw.
2. These two paragraphs put my personal story of Chapter 5 in a larger historical frame.

I benefited from increased opportunities for lower-class provincial boys after the war. But the contents of the education, its syllabus and teaching methods, were devised by James and John Stuart Mill to train civil servants for India a century before. When Victoria became Empress of India in 1870, seventeen out of twenty British civil servants worldwide, including Britain itself, worked in India. The Indians had had enough of the Empire by 1947. But the content of the escalator I rode to Manchester Grammar School and Cambridge University remained broadly the same. This lack of fit between historical decline and tenaciously held norms made my generation's rush to climb the social ladder doubly difficult. As a result, we failed to preserve the educational bonanza we inherited.

The United Kingdom and the British Empire

Just before the millennium, I met the US ambassador to France at a Paris tennis club. He asked me if Tony Blair would take the pound into Europe's new single currency, the euro. It wasn't a question of the currency, I said, but whether the country would hold together. The United Kingdom is the most unstable polity in the 'civilized' world and was already in a creeping constitutional crisis. This might combine any of the following: Britain's place in Europe; Scottish independence; reunification of Ireland; an unaccountable ruling class; the absolutist parliament with its feudal relic, the House of Lords; an antiquated voting system; a disastrous royal family. There was widespread resentment of London's monopoly of politics, administration, media, commerce and finance, while the provinces died from economic neglect.

When M.K. Gandhi came to London in 1931, he stayed in London's poor East End and announced that Indian peasants wouldn't tolerate the living conditions there. In a 1947 documentary, Lancashire textile workers were asked about American and Japanese competition. 'Shoddy goods', they replied. 'We have owned the world market for 150 years'. Some of the machines were almost that old. Their rulers told them they were 'the greatest people in the world'. This attitude lingers on. The Conservative Party depends on it. All my life I have been waiting for the penny to drop. But something always turns up to persuade my countrymen that we are still a global power.

The ambassador was pleased: 'The Brits always condescend to us on European questions. We should leave things to them, since we understand so little about the place. The next time I will ask them, what are you doing about your creeping constitutional crisis?'

There are two large islands off Europe's Atlantic coast. One is Albion, later known as Britain (Roman *Britannia* from the Celtic *Bretagne*), the other is Ireland. The two were sometimes known as Great and Little Britain. Albion is the ninth largest island in the world and the third most populous after Java and Honshu. Successive waves of immigration created an ethnic patchwork there whose synthesis is the English language.[3]

Maritime herders were the first wave. Their large stone ('megalithic') monuments extended from the western Mediterranean north to the Baltic Sea and south to the Senegal River. The most impressive, Stonehenge in western England, was built almost five thousand years ago. The language group known as 'Indo-European' has been largely discredited as a white imperialist myth,[4] but the first 'Indo-European' speakers to arrive in Britain were the Celts around 700 BC. They were followed by Romans, Anglo-Saxons, Vikings, Normans and lately 'Commonwealth' immigrants. English is a Germanic language, with a significant register of French and Latin used mainly by priests, lawyers, bureaucrats and academics. Successive historical layers of migration coexist in contemporary English as distinct registers. No-one asks what the megalith-builders contributed to the language over two millennia.

Diverted by September 11 and the Iraq War,[5] I forgot that Paris conversation. Then came the London bombings of 2005. I published pieces about Britain's national identity crisis.[6] The break-up of the United Kingdom is now much closer. Scotland is already bent on secession and the two Irelands are becoming reconciled. The UK's unravelling now recapitulates its violent origin three centuries ago.[7] Alexis de Tocqueville thought Britain in the 1830s was the most powerful state in Europe, but its administration was highly decentralized, a crowd of self-governing shires and municipalities.[8] Since 1945, a relentless accumulation of central power has taken place, while recent Tory governments have reduced local budgets in the name of 'austerity'. The coronavirus pandemic showed that neither London nor the provinces could control the disease, and their interaction was made worse by an authoritarian shift by the Prime Minister. This led to political clashes with the Labour mayor of Manchester and a United footballer, shortly before England was shut down again. My bet that Britain will soon be consumed by the politics of devolution is still on.

In seventeenth-century England, the Catholic aristocracy and Protestant middle class fought a civil war. King Charles was executed and his son restored to the monarchy. A European war of religions was fought between a Protestant coalition led by England and Holland against the Catholic monarchies

---

3. See Chapter 18.

4. C. A. Diop, *The African Origin of Civilization* (1974).

5. Hart, Appendix 2003d. See Chapter 1 and the movie *Vice* (2018).

6. Hart, Appendix 2005b.

7. On Brexit, see Hart, Appendix 2016e.

8. A. de Tocqueville, *Journeys to England and Ireland* (1835).

of France and Spain. Puritan settlers colonized North America. The Dutch prince, William of Orange, led the Protestant armies and then launched 'the Glorious Revolution' in England. He was installed as monarch with his wife, the English princess Mary. On his way, he inflicted a savage defeat on the Irish and settled Scottish Presbyterians (my ancestors)[9] in Northern Ireland to control the Catholic peasantry. The new Bank of England absorbed William's war debts.

The Scots had merged monarchies with the English before for a time. They now joined the race for overseas colonies. They selected Panama, the isthmus between the Atlantic and Pacific Oceans. A third of the country's liquidity was raised for their Darien colony. It collapsed with massive losses. The English then squeezed Scotland's coal exports, imposing a high tariff at the border. Political union between the two countries was proposed and the Scottish elites caved in. The United Kingdom was born in 1707. Scots proved to be enthusiastic and able servants of empire.

The eighteenth century culminated in a world war between England and France, when the Empire's focus switched from the New World to India. The English led an international coalition committed to abolishing slavery.[10] The United Kingdom now controlled the seas and became the world's financial centre, with the gold standard as its instrument. By the 1920s, the Empire comprised a fifth of the world's population and a quarter of the inhabited land surface. The Anglo-Indian superstate dominated geopolitics and forced its rivals to respond – the French in North Africa, the Germans in Persia and the Russians in Afghanistan.

The Empire claimed to bring higher standards to public life in the name of truth, justice and honesty, principles symbolized by the game of cricket. This was never true and the Brexit mess exposed the corrupt shambles of Westminster rule. The Empire always benefited from an English talent for organized brutality that is now manifested as racism at home and soccer hooliganism abroad.

The driving force of the nineteenth century was industrial capitalism. But the British Empire was built on mercantile colonialism by landlords, soldiers, financiers and traders based in the City of London. Modern industry in the north and Midlands, with Scotland, Northern Ireland and Wales, was subverted by an antiquated colonial system. Inevitably other industrial powers (Germany and the US) overtook Britain's lead. The same pattern underlies London's hegemony today. Two world wars finished off the British Empire. The election of the most left-wing government west of Moscow led the US to put an economic squeeze on Britain from 1945.

---

9. See Chapter 4.
10. See Chapter 10.

Since the 1950s the big question has been: what will become of the United Kingdom? There is always some excuse for not coming to grips with reality. Because of its longevity and historical prominence, Britain has a reputation for being stable. The unravelling of the Empire made Britain ripe for political breakdown. This seemed unlikely before 2016; but lately it has become accepted as an inexplicable fact, like the classic Maya collapse around 200 AD.[11] The constitutional crisis intensifies. The UK's place in the European Union (EU) is not the main issue. Institutional conflicts tear apart a society no longer held together by the glue of empire and global industrial leadership. I can extend the list I gave to the ambassador:

Loss of empire and global influence;
Corporate dominance and the collapse of the public sector;
An informal ruling class with no written constitution;
Europe and national sovereignty;
Scottish independence;
The reunification of Ireland;
The absolutist powers of the executive in parliament;
The House of Lords: parliament, the law and feudal property;
An irrational electoral system;
The monarchy and growth of republican sentiment;
The merger between Church and State;
The pound versus the euro and the dollar;
The concentration of power and wealth in London;
Regional devolution in England and Wales;
Racist paranoia over immigration;
The 'special relationship' with the American empire;
The judiciary standing alone against political mayhem.

A Norway–Scotland comparison I undertook with John Bryden confirmed that the Scots would lead the 'break up of Britain'.[12] Powerful forces maintain London's monopoly of politics, administration, finance, global plutocracy, commerce and the media. But the long history of towns and shires is remembered in the provinces and their intellectual centres, the universities.

Relations between the public and private sectors – government and business, workers and consumers – must move. Britain's curious mixture of feudalism and freebooting finance has spawned the dream of London as an offshore Singapore. The world's gangsters (especially Russians) park themselves and their money in London. The Europeans and Americans see the

---

11. T. Culbert, The Classic Maya Collapse (1973). https://en.wikipedia.org/wiki/Classic_Maya_collapse (accessed 15 September 2021).

12. J. Bryden and K. Hart, 'Money and Banking in Scotland and Norway' (2015); T. Nairn, The Break-up of Britain (1977).

City of London as the hub of the world's criminal economy. They are not wrong. This is where Thatcher came from. After Brexit, the pandemic and Europe's worst economic recession, not many imagine that Britain is going to be a prosperous and comfortable place to live in. The European Union has become an undemocratic bullies' club, run by and for bankers, bureaucrats and Germany. Maybe a decentralized Britain could do better.

How My Generation Let Down Our Students

My generation matured in the upward mobility of 'the sixties', which began in 1964 with the Beatles' US tour.[13] Before that, 'kitchen sink' drama and novels featured angry young men from the north. This social upheaval was driven by the Butler Education Act of 1944, the Baby Boom and rising prosperity in the late 1950s. I took little part in this 'cultural revolution'. Divisions of class, gender, race, religion, language and region did seem to be giving way then. But class inequality has been restored since. Oxbridge is still urged to increase recruitment from state schools. Did the temporary democratization of access to education benefit me? It did. But its content was antiquated. Any breathing space I found was despite my training, not because of it.

In 1969, when I got my PhD, there were twenty-three lecturing jobs available. One had no applicants. The new universities were still recruiting and their students had not yet reached the job market. This situation soon turned to one of job scarcity. The Tory government announced a higher education pay review, joining the universities, polytechnics and teachers' training colleges. The lecturers' union stayed out since we were 'part of the ruling class'. The Civil List dealt with pay for the royal family, admirals, judges, professors and the like. It was never likely that lower-class provincials would be admitted en masse. The polytechnics had a pay rise of 25 per cent and the universities nothing.

The union made concessions in exchange for small pay rises. Why we were giving away our work conditions for ephemeral pay increases? Activists claimed that most union members were scientists who were only interested in pay. Why were we placing our faith in the state? I argued for an alliance with the schoolteachers' unions. Most people thought university lecturers were intellectual snobs who had too many holidays. Politicians could shaft us with impunity. We needed a popular constituency. A Labour government then froze our pay when annual inflation was 25 per cent. This wiped out the small increments.

My generation failed to master the art of reproduction. We thought of ourselves as being cut off from our parents. A book about the student occupation of Turin University in 1968 confirmed this.[13] Its leader was later found in his father's law office. 'We felt like orphans. Our parents' generation had betrayed us. They embraced Mussolini's fascism and were defeated twice. We could take nothing from them and had to start afresh by ourselves.' In Britain, our parents won the war against fascism and smoothed our path into higher education. We owed them and our teachers a lot, but were in denial.

Coming from an imaginary 'nowhere', the task of upward social mobility absorbed all our energies. We had to accumulate a family, home and car, learn our trade and navigate the pitfalls of class. We didn't think about conserving our profession and families. We had no time to reflect on the important things. It was never our masters' intention to allow us into the ruling class. University teachers began a long descent into the proletariat. It started as bargaining about pay and status in the 1970s. Margaret Thatcher applied the *coup de grâce*.

Life in the British universities was still generous in the 1960s and 1970s. We didn't have heavy teaching loads and maintained ethical relations with our colleagues and students. Before the war, university lecturers . . . lectured. The point was to teach. The Cold War funded scientific research for food supplies, armaments and pharmaceuticals. A steady flow of capital-intensive research projects was good for academic morale. Social scientists bought into the new idea that 'research is king'. We were not as useful to the powers as the real scientists.

My story hinges on that turning point after 1970. Its gruesome denouement is better known. Margaret Thatcher picked off all interest groups that might obstruct market liberalization. Chief among these were the unions and local government, especially in the main cities. She cleansed her party of the Tory gentry ('the wets'). But she also took on the civil servants, the judges, the doctors and, of course, the universities. We represented a potential source of resistance to central government. The only institution she left unharmed, for obvious reasons, was the City of London.

The English ruling class, lacking a national bourgeoisie, was always ambivalent about the value of education. What would the masses do with it, if not undermine their power? In the 1980s the Tories tried to convert Britain into an offshore facility for transnational corporations. The tedium of the assembly line would banish subversive thoughts. University teachers settled in for trench warfare with the bureaucracy. One February day at Manchester University in the early 1970s, it was freezing and the thermostats were fixed at 58 °F. The secretaries were typing in gloves. I went to the main administration building and was hit by a wall of heat. The thermostats were set at 74 °F. I

---

13. L. Passerini, *Autobiography of a Generation* (1988).

knew then that we were at war with the bureaucrats and would lose. They had nothing better to do than rig the political game. They have been perfecting it ever since.

British cities have been emasculated since the Second World War. Access to higher education was democratized faster in France, Italy and Germany. Britain missed out on a modern university syllabus in the 1920s. The result was an amateur flexibility that was our strength and weakness. This tradition was brutally demolished in the 1990s. A revolution descended on the universities, a coercive mix of artificial markets and bureaucratic interference. The government wanted to concentrate its spending. University lecturers now earned less than secondary school teachers. We were put into fierce competition with each other. This audit culture is like painting the Forth Bridge. It never ends. As soon as one exercise is completed, another is on its way. Slowly the victims master the system and upgrade their scores. Then they are told that the money isn't available because there are too many winners.

The number of British universities was doubled by adding the polytechnics. This made it easier to discriminate between them. They all had to expand recruitment (Oxbridge refused). The proportion of an age cohort going to university tripled overnight. No more money was forthcoming, however. Mad bureaucratic directives and expanded enrolments have broken the university teachers' ethical commitment to their profession. A radical differentiation has taken place. Professors enjoy enhanced rewards and freedom. Young scholars perform cheap labour without prospects. The provincial arrivistes of yesteryear ignore the interests of the next generation. We now take leave for research and writing, while the university hires a young temporary replacement for a pittance.[14]

Tony Blair's New Labour government (neoliberal economics with mildly better social policies) introduced student fees. This emulated the US model of piling debt on students as a way of cowing them into submission. The financial squeeze on the universities continues. Many lecturers agitate for a return to the golden age before all hell broke loose. I know of no other class whose response to the neoliberal holocaust is to restore the status quo ante. The coronavirus pandemic has exposed the shambles for all to see. Many universities are going down along with academic publishers.

British anthropologists, displaying a touching reliance on the state, work only in the top fifteen universities. We hardly acknowledge our role as teachers. Fieldwork is king, except that the money for expensive overseas trips is scarce, so we write a stream of articles, chapters and conference papers instead. Students are expected to pay through the nose to study a subject

---

14. In the US, 'adjuncts' with no job security and low pay without benefits do the bulk of teaching.

unknown to the public and with few job prospects. I respect the young people who have found a toehold in academia today. Anthropology is an essential aid to emergent world society. We just need to learn how to communicate our knowledge.

Universities will struggle to keep their place in higher education. The names and buildings may remain; but their educational content will be unrecognizable. We, the beneficiaries of our parents' war and welfare state, threw it all away. The universities' decline is central to the collapse of British democracy. Voting alone does not give people democratic power. Denying this is just one way that education covers up truth at every level in our societies.[15]

The End of Something

In 1919, the three most strategic unions in Britain combined in the first multi-union national strike: miners (energy), dockers (import/export) and railwaymen (transport). Churchill ordered the army to shoot the strikers. They refused. After them, so did the police. The country came to a standstill and the strikers with their families converged on the Houses of Parliament one weekend. The Prime Minister, Lloyd-George, asked the leaders to his chambers. The Welsh miners' leader Tom Jones later wrote, 'It was a mistake, we should never have been separated from our people'. L-G opened up with 'Congratulations, gentlemen, you have won the state. But I must tell you that neither I with my colleagues here nor any member of the civil service will lift a finger to help you run it.' 'At that moment', says TJ, 'I knew we had lost'.

Why did they lose? They were only used to protesting against those in charge for the sake of incremental change, not a new social order. They didn't have a Lenin and he had two million Russian soldiers who quit the Eastern Front in July–September 1917, many bringing their weapons home.[16] The General Strike of 1926 was a pushover after that. The middle classes came out in droves to provide soup kitchens for the scabs who replaced the strikers. Thatcher illegally mobilized a third of the national police force to beat the coal miners in 1984.

'National capitalism' is ending now, but we too lack a vision of what might follow it. Politicians need money and money men need political cover. Central banks institutionalized their partnership. Educators insist that our societies are built on the separation of public and private interests. This has never been so. Neoliberalism has reached a 'Brezhnev moment', similar to when the Soviet Union collapsed in the 1980s. Like the politburo's apparatchiks then,

15. See Rousseau on education in Chapter 2.
16. See Chapter 10.

the system can no longer deliver even limited versions of its aims; powerful individuals grab what they can and run for cover. The Anglophone empires, past and present, epitomize this impasse. The Old Regime is now a better model for our world than the liberal revolutions that removed it. The British lead the way in reviving old social models once dismissed by a triumphant American and European bourgeoisie. We never made a break with the Old Regime, with the monarchy, aristocracy and landed property. Only when the United Kingdom follows the British Empire into the dustbin of history can my people start again. As for me, I am a writer and teacher, not a politician; I have taken up permanent residence in France after Brexit.

Chapter 18

EXPLORATIONS IN TRANSNATIONAL HISTORY

We live in an interconnected world where inequality is often based on claims to be exclusive and superior made by religions, nationalities, ethnicities, races and classes. Either humanity will make a viable world society in this century or there won't be a twenty-second. One major obstacle is an approach to history that puts one group so much into the foreground as to marginalize all the rest. The other is the compartmentalization of knowledge between academic disciplines whose denizens fiercely reject anything outside their own self-imposed blinkers. This habit ('modernism') was unknown to the nineteenth century's most ecumenical minds. It belongs to the last century's universities that are struggling to survive now.

Anthropology has become a narrow specialist discipline, but its history and greatest practitioners have addressed the idea and practice of studying humanity as a whole. It was never, for me, about local, national or even regional entities, but worlds past, present and future.[1] We must extend local knowledge in stages to more inclusive levels.[2] My preliminary excursions into world history have been piecemeal studies with the whole in mind. Given their scope, I had to abandon any pretension to disciplinary formalism, which was already weak. I would see how far I could get reading languages and scientific specialisms that I didn't 'know'. If I published the results, I would lose what was left of my academic authority. I didn't.

---

1. See my 'Voices from the Third World' course in Chapter 10.
2. See Chapter 15.

This chapter reports on three amateur projects, undertaken at Yale in the mid-1970s, whose common motive was to blow up nationalist history. The first proposes that for three millennia after Stonehenge was built, a significant part of the British population was of Mediterranean, even African origin. In the rush to declare that the English language is mainly Germanic, with some Latin and a smattering of Celtic, Scandinavian and ancient Greek thrown in, the legacy of this earlier stratum has never been seriously studied. The second sees the Norman conquest of England as a central plank of several Viking attempts to win back the Mediterranean from Arab and Byzantine control. The third traces Europe's first modern state to a Baltic tribe, the Burgundians, who flourished in the late Roman Empire, founded a genuinely European state and later became the Habsburgs. This has sounder historiographic credentials, but is also mostly hidden from view.

All these topics, even in the sketchy manner they are presented here, are unknown to the reading public. You will never have encountered the substance of these narratives before. We will not find a way forward if our idea of where we all came from remains trapped in modern nationalism. This is the message of my examples. All three offer radically new perspectives on the history of Britain and Europe. The nations that give their names to the countries we live in have always been part of the larger world, as we are now; but they prevent us from understanding the world we live in. We have to develop more inclusive narratives that tell history as it is, not as it is supposed to be. Giambattista Vico insisted in his *New Science* that, if we wish to understand civilizations, beginnings matter more than ends. Their founders' poetic vision preserved the vivid imagination of children. The rot sets in when individuals and societies reach adulthood.[3] The next two or three generations will have to make a world society. This is a turning point, a new beginning for humanity – or its end. At first, we will need poetry more than academic scholarship; but we will definitely need science to make it work.

The task of breaking down the imperialist separation of Europe from its African and Asian neighbours is still important; but it is not news. Mozart and many Victorians thought Egypt was the source of world civilization; and Niall Ferguson[4] has traced the history of today's financial instruments (bonds, stocks, etc.) through an oversimplified line from the Arabs via the Italian Renaissance and seventeenth-century England to the world. The Indian novelist and social anthropologist Amitav Ghosh[5] recreated the twelfth-century trade network linking India to Andalusia with Cairo as its

---

3. See Chapter 2.

4. N. Ferguson, *The Ascent of Money* (2008).

5. A. Ghosh, *In an Antique Land* (1992).

hub. Mansah Musa, a fourteenth-century king of Mali, as a pilgrim to Mecca, spent so much gold in Egypt that he caused runaway inflation there for several decades.[6] Deconstruction of European self-regard begins with the Arabs, Indians and Northern Europeans. The contribution of Africans to world history remains to be told when they are the winners.[7]

The historical roots of human interdependence go further back and wider than we think. This is another argument for a methodologically open anthropology. The work summarized here was never professionally specialized and, apart from recording my philological investigations on a thousand small white cards, my sources are too eclectic to withstand interrogation by specialist academics. I pine for when stories could be told to an open-minded public with more interest in stories than evidence. I must find a non-scholarly method for telling them. Gore Vidal's massive novel of the axial age, *Creation*, is one precedent. It has Persia as its focal point, taking in Zoroaster, the Ionian Greeks, Socrates, the Buddha, Confucius and the entire Eurasian continent.[8]

My main published sources for the English language study are Carl D. Buck and Calvert Watkins.[9] The traditional method for reaching the top in philology was to learn forty languages, beat off all comers in scholarship and then write the dictionary yourself with some poetic licence. This is a game I could never play. I did, however, teach courses in the US on 'The Transition from Bronze to Iron in the Eastern Mediterranean, 1600–500 BC' and 'Expansion into the Western Mediterranean, 1000–500 BC'.[10] I soon abandoned disciplinary limits to my researches. This meant having no presumptions about what I could get from works in any language. I could always glean something from organization, references and proper names. Now I have DeepL ('deep learning'), a German translator of the main European languages (with Arabic and Chinese to come) that, being based on Artificial Intelligence feedback processes, is much more reliable than the algorithms of the first-wave social media machines.

Observing no limits was fun, taking in what I could of X-ray crystallography, blood types, carbon dating, family and place names, megalithic archaeology, ecology and discoveries like an 850-page Scottish history of the black British that I picked up at a Philadelphia black book fair.[11] I keep

---

6. K. Hart, *West African Agriculture* (1982: 20). See Chapter 8.

7. With notable exceptions, such as Cheikh Anta Diop. See Chapter 16.

8. G. Vidal, *Creation: A Novel* (1981).

9. D. Buck, *A Dictionary of Selected Synonyms in the Principal Indo-European Languages* (1947); C. Watkins, 'Indo-European Roots Appendix' (1996).

10. See Chapter 8.

11. D. Mac Ritchie, *Ancient and Modern Britons*, 2 vols (1985 [1884]).

up with the history of science, since I teach statistics, have some maths and focus on the words of natural scientists who believe they are uninfluenced by society.[12]

The Origins of the British (through the English Language)

Stonehenge – the largest megalithic monument in a network going back to Malta around 4000 BC and spreading out on both sides of the western Mediterranean – was begun early in the third millennium BCE. By whom? Seafaring herders via North Africa and the eastern Mediterranean, precursors of the Phoenicians later. Copper and tin from Cornwall have been found in Egyptian implements of the first dynasty. Geoffrey of Monmouth, going back nearly two thousand years in the twelfth century,[13] says that 'Stonehenge came from Ireland, but before that it came from Africa'.

The English language has added registers over time, but does not synthesize them (as French does Latin and German). It is most unlikely that this period has disappeared from English. I suspect that it belonged to the Semitic language group. The megalith-builders bypassed the North Sea and took the western route to the Baltic. Perhaps they were blocked in the east or sought the climatic benefits of the Gulf Stream. Stonehenge was built inland on Salisbury Plain (which is rich in stone-age sites), close to the Bristol Channel, which divides Wales from south-west England, and the Irish Sea.

Searching for an early register of English, I identified possible words by looking for sailing and herding terms, then those with no attested links to Celtic, Germanic and Romance languages, to qualify a word was in Old or Middle English; eventually some phonemic and morphological regularities emerged. I listed a word as probable on these grounds; but the range of reference became much wider.

The Indo-European 'family' has no words like 'pig' and 'dog'; they share a unique suffix -ca in Old English. Most words are monosyllables of the CVC type.[14] The rare initial j (dj) is common in modern English (jug, job, jaw). 'Jack' has the most different meanings of any English word: manual labourer, sailor, object in games, bowling pin, flag, iris, lifting device, rabbit, plug socket, apple hooch, money, to masturbate; and many nautical, fishing and hunting terms. Its general meaning is 'man' or 'fellow'. The etymology for

---

12. K. Hart, https://www.academia.edu/44960305/From_bell_curve_to_power_law_distri bution_models_between_national_and_world_society.

13. Geoffrey of Monmouth, *The History of the Kings of Britain* (1136).

14. Consonant-Vowel-Consonant.

'straight' could be 'erection'. The name Jack is usually derived from Jacques, which means James, not John. Most 'short names' conform to the CVC model: Bill for William, Jim for James, Dick for Richard, Bob for Robert, Meg for Margaret, Kit for Catherine, Bess for Elizabeth – possibly hangovers from that earlier register. 'Mug' meant 'face', later a drinking vessel with a face on it, to mug was to frighten victims with faces. 'Sky' is usually traced to Old Norse, but the Vikings were in the same Mediterranean diaspora (like the Normans). 'Bird' has only one link to ancient Swedish (ditto) and in Middle English could refer to any young animal, including people (young women in some circles today). These keywords can't be found in Eurocentric dictionaries of synonyms.

I collected some two thousand words. The register has its own distinctive sound, as do the Germanic and Latin registers. The words and speech rhythms appear more strongly in regional dialects of the north and west today. I have long wondered why great British comedians come from north-west England: George Formby, Gracie Fields, Eric Morecambe.[15] The speech of conquered and marginalized peoples often seems funny to the winners. Think of black comedians in the US, and indeed of blacking up by whites for a laugh or the scandal of the English women's national soccer team, where white coaches used fake Caribbean accents when putting down black players.

Thomas Huxley, an eminent Victorian scientist, wrote about the two races that make up the British peoples, whom he called *xanthochroi* ('fair-skinned') and *melanochroi* ('dark-skinned').[16] The latter was a Mediterranean type

> . . . exhibited by many Irishmen, Welshmen and Bretons, by Spaniards, South Italians, Greeks, Armenians, Arabs and high-caste Brahmins. . . the result of intermixture. It is to the Xanthochroi and Melanochroi, taken together, that the absurd denomination of 'Caucasian' is usually applied.

Most British enumeration districts have 75 per cent or more A blood type (Northern European farmers) or 75 per cent plus O (Mediterranean sailor-herders)[17] and these are clustered on a south-east/north-west axis, divided by a line from the Wash to the Bristol Channel. A town in North Wales has the same specific blood type as a Berber town in Morocco. DNA analysis makes all of this much more precise.

---

15. Peter Chelsom's movie *Funny Bones* (1995) explores the British, American and French roots of comedy in Lancashire's prime seaside resort, Blackpool. I recommend it.

16. T. Huxley, 'On the Geographical Distribution of the Chief Modifications of Mankind', *Journal of the Ethnological Society of London* (1870).

17. I am O blood type.

The food staples of south-east Britain are traditionally pork and wheat/maize, and in the north-west sheep and oats/barley. The typical terrains are lowland and upland respectively. The choice of an Irish Sea route to the Baltic over the North Sea (which was only flooded five thousand years ago, after the ice melted) probably reflects this racial divergence, which the victorious 'whites' chose to deny. Nationalism papers over such differences; but they were acknowledged by scientific discourse in the heyday of racist empires that divided the world's mixed peoples into black and white.

William the Conqueror

To bring all this crank bricolage into more recent history, the English ruling class and the schoolchildren they brainwash have always traced our political history to Julius Caesar and William the Conqueror. But what was William doing when he crossed the sea from Normandy to Sussex? Recall who the Normans were: Vikings with ships (of course), but also with state-of-the-art heavy cavalry transported in those ships wherever they liked. In Normandy they guarded the entrance to the North Sea, but the ancestors of the Danes and Dutch blocked that route to the Baltic. William attacked southern England for this reason. Albion (the bigger island) stood between the Baltic and the Mediterranean, from which the Vikings had been excluded by the Arabs and the Byzantine Empire. He had to go west, young man.

King Harold's English army first had to march to north-east England, where they met King Harald Hardrada of Norway. They then marched south to be beaten on the Sussex coast. This is treated in school history books as typical English bad luck, like the national football team being drawn against Germany and Brazil in successive cup ties. The idea that King Harald and Duke William were coordinating is rarely considered. Also in 1066, the Normans under Count Robert began seizing Calabria in southern Italy, attacking the Byzantine Balkans, driving the emirate out of Sicily and annexing Malta. English historians don't bother with that history.

After confirming that his place men held London, William marched to west Wales, where he built castles protecting the north–south sea route through the Irish Sea. Vikings had already driven from the Baltic to the Black Sea via the Russian rivers and began besieging Constantinople. Jerusalem fell to the first crusade in 1099. Britain was a staging post in a continent-wide campaign to make the Mediterranean safe for Nordic looting by pushing two enemies out. The northern peoples, in a variety of guises, recaptured in three decades what the Arabs had seized four centuries earlier.

The whole story passed the English by, still feeling the elephant blindly from one local angle. Richard the Lionheart, backed by Robin Hood of Sherwood Forest, returned from the crusades to challenge his 'bad' brother King John and the dastardly Sheriff of Nottingham. Who would guess that Richard preferred foreign adventures and his French castles to ruling England, or that John was an effective monarch who signed the Magna Carta and was later targeted in the propaganda of rivals for the throne?

In 'A Day in the Life', John Lennon sings ironically: 'I saw a film today, oh boy / The English army had just won the war'. This pathetic nonsense is even worse in the Brexit era.[18] The Battle of Kursk was fought in July–August 1943, while Patton conquered Sicily. Stalin's and Hitler's war machines destroyed more material there than the whole First World War. This was how the German army was turned back. The main British contribution was the Royal Air Force's murderous bombings of German cities. Shostakovich was composing his monumental war symphony, the Eighth. I was two weeks old in July 1943.

From Burgundians to Habsburgs

Albion and Ireland, with Iberia, have always been destinations for waves of continental migrants. The same goes at the other end of Eurasia for the Japanese islands and Korean peninsula. I wondered what happened in the historically empty space between the north Italian and Dutch renaissances. I found there Lotharingia, the Rhineland and the Burgundians. My third project focused on the last. Around 200 CE they came via Poland from a small Baltic island, Bornholm, before settling on the Rhine at Worms as Wagner's fabulously wealthy royal *Nibelungen*.[19] They were defeated by Attila the Hun, joined him and resettled in Savoy. They guarded Roman villas against the other Germans and Rome's tax-hungry rulers; their customs alone were codified as the *Lex Romana Burgundiorum*.

After the Empire fell, they founded the Kingdom of the Burgundians, whose twin capitals were Geneva and Lyon. This was undermined by stronger regional powers and, as a minor duchy, they moved to a watershed whose rivers (the Saone and the Yonne) linked with the Rhone, Loire and Seine arteries. They exported Burgundy wine and founded the Cistercian monastic order. Wine was the highest-value commodity in ancient and medieval Mediterranean trade.

---

18. See Chapter 17.

19. Richard Wagner's 'The Ring of the Nibelungs', composed in 1848–73, had four parts: *The Rhine Gold*, *The Valkyries*, *Siegfried* and *The Twilight of the Gods*. The Nibelungs are the Burgundian royal house.

Four dukes of Burgundy pursued an expansionist policy in the fifteenth century. They acquired a patchwork of affluent territories to the north, notably Flanders, Brabant, and parts of the Rhineland and of northern France. As a new European power, the Belgian historian Henri Pirenne named them 'the Burgundian state'. The last Duke, Charles the Bold, managed to offend not only the French king (which was habitual), but also the Swiss Confederacy and the Duke of Lorraine. The latter combined to defeat and kill him at the Battle of Nancy in 1477. This was the end of the male line and Charles was succeeded by his daughter Marie, who made a stab at ruling the duchy before marrying the Holy Roman Emperor Maximilian in an effort to stave off the predations of Louis XI of France. Their base was now Bruges, the wealthiest city in Northern Europe. Their son Philip married Joanna, the daughter of Ferdinand and Isabella of Spain and his son became Charles V of Spain, Holy Roman Emperor, Archduke of Austria, Count of Flanders, Lord of the Netherlands and 'the last of the Burgundians'. Louis XI grabbed the lion's share of Burgundy, but lost Artois, regained in battle by Maximilian. Marie died early in a hunting accident.

The dukes of Burgundy pioneered the modern European state, combining extensive royal marriage networks with a transnational entourage of Italian notaries and bankers, Austrian gold miners and venture capitalists,[20] and Flemish textile manufacturers and historians. Charles took this alliance into the New World; but the Spanish nobles objected to his retinue having the lion's share of the American loot. Philip II, with noble backing, launched a coup against his father, who died soon afterwards. He then tried to force the Dutch and Flemish back into his kingdom. Verdi's opera *Don Carlo* tells how Philip married his son's fiancée, the French king's daughter, and then locked Carlos up. He in turn was sprung by his mates and took up the Flemish cause, encouraged by his grandfather's ghost. Is this story transnational enough?

What Is the Point of All This?

Much of my work in the last three decades has tried to make emergent world society more concretely historical (national capitalism, the digital revolution, the corporations, human economy). I focus on the period 1800–2100.[21] European global expansion since the sixteenth century ended in 1914–18. I need to go back to the early Bronze Age, to the invention of agriculture and before that. We, the offspring of agrarian civilizations, stumbled into

---

20. The Fugger family dominated European finance after the Medicis: M. Kluger, *The Fugger Dynasty in Augsburg* (2014).

21. See Chapter 16.

machines whose uses and potential we barely understand. Humanity will never find a way forward if our notions of where we came from are based on nationalism and racism. My examples here offer new perspectives on the history of Britain and Europe. Only in a new world society will world history take shape.

Somehow – and academic specialization undermines this – we have to develop more inclusive narratives of history as it is, not as it is supposed to be. Georg Lukács recounted a parable that has been widely cited, usually without attribution.[22] It concerns a type, 'the bourgeois sceptic' and takes place allegedly in Morocco's Atlas Mountains. A sage tells his audience that the world is supported on the backs of four elephants. One smart young man (the bourgeois sceptic) asks, 'What are the elephants standing on?' and is satisfied by the answer, 'a large turtle'. Stephen Hawking made a terrific joke about this, but did not acknowledge Lukács. When modern physicists are asked what the turtle stands on, they say 'it's turtles, turtles all the way down'.[23]

My work, if I can call it that, was triggered by the commonplace assertion that 'Europeans' relied heavily on Arabs or Islam for developments they represent as endogenous. I went back to Stonehenge, the Crusades and the Renaissance because they are familiar to Western readers and to the British, now pursuing a politics of imagined insularity. The first combined history (including a twelfth-century historian and some forgotten Victorians), linguistics and archaeology with modern analysis of metals, blood types, ecology, DNA and so on.

My explorations in transnational history start from the point that restrictions of human movement, miscegenation and significant international trade came very late, accompanied by the rise of nationalism and racist imperialism. Human beings are animals who generally move to where the food is, whereas plants and those who cultivate them expect the food to come to them. All anthropology's formative thinkers understood that the invention of agriculture and later of states, cities, writing and intensified production made a huge difference. Even then, as the Bronze Age and Norman examples show, human movement was more common than we now imagine. It still is, despite the efforts made by states to control people on the move.

Immanuel Kant's late essay *Perpetual Peace*[24] is a wonderful exploration of what world society could be like, and once was, without states. After all, a state is a state, a fixed point, not movement; this principle contradicts humanity's nature as a species. When some of us argue for widespread human interconnection, the representatives of normal society, who believe that being

---

22. G. Lukács, *The Historical Novel* (1955).

23. S. Hawking, *A Brief History of Time* (1988).

24. I. Kant, *Perpetual Peace* (1795). Mine is even sketchier than Kant's. See Chapter 2.

fixed in the ground is natural and movement unnatural, tell us to prove the historical connections. The burden is on them to show why Columbus was the first transatlantic voyager, when shipping technology had been basically the same for millennia.

The Phoenicians crossed the Atlantic and circumnavigated Africa. The Semitic root for iron is *brzl* (Hebrew *barzel*) and Brazil's coastline is red with it. Yet we are told its name comes from a Portuguese word for a red tree. I once organized a workshop on Africa's connections with the ancient world, featuring presentations on West Africa, Sudan, Ethiopia (Aksum) and the Swahili Coast. We have heard of Phoenicians, Romans and Arabs, but not much about the achievements of ancient Ghana, Mali and Songhay. 'Africa' was the Roman word for Carthage's territory in today's Tunisia.

Sudan is connected by the Nile to Egypt and in the south to the Lakes region, and also by the savannah to Senegal and the Atlantic Ocean. Aksum in the fourth-century had pottery from China and other artefacts from Spain and India. But the strongest outside links of the four were by sea from the Swahili Coast between the Horn and Zimbabwe. We now realize that the Indian Ocean was a more advanced world system, supporting impressive movement for longer than our global navigations.[25] Austronesian peoples from South East Asia settled Madagascar in the first millennium.

Perhaps it was inevitable, when the 'whites' ruled Africa, that their presence should be the benchmark of its history (precolonial, colonial, postcolonial, decolonization); but they don't rule Africa any more. A 'biopolitical' approach would emphasize the power/knowledge axis, commercial imperatives, historical memory and how identities are shaped and reified. Given the prevailing organization of power, production, knowledge and communications, I judged until now that there is no reception for my amateur explorations.[26]

In adult life, I have sometimes gone against the powers and made a small difference; but I failed more often. I argued around 1970 that economies are made by people, not just by states; and this eventually went mainstream as the informal economy.[27] But I had two years of fieldwork to back me up then. I then co-wrote a development programme for Papua New Guinea's independence that was opposed by the outside powers, but adopted by the local party that won independence. Around 1980, I wrote a book arguing that modern states in Africa would collapse if they continued to be based on small agriculture; many did subsequently fail. In 2000, I published a book on

25. P. Beaujard, *Les mondes de l'océan Indien* (2012).
26. Hart, Appendix 2017.
27. See Chapter 7.

the democratic potential of money in the internet era. In 2005, I attacked the global corporate conspiracy with no effect.[28]

I helped to launch an online club for anthropologists that attracted a global membership of twenty-two thousand. It failed because of weak administration and a dominant academic culture.[29] For years I have been writing a book about how demographic and economic expansion in this century could alter Africa's global prospects – the Africans like it and Western publishers won't touch it.[30] Oxfam made 'human economy' the key idea in their pitch for a seat at the world's high table. A brief footnote to our work was buried deep in the paper; they claimed that their approach was entirely different because it was non-academic.[31]

Each of us can make a difference; but adapting to the powers that be is a dead end. I am a classicist and I am part of the long human conversation about making a better world. I am neither optimistic nor pessimistic; we must work out who the sides are and then do what we can for our side. The powers are not as monolithic as they seem from the outside. Anthropologists can identify the weaknesses of the strong and the strengths of the weak, and sometimes may change the balance.

I am sure that the bureaucratic world of nation states, capitalist corporations and universities will not last. I write for those who envisage a different future and wish to address it, not alone, but as part of a diffuse human movement with the means of global networking at their disposal. I can decide what I want to write and how. It is a lot easier to get stuff out without the main gatekeepers involved. The voices in my head when I write speak to having lived and worked in twenty-four countries. I have imagined conversations with the writers who have shaped how I think. I don't write for particular audiences, but rather draw on a synthetic memory made up of all that I have done – teaching, writing and reading – and where I have gone.

I have an essay on the back burner, 'Death of the Audience' (*pace* Roland Barthes's death of the author);[32] but that's another story. Above all, I want to rectify the marginal place that self and the world occupy in anthropology, the humanities and the social disciplines. Most contemporary academic approaches outside the hard sciences are incurably defeatist.

Writing this chapter helped me to understand why the first volume of Edward Gibbon's great book on the fall of Rome caused such an uproar

---

28. K. Hart, *West Africa*; *The Memory Bank* (Appendix 2000a); Appendix 2005.
29. See Chapter 14.
30. See Chapter 16.
31. See Chapter 15.
32. R. Barthes, *The Death of the Author* (1967).

in England.[33] His compatriots identified with the Roman Empire and with Christianity. He showed that Christianity was a big reason why Rome fell. No wonder that David Hume could write to him:

> 'Your countrymen have given themselves up to barbarous and absurd faction . . . The prevalence of superstition in England prognosticates the fall of philosophy and the decay of taste.[34]

Gibbon returned to the Lausanne of his youth and wrote the last three volumes of his masterwork there.

33. See Chapter 1.
34. E. Gibbon, *Memoirs*, 91. See Chapter 1, Note 32 and context.

Chapter 19

MONEY IS HOW WE LEARN
TO BE MORE FULLY HUMAN

If language divides us, so too does money; but money, unlike language, has the power to unify the world. It already has – what else does the world market run on? In Chapter 15, I claimed that money is always personal and impersonal. That makes it an ideal instrument for bringing the two together. Just using it every day schools us in combining our double nature.

Max Weber saw no social force capable of resisting a highly centralized version of impersonal society. Society now operates at global, regional, national and local levels. We need new impersonal norms to guide our social interactions in such a world, while recognizing the importance of individual personalities. The stage is set for a new humanism capable of uniting these poles. We are still primitives; but eventually we will make society on our own terms, if we master the means of its development – people, machines and money.

What follows takes this idea further. First, I examine where private property, without which modern money and markets would be unthinkable, came from and what it has become. I then look at what money does in capitalist societies and how this differs from before. I draw a distinction between the few who 'make' money and the many who 'take' it. Money's character is revealed most strikingly in its crises. Three stories coexist concerning money speculation: (1) the economists' claim that you can't beat the markets; (2) the fact that you can with inside knowledge; and (3) that scientific methods guarantee steady profits from betting. Those who make markets must take prices from the market. A more autobiographical section discusses my experience with alternative currencies. Small-scale initiatives need large-scale bureaucracies. I add a note on betting and religion and conclude with some thoughts on money in a human economy.

Private Property Unbound

We experience the economy in modern society as a network of exchange relations. Most often these take place through the medium of money: the buyer hands over money to the seller in return for commodities. The sum of these transactions is sometimes referred to as 'the market', an abstract entity whose extent is unknowable. Only recently have people everywhere become part of a single nexus of exchange, 'the world market'. The idea of modern markets is that they can take place at any time, anywhere, between individuals who don't need to know each other. This assumption ('economic individualism') enables economists to construct mathematical models of behaviour outside time, place and society. The institutional conditions that make this assumption plausible are quite abnormal and were won at first in a few countries only after centuries of political struggle. The idea of buyers and sellers making free decisions in this way is remarkable, even when only a hat or pair of shoes is at stake. It gets more complicated when someone's ability to work or a family's home is being bought and sold.

The idea of personal agency in market situations is closely tied to private property.[1] This gives an owner the right to command exclusive rights over something against the rest of the world. We assume that, once we have bought something, we can do what we like with it; the seller in turn is free to dispose of the money we paid. Your personal possessions are yours. How did you get them and what makes them your own? Your watch feels like it is yours by being worn next to your skin. You probably bought it, or it was a gift from someone who bought it. Market exchange is the source of your right to own the watch. But what secures the market exchange? Most people rarely think about this, until something goes wrong. You get mugged and the stranger demands your watch. You now realize that the government underwrites your claim to own the watch and promises to keep your person and property safe. Eventually you settle back into thinking of your possessions as your own and forget about the social conditions that make it possible.

Private property secured by an anonymous state apparatus has been very rare in human history. More often, ownership is relative to membership of concrete social groups – clans or similar undifferentiated units. Take the following example. A Maasai warrior works as a nightwatchman in Kenya's capital, Nairobi. The Maasai are famous for having maintained a traditional

---

1. See Chapter 15.

way of life based on cattle-herding, and young men form groups of warriors whose task is to defend the village's herds against all comers. Nowadays many of them work temporarily for wages. This young man saves money and, before returning home, buys a watch. On arriving back home, he meets an age-mate who says, 'I like your watch: give it to me', and he must give it up. Why? Because all property in the village depends on the warriors to ward off predators, both animal and human; and their solidarity, essential in battle, is undermined by members whose interests diverge from the rest. Our ex-watchman must recognize that village life still rests on different principles than Nairobi's, and he hands over the watch.

In Western legal history the Romans invented private property. Before the Empire, property rights were mainly based on local kin groups' ability to assert their interests against similar groups. This was called *ius in personam* – rights over things are mediated by personal ties. Ownership came from production or consumption: something belonged to you because you had made it or because you needed to use it; and both rights were assured by membership of local groups. Merchants, however, owned things they had neither produced themselves nor would use personally, but intended to sell for money. They were exposed to the brigandage of any small group wishing to enforce its monopoly of local violence. In the interest of long-distance trade, the Roman state offered military protection to these traders. It supported their claim to *ius in rem*, rights over things unmediated by personal relationships. This is the same system of private property that we now take for granted.

The connections between persons and objects and persons in groups were weakened in law. Apart from the Romans, only the Chinese and perhaps the Aztecs developed private property law independently. The social ties that make ownership possible have now become invisible thanks to economic relations abstracted from social content. This takes us to the historical relationship between markets and liberal democracy.

In 1683, at the age of 51, John Locke was an unpublished Oxford academic and the client of a discredited politician. During the exclusion crisis of the Catholic King James II's accession to the throne, he fled for his life to Holland and was sacked by his college. He returned to England six years later after William of Orange's establishment of a Protestant monarchy in the Glorious Revolution of 1688. He published *Two Treatises of Government*,[2] was appointed to the Board of Trade and wrote influential pamphlets on money that helped to resolve the recoinage crisis of the 1690s. Before his death in 1704, he had become so famous that a correspondent could describe him without irony as 'the greatest man in the world'. The eighteenth-century Enlightenment was largely a response to Locke's work as an architect of the

---

2. J. Locke, *Two Treatises of Government* (1690),

middle-class revolution. The Americans wrote their constitution on the basis of his ideas. Now he is often regarded as an apologist for capitalism and author of a narrow 'possessive individualism' on which economic orthodoxy is founded today.

I don't find a story of economic individualism in the *Two Treatises*. John Locke's commonwealth was intended to preserve everyone's property in themselves and their possessions. 'The end of law is. . . to preserve and enlarge freedom'. Freedom is someone's '. . . liberty to dispose and order, as he lists, his person, actions, possessions and his whole property within the allowance of those laws under which he is, and therein not to be subject to the arbitrary will of another, but freely follow his own'. Locke's emphasis is on the political conditions of personal autonomy. Both treatises are extended essays on parent–child relations. In the first, Locke denies the right of absolute monarchs to claim to be the father of their subjects. In the second, he allows only one exception to the rule of autonomy of citizens – childhood. He asks how we can protect children so that they will grow up to be independent. He was best-known in eighteenth-century England for *Some Thoughts Concerning Education*.[3]

Locke also asked how one commonwealth acting alone can protect the property of foreigners passing through – who or what secures the property of the Dutchman in London? He founded national capitalism, long before Hegel and Bismarck. He wanted to establish global trade with Britain at its centre, above all, and to stabilize the means of communication and exchange – words and money. His targets were economic and semantic criminals. The state can hang counterfeiters, but what do you do with politicians who never say what they mean? Each undermines confidence in civil society. Only a perverse hindsight would represent this far-sighted political project as hiding the class dominance of capitalists behind a rhetoric of market democracy and natural rights.

What Money Does

Money – the main device in capitalist societies for making social relations objective – is also a benchmark for concrete narratives of subjective attachment. Hence, in divorce, argument often focuses on money as a proxy for personal pain. Its power lies in this synthesis of impersonal abstraction and personal meaning, objectification and subjectivity, analytical reason and synthetic narrative. Money is like religion,[4] channelling our desire to link our deepest thoughts and feelings to the object world that we share with everyone.

---

3. J. Locke, *Some Thoughts Concerning Education* (1693).
4. Hart, Appendix 2010b.

Money surely has redemptive features too. Money is a part of human nature, like language. It is an ocean extending our horizons; but the pressure to exert local control remains strong. Money's social value lies in moving between local and global spheres, not in separating them. It expresses our common humanity while anchoring us in daily life. All markets are potentially world markets, but money belongs in all levels of society.

Our societies are conventionally divided between market and home. The *market* is an impersonal sphere where abstract rationality rules. *Home* is a protected zone where intimate relations hold sway. Some adults go out to *work*, to 'make' the money for the household. The home economy spends this money and performs domestic tasks without payment. This is the moral and practical foundation of capitalism, public production vs private consumption. It asks too much of us to divide ourselves this way; and it takes enormous cultural effort to keep the two apart. This battle has never been finally won. Money is in both spheres; but so too is human personality.

Money's key feature is its fluent movement between life's social extremes, large and small. If you have some, you can buy almost anything with it. Money shows us society's abstract potential to be universal.[5] At the same time, it closes off particular transactions, anchoring them in time and space. Money schools us daily in moving between society's widest and narrowest regions.

A human economy brings together many initiatives in a unifying vision, expressed as a shared drive for a better world. It links each of us to emergent world society, one fit for all humanity. We need an economics that can address both levels and many in between. Money has the potential to mediate between these extremes.[6] Simmel saw money's potential to make universal society while being grounded in everyday life.[7] Forms of association, old and new, can bring democratic norms to economic practice. We cannot afford to return to the Cold War contradiction of market vs state.

The market is a bastion of human economy.[8] Many classical social theorists believed that markets break down traditional insularity. They extend society to become more inclusive. They provide some freedom for individuals and minorities. But markets without limits threaten democracy itself. Society must impose its rules on markets, and state guarantees of livelihood should coexist with voluntary self-organization based on mutuality, not just citizenship.[9]

---

5. G. Simmel, *The Philosophy of Money* (1900).

6. My best article on money is Hart, Appendix 2009b; see also 2000a and 2017.

7. Simmel (ibid.).

8. See Chapter 15.

9. J.-L. Laville, *L'Économie sociale et solidaire* (2019).

Number and money separate and depersonalize. According to Oswald Spengler, this is fundamental to civilization.[10] For the ancient Greeks number was *magnitude*, the essence of all things perceptible to the senses. Mathematics for them was about measurement in the here and now. All this changed with René Descartes.[11] His new number-idea was *function* – a world of relations between points in abstract space. Now a passionate Faustian tendency towards the infinite took hold. Abstract mathematical forms were freed from concrete reality, the better to control it. A parallel shift took place from thinking about goods to thinking about money. A businessman signs a piece of paper to mobilize remote forces. This gesture stands in an abstract relationship to the power of labour and machinery. It only takes the form of money numbers in a retrospective accountancy process.

Thinking through money generates money. It turns the world into a few money men who exploit workers, consumers and small owners. Anyone can 'make' money, but most people are its victims. People with little money still count it as a measure. Money men understand that its potential is less tangible. Let us label the actors 'makers of money' and the rest 'takers of money'. Two qualifications are necessary. Money-makers do not operate in a world of their own making; they have to take the market as they find it and then make it. Betting blurs the contrasts between makers and takers and between large and small scales. For 'money-takers', betting means not being a passive bystander. Even if they lose, they are sometimes active participants in Spengler's 'money force'.

Money Revealed by Its Crises

Nassim Nicholas Taleb is a homespun philosopher and successful financial trader. His book *The Black Swan* says that the history of markets is dominated by high-impact, hard-to-predict events ('uncertainty').[12] But financial traders deal in short-term routine fluctuations ('risk'). Scientific methods cannot handle rare events. Common psychology makes most people blind to these possibilities. We can, however, hedge against them. Elie Ayache, a French trader in New York, challenges Taleb in *The Blank Swan*.[13] Calculating trends in market prices and even hedging against rare events, he says, is pointless. The swan is neither black nor white. It is a blank sheet on which proactive

---

10. O. Spengler, *The Decline of the West* (1918).
11. 'The father of analytical geometry' and pioneer of calculus.
12. N. Taleb, *The Black Swan* (2007).
13. E. Ayache, *The Blank Swan* (2010).

traders write their derivatives. He wants to reinstate contingency over probability. I sympathize with this. Ayache also wrote an article entitled 'I Am a Creator'.[14] His approach to the standard model for pricing options is a reflexive one. One must make the market while being in it as a 'dynamic trader'. Market-makers are thinkers and creators. They need to produce prices as outputs of their models. A market-maker sets a price only if the market makes it.

Fortune's Formula covers the sweep of post-war US history: crime, hi-tech, insider trading, economists, prosecutors.[15] Its author, William Poundstone, starts from the Chicago mob's racing scams just after the war. Claude Shannon at Bell Labs gambled in stocks. Several of his followers went into scientific betting on financial markets. Paul Samuelson wrote the standard economics textbook.[16] Rudy Giuliani crusaded against insider trading. Michael Milken's junk bonds scheme failed in the end. Black-Scholes-Merton's firm, Long-Term Capital Management, crashed in the 1997–98 financial crisis. Poundstone shows that the rich rely on personal knowledge and contacts. Social science disciplines assume that impersonal forces govern society. Middle-class parents shield their children from direct experience of money. But poor parents can't afford to.

Samuelson asked a question of his many readers. Ten million New Yorkers go to sleep every night confident that the economy will be there tomorrow. How do they know? J.K. Galbraith[17] tells of a member of Kennedy's administration paid off with a bank directorship. After his first meeting, he was seen muttering 'I never knew'. What had he not known? Galbraith thinks he learned the first principle of modern banking. Take money from one party and lend it to another, then persuade both that they still have it.

In Frank Baum's famous allegory, money is a conjured up by unscrupulous wizards.[18] Most of us would rather not know. We believe we are standing on solid ground; money is real and durable. Or, reassured by their impenetrable jargon, we let experts handle the problem. In either case, understanding is unnecessary. When money loses its value because of inflation, what else can we rely on? Fear of the unknown begets a search for certainty. Scientific betting and do-it-yourself trading circuits are the most popular alternatives to working for wages and pensions. The difference between capitalists and small punters is that the former have large reserves.

---

14. From the movie *Barton Fink* (1991). http://www.ito33.com/sites/default/files/articles/0807_nail.pdf (accessed 16 September 2021).

15. W. Poundstone, *Fortune's Formula* (2005).

16. P. Samuelson, *Economics* (1948 and many subsequent editions).

17. J.K. Galbraith, *Money: Whence It Came and Whither It Went* (1975).

18. F. Baum, *The Wonderful Wizard of Oz* (1900).

Alternative Currencies

The era of national currencies is ending. For four decades now, central banks have concentrated on keeping asset prices up. But governments and banks no longer monopolize the issuing of money. A distributed global network of many types of institutions now generates a plethora of money instruments. Most people, however, have little of it to spend. Why not make your own money instead? Do-it-yourself money could restore some democracy to society. Thousands of community and complementary currencies have sprung up.[19] But most people cling stubbornly to the money they know. Why waste one's life on an unrewarding system unless it is inevitable?

I would rather understand money than have a lot of it. Money was the topic for a public lecture in the 1980s. One side of a coin ('heads') reveals money as an aspect of political society, the other ('tails') measures its value in exchange. Both state and market are indispensable to money. National economies suffer from ruinous swings between monetary theories stressing one to the exclusion of the other.[20] I mentioned the recent invention of Local Exchange Trading Systems (LETS) in British Columbia. Community currencies trade their own money in closed circuits. Firms issue air miles, loyalty cards and supermarket coupons to tie customers. Complementary currencies may be accepted in part payment by listed firms. Both add to purchasing power at little cost. LETS members issue money whenever they receive a service without payment.

I met Michael Linton, LETS's founder, in the 1990s. I thought of community currencies as stand-alone trading circuits in full flight from the capitalist economy. They were harassed by government agencies. But they embodied the spirit of utopian socialism in local communities. Michael sketched a different vision. He saw LETS linking individuals to exchange circuits reflecting their plural interests. These would be integrated with normal commerce and tax regimes. IT would bring the plastic revolution to LETS. We could make our own money and markets inside capitalism, but on a very different ethical basis.

I left Cambridge for Paris. The first outcome was my book on money.[21] I argued there that electronic money shifts power from its producers to its users.[22] Michael, Ernie Yacub and I agreed to write a book on LETS together.

---

19. M. Linton, http://subsol.c3.hu/subsol_2/contributors0/lintontext.html (accessed 16 September 2021); J. Blanc, 'Community and Complementary Currencies' (2010).

20. Hart, Appendix 1986.

21. Hart, Appendix 2000a.

22. N. Dodd, 'Laundering Money' (2005).

I wanted to explore 'open money'.[23] We worked together in 2000–2 and shared material for a book, *Common Wealth: Building Community and Economic Democracy with Open Money*. Nothing came of it; but I learned a lot.

We launched the Japan Open Money Project, sponsored by a magazine linked to Japan's second largest advertising agency.[24] I saw echoes there of capitalist firms' role in the early liberal revolutions.[25] Japan could support such a revolution today. I met the New Association Movement (NAM) and befriended Makoto Nishibe, an innovative economist working in LETS. I later helped translate *The Enigma of Money: Gold, Banknotes, Bitcoin*.[26] Kojin Karatani, drawing on Kant and Marx in *Transcritique*, advocates resistance to capitalism through LETS (Linton) and consumer boycotts (Gandhi).[27] Unlike strikes and street demonstrations, these are less vulnerable to violent repression.

Michael and I attended a 'Wizards of OS' event in Berlin.[28] We explored there the relationship between open money and the FLOSS movement.[29] He pursued applications from small international electronic payments with the European Commission and schools in London to the peso crisis and barter clubs in Argentina.[30] I consulted on the informal economy for the French Ministry of Culture. *Le Monde* saw social democracy's future in local exchange systems. The movement to open money was gathering pace. The gap separating LETS initiatives from global problems was narrowing!

In 2003 I gave the keynote at a Bangkok conference on 'Trade in Organic Products' held by the International Federation of Organic Agriculture Movements (IFOAM). Having read *The Memory Bank*, they thought I could address their most pressing problem. Certifying food as 'organic' was expensive, especially for international trade. Only Europe, the US and Japan had consumers who would pay the higher costs. But getting in was difficult. Five corporations including Nestlé supplied 95 per cent of international trade in organic products. Most conference participants came from Japan, Germany, New York State and Thailand. Each had flourishing community currencies and DIY markets. As a global green currency for fair trade in organic products, I came up with the *eco* – people's money for an ecological economy.

---

23. http://openmoney.org (accessed 16 September 2021).

24. *Kohkoku* magazine and the Hakuhodo Corporation.

25. See Chapter 16.

26. M. Nishibe, 'The Theory of Labour Money' (2005).

27. K. Karatani, *Transcritique: On Kant and Marx* (2005).

28. OS = Open Source; in Baum's classic, Oz is short for an ounce (of gold).

29. Free Libre Open Source Software.

30. Hart, Appendix 2002a (the peso and the euro).

A currency based on food and organic values could become a staple of alter-globalization. We eat a lot of food. It is a symbol of other values. Controlling market abuse of food has public virtue. Trust between believers could reduce the costs of certification. By supporting the integration of production and consumption, city and countryside, green currency could offer protection from unknowable market forces. I drew on Japanese practice. Nishibe's online LETS network had launched fair trade in organic bananas from an island between Japan and the Philippines. An action group called 'Power to the People' imported Palestinian olive oil and soaps. Organic rice and coffee were exchanged between countryside and city in Japan. My speech came out in an ecological magazine. This butterfly's flapping wings did not start a hurricane.[31]

Most people have little money to spend. Better to make your own money. A new approach was the direct way to restore democracy to participation in society. These could only succeed if they harnessed the internet's potential. Michael and his partners focused on developing the software and technology needed. Community currencies should join wider systems. The banks could do this, but they saw them as a threat.

In Michael Linton's vision, a proper currency service provider would do two things. Users could create their own systems in the space available. They would also have access to similar systems. A stand-alone community currency is like a radio or TV with only one station or a computer with one programme. A cross-clearing platform could support communication between different currencies. This would use its own money domain-naming system (MDNS), incorporating a hierarchy of national, regional and local domains. It would be linked to smart-card systems carrying fifteen different currencies. They would be offline, anonymous and designed for use by shops. A kernel of cross-platform protocols would become open-source software. But there were few skilled hands and no organization to establish standards.

For most CCs, the exchange circuit is closed. But markets using conventional money can't stop money draining away to remote power centres. LETS promotes local economy against the import/export pattern of normal markets. But community trading circuits could scale up to a much larger online membership. Closed-circuit networks would then adopt an open-source approach to community money. Local community and global network are twin features of Michael's approach. His vision for network society in the internet's infancy is Keynesian in scope.

---

31. K. Hart, 'Organic Trade: Toward a Global Green Currency?', *Ecology and Farming* (2004).

Harnessing Bureaucracy to Grassroots Democracy

The collapse of national capitalism is an opportunity for community currencies. But many take their form from an isolated location. A clubby committee
acts as a mini-central bank. Large-scale bureaucracies are also necessary for
economic democracy. We need to build bridges between local interests and
world society.

South Africa has pioneered a clearing system for invoices to address slow
payments for the self-employed.[32] A South African-born Lebanese entrepreneur, Neville Kerdachi, conceived of the Validation Clearance Bureau. He
had been a factor in Durban port, buying cargo invoices discounted against
payment delays and the risk of non-payment. The VCB is now a platform
linking buyers, sellers and banks. The service recipient puts an invoice into
the system, acknowledged by the provider. The bank issues up to 80 per
cent of its value to the latter. This boosts the provider's cash flow, enabling
purchase of more stock and building cash balances. It speeds up payment by
big buyers to small suppliers. They get a cheaper method for handling their
invoices. The system could be set up in any country. It has won approval from
the Bank of International Settlements and the World Bank.

There are some two hundred and fifty thousand black SMEs in South
Africa. This innovation addresses both their needs and those of big corporations like Walmart. Setting up small accounts is always labour-intensive
and slow. One corporate contract can help finance this process. Amazon and
iTunes combine blockbuster bestsellers with a million small items ('the long
tail'). The latter make up half of Amazon's revenues. Small businesses will not
prosper just by forming networks with similar organizations. Big firms and
governments can also play a part if their interests overlap. Large-scale hi-tech
solutions are often beyond the reach of grassroots initiatives. Small operators
benefit from linking up with big players. Most community currency and
organic food movements miss this point.

We must go beyond local institutions. Innovations in money and markets
are particularly well suited to this. The recent explosion of money, markets
and communications was and is very dangerous. But it brought us closer to
a world society capable of expressing human principles through new social
media.

A federation of self-help currencies would be one way forward. But a
few scattered activists lack the resources needed for scaling up coordination.
Community currencies are defensive. They offer a temporary refuge from the

---

32. Vishnu Padayachee was company chairman of Validation Clearing Bureau. See Chapter 11.

ravages of capitalism and rely on personal trust between members. They hope to oppose 'ruthless impersonality'. Some base their currency on time. This increases the gap between their trading circuit and the national economy. Virtual relations at distance and face-to-face interaction are not contradictory, but complement each other.

Proponents of alternative currencies are often asked if their trading circuits succeed economically. But, whatever the outcome, they are a great source of political education. They open their members' eyes to new possibilities. They teach them different norms and attitudes when handling money. Money divides economic spheres, but it also joins together what it has divided. We still need to reach the parts of the economy we don't know. There are powerful anti-human forces in the world. Similarly, Tahrir Square's 'Arab Spring', Occupy Wall Street and London's two-million-strong march against the Iraq War did not deliver what they promised. But they changed many people's political outlook, including mine. Experience of crowds and self-organized networks alters how people see the world. The singularity of national currencies has been slipping for decades.[33] Alternative currencies open their members' eyes to new possibilities. Despite their organizational weakness, this is the social significance of experiments like LETS.

A Note on Betting and Religion

To understand the social force of religion, we must enter the minds of believers. Searching for the source of money's power is like asking how God gets us to believe in Him. We made God up, as we make money up.[34] Since we can only know the past, why would anyone accept a promise whose future is unknowable? But we do, because we have to – faith is the glue sticking past and future together in the present. Simmel offers an explanation.[35] All the transactions we wish to calculate are made through money. It seems to be more stable, even though we know it isn't.

Conventional money flatters our sense of self-determination. With some, we exert power over the world. Yet there is comfort in money being out of our control. As an exogenous force of necessity, it clarifies judgement and action. Otherwise, the world would be frighteningly wide open. There is a parallel with slavery.[36] People feel that national monopoly currency must be inevitable. No-one would freely choose it. Alternatives make nonsense of devoting

33. K. Hart, 'Money in Twentieth-Century Anthropology' (2012).

34. Poe said, 'Writing fiction is more important than science, since God makes things up'.

35. Simmel (ibid.).

36. On the master–slave dialectic, see G.W.F. Hegel, *Phenomenology of Spirit* (1807).

your life to an unrewarding system. We cling to what we know. We want to be free, but we choose the illusion of freedom without responsibility. We prefer not to make our own money. We never have enough because 'they' keep it scarce. Persuading people to take the leap to do-it-yourself money involves confronting their deepest beliefs.

Rationality works best backwards. The future is unknowable. Yet modern societies train their members to control future time, if only to meet bureaucratic deadlines. Precise calculation of futures caused the 2008 crash. The scientific method applies reason to past events that are assumed to recur. This only works when the key variables are constants. The market economy, however, is ever-changing. Knowledge and experience may help us to manage uncertain futures. Betting is one way to gain such experience.

I took up betting on the horses when I was 12. It saw me through university. It seems incredible now that I survived, never mind prospered a little.[37] What saved me from my system was empiricism. I knew a lot about the horses. I would have made more without the system, but we all need a crutch to lean on. I later widened my range, but I only bet in fields that I know very well. My youthful betting gave me a different attitude to money. I was not a victim of the market economy. This shaped my approach to economic anthropology. Betting can teach us about money.

I have reflected lately on money as a form of religious life.[38] According to Durkheim,[39] religion binds us to an external force while empowering us to act. It stabilizes our interactions with the world and provides an anchor for our volatility. What we know well is everyday life. But this is subject to larger forces. We would influence these unknown causes of our fate or establish a connection with them. Religion helps us to bridge the gap between known and unknown in our lives. It links the world of ordinary experience to an extraordinary world beyond it. The main thing we don't know is how we belong to society. Through ritual we worship our shared existence and call it God. Everyday life is more stable when we draw on beliefs about these representations. Ritual instils them in us.

Roy Rappaport[40] did not believe that religion must rest on a division between 'sacred' and 'profane'. Nor do I. For him, religion was how we touch the wholeness of things ('holiness'). The human economy approach is a religious project in that sense.[41] We should build bridges from everyday life to the human predicament. Money extends the idea of society to the whole world.

---

37. Hart, Appendix 2013a.
38. Hart, Appendix 2010b.
39. E. Durkheim, *The Elementary Forms of Religious Life* (1912).
40. R. Rappaport, *Ritual and Religion*.
41. Hart, Appendix 2021. See Chapter 15.

Betting is a ritualized form of engagement with society through money. A street gambler and a Wall Street trader differ in degree, not kind. Betting inserts someone into money and markets as an agent who takes and makes them at the same time. There is some satisfaction in that, regardless of profit and loss. Many card games offer a similar experience that has applications beyond the card table. We make history, but not under circumstances of our own choosing.[42] I am a creator. So are we all creators.

Money for a Human Economy

We need ways of reaching the parts of the economy we don't know. Money is central to both home and work. Markets are not just about abstraction. Money's significance lies in its synthesis of impersonal abstraction and personal meaning. Its social power comes from mediating infinite potential and finite closure. Money is linked to democracy because its impersonality dissolves differences between people. Thinking of money as a durable ground to stand on may anchor identity in collective memory. It also helps us to generate the personal credit linking us as individuals to society. Money is an ocean that helps us to widen our horizons. The pressure to exert local control persists, however. Money's social value lies not in separating local and global spheres, but in moving between them. It reflects our humanity while anchoring us in the everyday. All markets are world markets, but money is compatible with all levels of society.[43]

Money mediates the two pairs that define national capitalism – state and market, home and world. We develop ourselves through them.[44] Money is a great equalizer, but it also fuels inequality. As memory, money links individuals to their communities. We can join past, present and future; fact and fiction; local and global. We should not perch on one pole, but learn to combine both in society. Exchange of meanings through language and of goods and services through money are now converging on the internet. The digital revolution could advance the human conversation about a better world. Money is the strategic way to learn how to be more fully human.

---

42. K. Marx, *The Eighteenth Brumaire of Louis Bonaparte* (1852).

43. https://www.berghahnbooks.com/downloads/intros/HartMoney_intro.pdf (accessed 16 September 2021); Hart, Appendix 2017.

44. F. Engels, *Socialism, Utopian and Scientific* (1880).

Chapter 20

LEARNING, REMEMBERING AND SHARING

I sum up here what a lifetime of learning has taught me, how I share it with others through teaching and writing, and some of the techniques of storage, retrieval and performance that I have picked up along the way. I start with how I spent my time as a young child and what I learned from it. I then turn to learning and teaching as an academic. How do we combine ideas and life, when they are usually kept in separate compartments? They move together through dialectic (conversation) and story. Memory and communication are strongly linked. I conclude by assessing the claims of organized knowledge and popular culture as sources of education.

What I Did with My Time as a Young Child

I started out solitary. I felt that I was mentally quicker than most people. I have never lost the confidence this gave me. Playing on the street was a shock. I was small, clever and introverted. That made me a target. I had to avoid the taunts and blows somehow. I used my mouth, was funny and sociable, made friends and allies. I joined in ball games and became quite skilled. I took the lead in quasi-criminal activities like raiding richer neighbourhoods for conkers and stealing milk bottles from doorsteps. This habit transferred to primary school, where I had to mitigate doing well in class. I visited the headmaster's study for punishment more than anyone. I was no teacher's pet.

I liked being top of the class and I could be sure of 'winning' in the school room. This estranged my peers and I wanted them to like me. The mix I developed was to be smart, funny and naughty in unpredictable ways. I courted my teachers' approval and made their lives difficult, as with Mum at home. This pattern endured in later life. One day I walked around the classroom believing that I was invisible. This was the first sign of my mind's ability to make a world of its own. Speed and totality of mental connection normally served me well. But it could make me lose touch with reality.

How did I fill my free hours in my first decade? I much preferred school to the summer holidays. My main diversions were reading, ball games, playing cards and music, especially singing. Readers are loners. Ball games involved my peers in the street and parks. Playing cards was a family affair or just me with my sister, grandma or Dad. Singing in groups was a family preoccupation. I was the head choirboy at church. But music meant more than singing.

I could read well by the time I was 4. People tended to distract each other at home. Mum would recruit us kids for any domestic task. I spent as much time as I could out of doors. But if I was reading when told to help out, I could often ignore the order. Mum would say to Dad, 'When he gets into a book, he's deaf to the world'. My sister was not granted this exemption. I collaborated in her unequal treatment.

I was encouraged to pursue a social strategy of abstraction. I could escape from domestic routine into the world of books. I wanted to get away anyway. But I had to read in that crowded living space. I learned how to shut it all out. If I was indifferent to my surroundings, Mum would clear up the mess. 'I'll do less for you before I do more', she said, but she did more and we both knew she would.

Books, newspapers, comics and magazines helped me to extend the limits of my narrow existence. I valued general knowledge for its own sake. Murder mysteries gave me the chance to second-guess the author. Science fiction offered a window on the future. I consumed massive amounts of information about sport. I memorized the facts of history and geography. I was not attracted to the worlds of nature and technology. I was very keen on crosswords and quizzes. Cryptic crossword puzzles test mastery of words, irony and cultural allusion. Our family played pencil-and-paper quizzes a lot, especially at parties. At 9 I had the reading age of a 14-year-old.

Abstracting myself through reading from the reality of domestic life was contradictory. Linguistic virtuosity and book knowledge gave me social power and individual freedom. I could escape my home to inhabit worlds of the imagination. Parents, teachers and adults praised me for this. But I knew that escape could only ever be partial. I had to live with the other street kids and in the playground. I didn't have to; I wanted to be one of them. The abstract world drew me away from people. The habit of concentration has served me well. But background family noise reassures me that I remain connected to the real world.

Playing cards was for indoors and ball games for outside. These involved family and the boys of my neighbourhood respectively. The historian A.J.P. Taylor, who grew up on the Lancashire coast, claimed that the only useful skill his father taught him was advanced dominoes. He also noted that when the Communist leader, a Manchester man, was kidnapped by Fascists, they spent the weekend playing solo whist together.[1] I learned a lot more from my Dad, but the Manchester I grew up in was crazy about playing cards.

As soon as I was 3 and could read and count, Dad taught me to play cribbage. It was played in pubs, involved scoring on a board with pegs and had its own vocabulary ('one for his knob' – a jack, 'Morgan's orchard' – two pairs, etc.). You kept a hand with the best potential fit for cards turned up or discarded. I often wept. I would hear Mum say, 'Why don't you let him win for once, Stanley', and he would reply, 'He will only win on merit'. I won my first game of cribbage when I was 6 or 7. This led to other games. Our favourites were whist, an ancestor of contract bridge, gambling at Newmarket and pontoon for sugar beans or chocolate drops. I played rummy with Grandma and everything with my sister. My training as a card player was thorough and I put it to profitable use later.

The fact that I had only one good eye was recognized before I was 1 year old. Dad refused to let this delay my training as a sportsman. From eighteen months he had me catching tennis balls in the back yard. Stereoscopic vision matters for close work, but not to assess the speed and direction of moving objects. I was a good cricketer at 5. Others overtook me when they matured. I had the equipment and knowledge. I played soccer a lot and hit a tennis ball against the end wall of our terrace for hours. From the age of 9 I watched international cricket and some of Manchester United's games. As a teenager I found the time for lacrosse, rugby, soccer, cricket, tennis, badminton, golf and competitive cycling. At Cambridge I captained my college's occasional cricket and darts teams, played squash and coxed a rowing eight. I forgot that I had only one eye.

Singing linked me to the music-making traditions of my class and region. On Sunday evenings, I joined Dad and my two aunts to sing, with Uncle Albert giving a strong lead at the piano. We would sing hymns, psalms, arias, spirituals, pop songs, nursery rhymes – anything and everything. Church was a main focus for organized singing. I had a good voice and once sang 'The Holly and the Ivy' solo on BBC radio. But my exposure to music went beyond this. Dad couldn't go to work without a dose of classical music from the BBC Third Programme. We would compete to identify the music first.

---

1. A.J.P. Taylor, *A Personal History* (1983).

He also had a box full of 78s, collected in the 1930s. We had no gramophone, but Grandma did – a standing cabinet wound manually. I played Dad's records there. They featured singers like Beniamino Gigli, Paul Robeson and Deanna Durbin. I sang along with *La donna è mobile*, *Nessun dorma*, the chorus of the Hebrew slaves. But I was obsessed with Dvořák's New World Symphony, conducted by Arturo Toscanini. It never failed to sweep me away, embedding America deeply in my imagination.

Reading nourished my intellectual ambition and offered a means of escape. Ball games gave me motor skills and teamwork. What did I learn from playing cards? Perhaps it trained us for the market economy with its numbers, fast calculation, managing risk and partnership. All the world's music was open to me as a maker and taker. People say I was always a bright boy. I know lots of bright boys who didn't make it.[2] I think of my intelligence as a natural endowment and nothing to brag about. I value ethical qualities – concentration and perseverance, the will to see something through to the end.

The big problem was how to reconcile my mind's propensity to abstract with staying rooted in the real world. I was, on balance, solitary until my late teens. I was then social until my mid-thirties and solitary again until my early fifties (because of mental illness). I was more balanced from then to my early seventies. As I write, the pendulum is swinging back towards the solitary pole.

Closing the Gap between Ideas and Life

This book is a plea for anthropologists and their students to be open to the next world revolution in knowledge. I was initially attracted by anthropology's range. I could study anything that took my fancy. I would join the world while following my own impulses. The best way of gaining wider experience was to teach. After my PhD, life became a long process of self-learning. Perhaps that is what anthropology is best for. I taught in order to learn; but I also learned about teaching.

Many university lecturers avoid direct energy exchange with their audience. Their main interest is to stick to their script. They read out a text, notes or slides, barely making eye contact with listeners who are busy writing it all down. Students read books and articles detached from their lives or from any kind of life. The invention of word processing gave me a new sense of being an artisan.[3] In my late forties, I decided to improvise my lectures. I took this in small steps over a year, slowly mastering fear of public failure. I preferred

---

2. C.L.R. James would sit wrapped in a blanket and sometimes say pensively, 'I was a bright boy'.

3. See Chapter 14.

lecturing to a crowd (first-year students) or conversing one-on-one (with graduate students) to small groups (seminars and specialized lectures). Reading out a script and live performance are light years apart.

Sometimes, after a lecture, a student would approach me, eyes shining. I would ask, 'What did you like about it?' Sure enough, I did not recognize their version as mine. The student had been pondering something important to them, maybe for years. My 'performance' involved a lot of movement. My words were visually 'live'. They sounded coherent. But listeners also took time out to reflect. One of them would have a 'eureka' moment. In their excitement they fetishized my lecture as its source. Some students told me they could take notes more easily from me than they could from lecturers who read them out. All that school Latin and algebra lent unconscious order to my performances.

My hardest task in writing this book has been to combine ideas and life. Karl Marx compared ideology with the camera obscura.[4] Ideology is the dogma that life comes from ideas, allowing specialists in ideas (priests, lawyers, politicians, bureaucrats, writers and teachers) to tell people how they should think. The camera in question produced an image that turned the world upside down, as ideology does. Ideas come from life, not the other way around, and this idea strengthened the masses in their struggle with the know-all classes.

I tried to close the gap between ideas and life. I told students that anthropology would be impossible unless they were a human being to start with. How could we study religion and economy, through art and technology to politics and the family? Sure, we read the professional literature. But no-one could hold it all together unless they drew on what they had learned from life in general. The dead texts they were made to read could be enlivened in several ways. I regularly lectured on the founders – on their published ideas, but also on their lives, historical situations and political purposes. I hoped that this brought reading closer to how the students experienced the world. They could imagine doing something similar. This is the opposite of the 'hose and bucket' system of education – forget who you are and what you think you know; we will fill you up with what you need to get through.

Paolo Freire (1921–97), a Brazilian philosopher, became for education what Frantz Fanon was for the anti-colonial movement. He published a score of books in Portuguese, some in English. The most significant are *Pedagogy of the Oppressed* and *Pedagogy of Freedom*.[5]

---

4. K. Marx and F. Engels, *The German Ideology* (1845: section A 4). https://www.marxists.org/archive/marx/works/1845/german-ideology/ (accessed 13 October 2021).

5. P. Freire, *Pedagogy of the Oppressed* (1970); *Pedagogy of Freedom* (1998).

Freire saw education as emancipation for the downtrodden. Both teachers and students had to overcome profound obstacles to learning. The first must abandon the 'banking system' of education that sees students as empty accounts filled by teachers with the human capital to see them through life. Equally, the oppressed have to confront programming that makes them the passive cause of their fate. The teachers need to 'expose and explain' the conditions pupils face in society, but their main task is to help them to become agents of radical change. Above all, teachers and students need to learn from each other. Education is not a one-way process, but a dialogue to which both sides bring knowledge. This all requires the 'development of critical consciousness' (*conscientizacao*).

> Freire remains a humanist in [that] his discourse is anthropocentric – for him humans alone have critical capacities. . . His is a humanist ethic insofar as class societies retard the development of the capacities of people to take control of their own destinies.[6]

Education must make students critical, curious and autonomous. Teachers must respect their students' personal autonomy, but they themselves embody an autonomy that is social, reflecting the universal ethics of the human person, since these are 'indispensable for human living and human social intercourse. . . [since] humanity's ontological vocation calls us out of and beyond ourselves'.[7] I cannot think of a better definition of anthropology's mission. It goes with a commitment to lifelong learning of the sort advocated by Immanuel Kant. Paulo Freire also invoked 'science' in a way that contradicts the technical specialization that passes for science in contemporary theory and institutional practice.

Freire's repeated commitment to 'scientific formation' is confusing for the products of mainstream education since he rejects the 'neutrality' and 'value freedom' on which Western social science is conventionally founded. For him science is critical, not positivistic. He was Rousseau's twentieth-century successor as a radical educator.

Dialectical Method

What you read is more likely to take root if it engages your existing interests. A reader's ability to absorb something new depends on their own history of reading until then. Human beings must learn to cope with an imper-

---

6. S. Aronowitz, Prologue to Freire, *Pedagogy of Freedom* (1998).
7. Freire (1998: 25).

sonal world. Personal and impersonal dimensions of living in society do not inhabit different places. They belong together. Speech moves between people as conversation. Writing makes a sharper and often more unequal distinction between sender and recipient. I try to write as I speak and vice versa. Both reflect my formal education, but they are both human too.

G.W.F. Hegel took dialectical method from Kant and perfected his own system in *The Science of Logic*.[8] The object of philosophy for him was not individuals, but societies. Societies move because they are in history. How can thought move systematically with its object? Dialectical method is part of human thinking in general, where it is known as conversation. The other method of thinking in movement is story. Hegel begins with experience, a disorganized muddle. He shows the error of mistaking the idea for reality.

We all know the word 'house', and we might think there is nothing more to owning one than saying 'my house'. But before long the roof will leak, the paint will peel and we must acknowledge that the house is a material process requiring attention. An idea gives form to experience. If it is a powerful idea, like the state or kinship or economy, it may come to be seen as being synonymous with society itself. A complementary category organizes what it is not (right/wrong, hot/cold, state/market). Their movement may stand for societies in history.

This is positive dialectic. In time the pair loses its power. The division between the two sides becomes blurred – state capitalism, market socialism. This is negative dialectic. Perhaps a new idea will organize reality and the process will start over. What to do with a house when words are not enough? Redecorate? Read poetry while it falls apart? Are a leaky roof and cracks in the walls the only reality? Or do we reclaim our ownership and learn how to fix the house?

It is as damaging to insist on a radical separation of individuals and society, or of life and ideas, as it is to collapse the difference between them. Of course, the meaning of the pair evolves in time. The institution of private property drives a wedge between our individuality and an active sense of belonging to society. It became convenient for business corporations to acquire the rights of individual persons in economic law.[9] As a result, political culture is confused about the relative rights and responsibilities of citizens and abstract entities wielding far more power. The consequences for democracy are disastrous.

---

8. Hegel's aim in *The Science of Logic* (1812–16) was to overturn Kant's dialectical approach, and Marx helped him to succeed.

9. See Chapter 14.

On Communication and Memory

I never abandoned the idea of improvising lectures.[10] I gave the anthropology lectures for first-year social scientists. I trained myself for a year. First, I reduced the preparation time from two hours to one hour, then from forty-five to thirty minutes. I dispensed with notes and rehearsed my lecture over breakfast (twenty minutes), then while walking to the lecture theatre (ten minutes). Finally, I reviewed my options while waiting for the audience to settle down. Only two things matter: what is the big idea and where to start? A performance is like a wave. Once you are on it, you can't get off. The movement rides on an energy exchange between performer and audience. The last couple would realize that everyone else was quiet and then I would begin.

Writing/speaking and reading/listening are interdependent, and each is creative. But the creativity of receivers is usually downplayed. In the 1960s the critic Roland Barthes attempted to dethrone authors as subjective agents.[11] I am interested in 'the death of the audience'. A book's readership is unpredictable these days. *The Memory Bank*[12] generated fan mail from Swiss bankers and Peruvian activists whom I could hardly imagine, never mind write for. I have internalized working in twenty-four countries, unconsciously for the most part. But when I write something false or incomprehensible, voices inside me from these places make themselves heard. Listening to those voices helps to make my writing accessible to unknown readers. At least I hope so, but I will never know for sure.

For most of history, information was scarce, handed down by experts.[13] In my old university, teachers carried scrolls in their gowns' deep pockets and read them out for payment. Students ended up with a personal copy. The ability to interpret these manuscripts was costlier. The print revolution put the Bible in the hands of vernacular readers. They made their own connection to God. Printing took a line of business away from the hacks with gowns. The emphasis in learning shifted to interpretation and understanding.

Newspapers, novels and pamphlets proliferated in the late eighteenth century.[14] This abundant information posed new problems. Reading now had to be selective. This was dangerous. Who knew which powerful person would take offence at being ignored? Immanuel Kant wrote his *Critiques* in this context.[15] He asked how to know the world, achieve our purposes and make judgements.

---

10. See Chapter 7.

11. R. Barthes, *The Death of the Author* (1967).

12. K. Hart, *The Memory Bank* (2000).

13. Hart, Appendix 2015a.

14. Ibid.

15. Especially I. Kant, *The Critique of Judgment* (1790).

He paved the way for the mass media. The sender/receiver relationship was still unequal, however. Today the internet provides many options for engaging with the world as a communicator in one's own right. Self-expression is still hamstrung by the censorship of authoritarian states and by bureaucratic capitalism, with its command-and-control methods and intellectual property regime. Many want to democratize how information is produced, distributed and consumed. But we have not shaken off deference to writers and lecturers.

A sense of 'self' depends on memory. My working memory consists of stories, images and facts. For an item to find a home, it must connect with what's already there. I also conceive of money as a 'memory bank'.[16] The idea comes from computing; but the word 'bank' links flows of water and money to those of information. All three are slower-moving residues of fast-moving flows. When compared with the chaotic movement of water molecules, cash in your pocket or a computer's cursor, these appear to be static. But they move too. Stability and movement, stocks and flows, ideas and life are inseparable. But they are not identical.

Modernity rests on believing that we have escaped from its prehistory. In fact, we have never been modern.[17] The institutions of Bronze Age civilizations are our institutions today: territorial states, landed property, warfare, racism, cities, money objects, long-distance trade, an emphasis on work, world religion and the nuclear family.[18] This agrarian package has become more lethal with the addition of machines. The conservatism of 'modern' societies is evident in our education systems.

Organized Knowledge

The German Romantics claimed that since the world was falling apart, there was no point in learning how to adapt to it. Better to improve what is between our ears ('self-learning'). It might help us cope with unforeseeable crises. I admire philosophers who kept a foot in both Enlightenment and Romantic camps, especially Rousseau and Kant. Max Weber published two essays, 'Science as a Vocation' and 'Politics as a Vocation'.[19] Science is based on reason, but the best scientists are enthusiasts. Politics is based on passion, but to be persuasive politicians should be reasonable. We all mix up reason and passion variably.

---

16. Hart, Appendix 2000a.

17. B. Latour, *We Have Never Been Modern* (1993).

18. Hart, Appendix 2002b.

19. Based on Munich lectures in 1918–19. H. Gerth and C. Wright Mills (eds), *From Max Weber* (1946).

Two great ideas drive modern history – *democracy* and *science*. They are linked. The first says that citizens must be free and equal so that they can be self-governing, the second that such societies can only flourish if knowledge is based on what is real. A democratic society has to break down intrinsic barriers to its own development. These are poverty, ignorance and injustice. To do so, it needs science. Science is a collective enterprise, building on the cumulative efforts of generations. When it is cut off from ordinary people, it wastes away. Education links the two. Free and equal citizens must be knowledgeable. And science is sustained by a political culture that values truth, learning and invention.

Science at first was *not* mystical beliefs – religion, superstition, stories. It was not uninspected traditions referring human existence to supernatural causes. It was not 'myth'. Not long ago, the drive sustaining science was anticlerical. Science is now often opposed to the creative arts – literature, poetry, the critical imagination. Ethnography is writing and reflection. We must find again a conception of science as a means of human development.[20] Social scientists emulate the scientific method, but forget, if they ever knew, what science is for. Most have lost their way. The result is an impasse. Natural scientists don't relate their research to the complex character of human existence. The humanists have given up trying to understand how the world works. Social scientists imitate a caricature of the natural scientist, but don't try to change how they think or learn. Neither can say anything useful about how nature and society interact.

I have a friend, a professor of material science, who uses twenty-five equations of a certain type to monitor minute changes of metals under experimental conditions. The British Treasury uses 150 of these equations to model the national economy. It's a sick joke. Human progress requires a new concept of science and its branches. The mechanization of brains already demands this. We could start by admitting that social science has failed. Maybe religion should be given another try.[21]

The Humanities and Popular Culture

The sciences and humanities are, respectively, universal and particular in their approaches to knowledge. But that does not mean that they are antagonistic or don't overlap in important ways. *Science* (French), *Scienza* (Italian) and *Wissenschaft* (German) do not share with English the same narrow version

---

20. T. Ingold (ed.), *Key Debates in Anthropology* (1996). I opened the first debate: Hart, Appendix 1988b.

21. Hart, Appendix 2021.

of scientific object and method. They generally mean organized knowledge. Anthropologists are well placed to join the next synthesis. We study – or ought to – humanity as a whole. A synthesis will probably call itself 'science', perhaps 'human sciences'. We must not tie ourselves to the relics of the last synthesis. The discovery of general truths can rest on examining particular cases, using personal judgement, extensive knowledge and rigorous thought. A judge's ruling in one case may establish legal precedent for a century. Immanuel Kant made a major scientific discovery in astronomy, but his revolution in metaphysics was based on a humanist approach. Great literature yields general truths from closely observed details.

The humanities once cultivated personal judgement based on reading the Western literary canon. But, facing a collapse in public interest, they now peddle abstruse jargons. If we want to cope as individuals with fast-breaking and unpredictable conditions, our self-learning must sometimes embrace both contingency and probability. Lessons from life come in many forms. Ato Quayson has this to say:

> You cannot understand human society properly without taking an interest in its most banal and ephemeral features. Hart and (C.L.R.) James both devoured all forms of popular culture. The explanatory power of critical humanism stripped of any illusions of grandeur derives from its primary organizing interest, that is, in men and women as they pursue their hopes, fears, and vague ideas.[22]

In the 1950s, some distinguished British academics admitted that they liked football. As I recall, A.J. Ayer first confessed on a television programme for intellectual snobs called 'The Brains Trust' to being an avid supporter of the London club, Spurs.

I owe the following vignettes to James's *American Civilization*, popular music and fiction.[23] The 1940s saw a cultural explosion in American movies, jazz, art, theatre and fiction. James thought the struggle for democracy was most intense in the US; and the main battleground was popular culture. Industry was controlled by capitalists; workers and consumers took what they could get. But the cultural industry is huge. Here people relate to capitalism on different terms. They spend their own money freely on a wide choice of entertainment, clothing, etc. Hollywood studios cannot anticipate which movies will sell most seats. The pop charts are as unpredictable. Economic democracy can be contested here on terms more favourable to the masses.

---

22. A. Quayson, Afterword, 'A Conversation around Keith Hart' (2019). https://culanth .org/fieldsights/swimming-into-the-current-the-movement-of-human-society-through-history (accessed 16 September 2021).

23. See Chapters 9 and 10.

Theodor Adorno was frankly elitist and despised what he called 'mass culture'. He believed that the masses were dupes of capitalist advertising. Adorno claimed, 'the more democratic (German) jazz is, the worse it becomes' and 'jazz and pogrom go hand in hand'.[24] James's attitude was the opposite. He took 'the struggle for happiness' to be for more democracy in people's everyday lives.

Popular culture was a stand-off between capitalists and working people. It led to compromises between them. The story of Marlene Dietrich's 'pants' (trousers) is iconic.[25] The men were away fighting and women had taken over industrial production. Marlene Dietrich sometimes wore pants in movies and nightclubs. In 1944 she wore them at a New York event. The clothing stores and mail order firms were immediately flooded with women's orders for pants. Capitalists did not anticipate this demand; they struggled to catch up with it. A distinctively American female fashion – wearing trousers – was born. Consumers are just dupes of manipulative capitalists?

Soon after the millennium, I was on an American Airlines plane taking off from Paris to Chicago. I tuned to a TV news channel, but soon lost interest and read my book. Later I noticed that my foot was tapping. There was an ad break on the screen. This cheered me up: I was going to the land whose popular music is always going somewhere. Chicago is my favourite city for this reason. London hijacked Manchester's industrial revolution for the dead end of colonial empire. Chicago took up markets on a grander scale.

AA frequent flyers were called 'roadrunners'. One compilation was 'road music for roadrunners'. In my American decade, I absorbed 'freedom' as a synthesis of idea and practice rooted in forward movement, especially in rock 'n' roll. I missed Tom Petty in the 1970s. He found recognition in Britain; and I found it in the US. I danced round the living room with Constance as a baby, singing along to *Full Moon Fever*. When my mother was dying, I sat in the hospital car park listening to Paul Simon's *Graceland* with tears streaming down my face and shouted 'I am a singer!' All we have against death is song. I found in Tom Petty's 'Runnin' Down a Dream'[26] the poetry and road music that launched this book.

We are driving down a road, our life journey, chasing an elusive dream. This book might help me understand what I have been running after since I was fixated on getting into Cambridge. We are not authors of our own destiny or even of our dreams. In one recurrent dream, I am in a wilderness: a ravine with rocks and trees above, a fast-flowing mountain stream below and a narrow path ahead. A brown bear blocks my path. I can smell its damp fur;

---

24. Adorno spent 1941–49 in the US.

25. C.L.R. James, *American Civilization* (1993: 145–46).

26. https://www.youtube.com/watch?v=Qv4-m-cIZf4 (accessed 16 September 2021).

it opens its mouth and I shield my face with my arm, which is clamped in immensely strong teeth. But I am not afraid and the dream ends. The wilderness is nature and the bear my nature, my unconscious mind. It is more powerful than my conscious self, but that's OK. A Korean friend's mother interprets dreams. He asked me, 'Which way was the stream flowing?' The way I was going. 'Oh, that's alright then.'

Forward movement by itself may be the only point. Where it leads is a mystery. Perhaps the mystery is the end of the road, death. Murder mysteries are my favourite fiction genre. I have a sketch for one on the back burner. My detective hero is not one who reveals how he worked it all out at the end. It is Jules Maigret. William Faulkner said that Georges Simenon is our Chekhov and I agree. Maigret hates being asked if he has clues for solving the case. His method is to insert himself into the social ambience of a crime and wait for the answers to come to him. Yes, he follows leads, usually without a solution in mind. That's all we can do. In one novel Maigret takes a room in a lodging house next to where a police colleague has been shot down. At night he looks out from his room:

> The air had a velvety smoothness that was almost palpable. No movement, no sound troubled the peace of Rue Lhomond. Somewhere, behind the houses, a rumble could be heard, the muffled sounds of cars, of brakes and car-horns, but all that was in another world; between the roofs of the houses, between the chimney-pots, there was a splendid vista of an infinity populated by stars. . . After a moment of stillness, you could pick up the pulsations of the house.[27]

Maigret soaks up what the place has to tell him, imagines a Paris he can't see and takes in a universe of stars, altogether. I spent two years in a West African slum. I thought I became a better fieldworker with time. But when I wrote it up, I only used my notes from the first year. These read like a detective story – I was asking big questions then, but later I drowned in the trivia of parish pump politics.

i can smell the world burning

i wake up restless
in the dead of night
not for the first time
and smell the world burning
nothing to see
no-one to touch

---

27. G. Simenon, *Maigret Takes a Room* (*Maigret en meublé*, 1951). Chapter 3 Loc 599.

dry birdcage mouth
and everywhere silence

then I hear the steady rumble
of spaceship earth
or just the fridges tuneless song
of life machines
and dreams of common flight

and still I can smell
this bonfire of dead trees[28]
exhaust of motor cars
pungent and acrid
the world burning
while we sleep

28. Video by Louise Hart and Arron Bleasedale, 2000. https://www.facebook.com/grou ps/161765339613/permalink/10159578734064614/ (accessed 16 September 2021).

AFTERWORD

My editor[1] suggested that this book needed a proper ending. So here it is. I learned long ago that a good poem or short story builds to the last line, which, if it is successful, casts a new light on the whole piece and invites the reader to reconsider what it was really about. It should come as no surprise that this ending is not closed, but rather opens up the past (the book's, my own and, to some extent, the world's), if not the future. In search of conclusions, I take off from R.G. Collingwood's logic of question and answer, in a looser way than he intended.

What Question Is This the Answer to?

Every day I walked past the Albert Memorial.[2] Everything about it was visibly misshapen, corrupt, crawling, verminous. Why had Scott done it? What was the relationship between what he did and what he tried to do? . . . Truth consists of questions and answers. Each answer must be 'the right' one to the question it professes to answer.[3]

---

1. Tony Mason is another Manchester man, whose supervision of this final version has been just right.

2. A monument to Victorian imperialism erected in memory of the queen's deceased husband. Its architect, Gilbert Scott, designed Manchester's Town Hall and St John's college chapel, neither in such bad taste.

3. R.G. Collingwood, *Autobiography* (1939: 29).

Why did I write this book? Jack Goody (1919–2015) published some thirty of them in his long life: the first, in his late thirties, was an ethnography of north-west Ghana; he edited a collection on Fortes's development cycle approach, and his best book, *Death, Property and the Ancestors* (1962), was a work of comparative jurisprudence anchored in his Ghanaian research. What do we have against our own death? We can bequeath housing to our descendants (which he did) and we can become an ancestor (by writing many books). In a decade from almost fifty years old, Jack published comparative studies of literacy, property and kinship (what else?) and moved into the history of precolonial states in Africa.[4] Between 1976 and 2012, he published over twenty books comparing Eurasia and Africa, the last of them when in his nineties. *Metals, Culture and Capitalism: An Essay on the Origins of the Modern World* broke new ground.[5] Here he explains that he had been interested in mining since he joined a regiment of Nottinghamshire coal miners in the Second World War. I helped with *Production and Reproduction* (1976) and revised two more to get past hostile readers: *The Culture of Flowers* (1993) and *The East in the West* (1996). I once asked him why he wrote so much and he replied, 'Because I started late and was behind [Edmund Leach]'.

It is unsurprising that I too wanted to write books. One English teacher at Manchester Grammar School, a fop who later became an Oxford don, told my mother when I was 15: 'I'm afraid English isn't Keith's thing, Mrs Hart.' My first journal article was returned completely rewritten. I was outraged and threatened to withdraw the article. The editor, a seasoned pro, countered with 'Would you please withdraw it? It's the worst-written article I have ever received.' I changed my tune instantly and told her to publish the rewrite. I took an analytical approach to words then and had not worked out how many registers the English language had, nor their regional and class connotations.

Over the years I worked on my technique, but there were long periods when I hardly published anything – my time at Yale and afterwards, especially the years of mental illness when I couldn't concentrate for sustained writing. These were the middle years when my published output normally should have peaked. I sometimes wondered what question I would ask myself on my deathbed. The answer was always the same: 'Have you written the books you were capable of?' At a Cambridge dinner in 1998, John Davis, then Warden of All Souls, Oxford, asked me

JD: Why are you moving to Paris, Keith? KH: Because I want to write. JD: But we all love you; your friends and students are here. KH: I don't want the only people who know what I think to have been in the same room as me.

---

4. K. Hart, 'The social anthropology of West Africa (1985).

5. Hart, Appendix 2014a.

I went to Paris to be a freelance writer. My first effort, *The Memory Bank*, was published as a trade hardback in London.[6] A New York literary agent, Joe Spieler, signed me up for a second book on how the relationship between stability and movement in society was being transformed by the internet. I called it *Still Moving* and he offered to support me for a year in the US, to learn how to write for an American audience. I kept this up for a while, but it placed strains on Sophie and me. We married in 2001 and had Constance in 2002. I soon pulled out of the New York arrangement. I told myself that I wanted to elaborate the conceptual framework of my work on money. Since the millennium, I have published over a hundred books, articles, chapters and posts on money and economy alone.[7] I now realize that it was a waste of effort – academics don't read any more; they cite my early work, but not the products of later periods. But I saved my family this time around.

I then turned to writing books for the general public again. Marshall Sahlins published *The Hit Man's Dilemma*, which sank without a trace.[8] In the same year I drafted a science fiction murder mystery, *Futures: The Death and Life of Don Quick*. A pastiche of the Western novel, it drew on Cervantes, Goethe, Mann, Gibbon and Roddenberry (*Star Trek*). I posted an excerpt on my website and put it to one side.[9] I occasionally revisited my autobiography, even though a first version in 1989 ended badly.[10] In 2007, I was a visiting professor at Wits University, Johannesburg and launched there a historical synthesis of Africa's development.[11]

In the following decade I developed this approach. A major catalyst was being invited to give the keynote address at a 2013 World Bank/World Customs Organization conference in Brussels on 'Informality, International Trade and Customs'.[12] Eventually I put together a book, *Africa 1800–2100: A History of the Future*, an expanded version of Chapter 16 in this volume. A French friend asked me what it was about. I told her it was about Africa moving up in the global charts and Europe moving down. Her face hardened, so I made a conciliatory gesture:

KH: Of course, Africa is a mess. FF: Yes, it's a mess! KH: Have you ever been there? FF: No.

---

6. Hart, Appendix 2000a.

7. https://thememorybank.co.uk/2019/03/04/writings-on-money-and-economy-2000-2018 (accessed 16 September 2021).

8. Hart, Appendix 2005.

9. https://thememorybank.co.uk/other/futures-prologue/ (accessed 16 September 2021).

10. See Chapter 9.

11. https://thememorybank.co.uk/2007/05/16/two-lectures-on-african-development/ (accessed 16 September 2021).

12. See Chapter 11.

I did no better with New York and London publishers. Europeans, especially the former imperial powers, know at some level that their societies are weaker and in decline. European surveys of depression are headed by France and Britain. They can accept the rise of China, which was on a par with them in the eighteenth century. But Africa is something else. The blacks must be forever consigned to the bottom rung of the world ladder. The whites' slide into the dustbin of history is almost acceptable if the blacks are eternally condemned to being worse off.

By now, with no institutional authority and disenchanted with academia, I focused on the three books I wanted to write before I die: the one on Africa and Europe, the autobiography and the science fiction murder mystery. Africans always liked my story. In Brussels, a lady diplomat from the Democratic Republic of Congo launched into an impromptu revolutionary speech in the tea room after my keynote. But no takers. I promoted my autobiography to number one. It would make my name and help to sell the other books. My first efforts were premature and easily dismissed. I tried UNISA Press in South Africa, but got a very personal putdown from one reader.[13] This is the ninth full version of my text in four years. By now it had dawned on me that I was a known academic, but not a known popular writer. I wanted to combine my life story with what I had learned about the world. This would not after all be a trade autobiography.

I haven't stopped hoping for general readers, but I now wanted to write an accessible text for beginner students in the humanities and social disciplines. Only later did it occur to me that it might contribute to debates about the future of anthropology. I worried that academic anthropology's dire public reputation would be a handicap; but I made that purpose more prominent. In all of this, I made a surprising discovery, that this book was not just a means to publishing other books. It was the only book I wanted to write, the book of my life in both senses – my own story, but also the one book that I must get right.

I know that my motives, *pace* Collingwood, will not determine the outcome. Readers will decide the book's fate. Reflecting on Vico's sad experience, I sometimes think that my only chance to be famous will be two centuries from now, when a Mexican author finds a reflection of himself in my book and spreads my fame, falsely imagining that the ideas he has found are mine, not his own. I can settle for being a bit player in the long human conversation. I dream of becoming a classical source, but I know that success is a lottery.

What question, then, is this book the answer to? I have followed my Dad's example in old age, if not when I was a youth. I wrote about what interests me, taking in as much as I could without losing the thread. I learned a lot

---

13. My friend Hetta Pieterse did her best for me as editor; it wasn't her fault.

and that makes me feel better. Whether anyone else will join me is out of my control.

I love Collingwood and his Albert Memorial story. He is a congenial companion for the last stage of my journey. But he was a logician and I am not. I find it pointless to ask whether the end result is the 'right' answer to what I had in mind when I started out. I prefer the analogy of climbing a mountain. We can see the top from the bottom and get a great view from the top. In between, all we see is one foot stepping in front of the other. Any large work of the mind is like this, whatever vision we once had and might have when we finish. Most of the actual work is tedious; any guiding perspective goes missing.

I do, however, have an answer for 'What relation was there between what I have done and what I tried to do?' I take from Collingwood the idea that it sometimes pays to step back and ask 'What question was this supposed to be the answer to?' I have done that a dozen times while writing this book. What we start with is a prospectus, a plausible fiction. How could anyone know how the finished article will turn out, even less why?

The Albert Memorial story is good for me to think with, but in ways unintended by its author. A reader triangulates text and author with what is already stored in their memory. Collingwood wanted to displace the 'realists' in his field. Realism means something else to me. Meyer Fortes, after I fell into the swamp of my middle years, told me that I was the last person he expected to go mad. 'A rationalist yes, Keith; but I never met anyone as down-to-earth as you – you are a realist.' Here was a man with an LSE doctorate in psychology and an American psychiatrist wife and he didn't know that realism is a kind of idealism, just as vulnerable as any other to the vagaries of life. He didn't know that I identified with Raskolnikov and Lawrence of Arabia, fell in love with India because of a novel and made a vocation of scientific betting. The big question of my life – the WTF moment – was how I could have sacrificed my family life for an academic career. I cracked up because until then I thought I had all the answers; finding out that I didn't was a brutal shock. The rational realist in me made that mistake and life bit me hard where it hurts.

While we are on the topic of realism, I began a lifelong engagement with French literature and cinema as a Cambridge student. I ran my college film society; well, I was its treasurer, since no-one else wanted to handle the money. The important thing was to choose the films. A quarrelsome committee drew up a list for me to order the next term's programme during the vacation. I would replace half of it with my own selections and let them keep the rest. I told them some had not been available. They never supplied a back-up list.

Triangles were then a speciality of French New Wave cinema – memorably in *Last Year at Marienbad*.[14] I loved the sumptuous decor and pure mystifi-

---

14. Directed by Alain Resnais in 1961.

cation of *Marienbad*. A man tries to persuade a woman that they fell in love there last year and she made him promise to wait a year. She is with another man, maybe her husband, and now resists this story. At one point the husband shoots her, at another he doesn't. I vividly recall a television programme in which Alain Robbe-Grillet, the co-writer, was quizzed by journalists about that movie. One of them excitedly told the auteur, 'I know what really happened. They both died the previous year and are now ghosts.' Robbe-Grillet replied, 'What interests me is that you need to know what really happened'.

R.G. Collingwood (1889–1943) was born and died in the Lake District. His father worked closely with John Ruskin. He went to Rugby School and read classics ('greats') at Oxford. He became a philosopher, historian and archaeologist. His *Principles of Art* (1938) was influenced by the Italian idealist philosopher Benedetto Croce. Collingwood's aesthetic theory held that the artist's role in his community is to help people focus on their emotions. His posthumous *The Idea of History* (1946) was an important contribution to the philosophy of history.[15] He held that history was a science in the European sense of organized knowledge, here a science of human thought and action. He liked Vico a lot.

Collingwood and I have a magical relationship, similar to that of my daughters, 'the magical twins', born on the same day twenty-eight years apart. He died at 53 of multiple strokes in Coniston, the Lake District, the same year that I was born. We spent our summer holidays there when I was very young. I began to walk in the garden of Mrs Battie's Coniston guest house on my first birthday and have a photograph to prove it. I don't believe in the transmigration of souls; but magical thinking is a reliable writing tool for me.

I also know what science is – getting something right again and again within an acceptable margin of error, until it doesn't work anymore and we have to try something else. Magic and science occupy different compartments for me. I don't mix them up. But writing this book showed me that eclecticism is not good enough. Anthropology must rejoin the humanities with some conviction. Its sojourn as an impersonal social science was an aberration of the last century, the deadliest humanity has ever known.

---

15. R.G. Collingwood, *Principles of Art* (1938); *The Idea of History* (1946).

APPENDIX

Hart Papers Online (By Year)

https://goldsmiths.academia.edu/KeithHart (search for paper by full title)

1973   'Informal Income Opportunities and Urban Employment in Ghana'

1980s/90s 'Six Poems'

1986   'Heads or Tails? Two Sides of the Coin'

1988a   'Kinship, Contract and Trust: The Economic Organization of Migrants in an African City Slum'

1988b   'Social Anthropology as a Generalizing Science'

1990a   'Blacks in the World Economy: An Update of C.L.R. James on Negro Revolt (1938)'

1990b   'The Idea of Economy: Six Modern Dissenters'

1998   'The 1898 Cambridge Expedition to the Torres Straits in British Social Anthropology'

2000a   *The Memory Bank*

2000b   'Industrial Labour in India: The View From 19th-Century Lancashire'

2002a   'A Tale of Two Currencies'

2002b   'World Society as an Old Regime'

2003a   'Anthropology and the Crisis of the Intellectuals'

2003b   'British Social Anthropology's Nationalist Project'

2003c   'Manchester on My Mind'

2003d   'Notes on the Counter-Revolution'

2003e   'Studying World Society as a Vocation'

2004a   'An Anthropology of the Internet'

2004b   'How My Generation Let Down Our Students'

2004c   'The Political Economy of Food in an Unequal World'

2004d   'The Social Meaning of the Power Law'

2004e   'What Anthropologists Really Do'

2005   *The Hit Man's Dilemma*

2006a   'An Anthropologist in the World Revolution'

2006b   'Agrarian Civilization and Modern World Society'

2006c   'Bureaucratic Form and the Informal Economy'

2006d   'Common Wealth: Building Economic Democracy with Community Currencies'

2007a   'Keith Hart Answers Eleven Questions on Economic Anthropology'

2007b   'Marcel Mauss: In Pursuit of the Whole'

2007c   'Money is Always Personal and Impersonal'

2007d   'Towards an Alternative Economics: The View From France'

2008a   'Between Bureaucracy and the People: A Political History of Informality'

2008b   'Exchange in a Human Economy'

2008c   'Intellectual Property'

2008d   'Karl Polanyi's Legacy'

2009b   'The Persuasive Power of Money'

2009c   'An Anthropologist in the World Revolution'

2010a   'Building the Human Economy Together'

2010b   'Money as a Form of Religious Life'

2010c   'South Africa in Africa'

2010d   'Africa's Urban Revolution and the Informal Economy'

2010e   'Kant, "Anthropology" and the New Human Universal'

2011a   'Jack Goody's Vision of World History and African Development Today'

2011b   'Seeing Culture Everywhere: A Review'

2011c   'The Financial Crisis and the End of All-Purpose Money'

2012a   '"Anthropology" in Companion to Marxist Economics'

2012b   'David Graeber and the Anthropology of Unequal Society'

2012c   'Opening Anthropology'

2013a   'A Betting Man's Reflections on Money'

2013b   'A History of South African Capitalism in National and Global Perspective'

2014a   'Jack Goody: The Anthropology of Unequal Society'

2014b   'Marcel Mauss's Economic Vision 1920–1925: Anthropology, Politics, Journalism'

2014c   'Religion and Economy'

2014d   'The Anthropology of Money and Finance: Between Ethnography and World History'

2014e   'The Globalization of Apartheid: South Africa, Europe and the World'

2014f   'The Rise and Fall of Europe'

2015a   'Cultural Critique in Anthropology'

2015b   'Economy For and Against Democracy: Introduction'

2015c   'Gandhi as a Global Thinker: Anthropological Legacies of the Anti-Colonial Revolution'

2015d   'How the Informal Economy Took Over the World'

2015e   'Human Economy: The Revolutionary Struggle For Happiness'

2015f   'Money in the Making of World Society'

2015g   'New Preface to Globalization from Below'

2015h   'The Open Anthropology Cooperative: Towards an Online Public Anthropology'

2015i   'Waiting for Emancipation: the Prospects for Liberal Revolution in Africa'

2016a   'Money in the Making of a Human Economy: Beyond National Capitalism'

2016b   'Manifesto for a Human Economy'

2016c   'Preface to the Coming World Crisis'

2016d   'Review Article: The Anthropology of Debt'

2016e   'Where Once Was an Empire (Brexit)'

2017	'Europe's Links to Classical Antiquity, the Arabs and Long Before Them'
2018a	'After 2008: Market Fundamentalism at the Cross-Roads'
2018b	'Austerity: An Economy of Words?'
2018c	'Decolonizing Cambridge University'
2018d	'Structural Dynamics: Forms, Networks, Numbers (Meyer Fortes in the 1940s)'
2018e	'The Rise and Fall of National Capitalism'
2019a	'Rivers is Our Forgotten Founding Father'
2019b	'The Euro Crisis: An Episode in the Global History of Money'
2020a	'Clarkson, Cambridge and the International Movement for Human Rights'
2020b	'David Graeber (1961–2020)'
2021	'Human Economy as a Religious Project'

References

Achebe, C. 2006 [1958]. *Things Fall Apart*. London: Penguin.

Achebe, C. 2011. *The Education of a British-Protected Child*. London: Penguin.

Adams, H. 1999 [1918]. *The Education of Henry Adams*. Oxford: Oxford University Press.

Adams, H. 2011 [1889–91]. *History of the United States of America, 1801–1817* (9 vols). Cambridge: Cambridge University Press.

Anderson, P. 2012. 'Gandhi Centre Stage', *London Review of Books* 34.13: 3–11.

Aronowitz, S. 1997. 'Foreword', in P. Freire, *Pedagogy of the Oppressed*. London: Penguin.

Asbury, H. 2002 [1927]. *The Gangs of New York: An Informal History of the Underworld*. New York: Arrow.

Ayache, E. 2010. *The Blank Swan: The End of Probability*. Oxford: Wiley-Blackwell.

Ayer, A.J. 1977. *Part of My Life: Memoirs of a Philosopher*. Oxford: Oxford University Press.

Bakewell, S. 2010. *How to Live: A Life of Montaigne, One Question and Twenty Attempts at an Answer*. London: Chatto and Windus.

Barker, P. 2014. *The Regeneration Trilogy: Regeneration, The Eye in the Door and The Ghost Road*. London: Viking.

Barthes, R. 1977 [1967]. *The Death of the Author*. London: Fontana.

Baum, F. 2007 [1900]. *The Wonderful Wizard of Oz*. London: Penguin.

Beaujard, P. 2012. *Les mondes de l'océan Indien*. Paris: Armand Colin.

Berger, J. 1965. *Success and Failure of Picasso*. Harmondsworth: Penguin.

Biskind, P. 2007 [1998]. *Easy Riders, Raging Bulls: How the Sex-Drugs-and Rock 'n' Roll Generation Saved Hollywood*. London: Bloomsbury.

Blanc, J. 2010. 'Community and Complementary Currencies', in K. Hart, J.-L. Laville and A. D. Cattani (eds), *The Human Economy: A Citizen's Guide*. Cambridge: Polity, 303–12.

Bloom, A. 1978. 'The Education of Democratic Man: Emile', *Daedalus* 107.3: 135–53.

Breidenbach, J. and A. Gyiri. 2009. *Seeing Culture Everywhere: From Genocide to Consumer Habits*. Seattle, WA: University of Washington Press.

Brush, C. 1994. *From the Perspective of the Self: Montaigne's Self-Portrait*. New York: Fordham University Press.

Bryden, J. and K. Hart. 2004. *A New Approach to Rural Development in Europe: Germany, Greece, Scotland, Sweden*. Lewiston, NY: Edward Mellen.

Bryden J. and K. Hart. 2015. 'Money and Banking in Scotland and Norway', in J. Bryden, O. Brox and L. Riddoch (eds), *Northern Neighbours: Norway and Scotland since 1800*. Edinburgh: Edinburgh University Press, pp. 19–31.

Buchner, E. 2010 [1904]. *The Educational Theory of Immanuel Kant*. Whitefish, MT: Ketteridge.

Buck, D. 1947. *A Dictionary of Selected Synonyms in the Principal Indo-European Languages*. Chicago: University of Chicago Press.

Caillé, A., K. Hart and P. Chanial (eds). 2010. 'Marcel Mauss vivant', *Revue du MAUSS* 36.

Caldwell, J.C. et al. 2006. *Demographic Transition Theory*. Dordrecht: Springer.

Campbell, J. 2008 [1949]. *Hero with a Thousand Faces*. Novato, CA: New World.

Camus, A. 2002 [1947]. *The Plague*. London: Penguin.

Carrier, J. and D. Miller. 1998. *Virtualism: A New Political Economy*. London: Routledge.

Castells, M. 2000. *The Rise of the Network Society*. London: Routledge.

Clifford, J. and G. Marcus (eds). 2010 [1986]. *Writing Culture: The Poetics and Politics of Ethnography*. Berkeley, CA: University of California Press.

Coleman, G. 2013. *Coding Freedom: The Ethics and Aesthetics of Hacking*. Princeton, NJ: Princeton University Press.

Collingwood, R.G. 1958 [1938]. *Principles of Art*. Oxford: Oxford University Press.

Collingwood, R.G. 2014 [1946]. *The Idea of History*. Eastford, CT: Martino.

Collingwood, R.G. 2017 [1939]. *Autobiography*. Oxford: Oxford University Press.

Comte, A. 1997 [1830–42]. *Auguste Comte and Positivism: The Essential Writings*. Piscataway, NJ: Transaction.

Conroy, J. 2020. *The Informal Economy in Development: Evidence from German, British and Australian New Guinea*. Canberra: Development Policy Centre, ANU.

Costelloe, T. 1995. 'Giambattista Vico', *Stanford Encyclopedia of Philosophy*. Palo Alto, CA: Stanford University.

Cronon, W. 1992. *Nature's Metropolis: Chicago and the Great West*. New York: W.W. Norton.

Crutchfield, J. 2002. 'What Lies Between Order and Chaos?' Santa Fe, NM: Santa Fe Institute.

Dasgupta, A. 2015 [1994]. *Gandhi's Economic Thought*. London: Routledge.

De Soto, H. 2000. *The Mystery of Capital: Why Capitalism Triumphs in the West and Fails Everywhere Else*. New York: Bantam.

De Soto, H. 2002 [1989]. *The Other Path: The Economic Answer to Terrorism*. New York: Basic Books.

Desai, A. and G. Vahed. 2015. *The South African Gandhi: Stretcher-Bearer of Empire*. Palo Alto, CA: Stanford University Press.

Desan, P. 2014. *Montaigne: Une biographie politique*. Paris: Odile Jacob.

Diop, C.A. 1974. *The African Origin of Civilization: Myth or Reality?* Chicago: Laurence Hill.

Dodd, N. 2005. 'Laundering Money: On the Need for Conceptual Clarity within the Sociology of Money', *European Journal of Sociology* 46.3: 387–411.

Dostoevsky, F. 1993 [1864]. *Crime and Punishment*. London: Everyman.

Du Bois, W.E.B. 1999 [1920]. *Darkwater: Voices from within the Veil*. New York: Dover.

Du Bois, W.E.B. 2008 [1903]. *The Souls of Black Folk*. Oxford: Oxford University Press.

Durkheim, E. 2001 [1912]. *The Elementary Forms of Religious Life*. Oxford: Oxford University Press.

Durkheim, E. 2013 [1893]. *The Division of Labour in Society*. London: Palgrave.

Earle, J., C. Moral and Z. Ward-Perkins. 2016. *The Econocracy: The Perils of Leaving Economics to the Experts*. Manchester: Manchester University Press.

Eliot, T.S. 1974. 'Journey of the Magi', *Collected Poems 1909–1962*. London: Faber and Faber.

Eliot, T.S. 2010 [1948]. *Notes Towards the Definition of Culture*. London: Faber and Faber.

Ellison, R. 2001 [1952]. *Invisible Man*. London: Penguin.

Engels, F. 2009 [1845]. *The Condition of the Working Class in England in 1844*. Oxford: Oxford University Press.

Engels, F. 2010 [1884]. *Origin of the Family, Private Property and the State*. London: Penguin.

Engels, F. 2020 [1880]. *Socialism, Utopian and Scientific*. https://www.marxists.org/archive/marx/works/1880/soc-utop/index.htm (accessed 13 October 2021).

Equiano, O. 2003 [1789]. *An Interesting Narrative and Other Writings*. London: Penguin.

Evans-Pritchard, E. 1940. *The Nuer: Description of the Modes of Livelihood and Political Institutions of a Nilotic People*. Oxford: Oxford University Press.

Evens, T. and D. Handelman. 2006. *The Manchester School: Practice and Ethnographic Praxis*. Oxford: Berghahn.

Fanon, F. 2001 [1961]. *The Wretched of the Earth*. London: Penguin.

Fanon, F. 2017. *Alienation and Freedom*. London: Bloomsbury.

Fanon, F. 2021 [1952]. *Black Skin, White Masks*. London: Penguin.

Ferguson, N. 2008. *The Ascent of Money. A Financial History of the World*. London: Penguin.

Feyerabend, P. 2010 [1975]. *Against Method: Outline of an Anarchist Theory of Knowledge*. New York: Verso.

Forster, E.M. 2005 [1924]. *A Passage to India*. London: Penguin.

Forster, E.M. 2012 [1910]. *Howards End*. London: Penguin.

Fortes, M. 1969. *Kinship and the Social Order: The Legacy of L.H. Morgan*. London: Routledge.

Foucault, M. 2001 [1970]. *The Order of Things*. London: Routledge.

Fournier, M. 2006. *Marcel Mauss: A Biography*. Princeton, NJ: Princeton University Press.

Franklin, B. 1916 [1790]. *The Autobiography of Benjamin Franklin*. New York: Henry Holt.

Freire. P. 1998. *Pedagogy of Freedom: Ethics, Democracy and Civic Courage*. Lanham, MD: Rowman & Littlefield.

Freire, P. 2017 [1970]. *Pedagogy of the Oppressed*. London: Penguin.

Galbraith, J.K. 1975. *Money: Whence It Came and Whither It Went*. Boston: Houghton Mifflin.

Gandhi, M.K. 2001 [1927]. *An Autobiography: The Story of My Experiments with Truth*. London: Penguin.

Geertz, C. 1988. *Works and Lives: The Anthropologist as Author*. Cambridge: Polity.

Geoffrey of Monmouth. 1977 [1136]. *The History of the Kings of Britain: Including the Stories of King Arthur and the Prophecies of Merlin*. London: Penguin.

Geras, N. 2020 [1998]. *The Contract of Mutual Indifference: Political Philosophy after the Holocaust*. Manchester: Manchester University Press.

Gerth, H. and C.W. Mills (eds). 1991 [1948]. *From Max Weber: Essays in Sociology*. London: Routledge.

Ghosh, A. 1992. *In an Antique Land*. Delhi: Ravi Dayal.

Gibbon, E. 1984 [1796]. *Memoirs of My Life and Writings*. London: Penguin.

Gibbon, E. 2001 [1776–89]. *The History of the Decline and Fall of the Roman Empire* (6 vols). London: Penguin.

Gill, S. 2020. *William Wordsworth: A Life*. Oxford: Oxford University Press.

Gilroy, P. 1993. *The Black Atlantic: Modernity and Double Consciousness*. London: Verso.

Godin, S. 2008. *Tribes: We Need You to Lead Us*. London: Piatkus.

Goldman, W. 1996 [1983]. *Adventures in the Screen Trade: A Personal View of Hollywood*. London: Abacus.

Goody, J. 1976. *Production and Reproduction: Comparative Studies of the Domestic Domain*. Cambridge: Cambridge University Press.

Goody, J. 2012. *Metals, Culture and Capitalism: An Essay on the Origins of the Modern World*. Cambridge: Cambridge University Press.

Graeber, D. 2001. *Toward an Anthropological Theory of Value: The False Coin of Our Own Dreams*. London: Palgrave.

Grimshaw, A. (ed.). 1992. *The C.L.R. James Reader*. Oxford: Wiley-Blackwell.

Grimshaw, A. 1994. *Servants of the Buddha: Winter in a Himalayan Convent*. London: Robert Hale.

Grimshaw, A. 2010 [2001]. *The Ethnographer's Eye: Ways of Seeing in Anthropology*. Cambridge: Cambridge University Press.

Hann, C. and K. Hart. 2011. *Economic Anthropology: History, Ethnography, Critique*. Cambridge: Polity.

Hannerz, U. 1974. *Caymanian Politics: Structure and Style in a Changing Island Society*. Stockholm: Department of Social Anthropology.

Hardy, T. 2008 [1895]. *Jude the Obscure*. Oxford: Oxford University Press.

Harris, J. and M. Todaro. 1970. 'Migration, Unemployment and Development: A Two-Sector Analysis', *American Economic Review* 60.1: 126–42.

Hart, K. 1978. 'The Economic Basis of Tallensi Social History in the Early Twentieth Century', in G. Dalton (ed.), *Research in Economic Anthropology*, Vol. 1. Greenwich, CT: JAI, 185–216.

Hart, K. 1982. *The Political Economy of West African Agriculture*. Cambridge: Cambridge University Press.

Hart, K. 1985. 'The Social Anthropology of West Africa', *Annual Review of Anthropology* 14: 243–73.

Hart, K. 1999. 'Foreword', in R. Rappaport, *Ritual and Religion*, xiv–xix.

Hart, K. 2005. *The Hit Man's Dilemma: Or Business Personal and Impersonal*. Chicago: Prickly Paradigm.

Hart, K. 2008, 'The Human Economy'. https://www.theasa.org/publications/asaonline/arti cles/asaonline_0101.shtml (accessed 17 September 2021).

Hart, K. 2011. 'On Not Accepting Money from African Dictators: A Case Study in Moral Politics', *Anthropology Today* 27.3: 1–2.

Hart, K. 2012. 'Money in Twentieth-Century Anthropology', in James G. Carrier (ed.), *A Handbook of Economic Anthropology* (2nd edition). Cheltenham: Edward Elgar, 166–82.

Hart, K. 2016. 'Afrique: En attendant l'émancipation', in J.-L. Laville and J. Coraggio (eds), *Les Gauches du XXIe Siècle*. Lormont: Le Bord de l'Eau, 351–65.

Hart, K. 2017. 'Greybacks', in B. Maurer and L. Swartz (eds), *Paid: Tales of Dongles, Checks, and Other Money Stuff*. Cambridge, MA: The MIT Press, 21–220.

Hart, K. 2020. 'David Graeber: Obituary', *Anthropology Today* 36.6: 33–34.

Hart, K. (ed.). 1989. *Women and the Sexual Division of Labour in the Caribbean*. Kingston: Canoe Press.

Hart, K. (ed.). 2015. *Economy For and Against Democracy*. New York: Berghahn.

Hart, K. (ed.). 2017. *Money in a Human Economy*. New York: Berghahn.

Hart, K. and C. Kottak. 1999. 'Obituary for Roy A. ("Skip") Rappaport (1926–1997)', *American Anthropologist* 101.1: 159–61.

Hart, K. and J. Lewis (eds). 1995. *Why Angola Matters*. London: James Currey.

Hart, K. and V. Padayachee. 2000. 'Indian Business in South Africa after Apartheid: New and Old Trajectories', *Comparative Studies in Society and History* 42.4: 683–712.

Hart, K. and W. James. (eds) 2014. Special issue, 'Marcel Mauss: A Living Inspiration', *Journal of Classical Sociology* 14.1.

Hart, N. 1976. *When Marriage Ends: A Study in Status Passage*. London: Tavistock.

Haslam, D. 1999. *Manchester, England*. London: Fourth Estate.

Hawking, S. 1988. *A Brief History of Time: From the Big Bang to Black Holes*. London: Bantam.

Hazlitt, W. 1822. 'On Going a Journey: Table Talk No.1', *New Monthly Magazine* (London).

Hegel, G.W.F. 1967 [1821]. *The Philosophy of Right*. Oxford: Oxford University Press.

Hegel, G.W.F. 2015 [1812–16]. *Science of Logic*. Cambridge: Cambridge University Press.

Hegel, G.W.F. 2018 [1807]. *Phenomenology of Spirit*. Cambridge: Cambridge University Press.

Heidegger, M. 1983 [1929]. *Fundamental Concepts of Metaphysics: World, Finitude, Solitude*. Bloomington, IN: Indiana University Press.

Hicks, J. 1968. *A Theory of Economic History*. Oxford: Oxford University Press.

Hilton, B. 1986. *The Age of Atonement: The Influence of Evangelicalism on Social and Economic Thought, 1795–1865*. Oxford: Oxford University Press.

Himes, C. 1997 [1947]. *Lonely Crusade*. New York: Thunder's Mouth.

Hubbard, L. Ron. 2007 [1950]. *Dianetics: The Modern Science of Metal Health*. Glostrup, Denmark: New Era.

Hugo, V. 1988 [1874]. *Ninety-Three*. New York: Carroll and Graf.

Hume, D. 2015 [1777]. *My Own Life*. New York: Cosmo Classics.

Huxley, T. 1870. 'On the Geographical Distribution of the Chief Modifications of Mankind', *Journal of the Ethnological Society of London* 2.4: 404–12.

Ingold, T. (ed.). 1996. *Key Debates in Anthropology*. London: Routledge.

James, C.L.R. 1977. *Nkrumah and the Ghana Revolution*. London: Allison and Busby.

James, C.L.R. 1985 [1938]. *The History of Negro Revolt*. London: Creation for Liberation.

James, C.L.R. 1986. *Cricket*, ed. Anna Grimshaw. London: Allison and Busby.

James, C.L.R. 1993. *American Civilization*, ed. A. Grimshaw and K. Hart. Oxford: Blackwell.

James, C.L.R. 1997 [1953]. *Mariners, Renegades and Castaways: The Story of Herman Melville and the World We Live In*. Hanover, NH: University Press of New England.

James, C.L.R. 1999 [1963]. *Beyond a Boundary*. London: Vintage.

James, C.L.R. 2001 [1938]. *The Black Jacobins: Toussaint L'Ouverture and the San Domingo Revolution*. London: Penguin.

James, C.L.R. 2004 [1948]. *Notes on Dialectics: Hegel, Marx, Lenin*, ed. J. McClendon. Lanham, MD: Lexington.

James, C.L.R. 2013 [1960]. *Modern Politics*. Chicago: Charles H. Kerr.

Johns, A. 2009. *Piracy: The Intellectual Property Wars from Gutenberg to Gates*. Chicago: University of Chicago Press.

Jolly, R., E. de Kadt, H. Singer and F. Wilson (eds). 1973. *Third World Employment: Problems and Strategies*. Harmondsworth: Penguin.

Kant, I. 1993 [1784]. 'The Idea of a Universal History with a Cosmopolitan Purpose', *The Philosophy of Kant: Moral and Political Writings*. New York: Modern Library.

Kant, I. 1999 [1781]. 'Preface', *Critique of Pure Reason*. Cambridge: Cambridge University Press.

Kant, I. 2002 [1790]. *The Critique of Judgment*. Cambridge: Cambridge University Press.

Kant, I. 2003 [1795]. *Perpetual Peace: A Philosophical Sketch*. Indianapolis, IN: Hackett.

Kant, I. 2006 [1798]. *Anthropology from a Pragmatic Point of View*. Cambridge: Cambridge University Press.

Karatani, K. 2005. *Transcritique: On Kant and Marx*. Cambridge, MA: MIT Press.

Keynes, J.M. 2012 [1936]. *The General Theory of Employment, Interest and Money*. London: Wordsworth.

Kincaid, J. 1997 [1985]. *Annie John: A Novel*. New York: Farrar, Straus and Giroux.

Kluger, M. 2014. *The Fugger Dynasty in Augsburg: Merchants, Mining Entrepreneurs, Bankers and Benefactors*. Augsburg: Context.

Laing, R.D. 2001 [1960]. *The Divided Self: An Existentialist Study of Sanity and Madness*. London: Penguin.

Laing, R.D. 2016 [1964]. *Sanity, Madness and the Family*. London; Routledge.

Lamming, G. 2017 [1953]. *In the Castle of My Skin*. London: Penguin.

Langham, I. 1981. *The Building of British Social Anthropology: William Rivers and His Disciples in Kinship Studies*. London: Reidel.

Larkin, P. 2007. *The Poems*. London: Palgrave.

Latour, B. 1993. *We Have Never Been Modern*. Cambridge, MA: Harvard University Press.

Laville, J.-L. 2019. *L'Économie sociale et solidaire: Pratiques, théories, débats*. Paris: Seuil.

Law, R. (ed.). 1995. *From Slave Trade to 'Legitimate' Commerce: The Commercial Transition in Nineteenth-Century West Africa*. Cambridge: Cambridge University Press.

Lawrence, T.E. 2012 [1926]. *Seven Pillars of Wisdom*. Toronto: Aegitas.

Leach, E. 1968. *A Runaway World? 1967 Reith Lectures*. London: BBC.

Leighton, I. (ed.). 1965. *The Aspirin Age, 1919–1941*. New York: Simon and Schuster.

Lenin, V.I. 1961 [1899]. *The Development of Capitalism in Russia*. Moscow: Foreign Languages Publishing House.

Lévi-Strauss, C. 2012 [1955]. *Tristes Tropiques*. London: Penguin.

Lewis, W.A. 1954. 'Economic Development with Unlimited Supplies of Labour', *The Manchester School* 22.2: 139–91.

Lewis, W.A. 1978. *The Evolution of the International Economic Order*. Princeton, NJ: Princeton University Press.

Lindqvist, S. 2018 [1992]. *Exterminate All the Brutes: One Man's Odyssey into the Heart of Darkness and the Origins of European Genocide*. London: Granta.

List, F. 2016 [1841]. *The National System of Political Economy*. New York: Wentworth Press.

Locke, J. 1988 [1690]. *Two Treatises of Government*. Cambridge: Cambridge University Press.

Locke, J. 2017 [1693]. *Some Thoughts Concerning Education*. Dumfries: Andros.

Lovelace, E. 1979. *The Dragon Can't Dance*. London: Faber and Faber.

Luhrman, T. 1990. 'Our Master, Our Brother: Lévi-Strauss's Debt to Rousseau', *Cultural Anthropology* 5.4: 396–413.

Lukács, G. 1963 [1955]. *The Historical Novel*. Dublin: Merlin.

Mac Ritchie, D. 1985 [1884]. *Ancient and Modern Britons* (2 vols). Los Angeles: France Preston.

Malinowski, B. 1921. 'Primitive Economics of the Trobriand Islands', *The Economic Journal* 31.121: 1–16.

Malinowski, B. 2014 [1922]. *Argonauts of the Western Pacific: An Account of Native Enterprise and Adventure in New Guinea*. Oxford: Benediction.

Marshall, A. 1890. *Principles of Economics* (8th edition). New York: Cosimo.

Marx, K. 1963 [1852]. *The Eighteenth Brumaire of Louis Bonaparte*. New York: International Publishers.

Marx, K. 1970 [1867]. *Capital: The Critique of Political Economy*. London: Lawrence and Wishart.

Marx, K. and F. Engels. 1998 [1848]. *The German Ideology*. Amherst, MA: Prometheus.

Mauss, M. 1950. *Essais de sociologie*, ed. C. Lévi-Strauss. Paris: Presses Universitaires de France.

Mauss. M. 1968. *Oeuvres: Le Sens Commun* (3 vols). *1. Les fonctions sociales du sacré; 2. Représentations collectives et diversité des civilisations; 3. Cohésion sociale et divisions de la sociologie*. Paris: Éditions du Minuit.

Mauss, M. 1997. *Écrits politiques*, ed. M. Fournier. Paris: Fayard.

Mauss, M. 2003 [1909]. *On Prayer*. Oxford: Berghahn.

Mauss, M. 2016 [1925]. *The Gift: Expanded Edition*, ed. J. Guyer. Chicago: University of Chicago Press.

Mayhew, H. 2012 [1851]. *London Labour and the London Poor*. Oxford: Oxford University Press.

McCrea, G. 2015. *Mrs Engels: A Novel*. London: Scribe.

McNeill, D. 2020. *Fetishism and the Theory of Value: Reassessing Marx in the 21st Century*. London: Palgrave.

McPherson, C.B. (ed.). 1999 [1978]. *Property: Mainstream and Critical Perspectives*. Toronto: University of Toronto Press.

Miller D. and D. Slater. 2000. *The Internet: An Ethnographic Approach*. London: Routledge.

Montaigne, M. de. 1957 [1580–95]. *Essays*, in *Complete Works of Montaigne*. Palo Alto, CA: Stanford University Press.

Nabokov, V. 2000 [1951]. *Speak, Memory: An Autobiography Revisited*. London: Penguin.

Nairn, T. 1977. *The Break-up of Britain: Crisis and Neo-Nationalism*. London: Verso.

The New Testament: King James Version. 1998. London: Everyman.

Nietzsche, F. 2020 [1882]. *The Gay Science*. New York: Dover.

Nishibe, M. 2005. 'The Theory of Labour Money: Implications of Marx's Critique for LETS', in H. Uchida (ed.), *Marx for the 21st Century*. London: Routledge, 89–105.

Novak, M. 1982. *English Literature in the Age of Disguise*. Berkeley, CA: University of California Press.

Parekh, B. 1989. *Gandhi's Political Philosophy: A Critical Examination*. London: Palgrave.

Passerini, L. 1996 [1988]. *Autobiography of a Generation: Italy, 1968*. Middletown, CT: Wesleyan University Press.

Perkins, J. 2004. *Confessions of an Economic Hit Man: How America Really Took Over the World*. London: Penguin.

Pirenne, H. 2014 [1925]. *Medieval Cities: Their Origins and the Survival of Trade*. Princeton, NJ: Princeton University Press.

Pleyers, G. 2011. *Alter-Globalization: Becoming Actors in the Global Age*. Cambridge: Polity.

Polanyi, K. 1957. 'Economy as Instituted Process', in K. Polanyi, C. Arensberg and H. Pearson (eds), *Trade and Market in the Early Empires: Economies in History and Theory*. Glencoe, IL: Free Press, 243–72.

Polanyi, K. 2001 [1944]. *The Great Transformation: The Political and Economic Origins of Our Times*. Boston: Beacon.

Polanyi, K. with A. Rotstein. 1966. *Dahomey and the Slave Trade: An Analysis of an Archaic Economy*. Seattle, WA: University of Washington Press.

Poundstone, W. 2005. *Fortune's Formula: The Untold Story of the Scientific Betting System That Beat the Casinos and Wall Street*. New York: Hill & Wang.

Radcliffe-Brown, A. 2013 [1922]. *The Andaman Islanders*. Cambridge: Cambridge University Press.

Rappaport, R. 1999. *Ritual and Religion in the Making of Humanity*. Cambridge: Cambridge University Press.

Rempel, H. 1974. 'Review of Jolly et al., *Third World Employment*', *Manpower and Unemployment Research in Africa* 7.2: 42–44.

Renfrew, A.C. 1987. *Archaeology and Language: The Puzzle of the Indo-European Origins*. London: Pimlico.

Rey, P.-P. 1973. *Les alliances de classes*. Paris: Maspero.

Rey, P.-P. 1979. 'Class Contradictions in Lineage Societies', *Critique of Anthropology* 13–14: 41–60.

Ricardo, D. 2004 [1817]. *Principles of Political Economy*. New York: Dover.

Richler, M. 1971. *St Urbain's Horseman*. Toronto: McClelland and Stewart.

Rivers, W. 1912. 'Methodology', *Notes and Queries on Anthropology*. London.

Rivers, W. 2018 [1923]. *Conflict and Dream*. Emeryville, CA: Alibris.

Rivers, W. 2018 [1906] *The Todas*. Cambridge: Cambridge University Press.

Rouch, J. 1956. *Migrations au Ghana: Gold Coast enquête 1953–1955*. Paris: CNRS.

Rousseau, J.-J. 1984 [1754]. *Discourse on Inequality*. London: Penguin.

Rousseau, J.-J. 1986 [1761]. *La Nouvelle Heloïse: Or Julie: The New Heloïse*. University Park, PA: Pennsylvania State University Press.

Rousseau, J.-J. 1987 [1761]. *The Social Contract*. London

Rousseau, J.-J. 1991 [1762]. *Emile: On Education*. London: Penguin.

Rousseau, J.-J. 2008 [1782]. *The Confessions*. Oxford: Oxford University Press.

Rousseau, J.-J. 2011 [1782]. *Reveries of a Solitary Walker*. Oxford: Oxford University Press.

Said, E. 1991 [1978]. *Orientalism: Western Conceptions of the Orient*. London: Penguin.

Samuelson, P. 1997 [1948]. *Economics: An Introductory Analysis*. Cambridge: Cambridge University Press.

Seddon, D. (ed.). 2012 [1978]. *Relations of Production: Marxist Approaches to Economic Anthropology*. London: Routledge.

Shattuck, R. 1968 [1955]. *The Banquet Years: The Origins of the Avant-Garde in France, 1885–1914*. New York: Random House.

Shaxson, N. 2012. *Treasure Islands: Tax Havens and the Men Who Stole the World*. New York: Vintage.

Shostak, M. 1990 [1981]. *Nisa: The Life and Words of a !Kung Woman*. London: Routledge.

Sigaud, L. 2002. 'The Vicissitudes of The Gift', *Social Anthropology* 10.3: 335–58.

Silverman, K. 2003. 'Introduction', in *Benjamin Franklin's Autobiography and Other Writings*. London: Penguin.

Simenon, G. 2016 [1951]. *Maigret Takes a Room*. London: Penguin.

Simmel, G. 1976 [1903]. 'The Metropolis and Mental Life', in *Metropolis: The Sociology of Georg Simmel*. Glencoe, IL: Free Press.

Singer, H., R. Jolly et al. 1972. *Employment, Incomes and Equality*. Geneva: International Labour Office.

Slobodin, R. 1978. *W.H.R. Rivers*. New York: Columbia University Press.

Smith, R.T. 2014 [1955]. *The Matrifocal Family: Power, Pluralism and Politics*. London: Routledge.

Spengler, O. 1991 [1918]. *The Decline of the West: Form and Actuality*. Oxford: Oxford University Press.

Spooner, L. 2011 [1855]. *The Law of Intellectual Property: Or an Essay on the Right of Authors and Inventors to a Perpetual Property in Their Ideas*. Online: Vulgus Press.

Steiner, P. and F. Vatin. 2012. *Traité de sociologie économique*. Paris: Presses Universitaires de France.

Steuart, J. 1767. *An Inquiry into the Principles of Political Oeconomy: Being an Essay on the Science of Domestic Policy in Free Nations*. London: Millar and Cadell.

Stocking, G. 1995. *After Tylor: British Social Anthropology, 1888–1951*. Madison, WI: University of Wisconsin Press.

Taleb, N. 2007. *The Black Swan*. London: Allen Lane.

Taylor, A.J.P. 1983. *A Personal History*. London: Hamish Hamilton.

Tocqueville, A. 1979 [1835]. *Journeys to England and Ireland*. London: Routledge.

Tocqueville, A. 2003 [1840]. *Democracy in America* (2 vols). London: Penguin.

Toulmin, S. 1992. *Cosmopolis: The Hidden Agenda of Modernity*. Chicago: University of Chicago Press.

Trotsky, L. 2017 [1932]. *History of the Russian Revolution* (3 vols). London: Penguin.

Turner, H. et al. 1980. *The Last Colony, But Whose? Labour Movement, Labour Market and Labour Relations in Hong Kong*. Cambridge: Cambridge University Press.

Vico, G. 1963 [1725]. *The Autobiography of Giambattista Vico*. Ithaca, NY: Cornell University Press.

Vico, G. 1999 [1744]. *New Science*. London: Penguin.

Vidal, G. 1981. *Creation: A Novel*. New York: Random House.

Watkins, C. 1996. 'Indo-European Roots Appendix', *American Heritage Dictionary of the English Language*. Boston: Houghton Mifflin, 2081–134.

Webb, B. 1980 [1926]. *My Apprenticeship*. Cambridge: Cambridge University Press.

Weber, M. 1978 [1922]. *Economy and Society* (2 vols). Berkeley, CA: University of California Press.

Weinberger, D. 2008. *Everything is Miscellaneous: The Power of the New Digital Disorder*. New York: Henry Holt.

Weschler, L. 2000. *Boggs: A Comedy of Values*. Chicago: University of Chicago Press.

Whittle, P. 1997. 'A Founding Father Worth Remembering', *Science as Culture*. http://human-nature.com/science-as-culture/whittle.html (temporarily unavailable, 3 October 2021)

Wilson, E. 1989. *Thomas Clarkson: A Biography*. London: Macmillan.

Wordsworth, W. 1802. 'To Toussaint L'Ouverture'. https://www.poemanalysis.com/william-wordsworth/to-toussaint-louverture (accessed 17 September 2021).

Wordsworth, W. 1996 [1850]. *The Prelude: Four Texts*. London: Penguin.

Wright, R. 2000 [1940]. *Native Son*. New York: Vintage.

Yeats, W.B. 1920. 'The Second Coming'. https://www.poetryfoundation.org/43290/the-second-coming (accessed 3 October 2021).

Name Index

SUBJECT INDEX